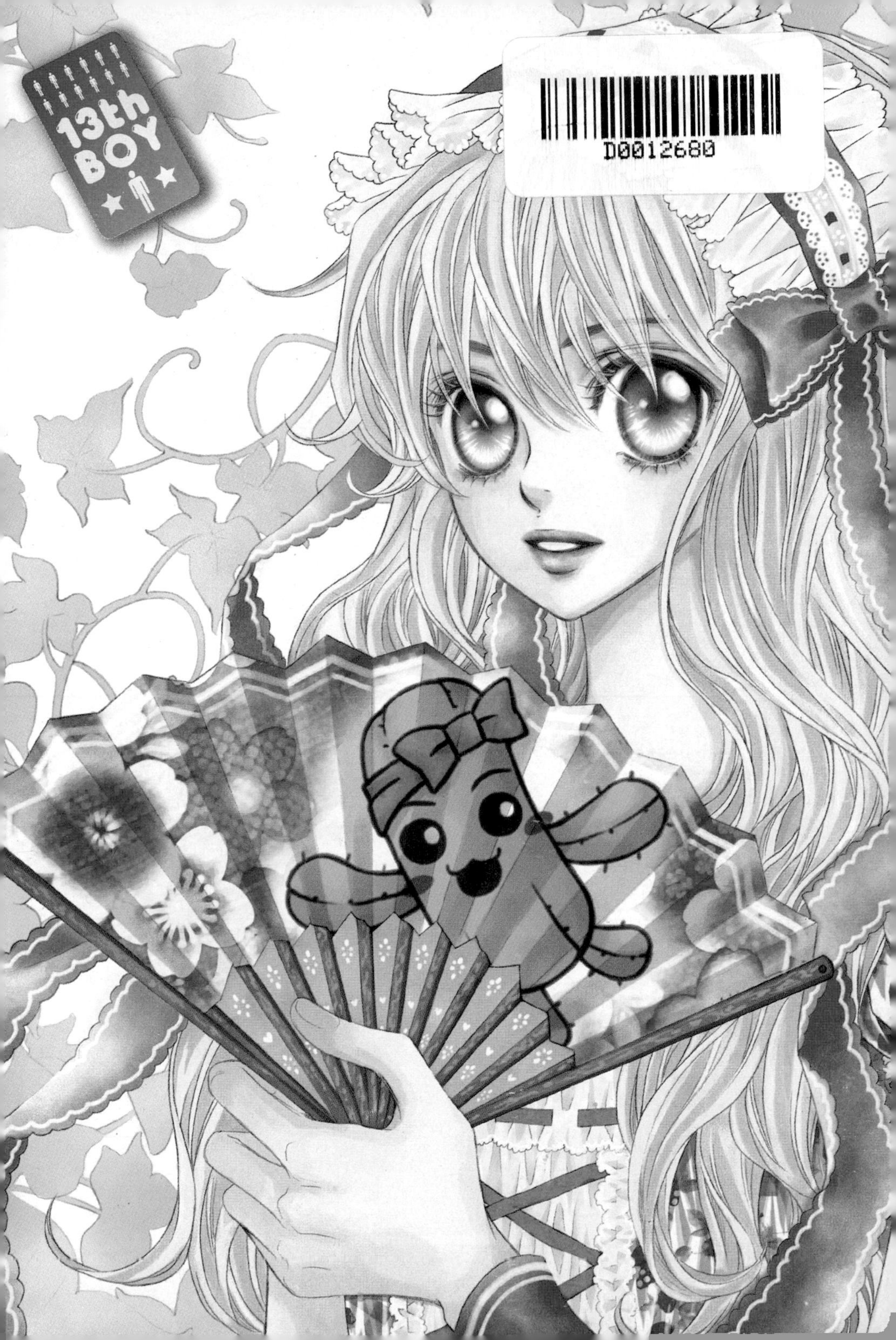
13th BOY

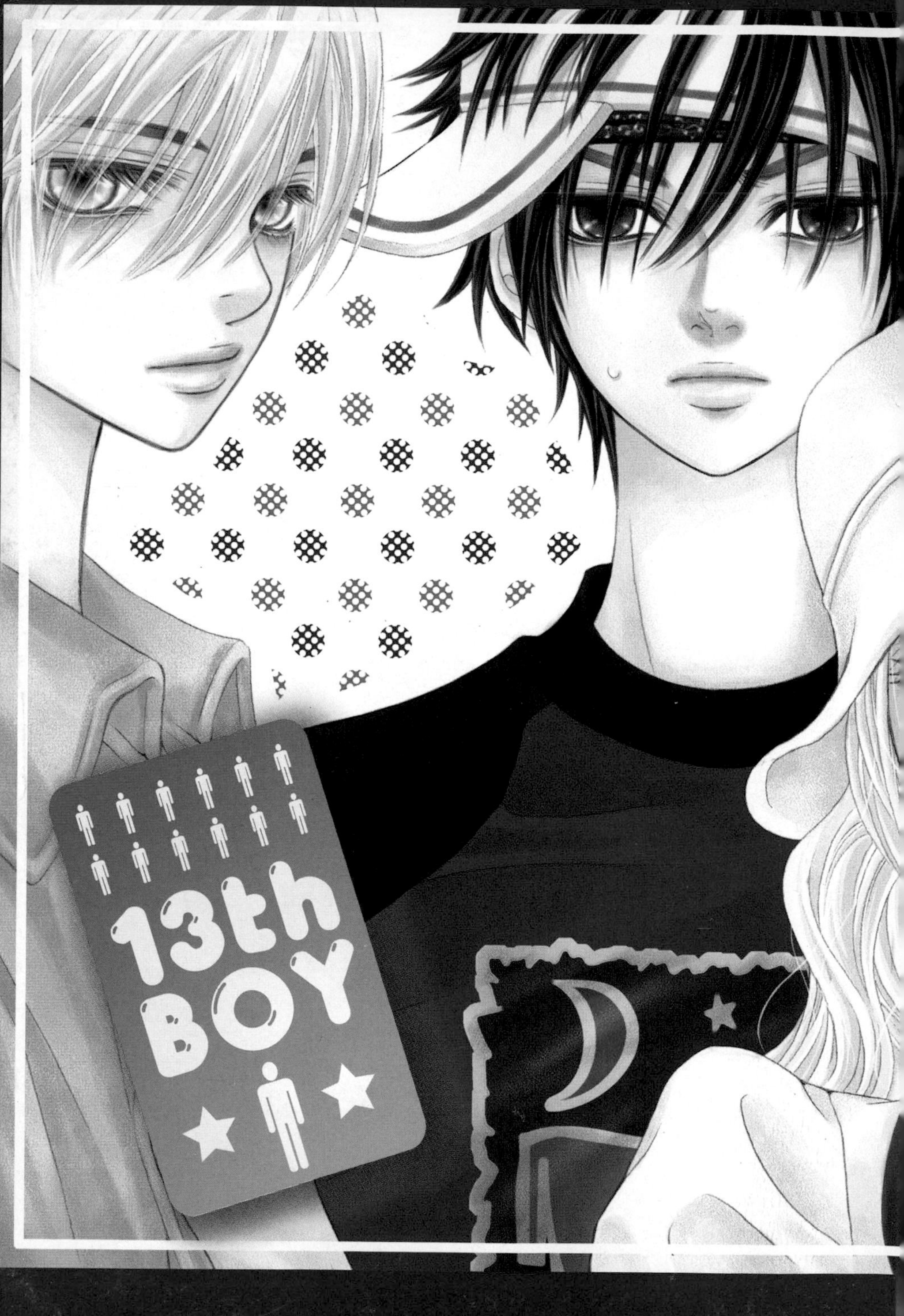
13th BOY

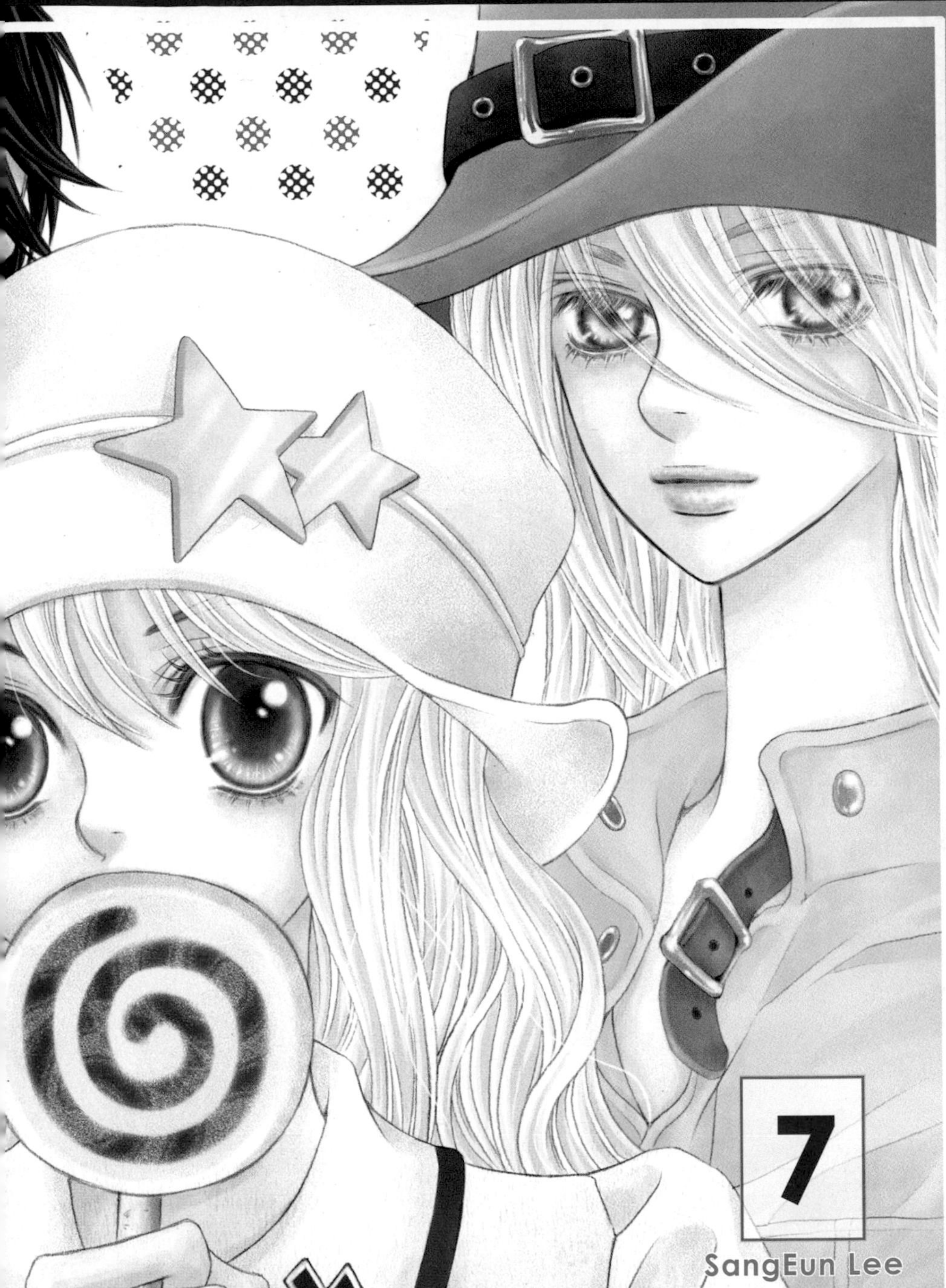
7
SangEun Lee

13th BOY ♥ CONTENTS

STEP 24. *BEATRICE IN THE CLOSET*   7

STEP 25. *SECRETS AND LIES*   40

STEP 26. *I'M A MAN*   74

STEP 27. *LOVE IS LIKE RAINDROPS OUTSIDE THE WINDOW~! ♫*   97

STEP 28. *HEE-SO EUN'S MELANCHOLY*   156

BONUS STEP *BEHIND THE SCENES OF <13TH BOY>! LET'S TAKE A LOOK~! ♥ ~EPISODE 4~*   174

13TH BOY

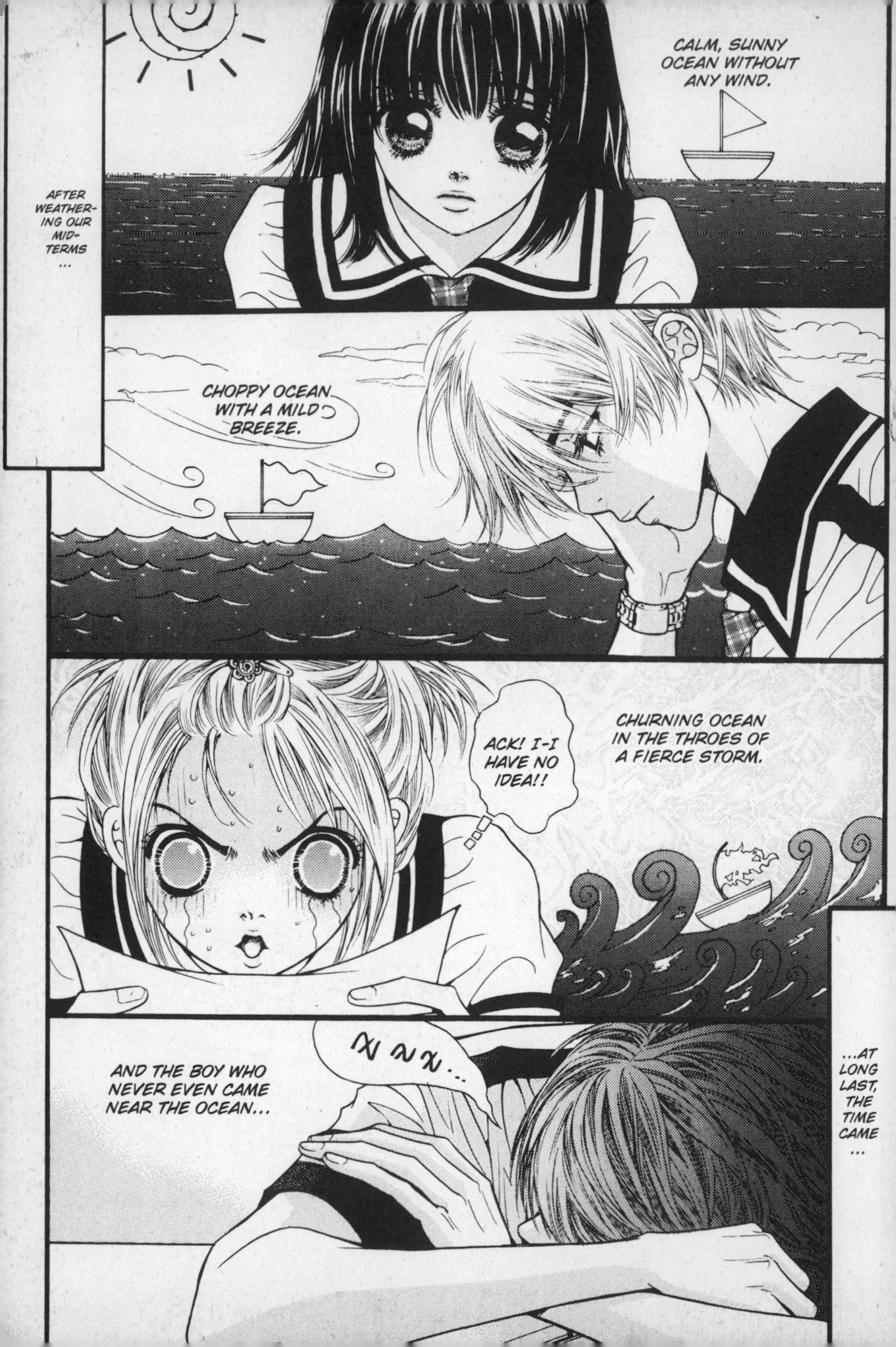

AFTER WEATHERING OUR MIDTERMS...
CALM, SUNNY OCEAN WITHOUT ANY WIND.
CHOPPY OCEAN WITH A MILD BREEZE.
ACK! I-I HAVE NO IDEA!!
CHURNING OCEAN IN THE THROES OF A FIERCE STORM.
AND THE BOY WHO NEVER EVEN CAME NEAR THE OCEAN...
...AT LONG LAST, THE TIME CAME...

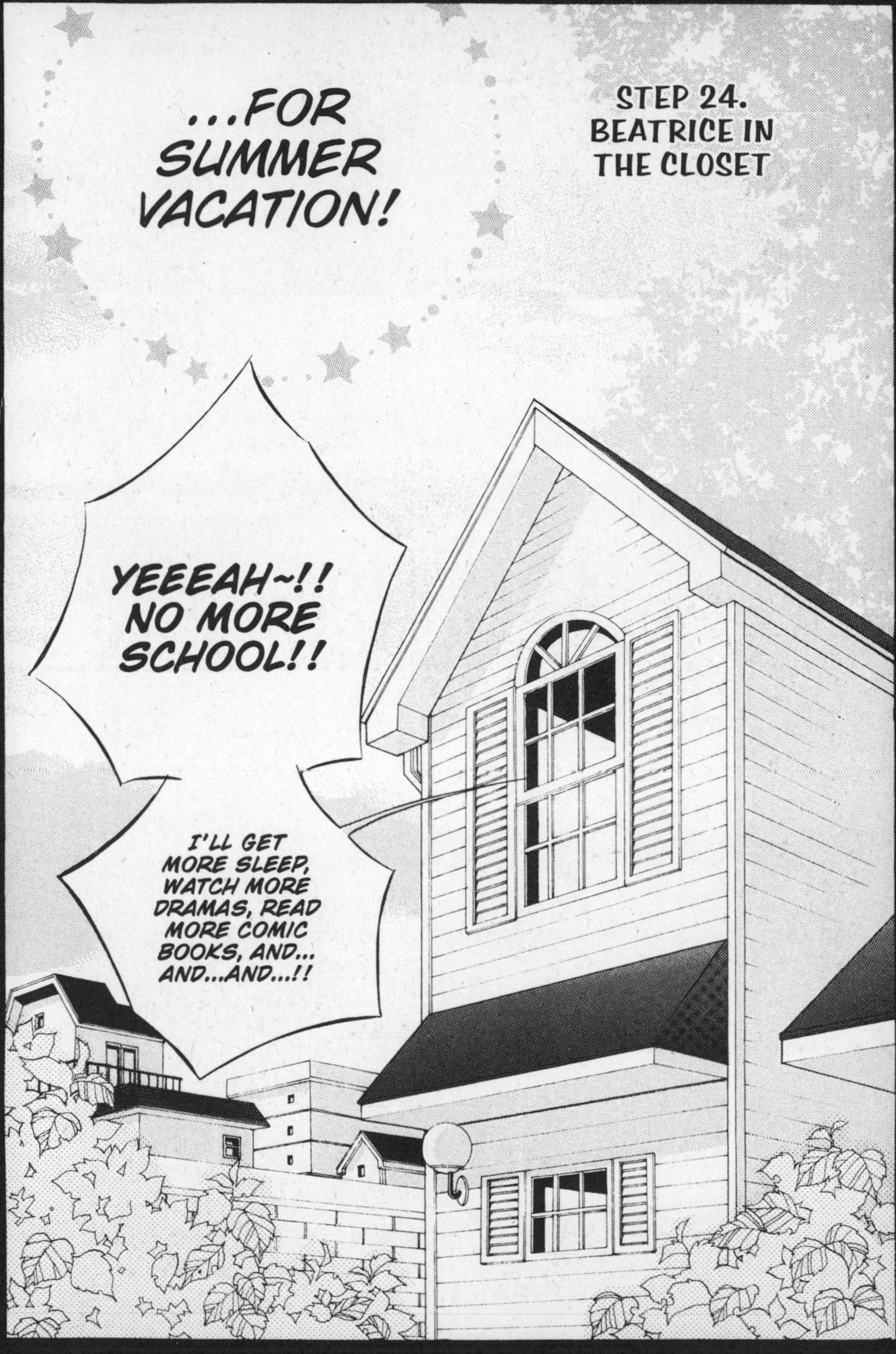

...FOR SUMMER VACATION!
STEP 24. BEATRICE IN THE CLOSET
YEEEAH~!! NO MORE SCHOOL!!
I'LL GET MORE SLEEP, WATCH MORE DRAMAS, READ MORE COMIC BOOKS, AND... AND...AND...!!

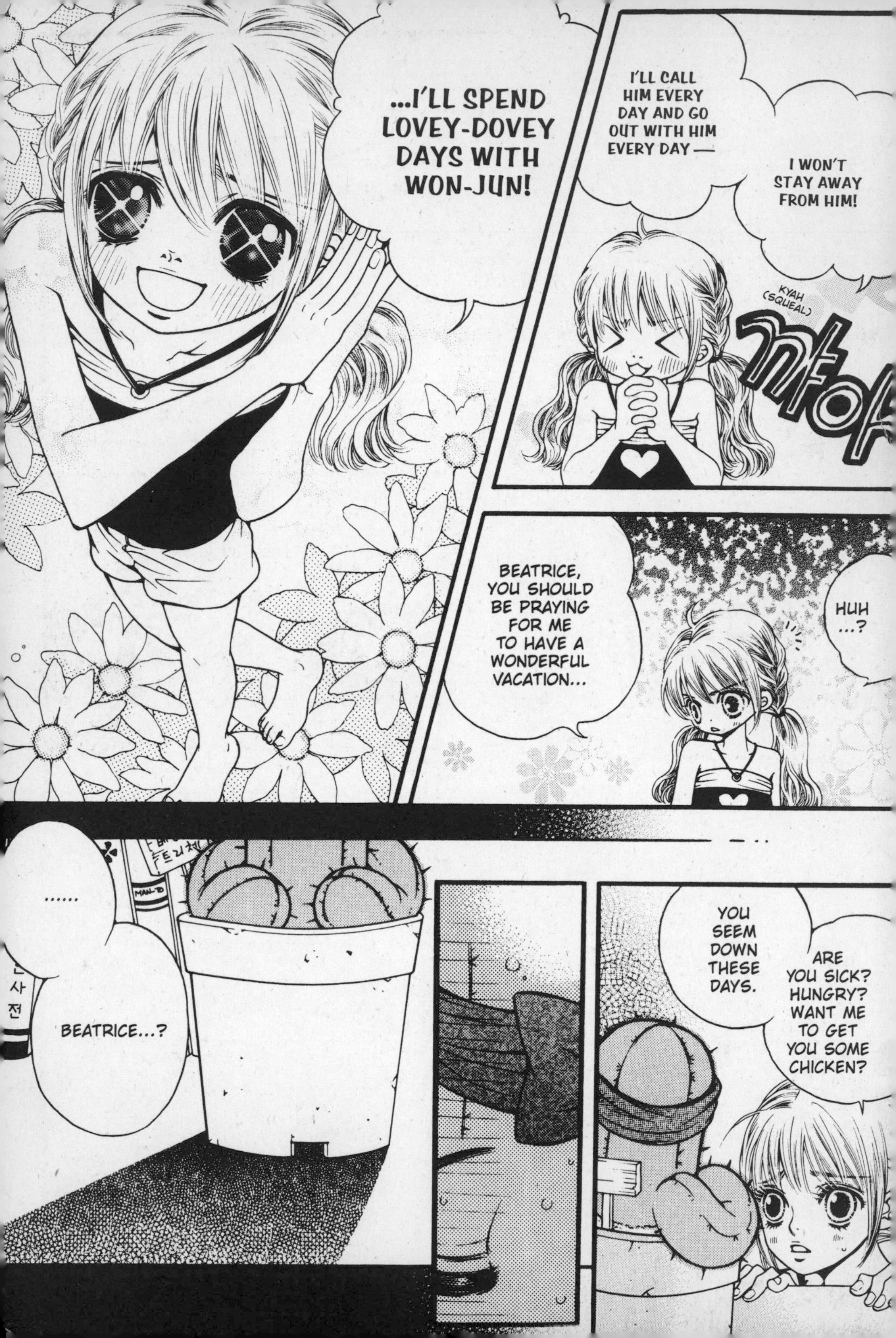
...I'LL SPEND LOVEY-DOVEY DAYS WITH WON-JUN!
I'LL CALL HIM EVERY DAY AND GO OUT WITH HIM EVERY DAY —
I WON'T STAY AWAY FROM HIM!
KYAH (SQUEAL)
BEATRICE, YOU SHOULD BE PRAYING FOR ME TO HAVE A WONDERFUL VACATION...
HUH ...?
......
BEATRICE...?
YOU SEEM DOWN THESE DAYS.
ARE YOU SICK? HUNGRY? WANT ME TO GET YOU SOME CHICKEN?

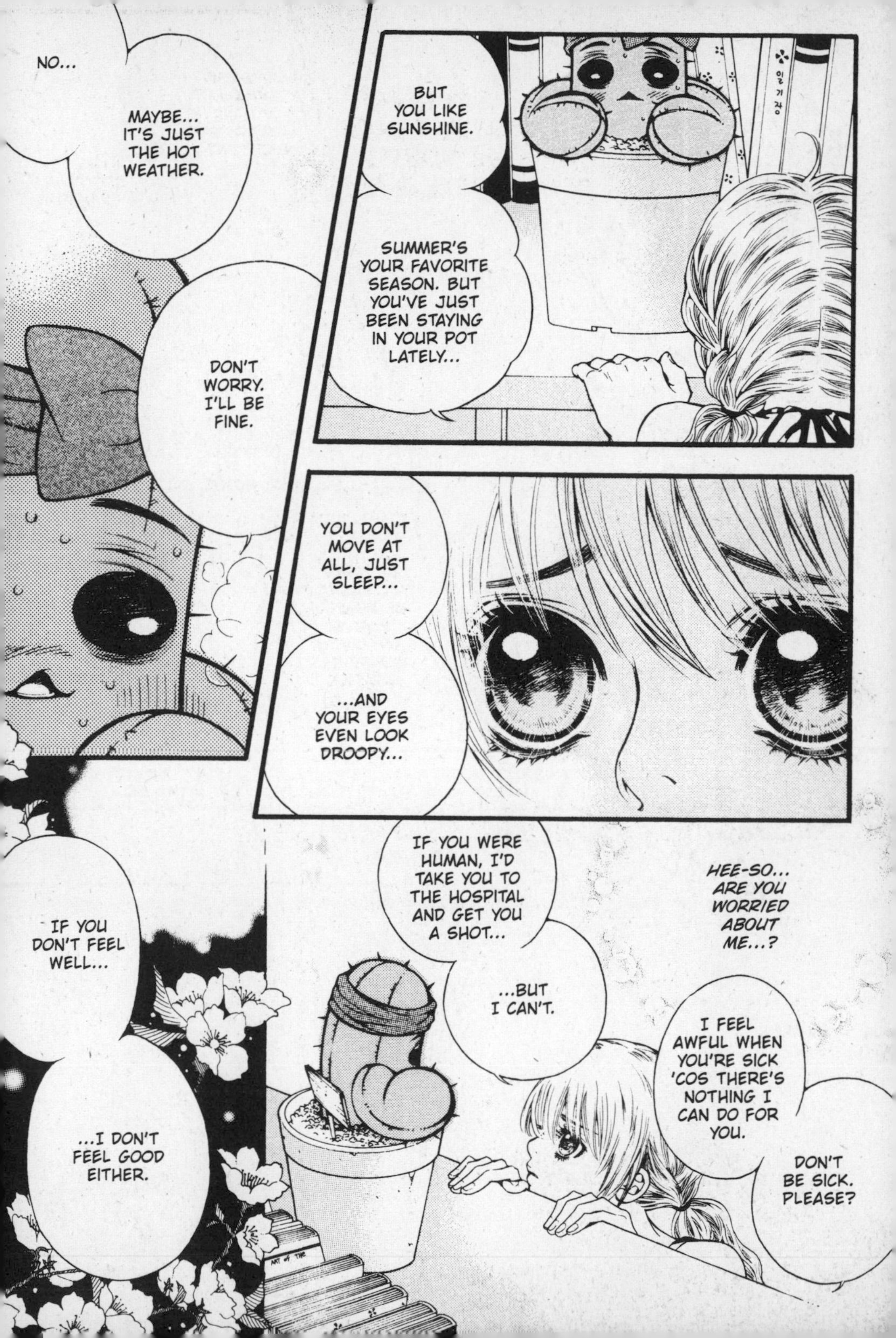
NO...
MAYBE... IT'S JUST THE HOT WEATHER.
DON'T WORRY. I'LL BE FINE.
BUT YOU LIKE SUNSHINE.
SUMMER'S YOUR FAVORITE SEASON. BUT YOU'VE JUST BEEN STAYING IN YOUR POT LATELY...
YOU DON'T MOVE AT ALL, JUST SLEEP...
...AND YOUR EYES EVEN LOOK DROOPY...
IF YOU DON'T FEEL WELL...
...I DON'T FEEL GOOD EITHER.
IF YOU WERE HUMAN, I'D TAKE YOU TO THE HOSPITAL AND GET YOU A SHOT...
...BUT I CAN'T.
HEE-SO... ARE YOU WORRIED ABOUT ME...?
I FEEL AWFUL WHEN YOU'RE SICK 'COS THERE'S NOTHING I CAN DO FOR YOU.
DON'T BE SICK. PLEASE?

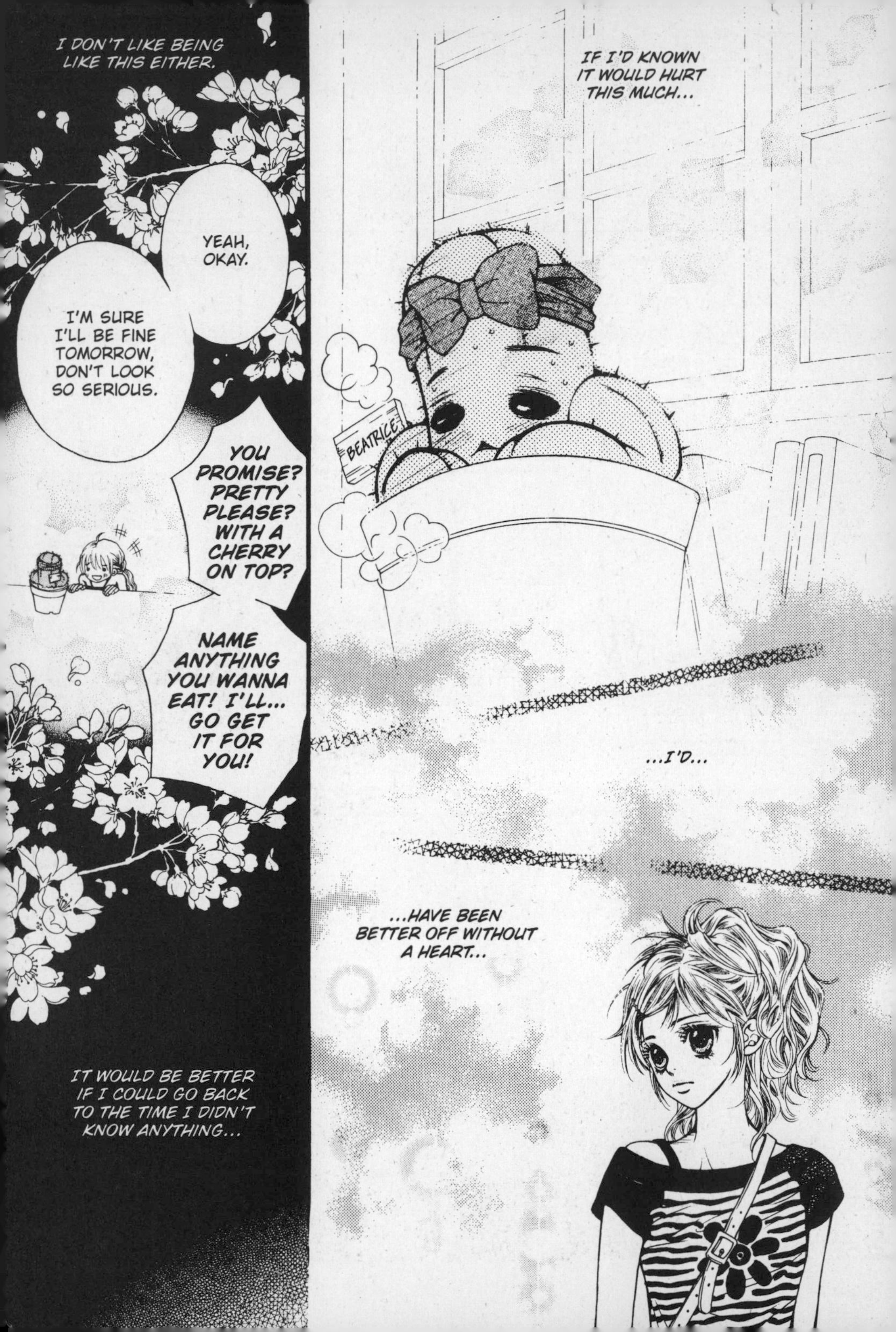
I DON'T LIKE BEING LIKE THIS EITHER.
YEAH, OKAY.
I'M SURE I'LL BE FINE TOMORROW, DON'T LOOK SO SERIOUS.
YOU PROMISE? PRETTY PLEASE? WITH A CHERRY ON TOP?
NAME ANYTHING YOU WANNA EAT! I'LL... GO GET IT FOR YOU!
IT WOULD BE BETTER IF I COULD GO BACK TO THE TIME I DIDN'T KNOW ANYTHING...
IF I'D KNOWN IT WOULD HURT THIS MUCH...
BEATRICE
...I'D...
...HAVE BEEN BETTER OFF WITHOUT A HEART...

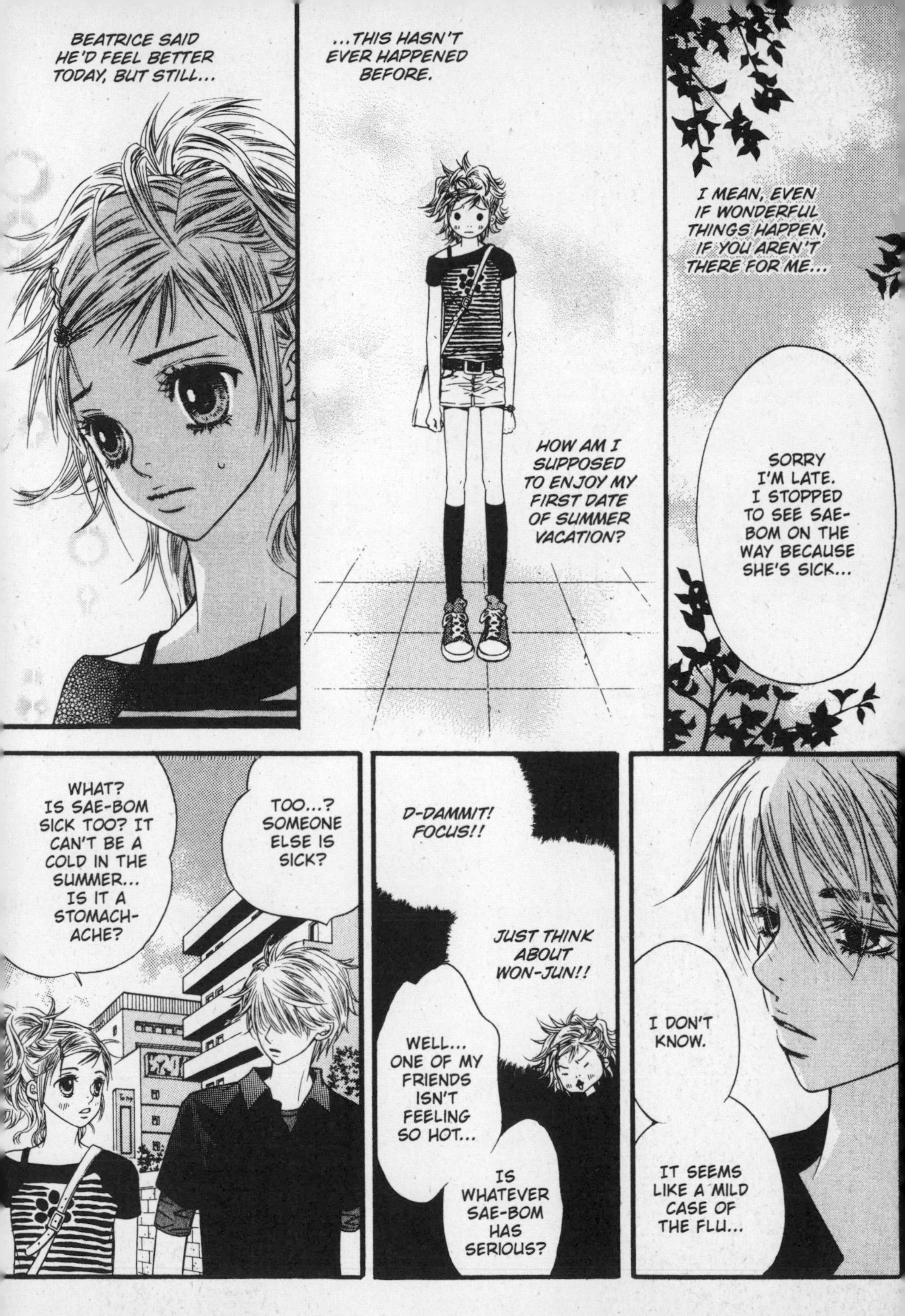
BEATRICE SAID HE'D FEEL BETTER TODAY, BUT STILL...
...THIS HASN'T EVER HAPPENED BEFORE.
HOW AM I SUPPOSED TO ENJOY MY FIRST DATE OF SUMMER VACATION?
I MEAN, EVEN IF WONDERFUL THINGS HAPPEN, IF YOU AREN'T THERE FOR ME...
SORRY I'M LATE. I STOPPED TO SEE SAE-BOM ON THE WAY BECAUSE SHE'S SICK...
WHAT? IS SAE-BOM SICK TOO? IT CAN'T BE A COLD IN THE SUMMER... IS IT A STOMACH-ACHE?
TOO...? SOMEONE ELSE IS SICK?
D-DAMMIT! FOCUS!!
JUST THINK ABOUT WON-JUN!!
WELL... ONE OF MY FRIENDS ISN'T FEELING SO HOT...
IS WHATEVER SAE-BOM HAS SERIOUS?
I DON'T KNOW.
IT SEEMS LIKE A MILD CASE OF THE FLU...

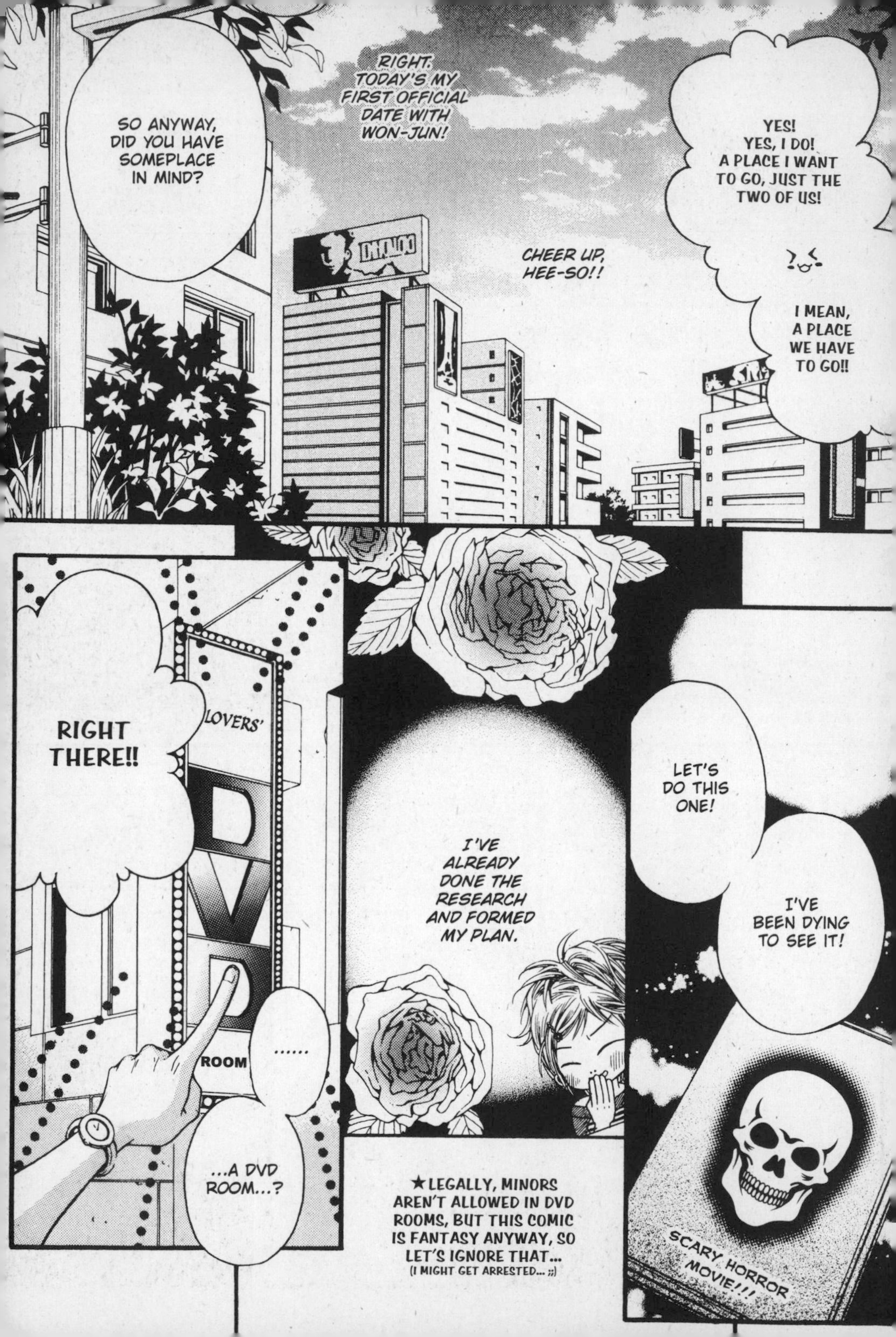
SO ANYWAY, DID YOU HAVE SOMEPLACE IN MIND?
RIGHT. TODAY'S MY FIRST OFFICIAL DATE WITH WON-JUN!
CHEER UP, HEE-SO!!
YES! YES, I DO! A PLACE I WANT TO GO, JUST THE TWO OF US!
I MEAN, A PLACE WE HAVE TO GO!!
RIGHT THERE!!
LOVERS'
DVD
ROOM
......
...A DVD ROOM...?
I'VE ALREADY DONE THE RESEARCH AND FORMED MY PLAN.
★LEGALLY, MINORS AREN'T ALLOWED IN DVD ROOMS, BUT THIS COMIC IS FANTASY ANYWAY, SO LET'S IGNORE THAT...
(I MIGHT GET ARRESTED... ;;)
LET'S DO THIS ONE!
I'VE BEEN DYING TO SEE IT!
SCARY HORROR MOVIE!!!

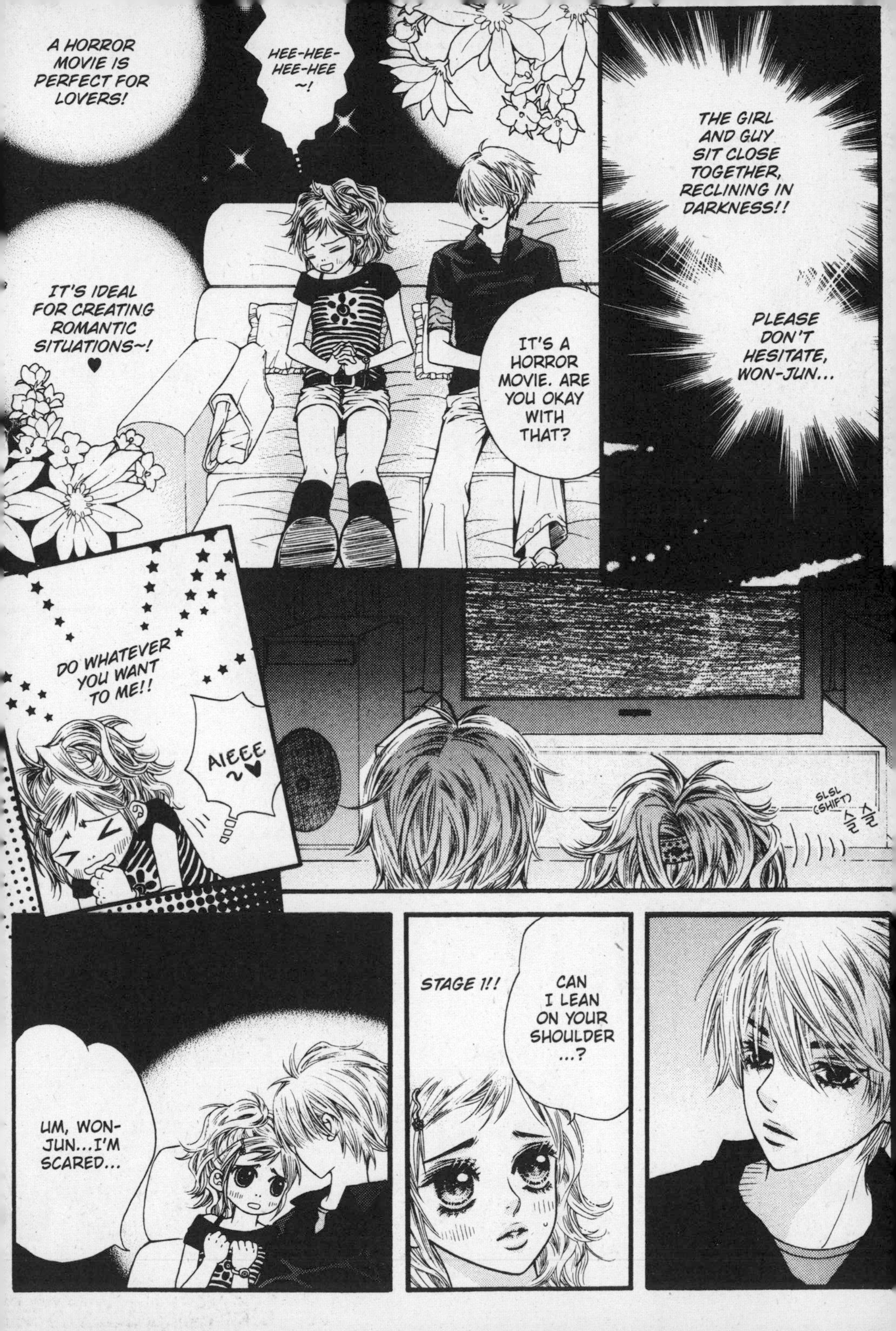
A HORROR MOVIE IS PERFECT FOR LOVERS!
HEE-HEE-HEE-HEE ~!
IT'S IDEAL FOR CREATING ROMANTIC SITUATIONS~! ♥
IT'S A HORROR MOVIE. ARE YOU OKAY WITH THAT?
THE GIRL AND GUY SIT CLOSE TOGETHER, RECLINING IN DARKNESS!!
PLEASE DON'T HESITATE, WON-JUN...
DO WHATEVER YOU WANT TO ME!!
AIEEE ~♥
SLSL (SHIFT)
슬 슬
UM, WON-JUN...I'M SCARED...
STAGE 1!!
CAN I LEAN ON YOUR SHOULDER ...?

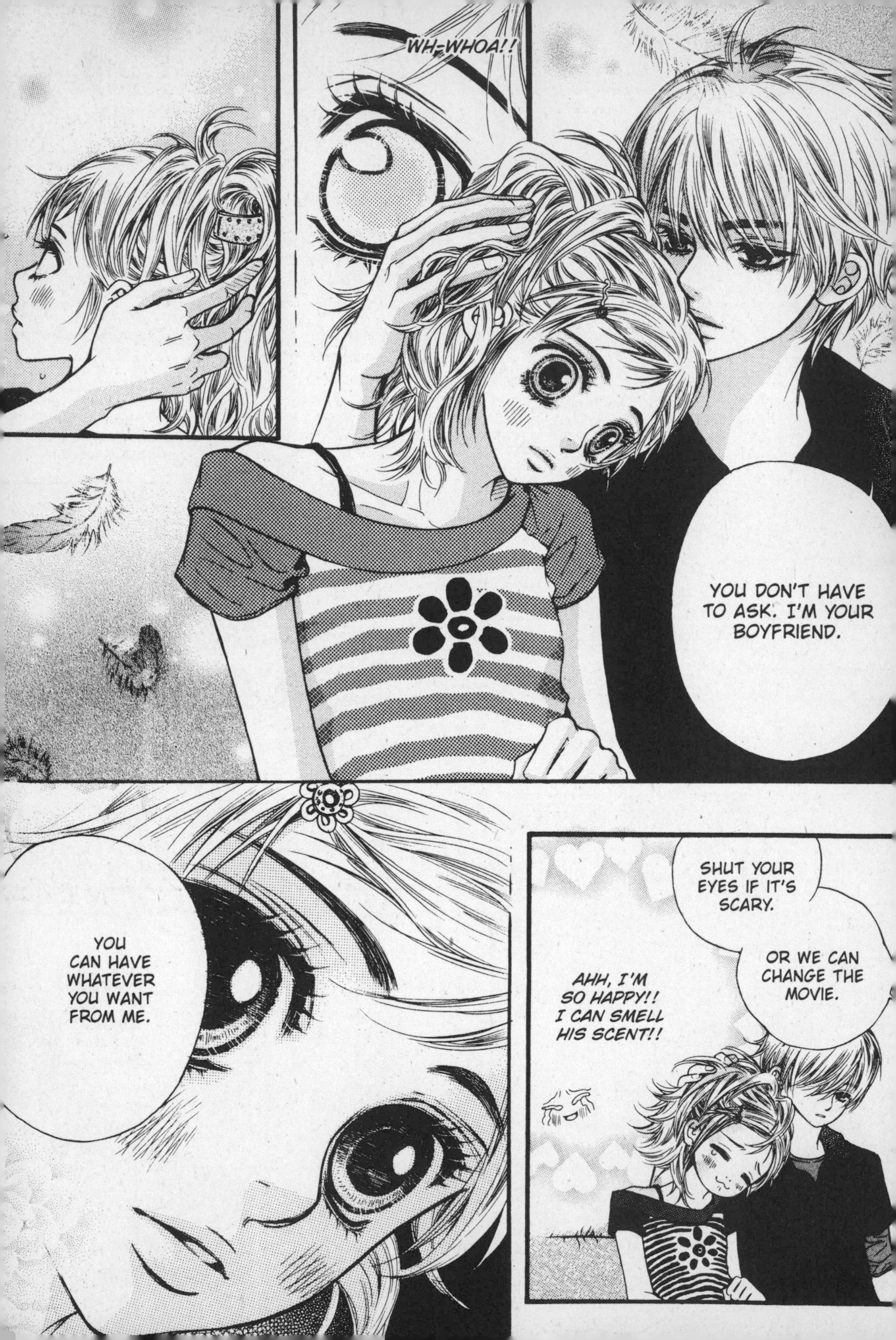
WH-WHOA!!
YOU DON'T HAVE TO ASK. I'M YOUR BOYFRIEND.
YOU CAN HAVE WHATEVER YOU WANT FROM ME.
SHUT YOUR EYES IF IT'S SCARY.
AHH, I'M SO HAPPY!! I CAN SMELL HIS SCENT!!
OR WE CAN CHANGE THE MOVIE.

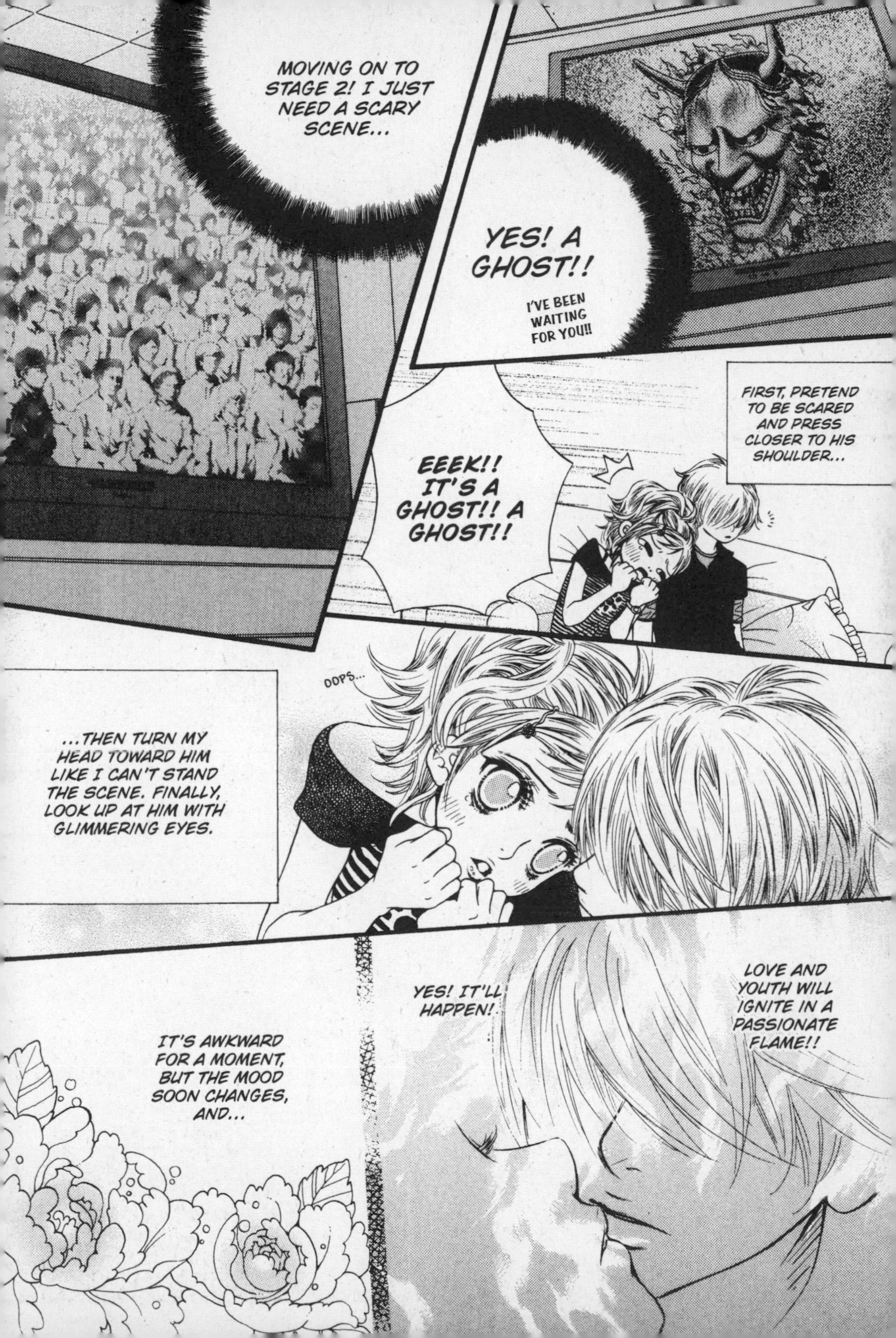
MOVING ON TO STAGE 2! I JUST NEED A SCARY SCENE...
YES! A GHOST!!
I'VE BEEN WAITING FOR YOU!!
EEEK!! IT'S A GHOST!! A GHOST!!
FIRST, PRETEND TO BE SCARED AND PRESS CLOSER TO HIS SHOULDER...
...THEN TURN MY HEAD TOWARD HIM LIKE I CAN'T STAND THE SCENE. FINALLY, LOOK UP AT HIM WITH GLIMMERING EYES.
OOPS...
IT'S AWKWARD FOR A MOMENT, BUT THE MOOD SOON CHANGES, AND...
YES! IT'LL HAPPEN!
LOVE AND YOUTH WILL IGNITE IN A PASSIONATE FLAME!!

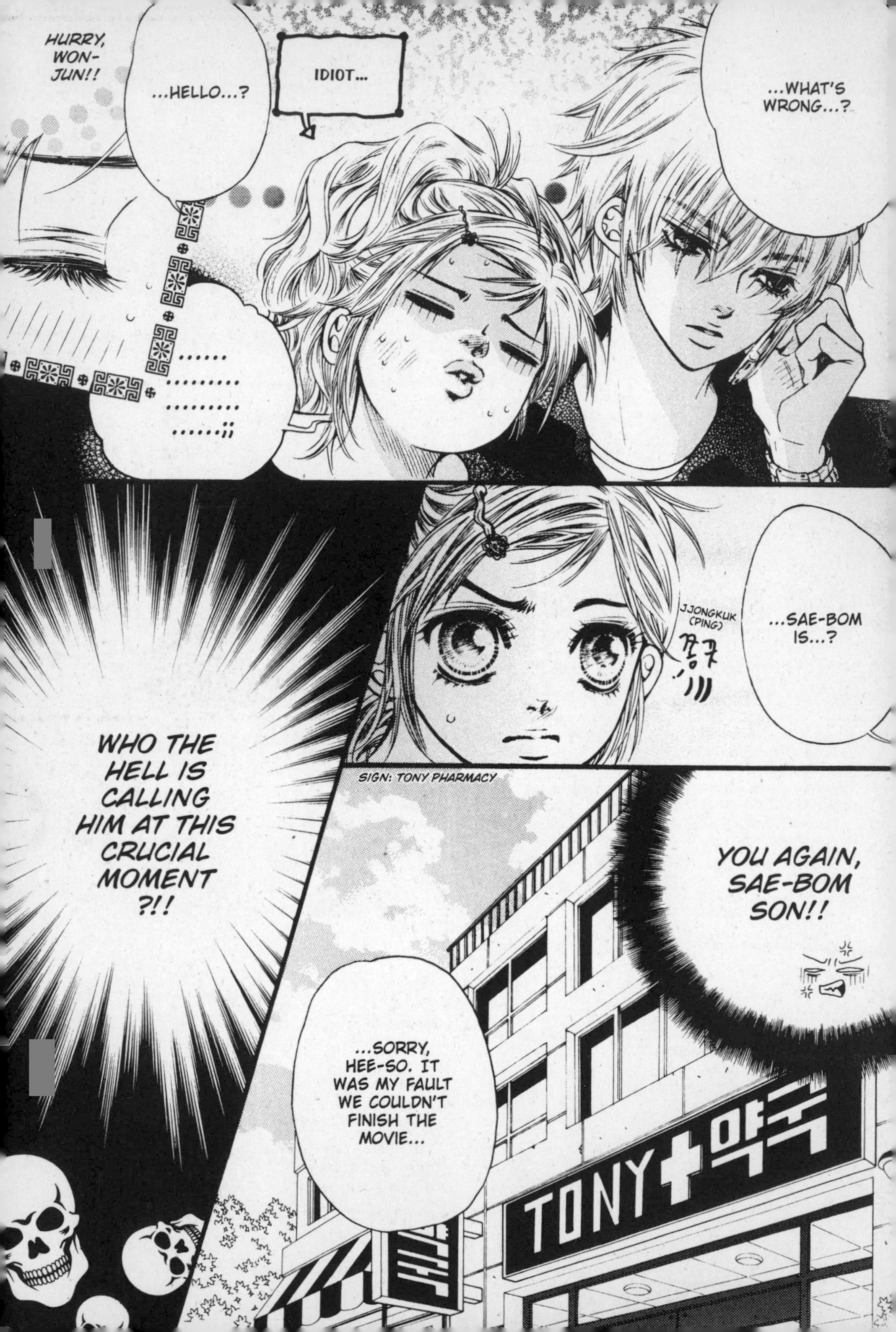
HURRY, WON-JUN!!
...HELLO...?
IDIOT...
...WHAT'S WRONG...?
......
....
....
.......;;
WHO THE HELL IS CALLING HIM AT THIS CRUCIAL MOMENT ?!!
JJONGKUK (PING)
...SAE-BOM IS...?
SIGN: TONY PHARMACY
YOU AGAIN, SAE-BOM SON!!
...SORRY, HEE-SO. IT WAS MY FAULT WE COULDN'T FINISH THE MOVIE...
TONY 약국

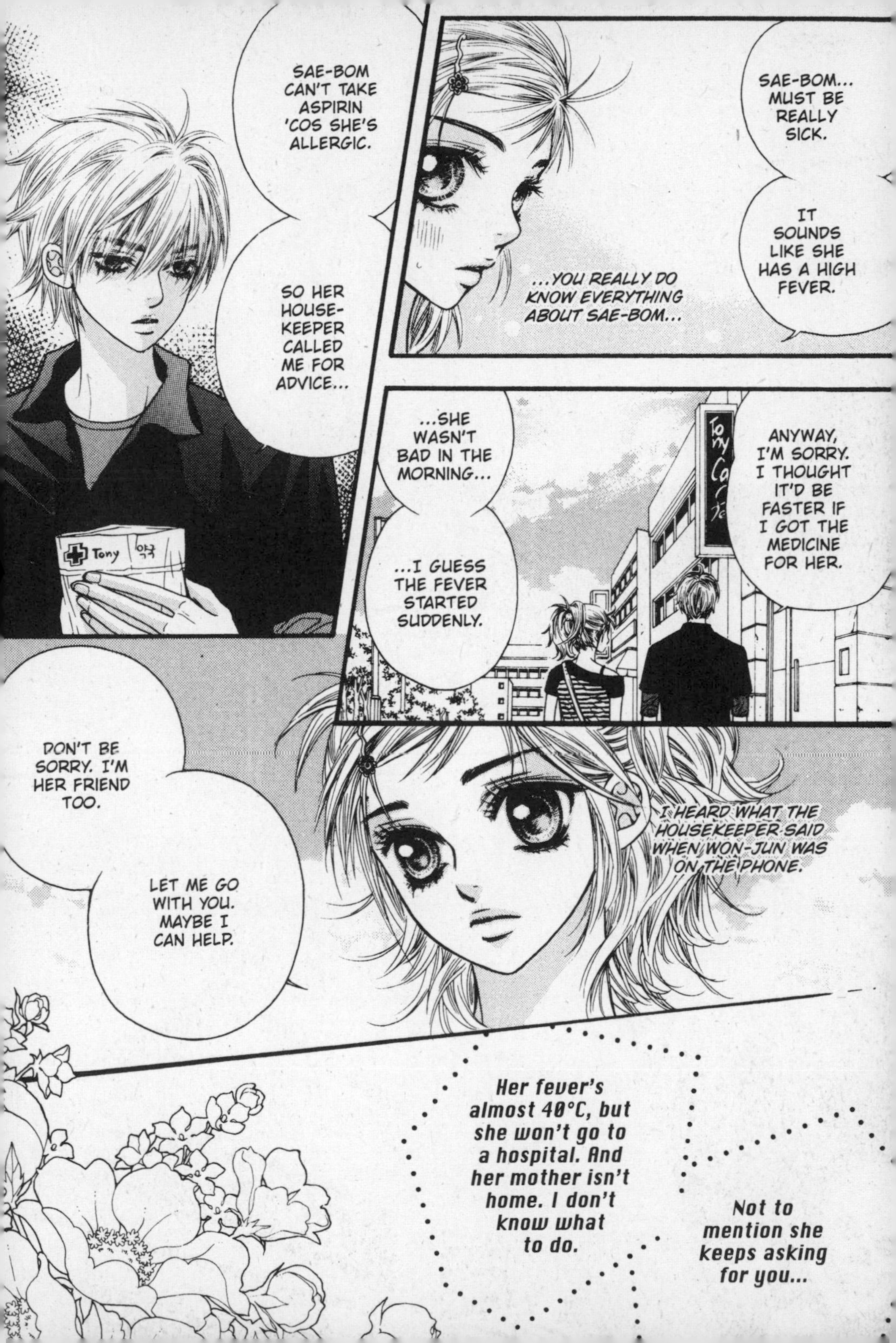
SAE-BOM CAN'T TAKE ASPIRIN 'COS SHE'S ALLERGIC.
SO HER HOUSE-KEEPER CALLED ME FOR ADVICE...
Tony 약국
...YOU REALLY DO KNOW EVERYTHING ABOUT SAE-BOM...
SAE-BOM... MUST BE REALLY SICK.
IT SOUNDS LIKE SHE HAS A HIGH FEVER.
...SHE WASN'T BAD IN THE MORNING...
...I GUESS THE FEVER STARTED SUDDENLY.
ANYWAY, I'M SORRY. I THOUGHT IT'D BE FASTER IF I GOT THE MEDICINE FOR HER.
DON'T BE SORRY. I'M HER FRIEND TOO.
LET ME GO WITH YOU. MAYBE I CAN HELP.
I HEARD WHAT THE HOUSEKEEPER SAID WHEN WON-JUN WAS ON THE PHONE.
Her fever's almost 40°C, but she won't go to a hospital. And her mother isn't home. I don't know what to do.
Not to mention she keeps asking for you...

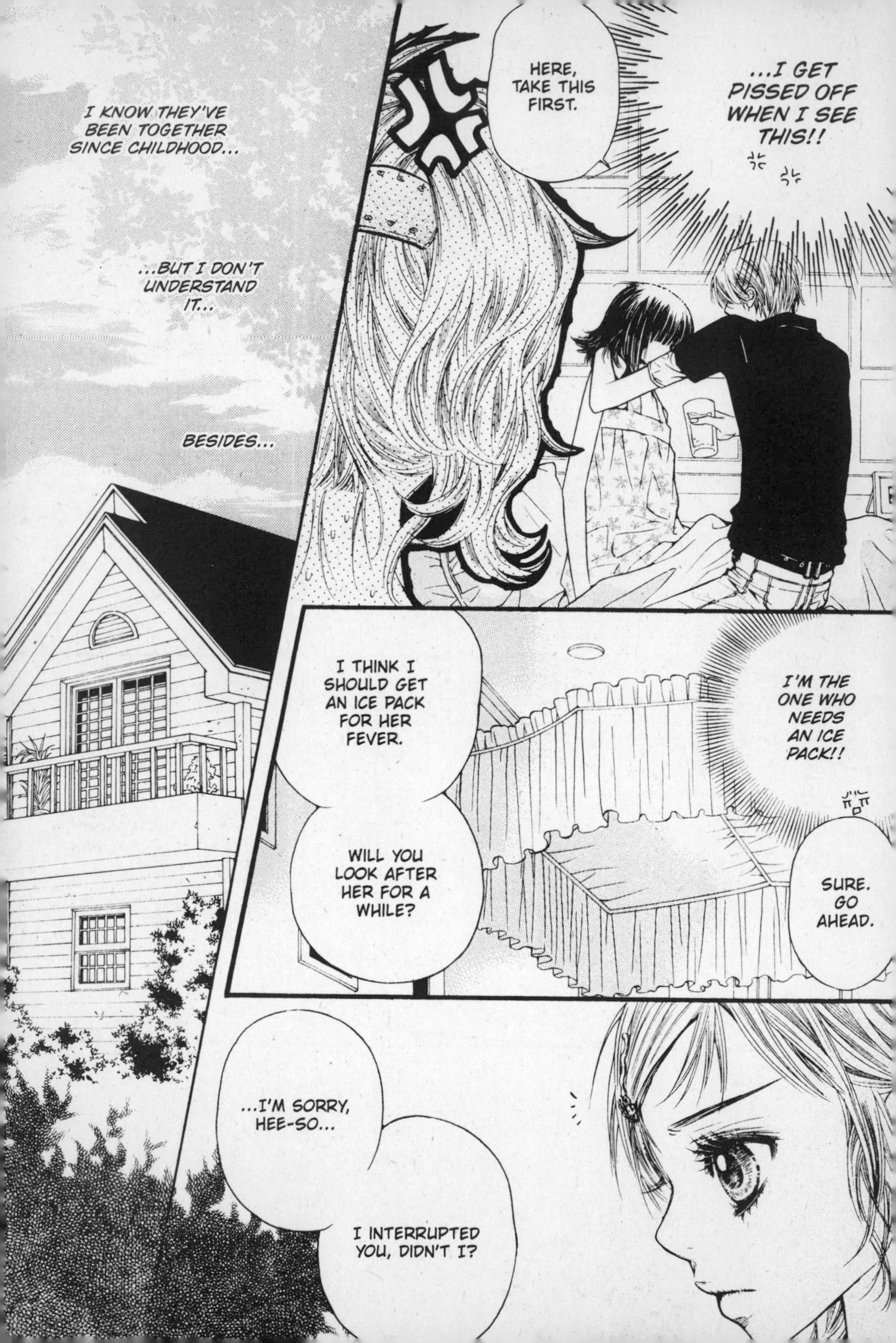
I KNOW THEY'VE BEEN TOGETHER SINCE CHILDHOOD...
...BUT I DON'T UNDERSTAND IT...
BESIDES...
HERE, TAKE THIS FIRST.
...I GET PISSED OFF WHEN I SEE THIS!!
I THINK I SHOULD GET AN ICE PACK FOR HER FEVER.
WILL YOU LOOK AFTER HER FOR A WHILE?
I'M THE ONE WHO NEEDS AN ICE PACK!!
SURE. GO AHEAD.
...I'M SORRY, HEE-SO...
I INTERRUPTED YOU, DIDN'T I?

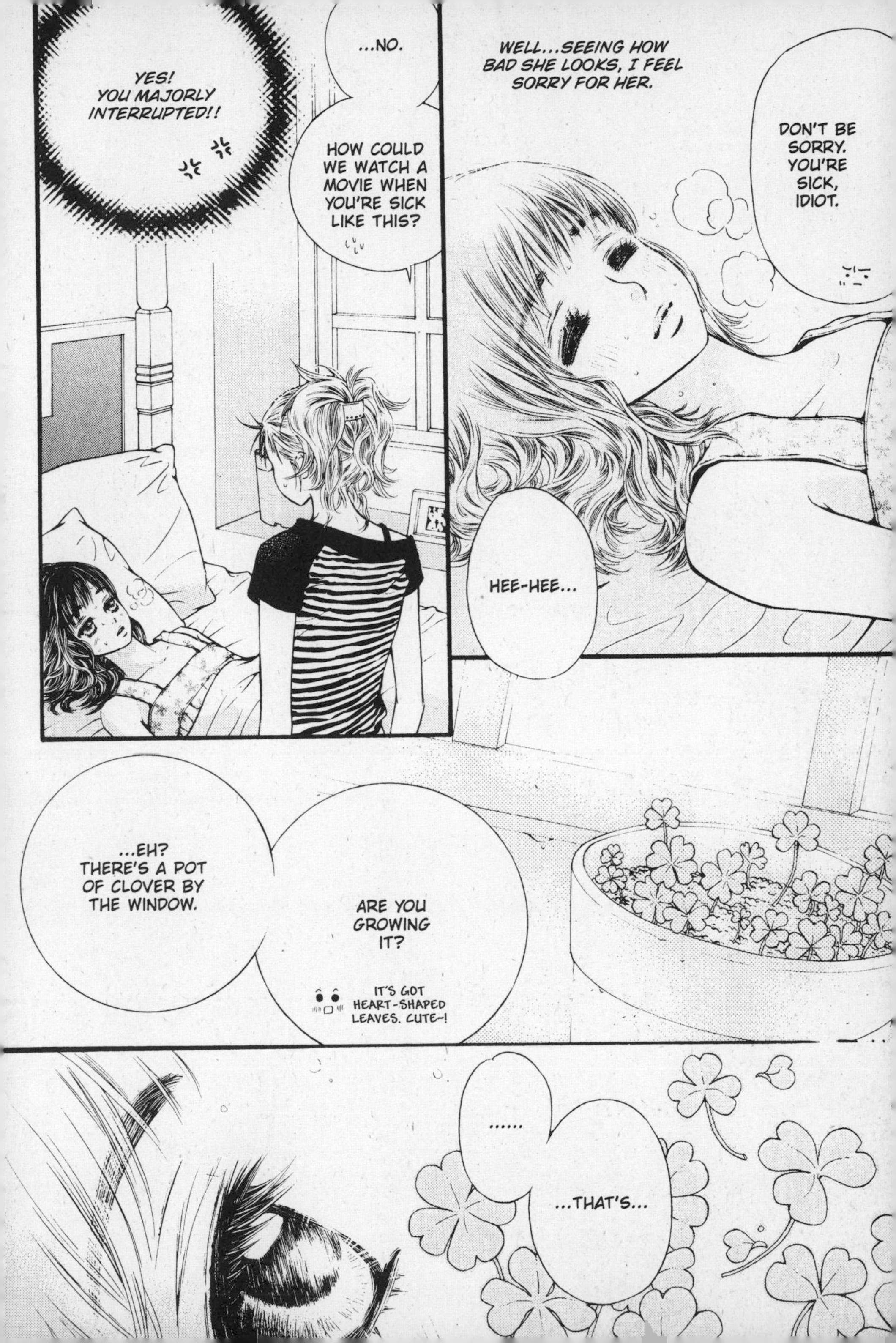
YES! YOU MAJORLY INTERRUPTED!!
...NO.
HOW COULD WE WATCH A MOVIE WHEN YOU'RE SICK LIKE THIS?
WELL...SEEING HOW BAD SHE LOOKS, I FEEL SORRY FOR HER.
DON'T BE SORRY. YOU'RE SICK, IDIOT.
HEE-HEE...
...EH? THERE'S A POT OF CLOVER BY THE WINDOW.
ARE YOU GROWING IT?
IT'S GOT HEART-SHAPED LEAVES. CUTE-!
......
...THAT'S...

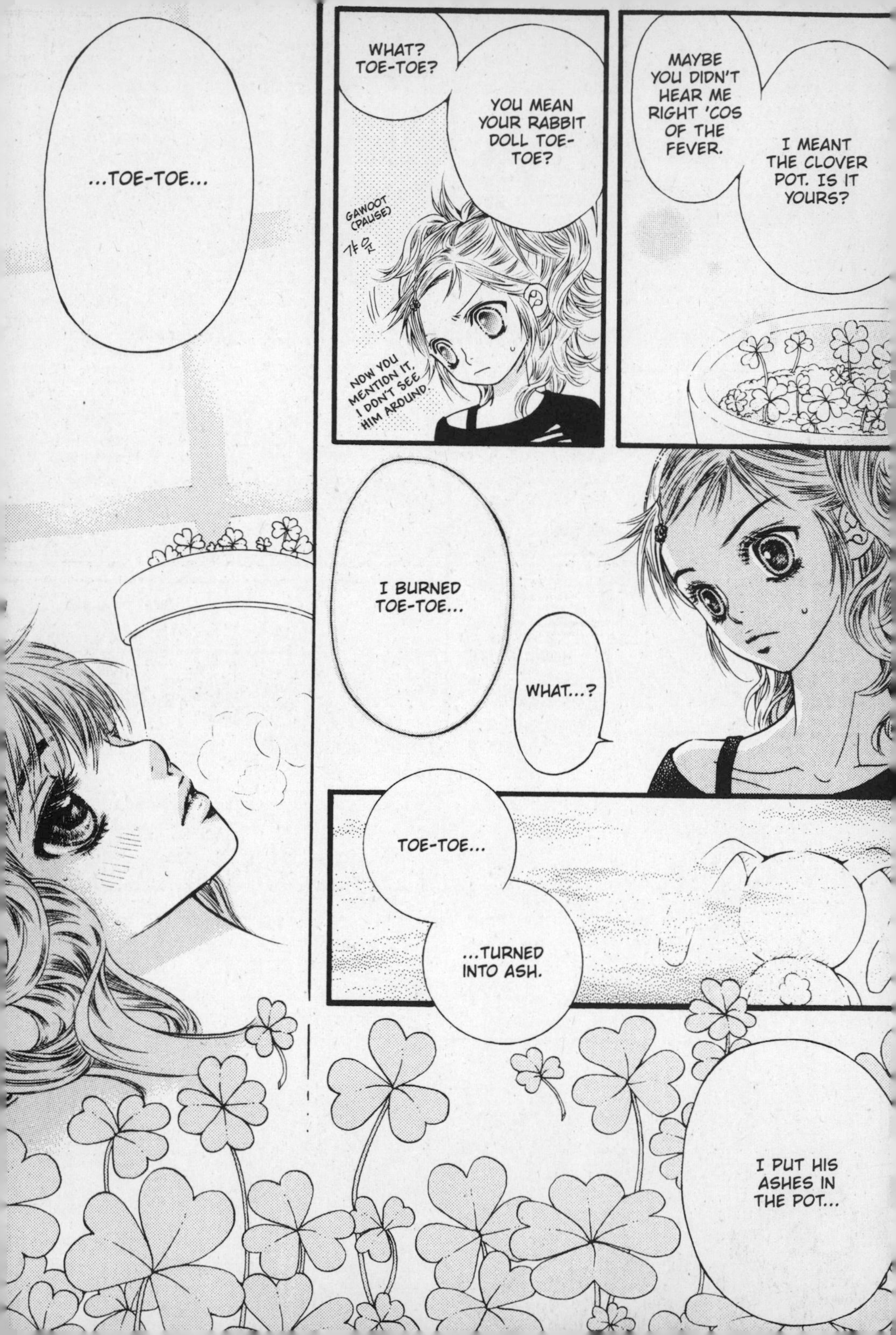
...TOE-TOE...
WHAT? TOE-TOE?
YOU MEAN YOUR RABBIT DOLL TOE-TOE?
GAWOOT (PAUSE)
갸웃
NOW YOU MENTION IT, I DON'T SEE HIM AROUND.
MAYBE YOU DIDN'T HEAR ME RIGHT 'COS OF THE FEVER.
I MEANT THE CLOVER POT. IS IT YOURS?
I BURNED TOE-TOE...
WHAT...?
TOE-TOE...
...TURNED INTO ASH.
I PUT HIS ASHES IN THE POT...

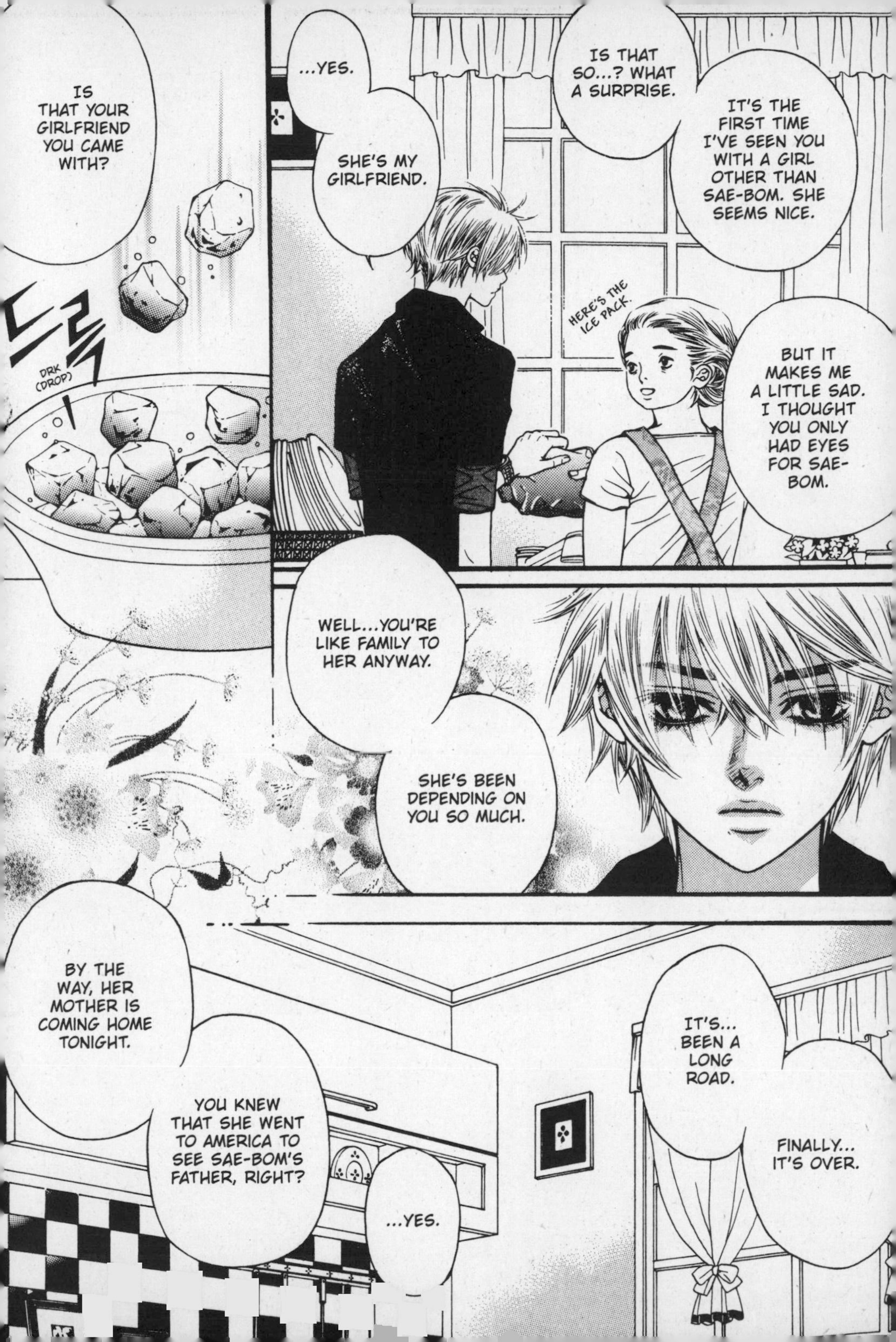

IS THAT YOUR GIRLFRIEND YOU CAME WITH?
드르륵
DRK (DROP)
...YES.
SHE'S MY GIRLFRIEND.
IS THAT SO...? WHAT A SURPRISE.
IT'S THE FIRST TIME I'VE SEEN YOU WITH A GIRL OTHER THAN SAE-BOM. SHE SEEMS NICE.
HERE'S THE ICE PACK.
BUT IT MAKES ME A LITTLE SAD. I THOUGHT YOU ONLY HAD EYES FOR SAE-BOM.
WELL...YOU'RE LIKE FAMILY TO HER ANYWAY.
SHE'S BEEN DEPENDING ON YOU SO MUCH.
BY THE WAY, HER MOTHER IS COMING HOME TONIGHT.
YOU KNEW THAT SHE WENT TO AMERICA TO SEE SAE-BOM'S FATHER, RIGHT?
...YES.
IT'S... BEEN A LONG ROAD.
FINALLY... IT'S OVER.

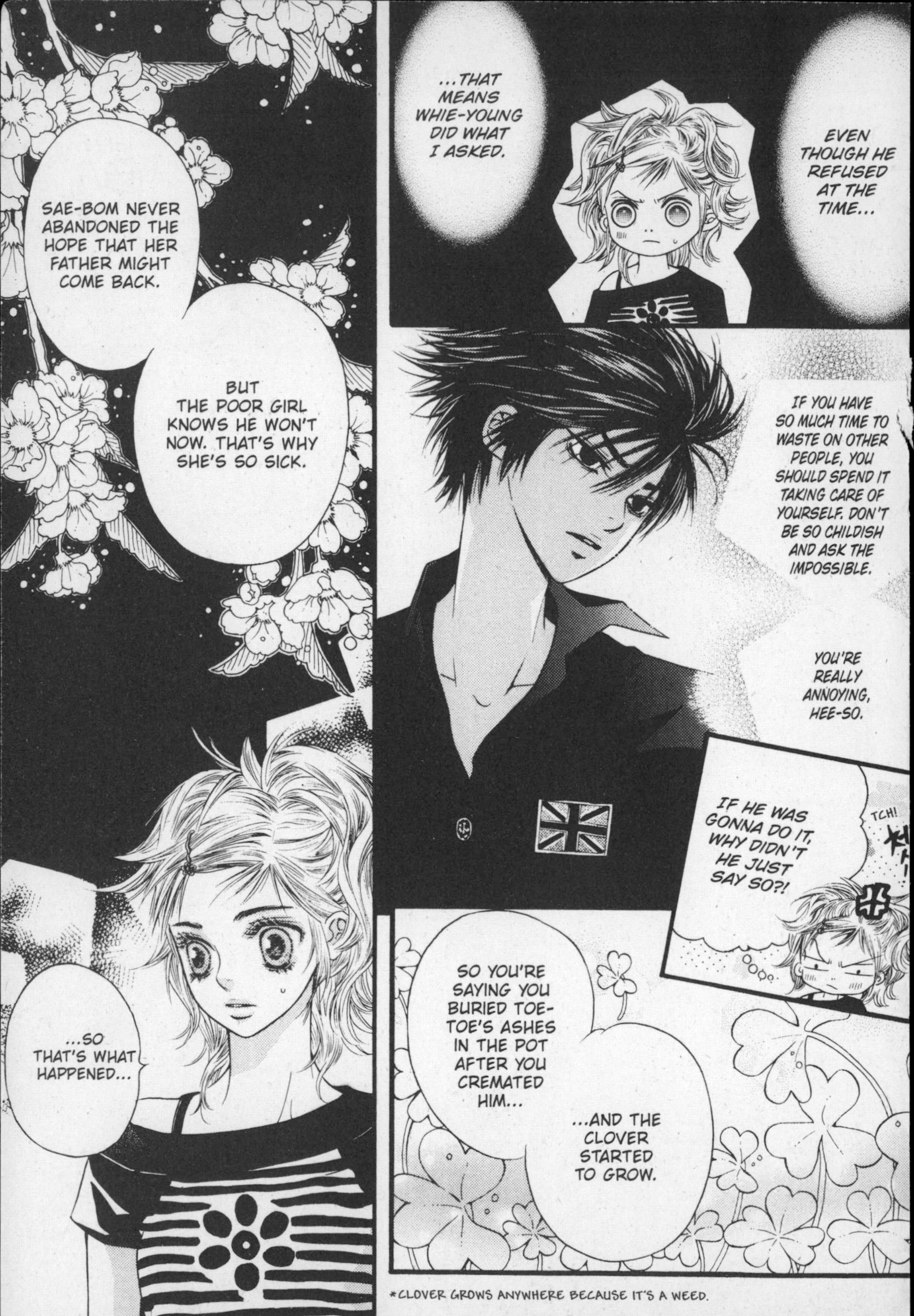
SAE-BOM NEVER ABANDONED THE HOPE THAT HER FATHER MIGHT COME BACK.
BUT THE POOR GIRL KNOWS HE WON'T NOW. THAT'S WHY SHE'S SO SICK.
...SO THAT'S WHAT HAPPENED...
...THAT MEANS WHIE-YOUNG DID WHAT I ASKED.
EVEN THOUGH HE REFUSED AT THE TIME...
IF YOU HAVE SO MUCH TIME TO WASTE ON OTHER PEOPLE, YOU SHOULD SPEND IT TAKING CARE OF YOURSELF. DON'T BE SO CHILDISH AND ASK THE IMPOSSIBLE.
YOU'RE REALLY ANNOYING, HEE-SO.
IF HE WAS GONNA DO IT, WHY DIDN'T HE JUST SAY SO?!
TCH!
SO YOU'RE SAYING YOU BURIED TOE-TOE'S ASHES IN THE POT AFTER YOU CREMATED HIM...
...AND THE CLOVER STARTED TO GROW.

*CLOVER GROWS ANYWHERE BECAUSE IT'S A WEED.

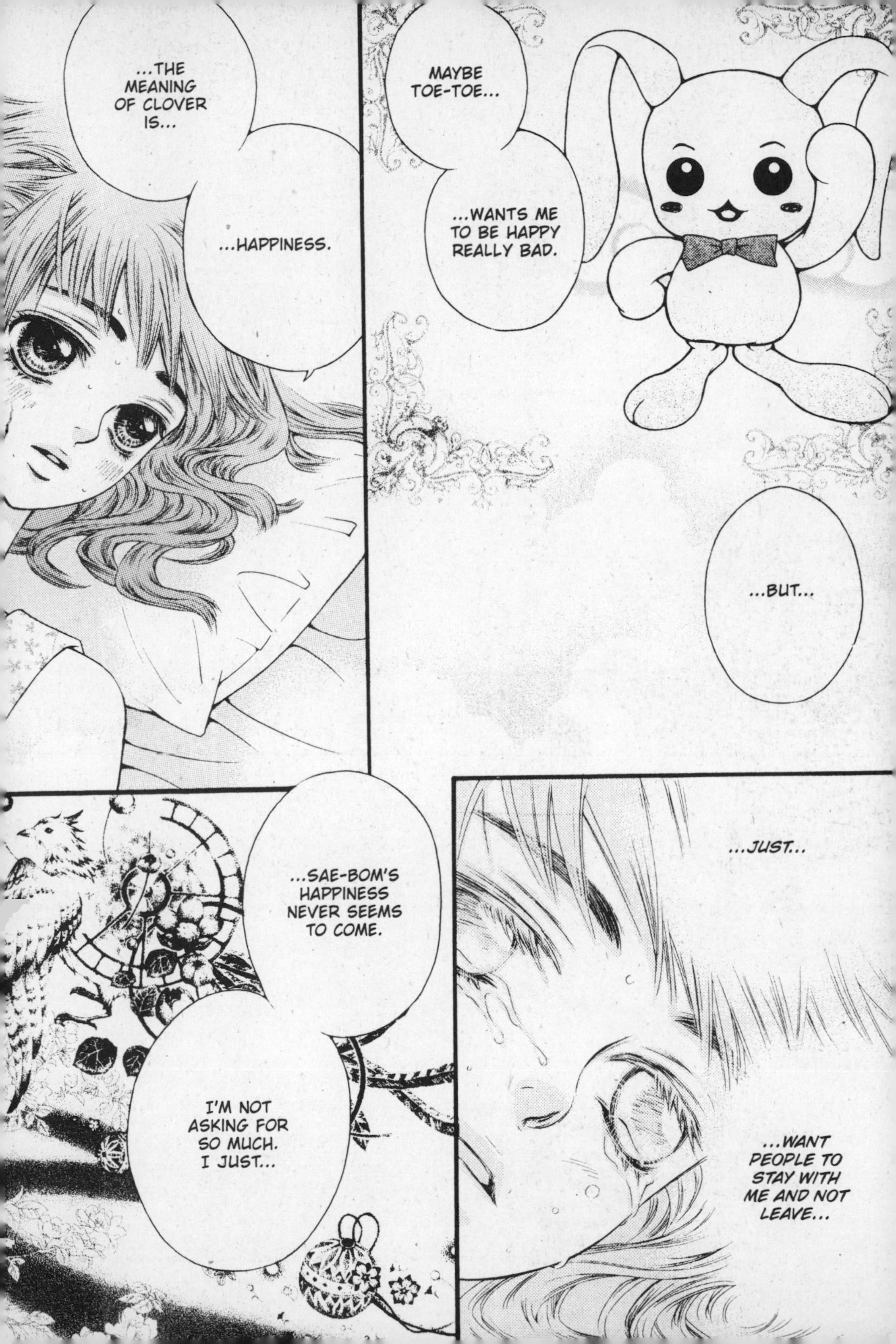
...THE MEANING OF CLOVER IS...
...HAPPINESS.
MAYBE TOE-TOE...
...WANTS ME TO BE HAPPY REALLY BAD.
...BUT...
...SAE-BOM'S HAPPINESS NEVER SEEMS TO COME.
I'M NOT ASKING FOR SO MUCH. I JUST...
...JUST...
...WANT PEOPLE TO STAY WITH ME AND NOT LEAVE...

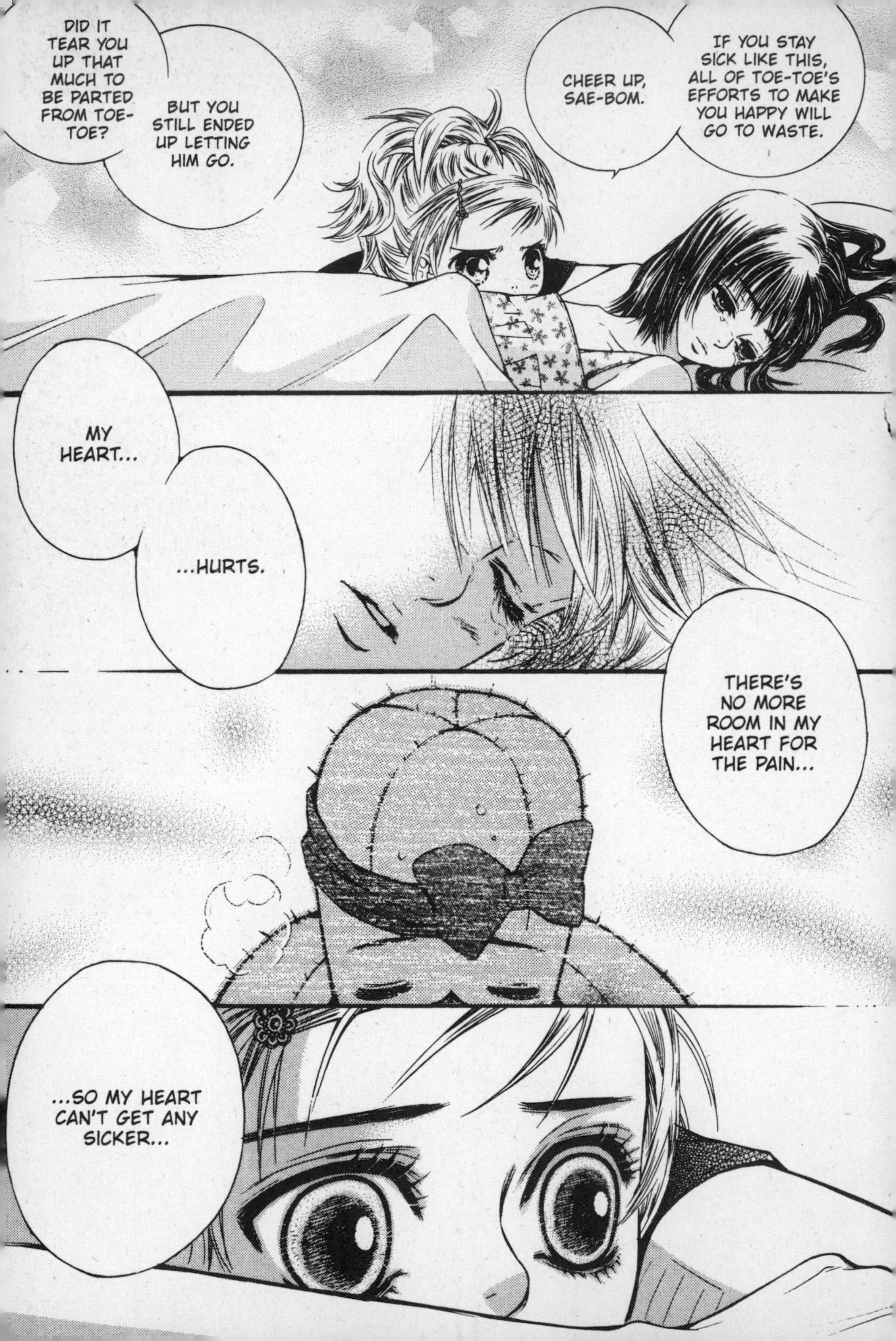
DID IT TEAR YOU UP THAT MUCH TO BE PARTED FROM TOE-TOE?
BUT YOU STILL ENDED UP LETTING HIM GO.
CHEER UP, SAE-BOM.
IF YOU STAY SICK LIKE THIS, ALL OF TOE-TOE'S EFFORTS TO MAKE YOU HAPPY WILL GO TO WASTE.
MY HEART...
...HURTS.
THERE'S NO MORE ROOM IN MY HEART FOR THE PAIN...
...SO MY HEART CAN'T GET ANY SICKER...

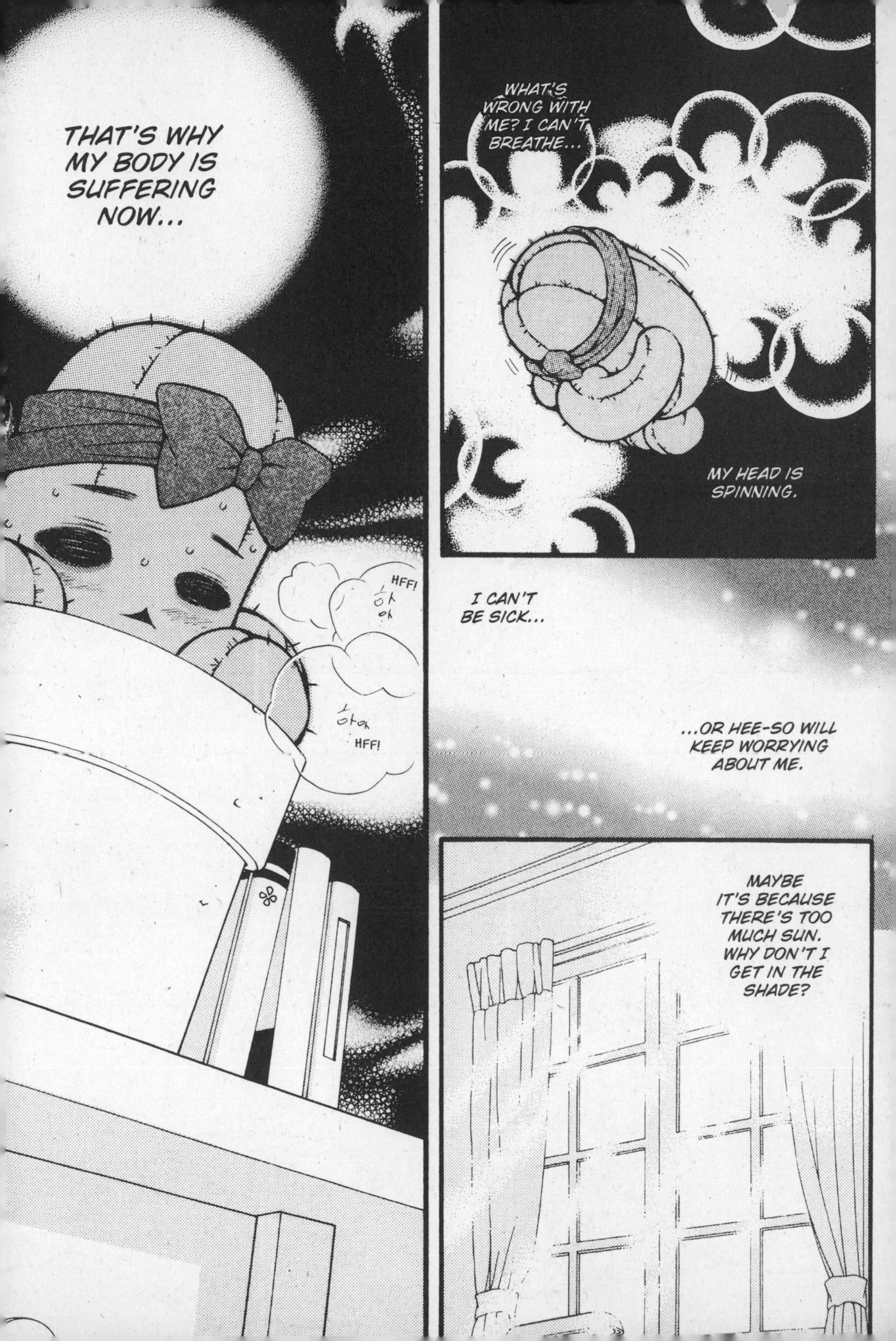
THAT'S WHY MY BODY IS SUFFERING NOW...
HFF!
HFF!
WHAT'S WRONG WITH ME? I CAN'T BREATHE...
MY HEAD IS SPINNING.
I CAN'T BE SICK...
...OR HEE-SO WILL KEEP WORRYING ABOUT ME.
MAYBE IT'S BECAUSE THERE'S TOO MUCH SUN. WHY DON'T I GET IN THE SHADE?

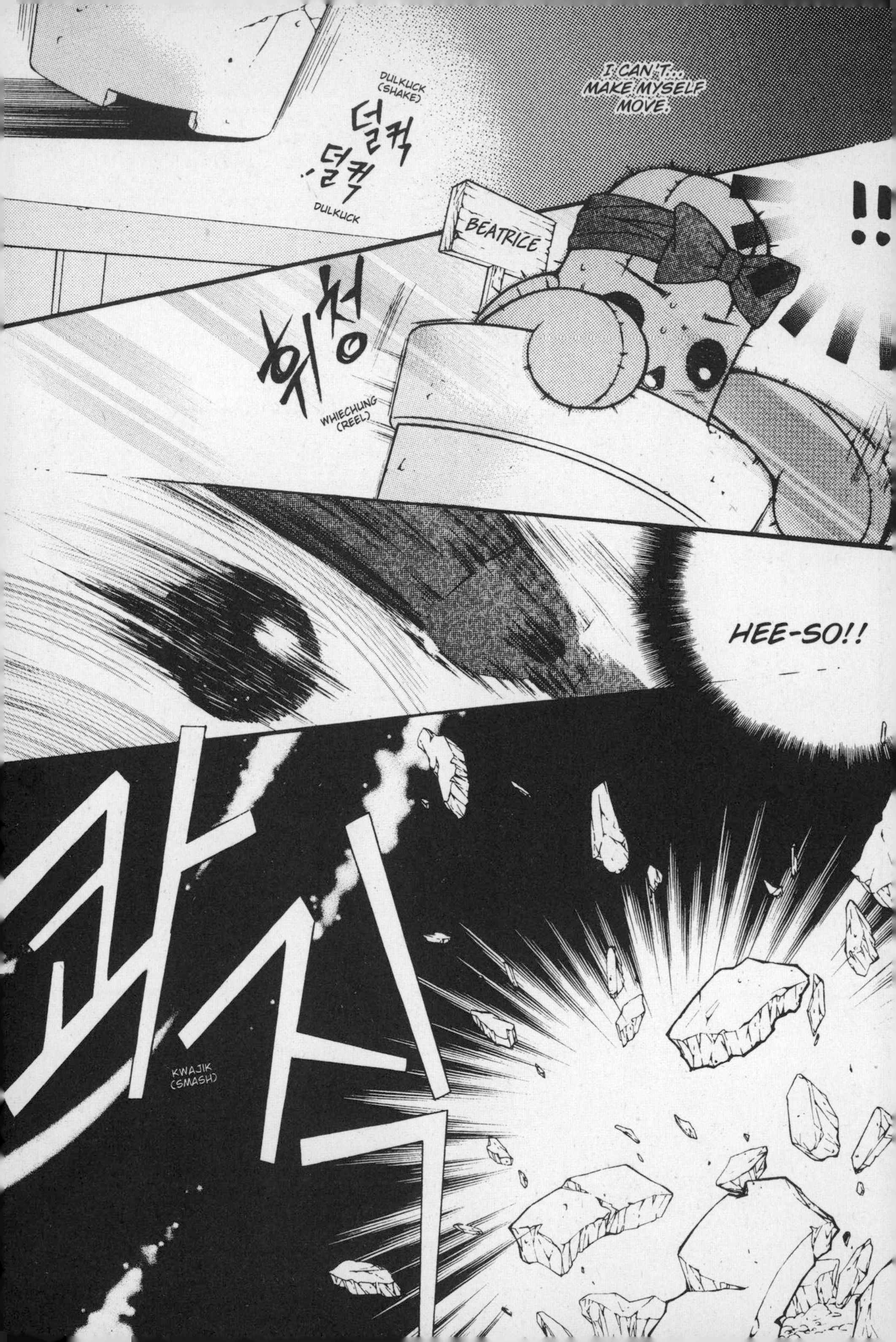
DULKUCK (SHAKE)
덜컥
덜컥
DULKUCK
BEATRICE
I CAN'T... MAKE MYSELF MOVE.
!!
휘청
WHIECHUNG (REEL)
HEE-SO!!
콰직
KWAJIK (SMASH)

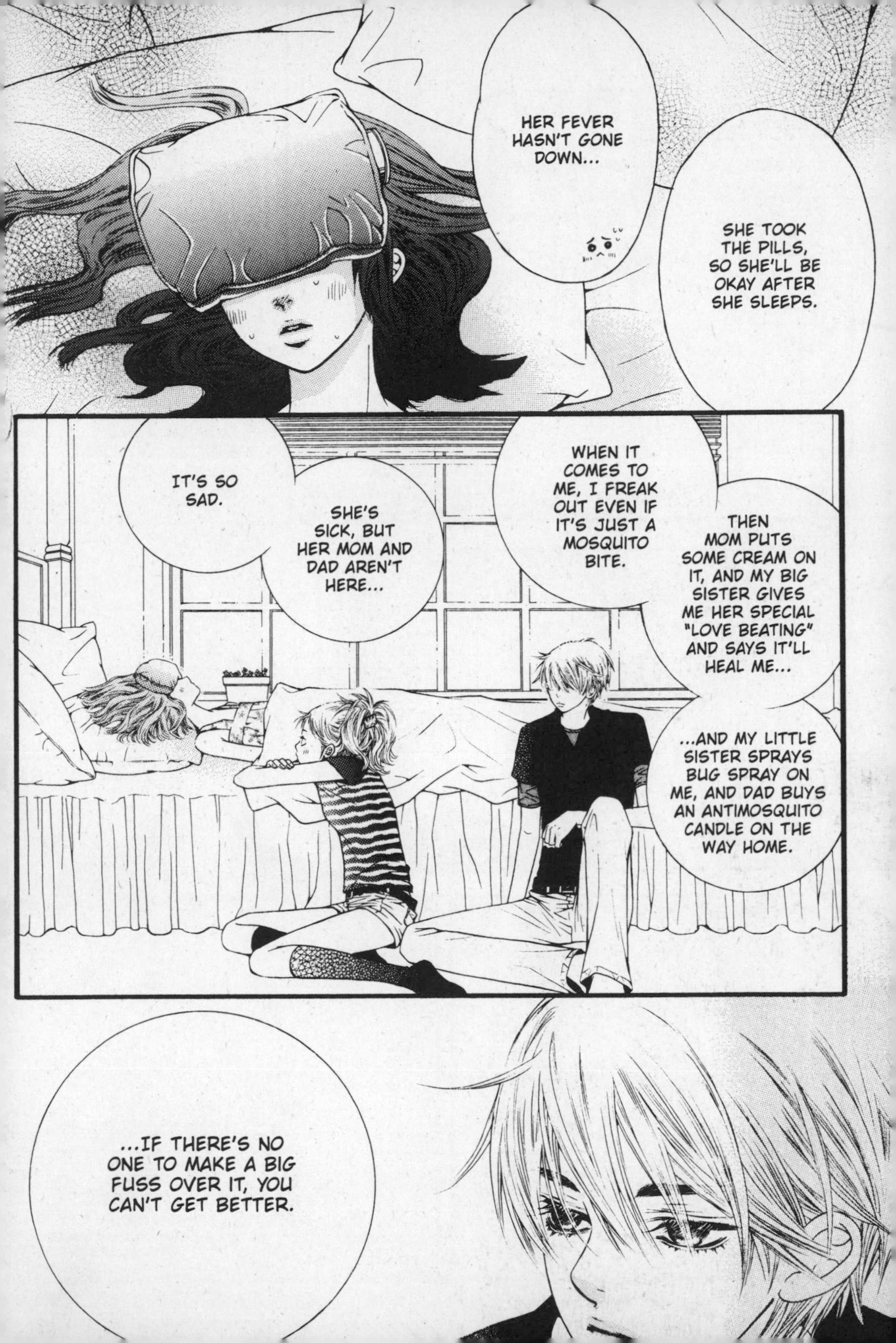
HER FEVER HASN'T GONE DOWN...
SHE TOOK THE PILLS, SO SHE'LL BE OKAY AFTER SHE SLEEPS.
IT'S SO SAD.
SHE'S SICK, BUT HER MOM AND DAD AREN'T HERE...
WHEN IT COMES TO ME, I FREAK OUT EVEN IF IT'S JUST A MOSQUITO BITE.
THEN MOM PUTS SOME CREAM ON IT, AND MY BIG SISTER GIVES ME HER SPECIAL "LOVE BEATING" AND SAYS IT'LL HEAL ME...
...AND MY LITTLE SISTER SPRAYS BUG SPRAY ON ME, AND DAD BUYS AN ANTIMOSQUITO CANDLE ON THE WAY HOME.
...IF THERE'S NO ONE TO MAKE A BIG FUSS OVER IT, YOU CAN'T GET BETTER.

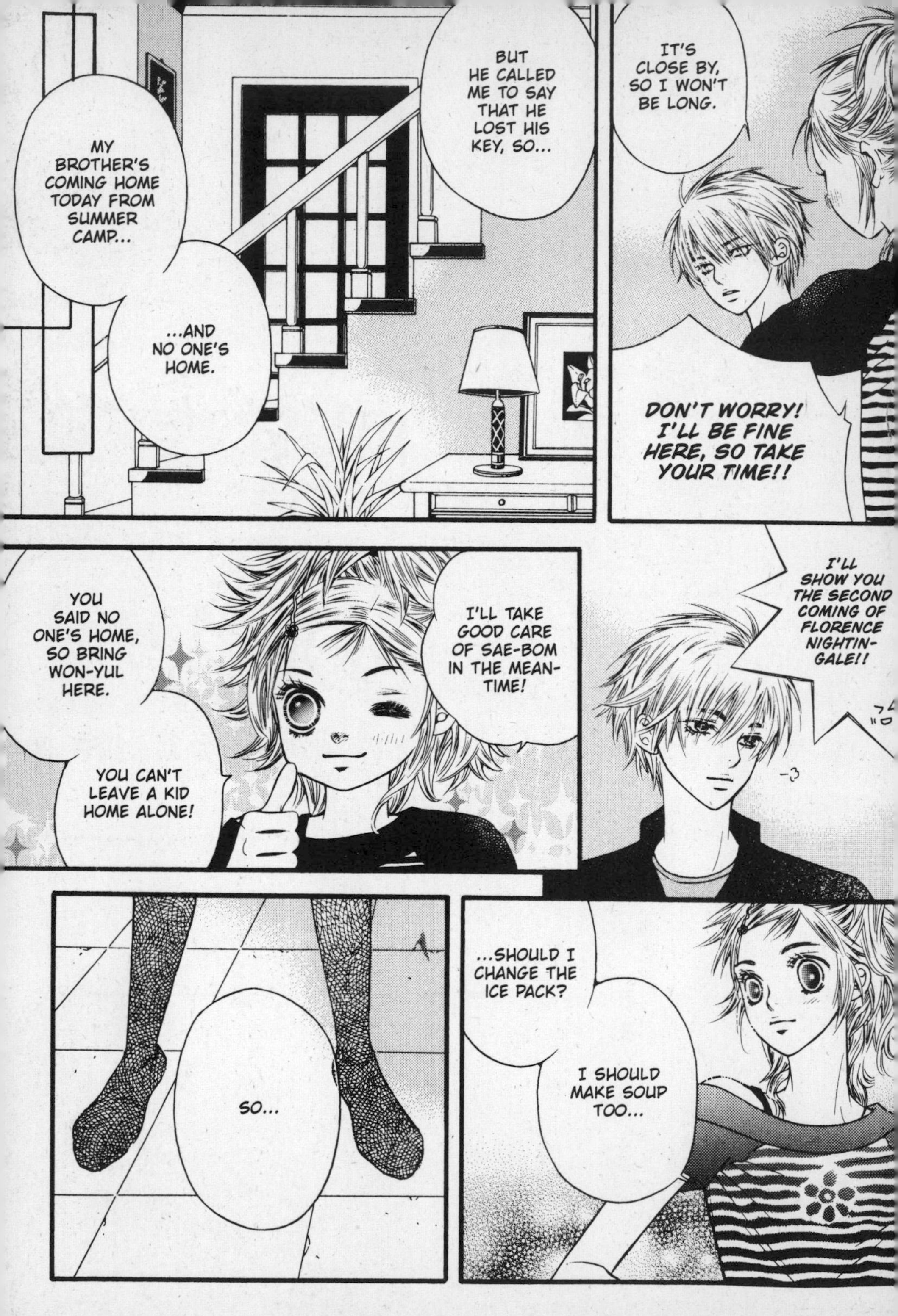
MY BROTHER'S COMING HOME TODAY FROM SUMMER CAMP...
BUT HE CALLED ME TO SAY THAT HE LOST HIS KEY, SO...
...AND NO ONE'S HOME.
IT'S CLOSE BY, SO I WON'T BE LONG.
DON'T WORRY! I'LL BE FINE HERE, SO TAKE YOUR TIME!!
YOU SAID NO ONE'S HOME, SO BRING WON-YUL HERE.
YOU CAN'T LEAVE A KID HOME ALONE!
I'LL TAKE GOOD CARE OF SAE-BOM IN THE MEAN-TIME!
I'LL SHOW YOU THE SECOND COMING OF FLORENCE NIGHTIN-GALE!!
SO...
...SHOULD I CHANGE THE ICE PACK?
I SHOULD MAKE SOUP TOO...

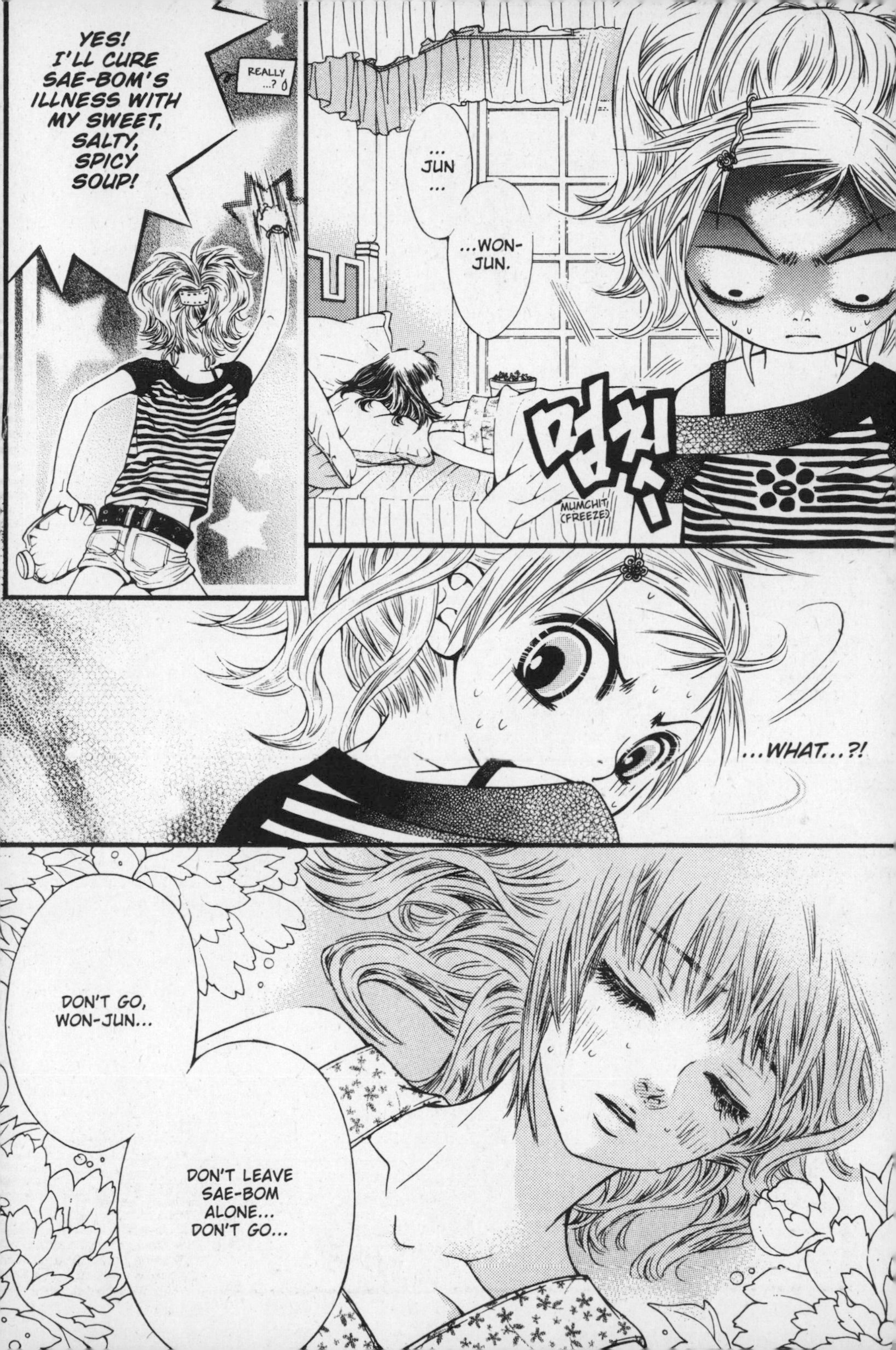
YES! I'LL CURE SAE-BOM'S ILLNESS WITH MY SWEET, SALTY, SPICY SOUP!
REALLY ...?
... JUN ...
...WON-JUN.
멈칫!
MUMCHIT (FREEZE)
...WHAT...?!
DON'T GO, WON-JUN...
DON'T LEAVE SAE-BOM ALONE... DON'T GO...

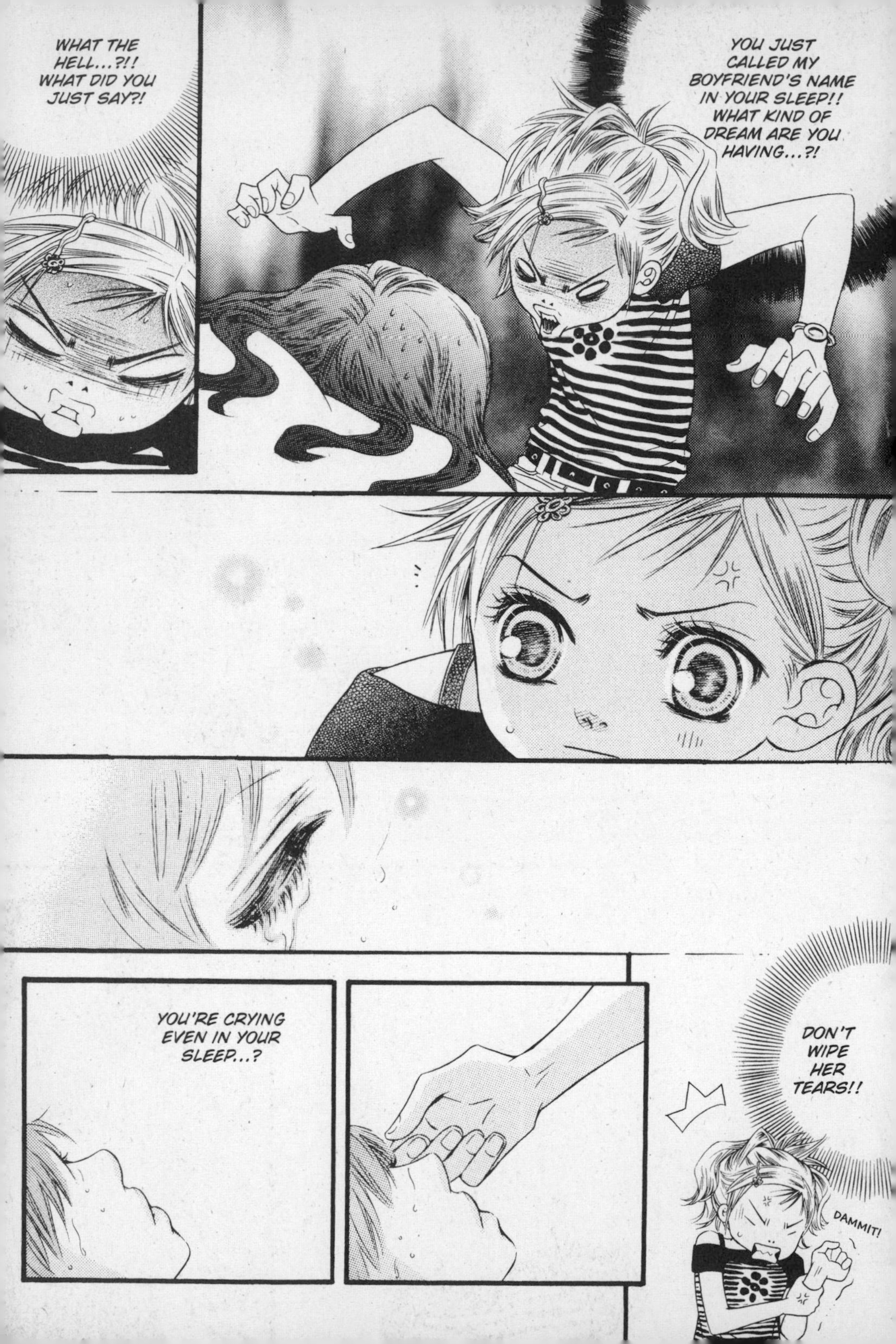
WHAT THE HELL...?!! WHAT DID YOU JUST SAY?!
YOU JUST CALLED MY BOYFRIEND'S NAME IN YOUR SLEEP!! WHAT KIND OF DREAM ARE YOU HAVING...?!
YOU'RE CRYING EVEN IN YOUR SLEEP...?
DON'T WIPE HER TEARS!!
DAMMIT!

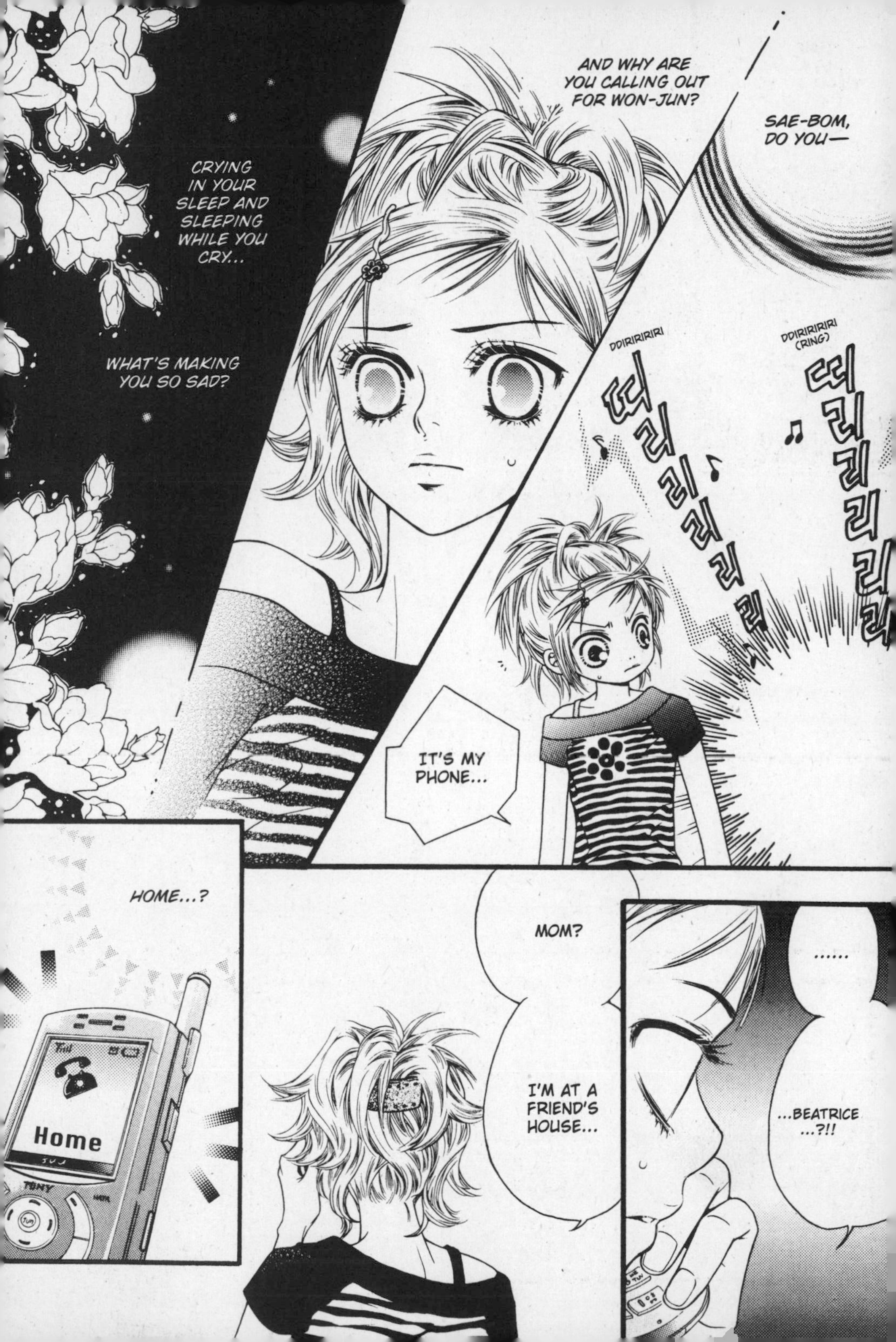
CRYING IN YOUR SLEEP AND SLEEPING WHILE YOU CRY...
WHAT'S MAKING YOU SO SAD?
AND WHY ARE YOU CALLING OUT FOR WON-JUN?
SAE-BOM, DO YOU—
DDIRIRIRIRI
DDIRIRIRIRI (RING)
IT'S MY PHONE...
HOME...?
Home
MOM?
I'M AT A FRIEND'S HOUSE...
......
...BEATRICE ...?!!

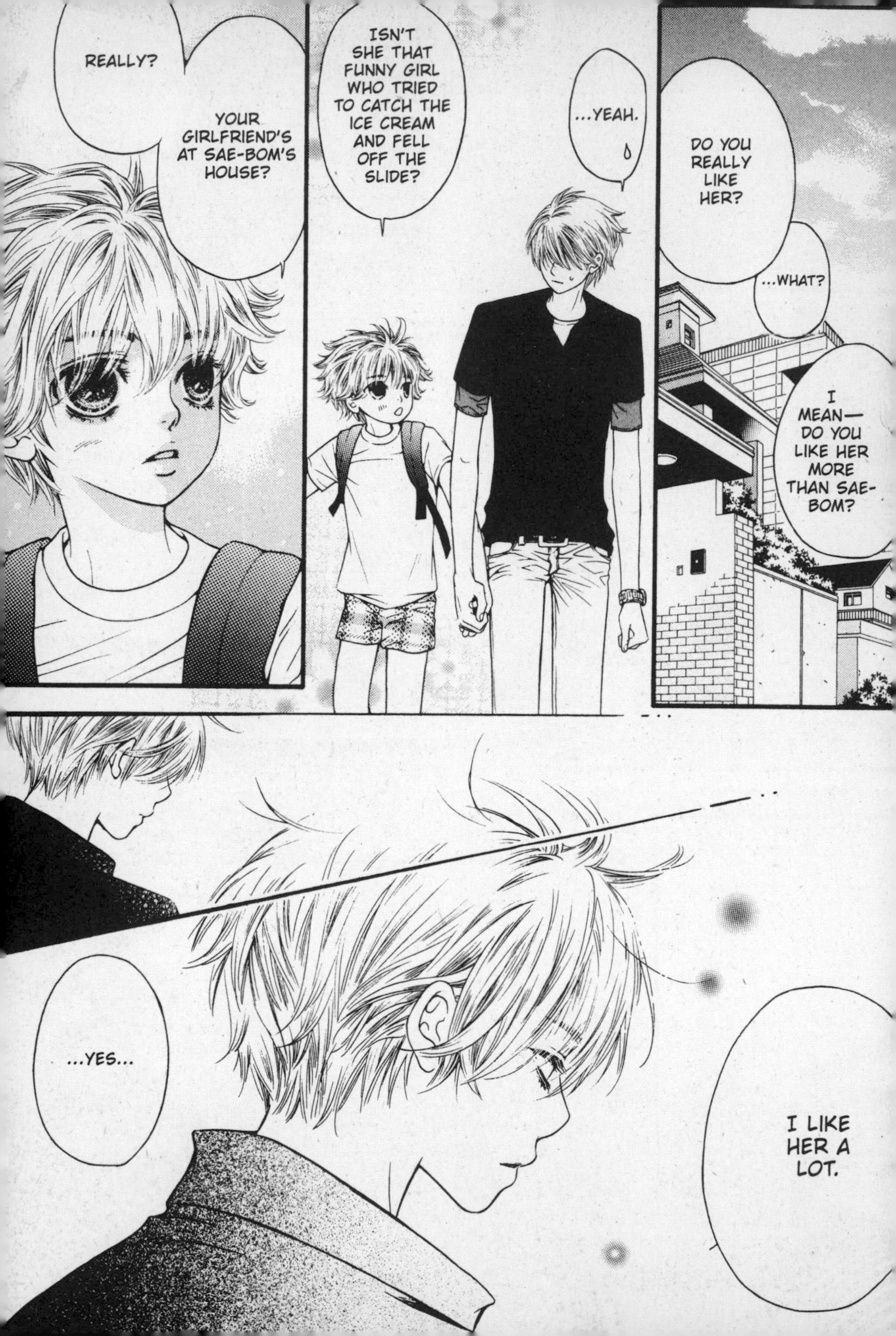
REALLY?
YOUR GIRLFRIEND'S AT SAE-BOM'S HOUSE?
ISN'T SHE THAT FUNNY GIRL WHO TRIED TO CATCH THE ICE CREAM AND FELL OFF THE SLIDE?
...YEAH.
DO YOU REALLY LIKE HER?
...WHAT?
I MEAN— DO YOU LIKE HER MORE THAN SAE-BOM?
...YES...
I LIKE HER A LOT.

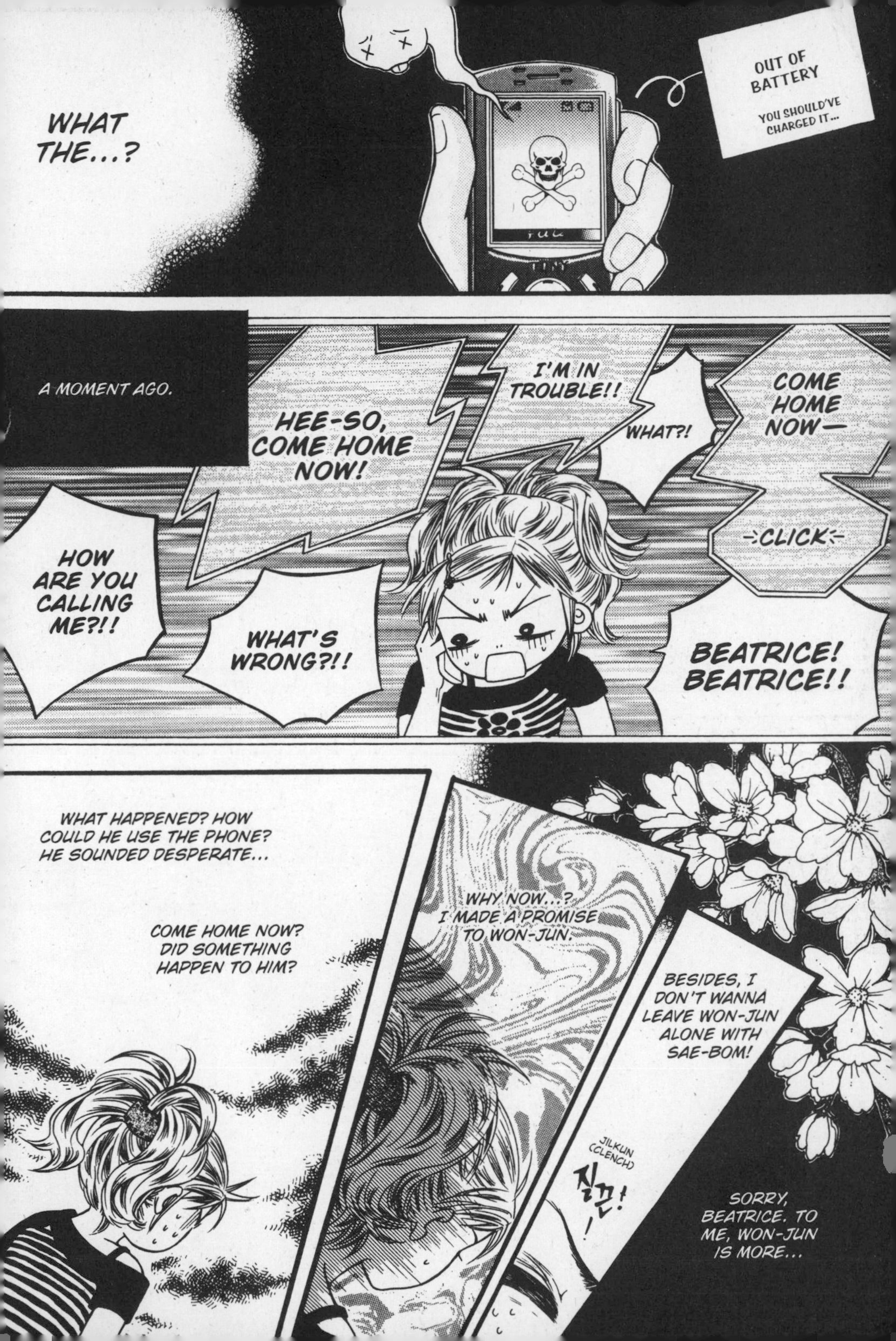
WHAT THE...?
OUT OF BATTERY
YOU SHOULD'VE CHARGED IT...
A MOMENT AGO.
HEE-SO, COME HOME NOW!
I'M IN TROUBLE!!
WHAT?!
COME HOME NOW—
-CLICK-
HOW ARE YOU CALLING ME?!!
WHAT'S WRONG?!!
BEATRICE! BEATRICE!!
WHAT HAPPENED? HOW COULD HE USE THE PHONE? HE SOUNDED DESPERATE...
COME HOME NOW? DID SOMETHING HAPPEN TO HIM?
WHY NOW...? I MADE A PROMISE TO WON-JUN.
BESIDES, I DON'T WANNA LEAVE WON-JUN ALONE WITH SAE-BOM!
JILKUN (CLENCH)
질끈!
SORRY, BEATRICE. TO ME, WON-JUN IS MORE...

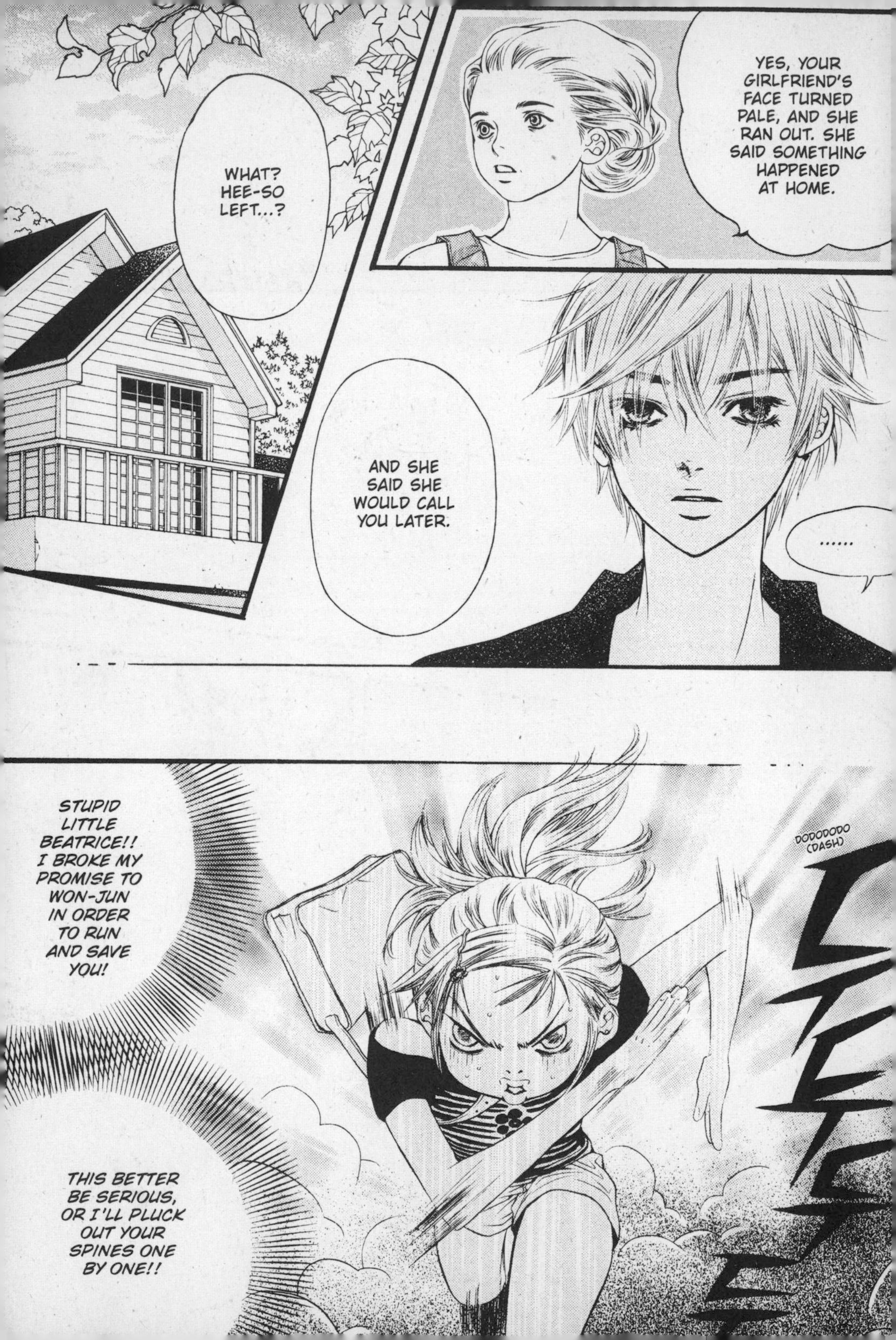

WHAT? HEE-SO LEFT...?
YES, YOUR GIRLFRIEND'S FACE TURNED PALE, AND SHE RAN OUT. SHE SAID SOMETHING HAPPENED AT HOME.
AND SHE SAID SHE WOULD CALL YOU LATER.
......
STUPID LITTLE BEATRICE!! I BROKE MY PROMISE TO WON-JUN IN ORDER TO RUN AND SAVE YOU!
DODODODO (DASH)
THIS BETTER BE SERIOUS, OR I'LL PLUCK OUT YOUR SPINES ONE BY ONE!!

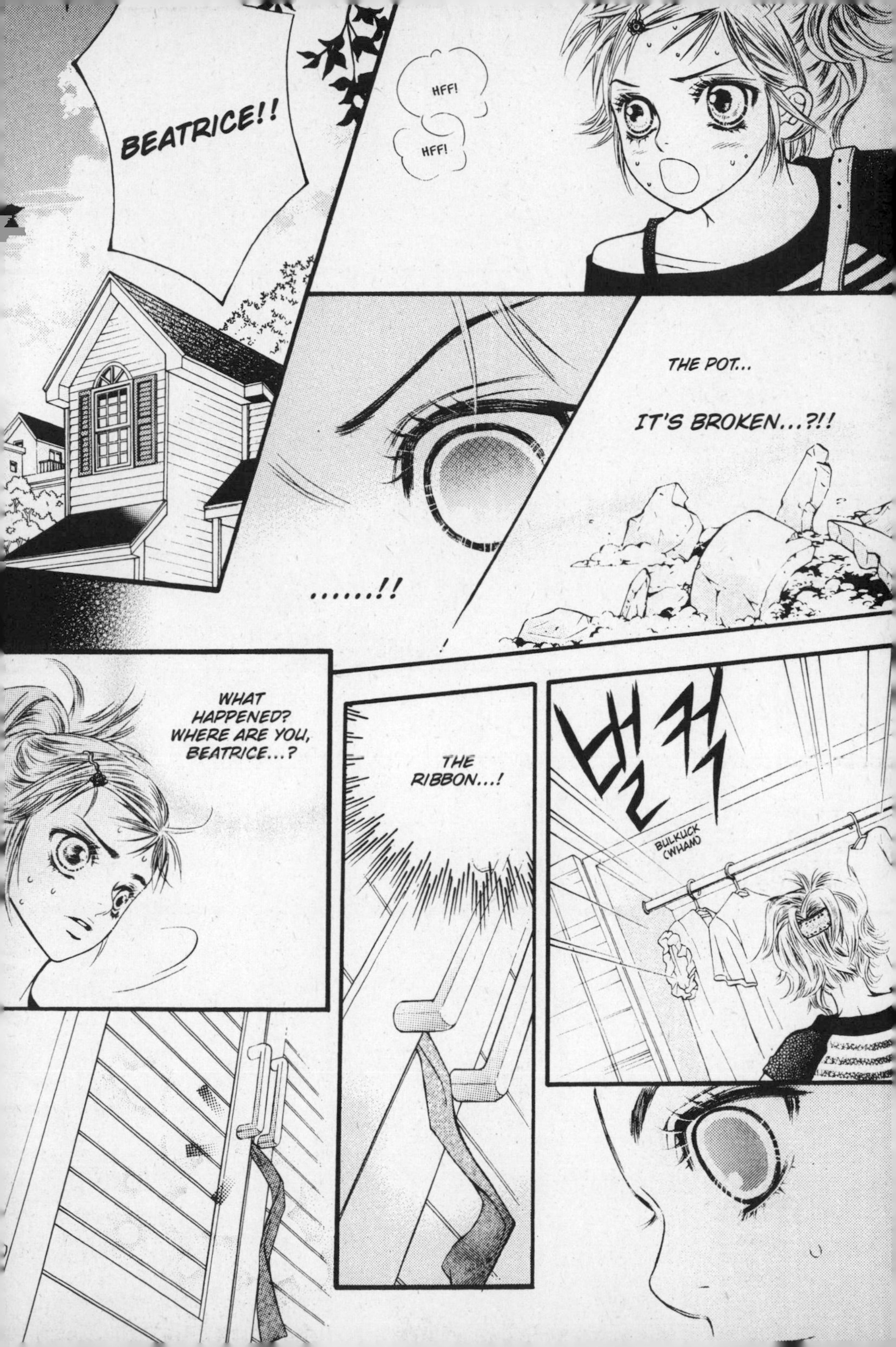
BEATRICE!!
HFF!
HFF!
THE POT...
IT'S BROKEN...?!!
......!!
WHAT HAPPENED? WHERE ARE YOU, BEATRICE...?
THE RIBBON...!
벌컥
BULKUCK (WHAM)

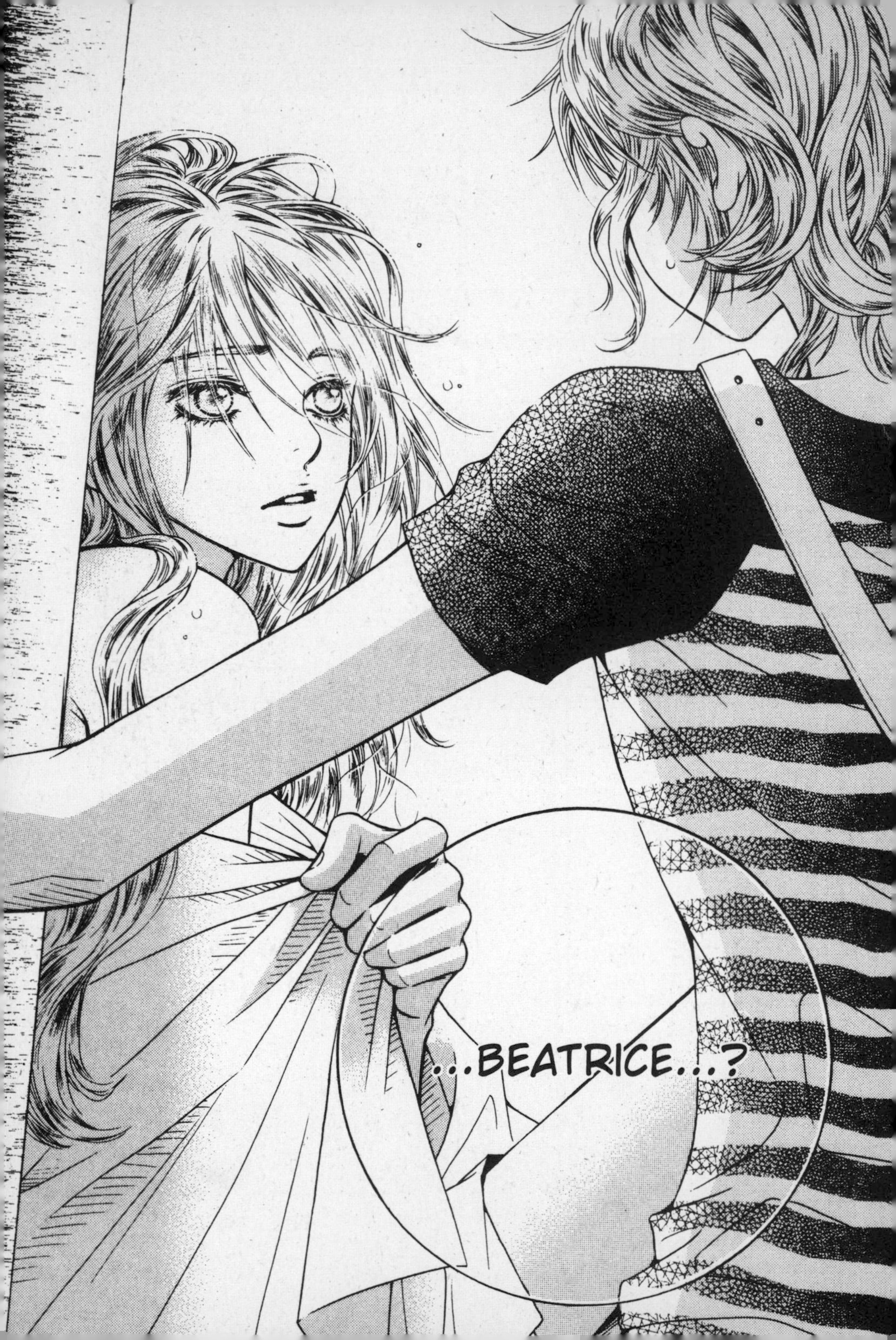
...BEATRICE...?

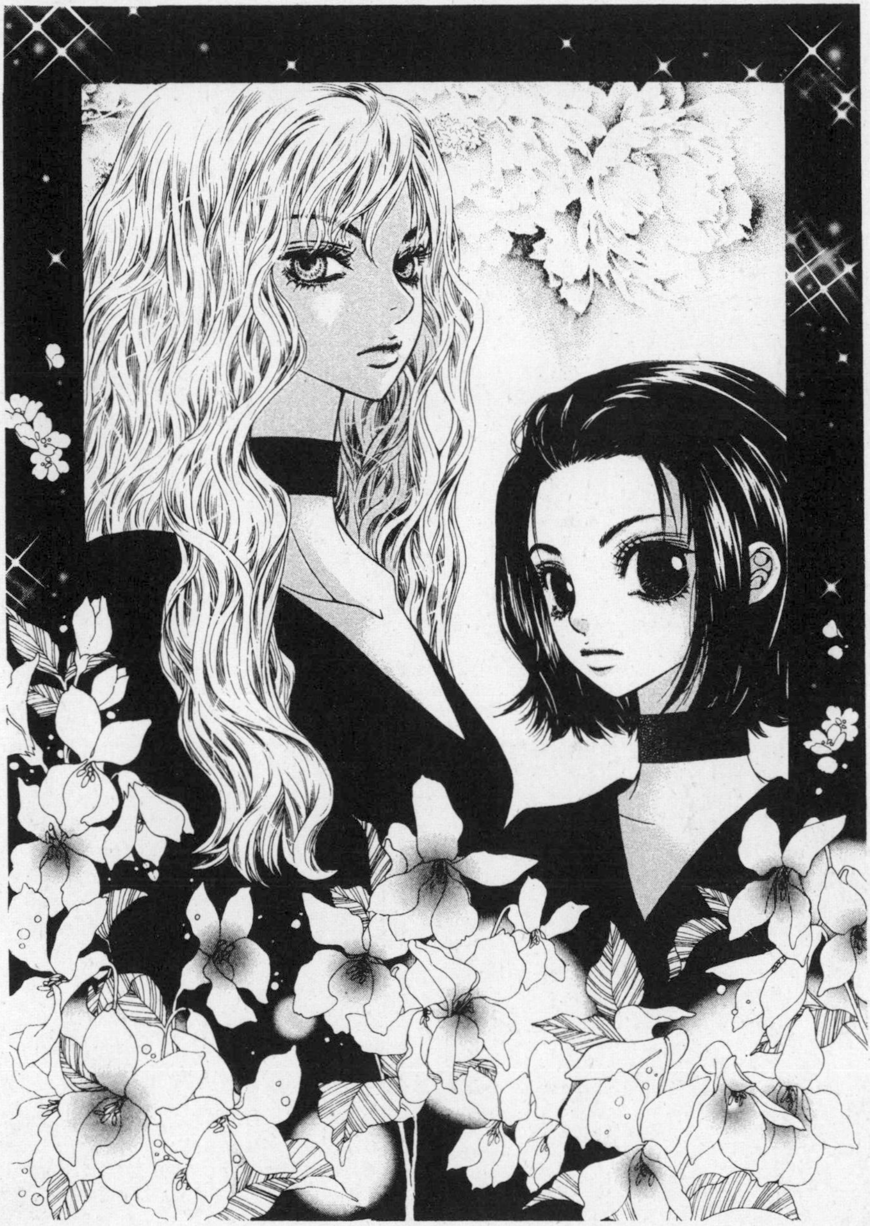

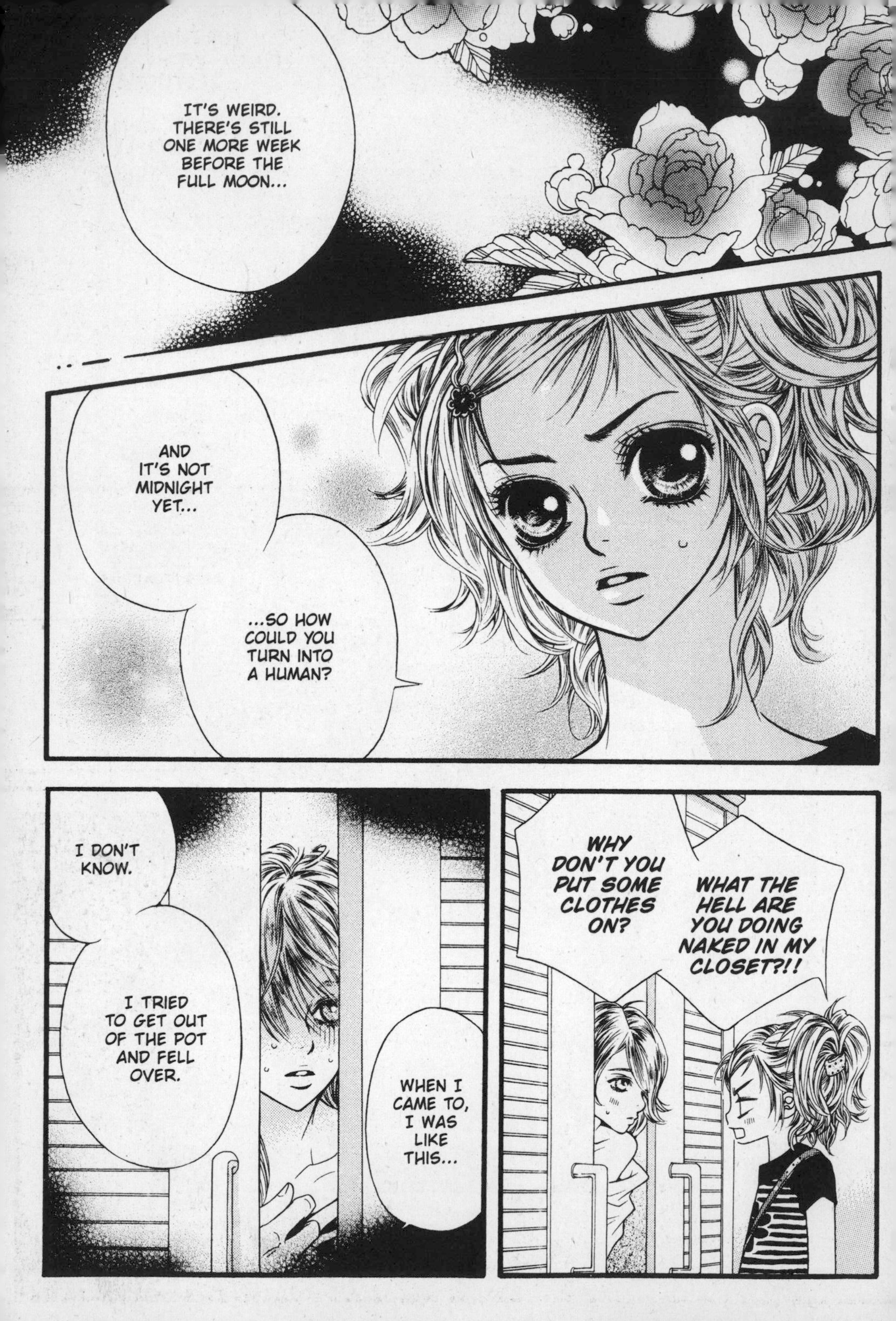
IT'S WEIRD. THERE'S STILL ONE MORE WEEK BEFORE THE FULL MOON...
AND IT'S NOT MIDNIGHT YET...
...SO HOW COULD YOU TURN INTO A HUMAN?
I DON'T KNOW.
I TRIED TO GET OUT OF THE POT AND FELL OVER.
WHEN I CAME TO, I WAS LIKE THIS...
WHY DON'T YOU PUT SOME CLOTHES ON?
WHAT THE HELL ARE YOU DOING NAKED IN MY CLOSET?!!

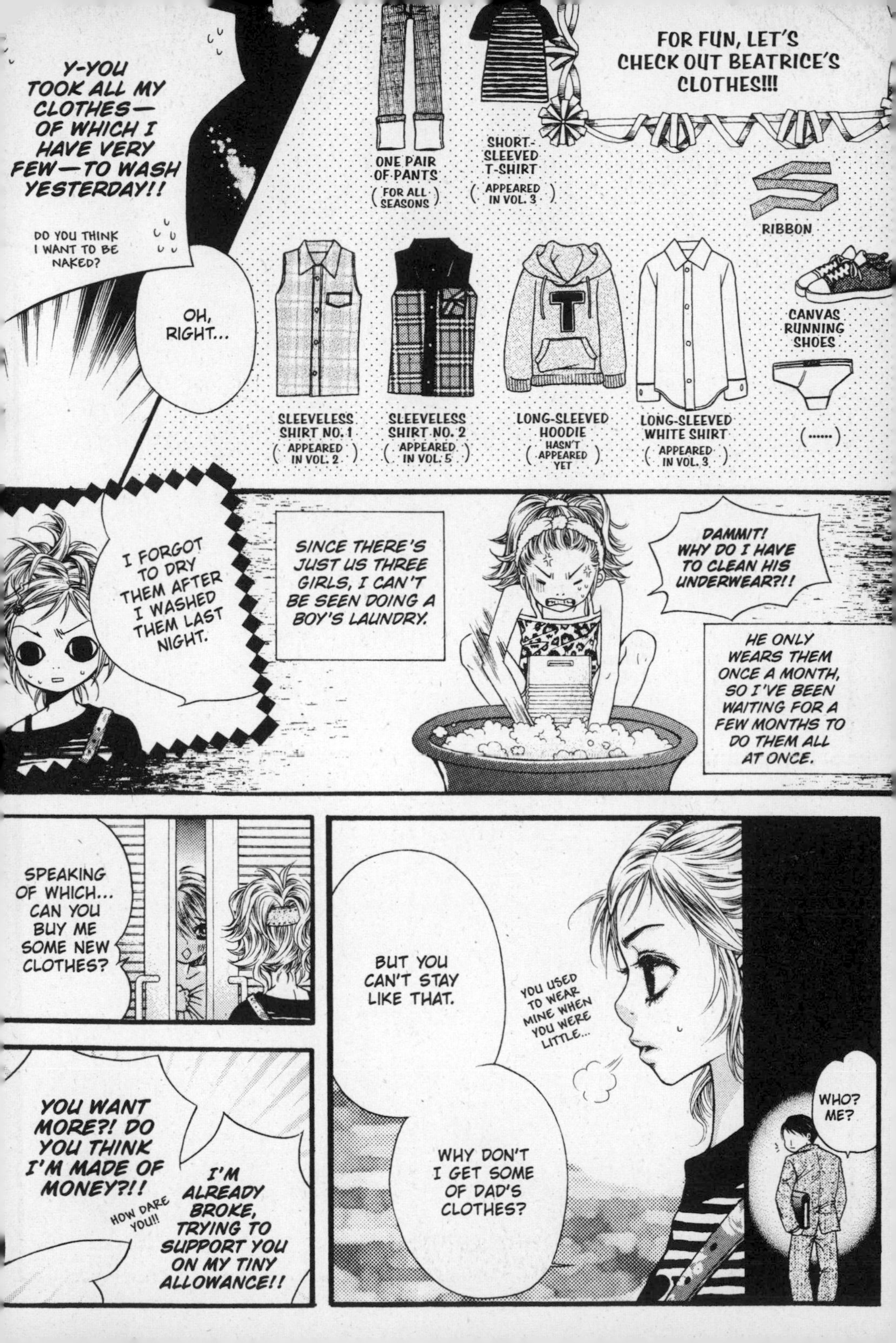
Y-YOU TOOK ALL MY CLOTHES—OF WHICH I HAVE VERY FEW—TO WASH YESTERDAY!!
DO YOU THINK I WANT TO BE NAKED?
OH, RIGHT...
ONE PAIR OF PANTS (FOR ALL SEASONS)
SHORT-SLEEVED T-SHIRT (APPEARED IN VOL. 3)
FOR FUN, LET'S CHECK OUT BEATRICE'S CLOTHES!!!
RIBBON
CANVAS RUNNING SHOES
SLEEVELESS SHIRT NO. 1 (APPEARED IN VOL. 2)
SLEEVELESS SHIRT NO. 2 (APPEARED IN VOL. 5)
LONG-SLEEVED HOODIE (HASN'T APPEARED YET)
LONG-SLEEVED WHITE SHIRT (APPEARED IN VOL. 3)
(......)
I FORGOT TO DRY THEM AFTER I WASHED THEM LAST NIGHT.
SINCE THERE'S JUST US THREE GIRLS, I CAN'T BE SEEN DOING A BOY'S LAUNDRY.
DAMMIT! WHY DO I HAVE TO CLEAN HIS UNDERWEAR?!!
HE ONLY WEARS THEM ONCE A MONTH, SO I'VE BEEN WAITING FOR A FEW MONTHS TO DO THEM ALL AT ONCE.
SPEAKING OF WHICH... CAN YOU BUY ME SOME NEW CLOTHES?
YOU WANT MORE?! DO YOU THINK I'M MADE OF MONEY?!!
HOW DARE YOU!!
I'M ALREADY BROKE, TRYING TO SUPPORT YOU ON MY TINY ALLOWANCE!!
BUT YOU CAN'T STAY LIKE THAT.
YOU USED TO WEAR MINE WHEN YOU WERE LITTLE...
WHY DON'T I GET SOME OF DAD'S CLOTHES?
WHO? ME?

STEP 25. SECRETS AND LIES

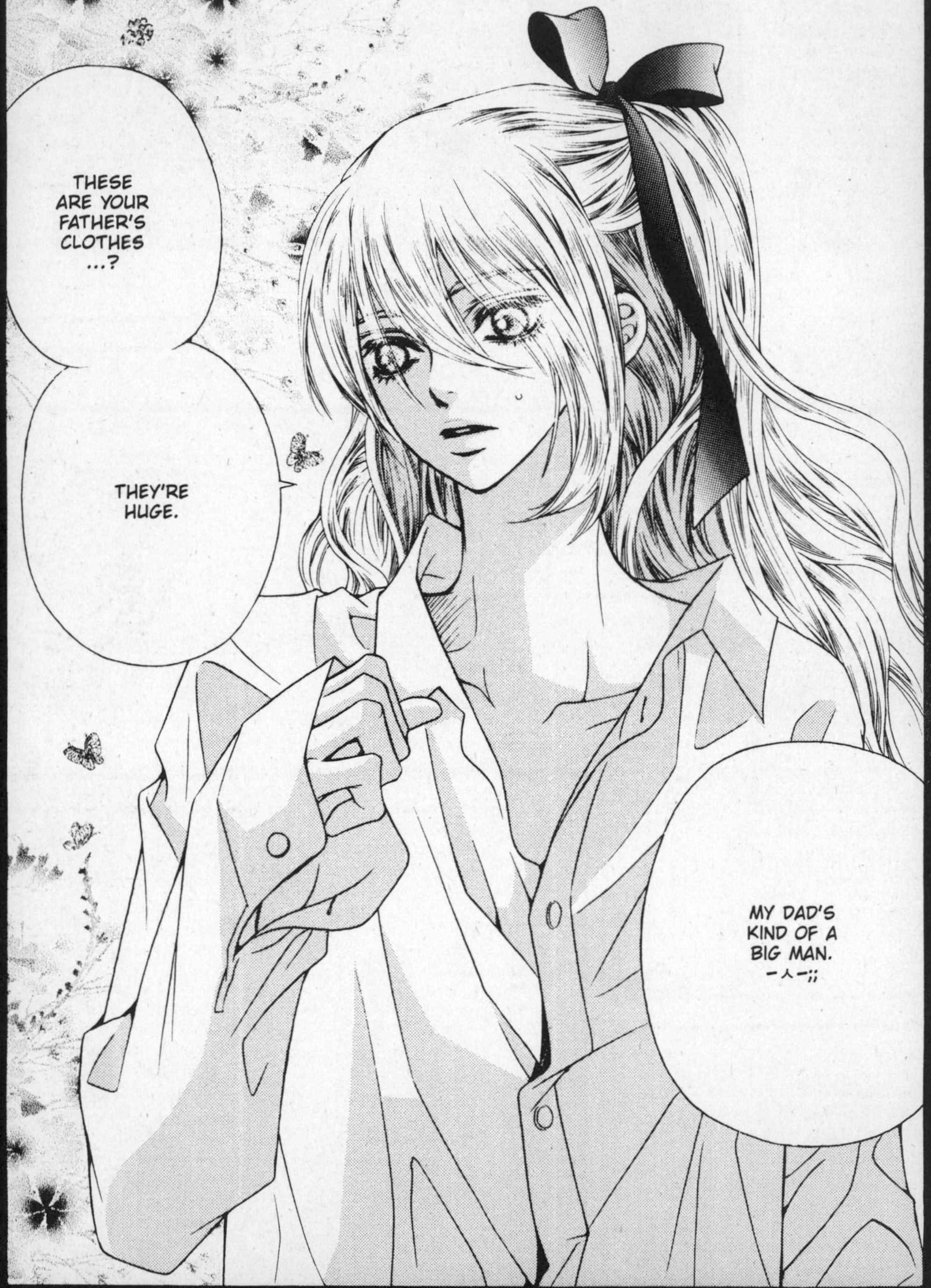
THESE ARE YOUR FATHER'S CLOTHES ...?
THEY'RE HUGE.
MY DAD'S KIND OF A BIG MAN.
ー人ー;;

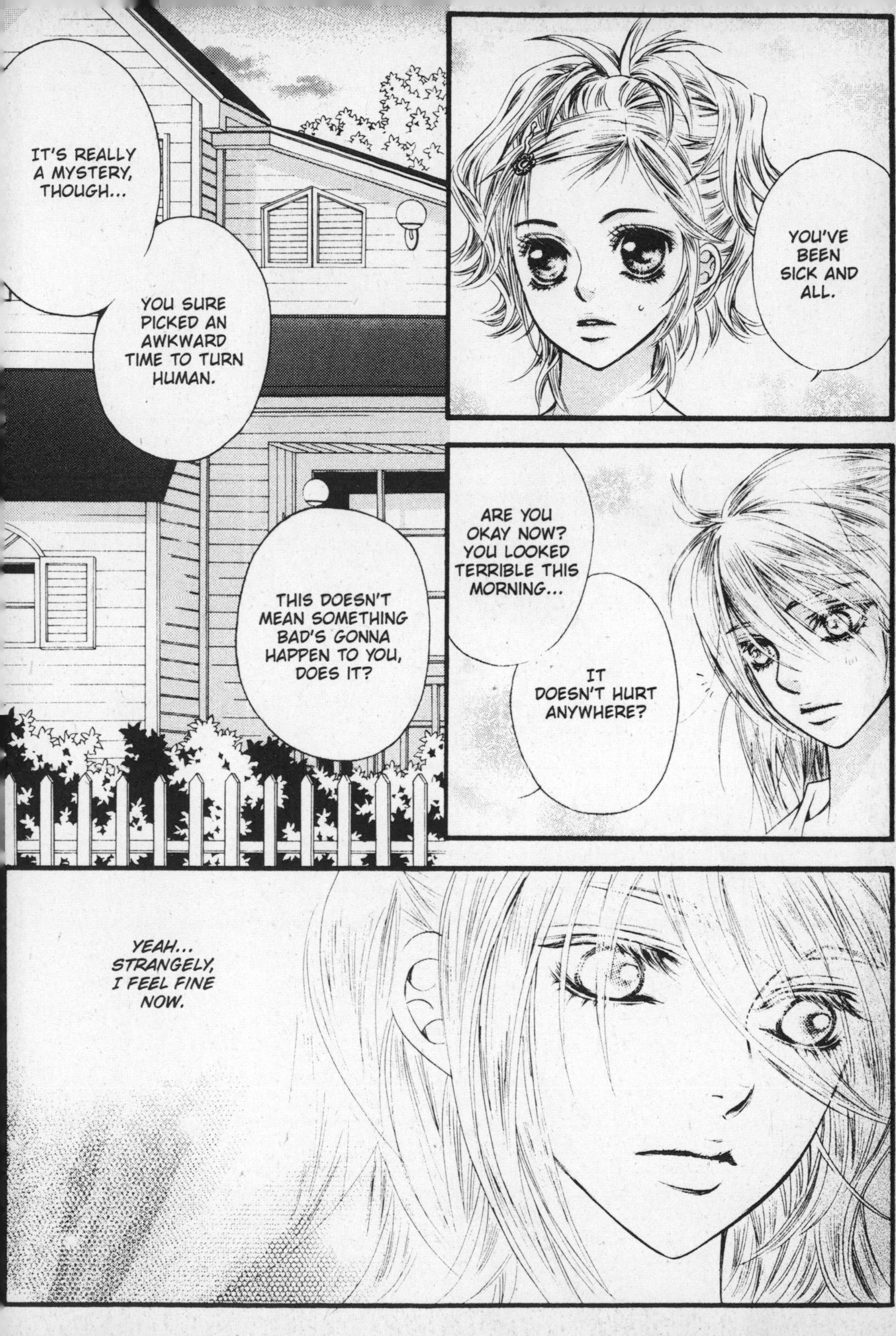
IT'S REALLY A MYSTERY, THOUGH...
YOU SURE PICKED AN AWKWARD TIME TO TURN HUMAN.
THIS DOESN'T MEAN SOMETHING BAD'S GONNA HAPPEN TO YOU, DOES IT?
YOU'VE BEEN SICK AND ALL.
ARE YOU OKAY NOW? YOU LOOKED TERRIBLE THIS MORNING...
IT DOESN'T HURT ANYWHERE?
YEAH... STRANGELY, I FEEL FINE NOW.

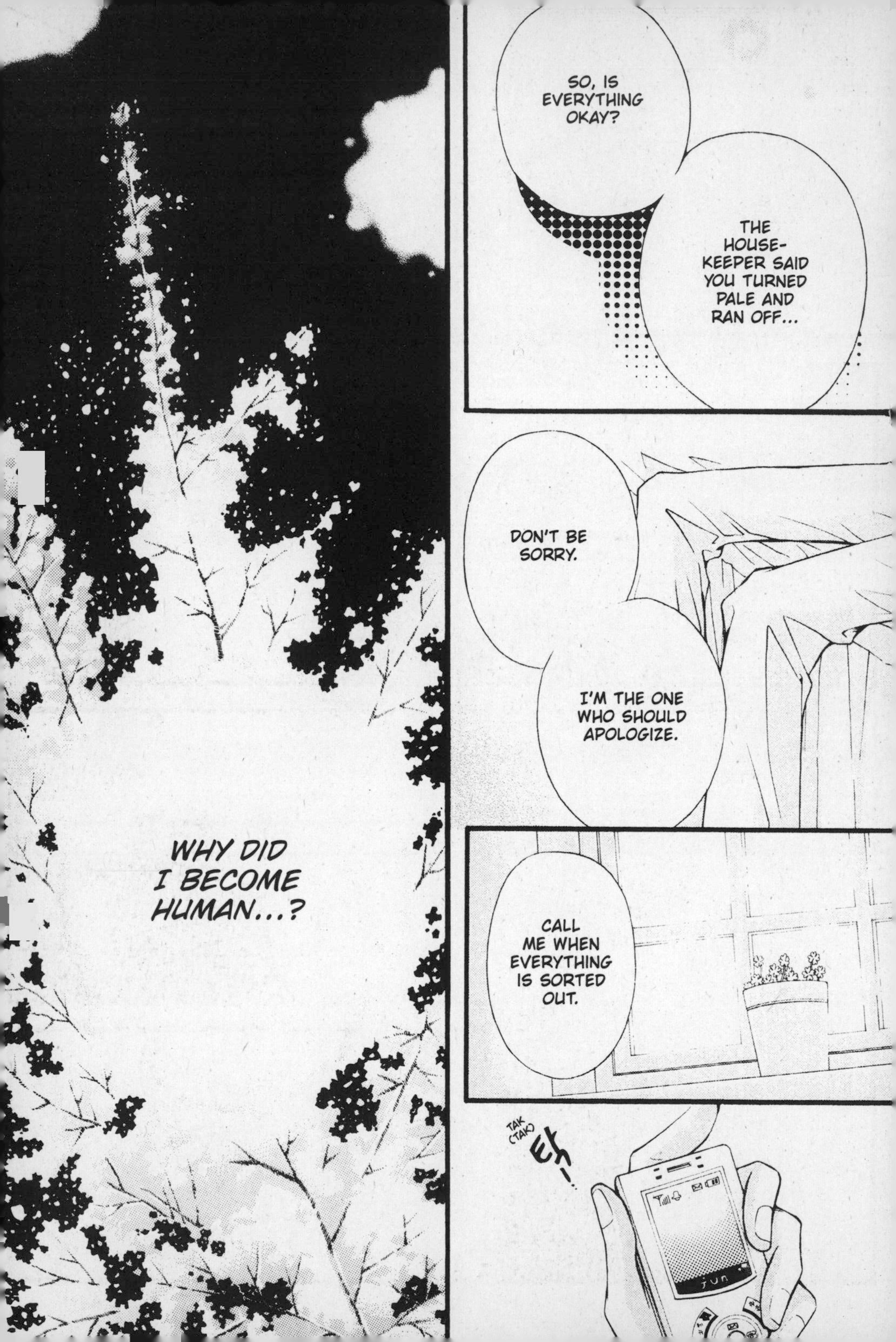
WHY DID I BECOME HUMAN...?
SO, IS EVERYTHING OKAY?
THE HOUSE-KEEPER SAID YOU TURNED PALE AND RAN OFF...
DON'T BE SORRY.
I'M THE ONE WHO SHOULD APOLOGIZE.
CALL ME WHEN EVERYTHING IS SORTED OUT.
TAK (TAK)

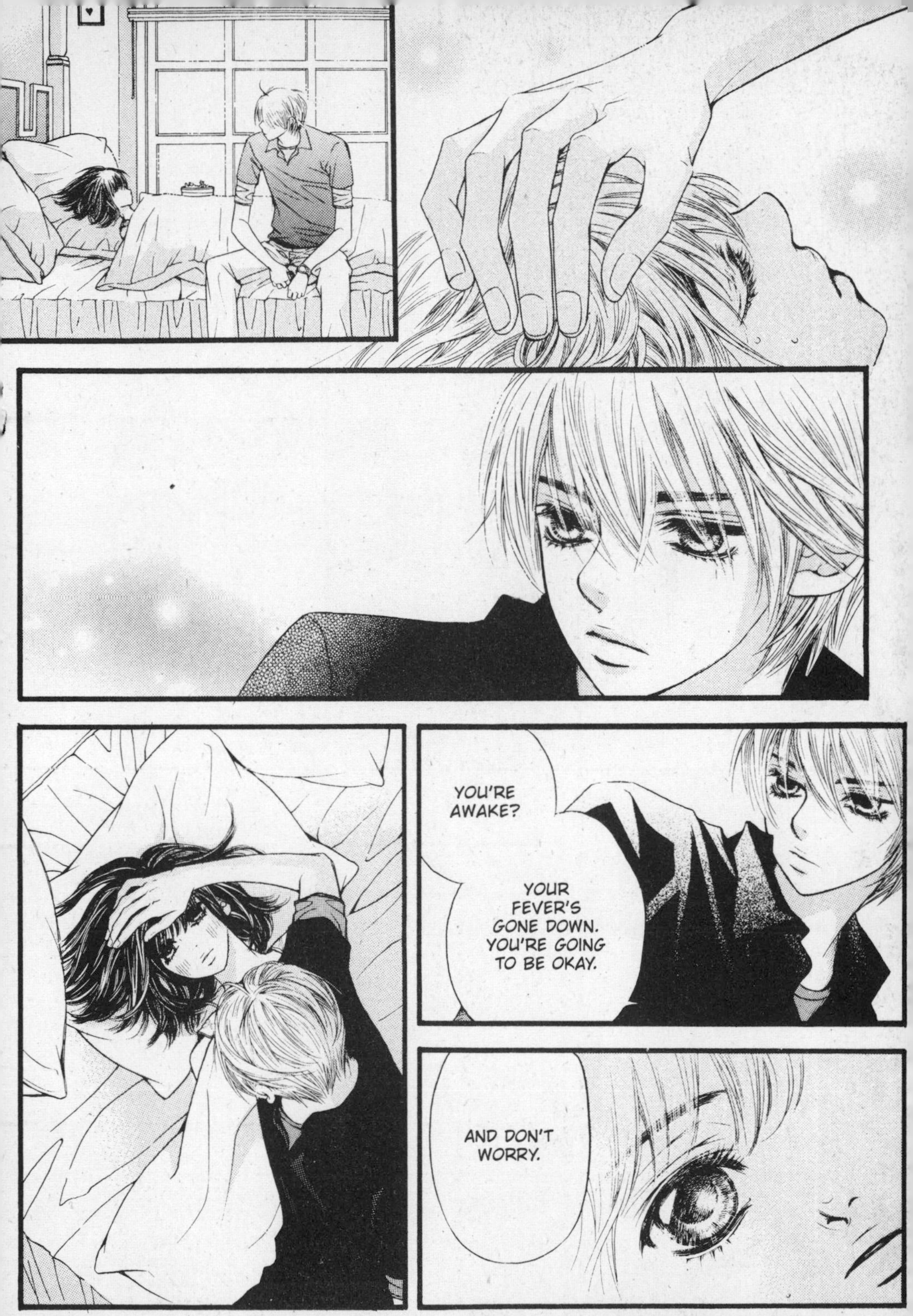
YOU'RE AWAKE?
YOUR FEVER'S GONE DOWN. YOU'RE GOING TO BE OKAY.
AND DON'T WORRY.

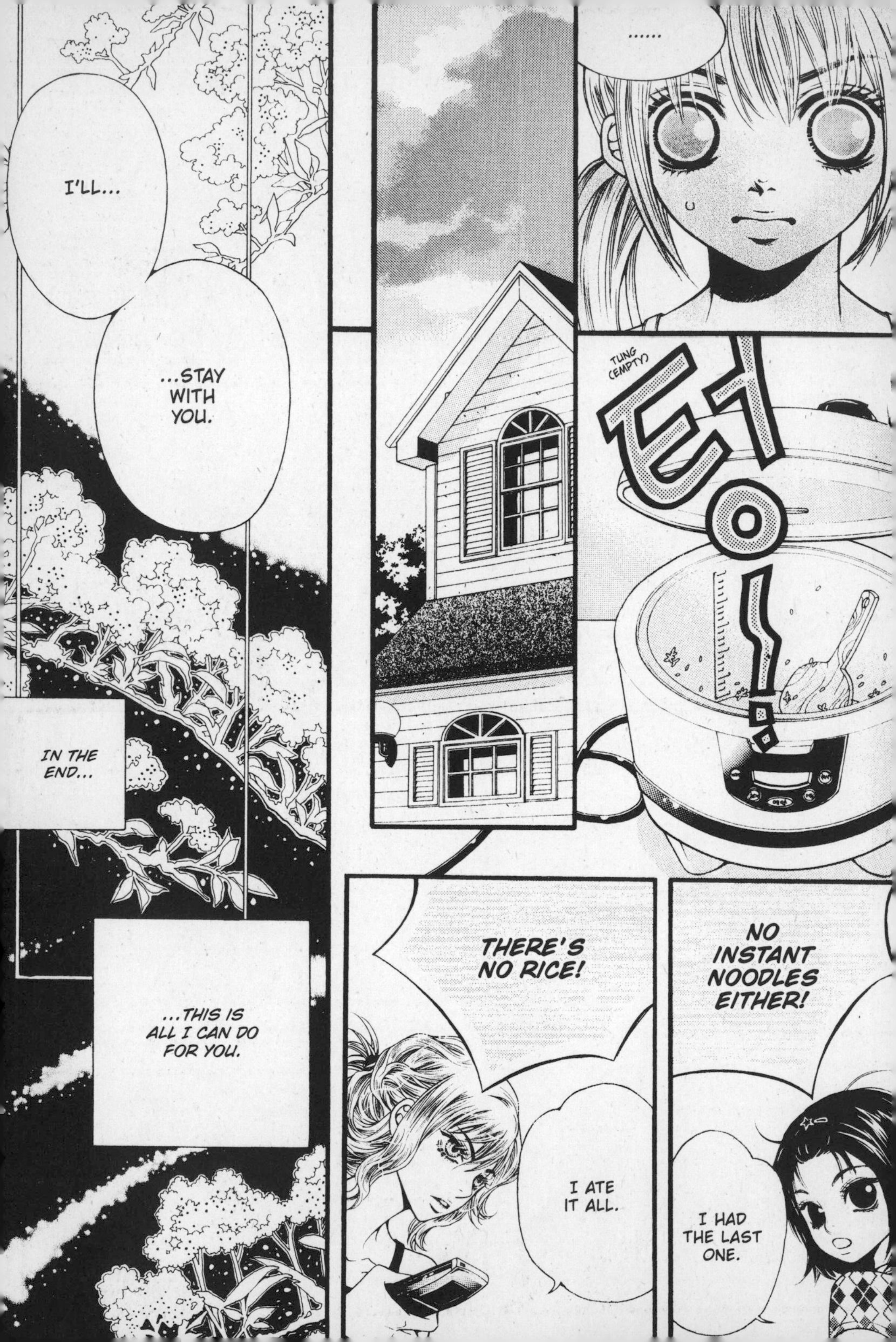
I'LL...
...STAY WITH YOU.
IN THE END...
...THIS IS ALL I CAN DO FOR YOU.
......
TUNG (EMPTY)
텅!
THERE'S NO RICE!
I ATE IT ALL.
NO INSTANT NOODLES EITHER!
I HAD THE LAST ONE.

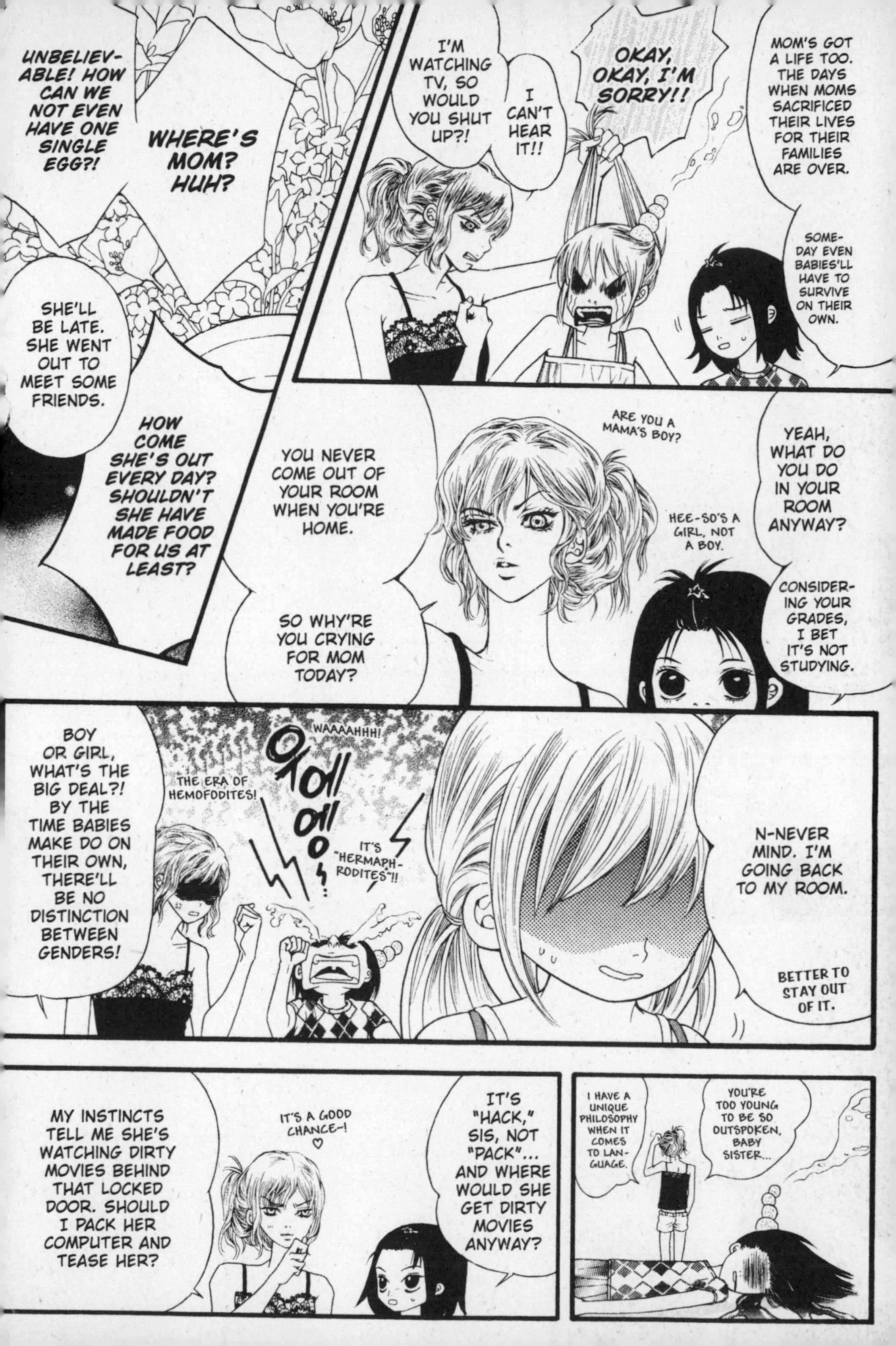

UNBELIEVABLE! HOW CAN WE NOT EVEN HAVE ONE SINGLE EGG?!
WHERE'S MOM? HUH?
SHE'LL BE LATE. SHE WENT OUT TO MEET SOME FRIENDS.
HOW COME SHE'S OUT EVERY DAY? SHOULDN'T SHE HAVE MADE FOOD FOR US AT LEAST?
I'M WATCHING TV, SO WOULD YOU SHUT UP?!
I CAN'T HEAR IT!!
OKAY, OKAY, I'M SORRY!!
MOM'S GOT A LIFE TOO. THE DAYS WHEN MOMS SACRIFICED THEIR LIVES FOR THEIR FAMILIES ARE OVER.
SOMEDAY EVEN BABIES'LL HAVE TO SURVIVE ON THEIR OWN.
YOU NEVER COME OUT OF YOUR ROOM WHEN YOU'RE HOME.
SO WHY'RE YOU CRYING FOR MOM TODAY?
ARE YOU A MAMA'S BOY?
HEE-SO'S A GIRL, NOT A BOY.
YEAH, WHAT DO YOU DO IN YOUR ROOM ANYWAY?
CONSIDERING YOUR GRADES, I BET IT'S NOT STUDYING.
BOY OR GIRL, WHAT'S THE BIG DEAL?! BY THE TIME BABIES MAKE DO ON THEIR OWN, THERE'LL BE NO DISTINCTION BETWEEN GENDERS!
THE ERA OF HEMOFODITES!
WAAAAHHH!
악에엥
IT'S "HERMAPHRODITES"!!
N-NEVER MIND. I'M GOING BACK TO MY ROOM.
BETTER TO STAY OUT OF IT.
MY INSTINCTS TELL ME SHE'S WATCHING DIRTY MOVIES BEHIND THAT LOCKED DOOR. SHOULD I PACK HER COMPUTER AND TEASE HER?
IT'S A GOOD CHANCE~! ♡
IT'S "HACK," SIS, NOT "PACK"... AND WHERE WOULD SHE GET DIRTY MOVIES ANYWAY?
I HAVE A UNIQUE PHILOSOPHY WHEN IT COMES TO LANGUAGE.
YOU'RE TOO YOUNG TO BE SO OUTSPOKEN, BABY SISTER...

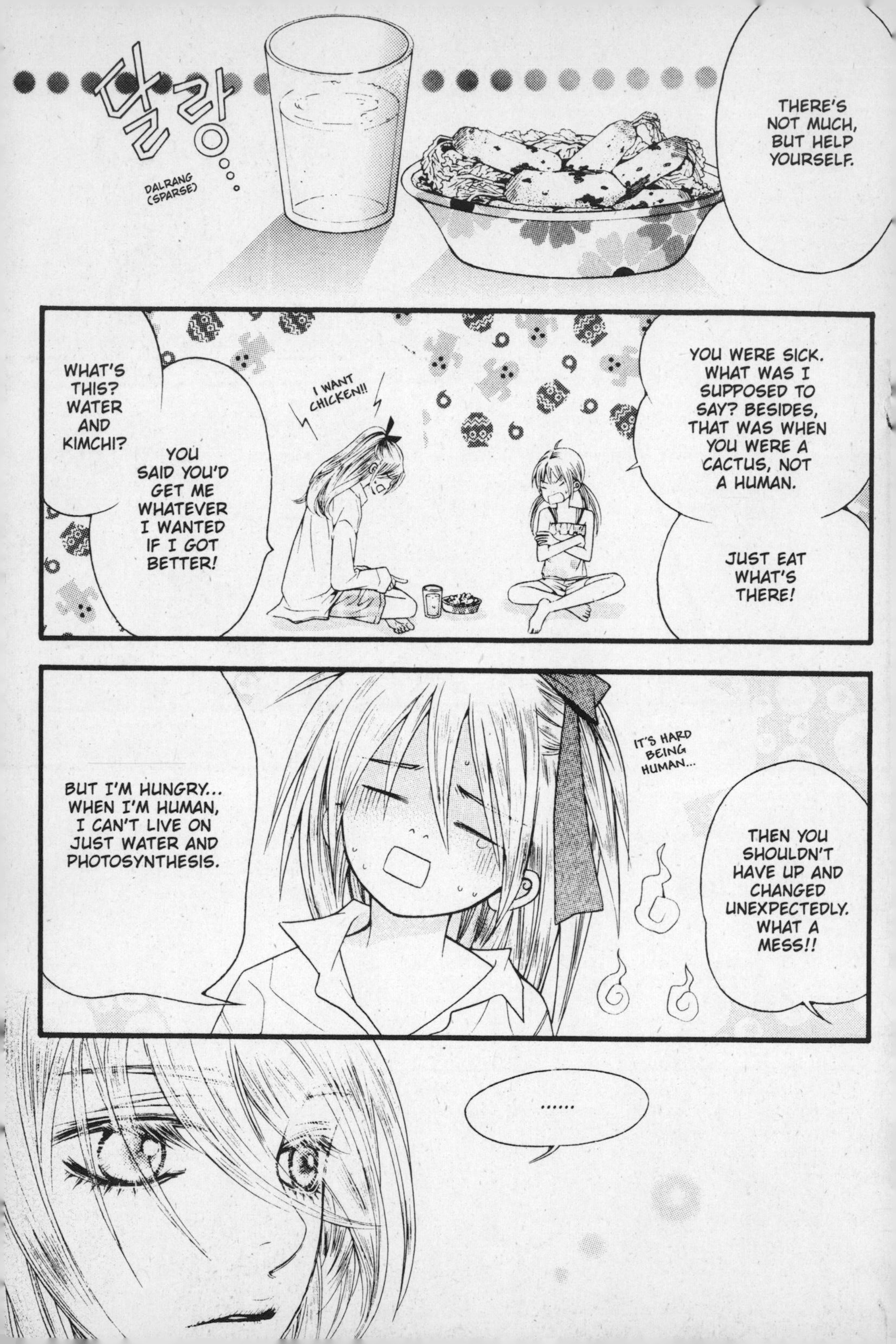
달랑
DALRANG (SPARSE)
THERE'S NOT MUCH, BUT HELP YOURSELF.
WHAT'S THIS? WATER AND KIMCHI?
YOU SAID YOU'D GET ME WHATEVER I WANTED IF I GOT BETTER!
I WANT CHICKEN!!
YOU WERE SICK. WHAT WAS I SUPPOSED TO SAY? BESIDES, THAT WAS WHEN YOU WERE A CACTUS, NOT A HUMAN.
JUST EAT WHAT'S THERE!
BUT I'M HUNGRY... WHEN I'M HUMAN, I CAN'T LIVE ON JUST WATER AND PHOTOSYNTHESIS.
IT'S HARD BEING HUMAN...
THEN YOU SHOULDN'T HAVE UP AND CHANGED UNEXPECTEDLY. WHAT A MESS!!
......

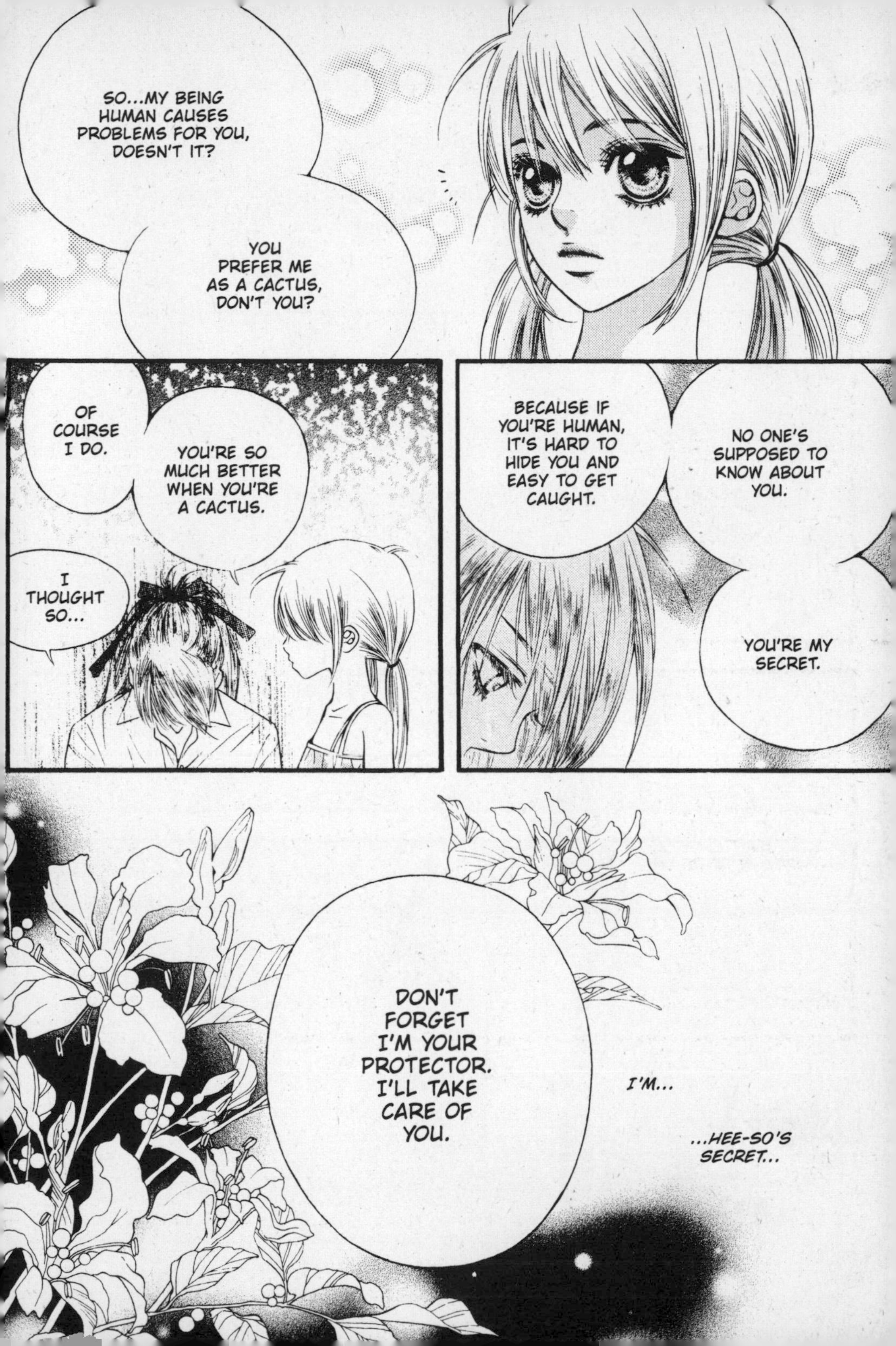
SO...MY BEING HUMAN CAUSES PROBLEMS FOR YOU, DOESN'T IT?
YOU PREFER ME AS A CACTUS, DON'T YOU?
OF COURSE I DO.
YOU'RE SO MUCH BETTER WHEN YOU'RE A CACTUS.
I THOUGHT SO...
BECAUSE IF YOU'RE HUMAN, IT'S HARD TO HIDE YOU AND EASY TO GET CAUGHT.
NO ONE'S SUPPOSED TO KNOW ABOUT YOU.
YOU'RE MY SECRET.
DON'T FORGET I'M YOUR PROTECTOR. I'LL TAKE CARE OF YOU.
I'M...
...HEE-SO'S SECRET...

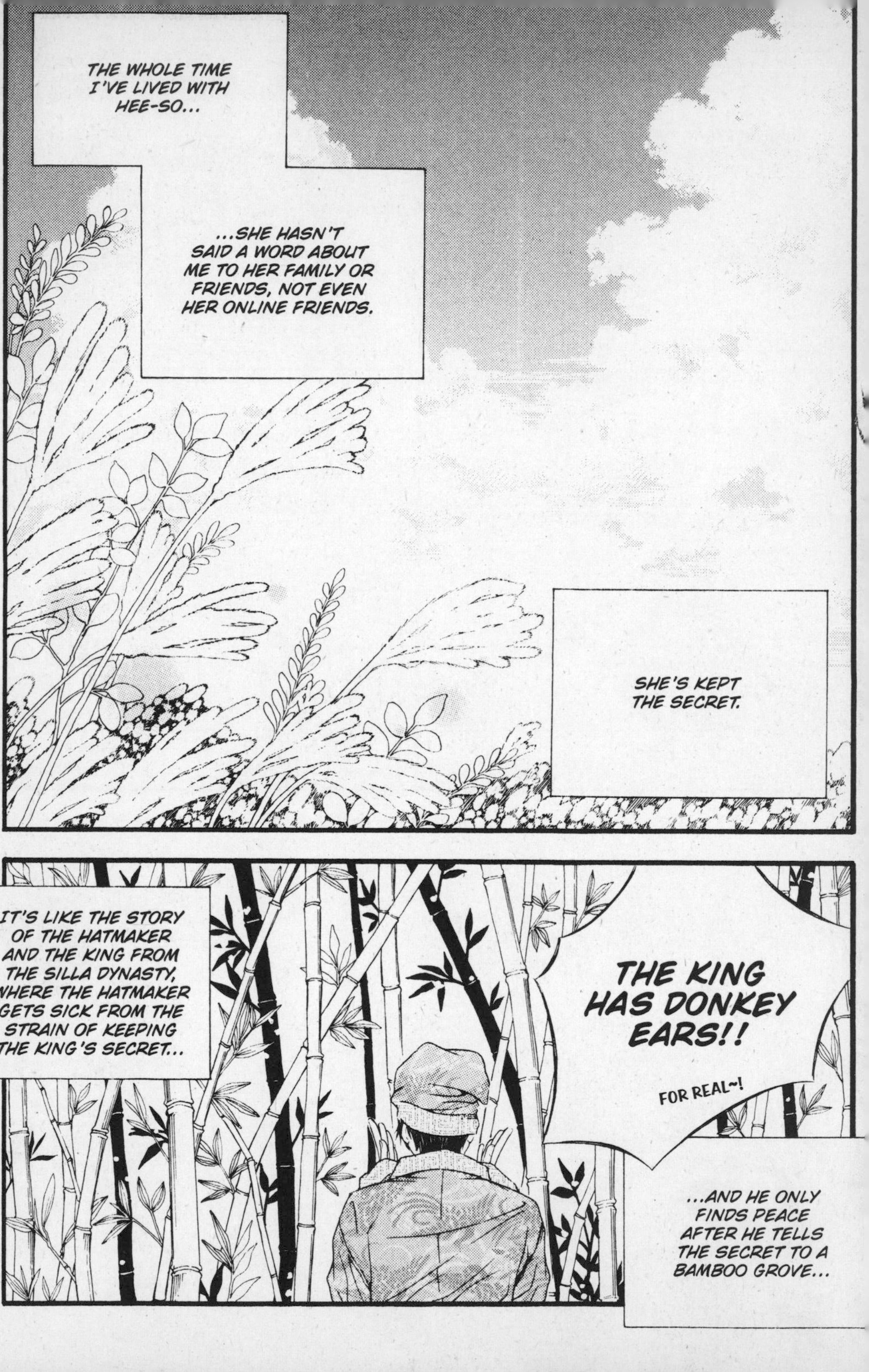
THE WHOLE TIME I'VE LIVED WITH HEE-SO...
...SHE HASN'T SAID A WORD ABOUT ME TO HER FAMILY OR FRIENDS, NOT EVEN HER ONLINE FRIENDS.
SHE'S KEPT THE SECRET.
IT'S LIKE THE STORY OF THE HATMAKER AND THE KING FROM THE SILLA DYNASTY, WHERE THE HATMAKER GETS SICK FROM THE STRAIN OF KEEPING THE KING'S SECRET...
THE KING HAS DONKEY EARS!!
FOR REAL~!
...AND HE ONLY FINDS PEACE AFTER HE TELLS THE SECRET TO A BAMBOO GROVE...

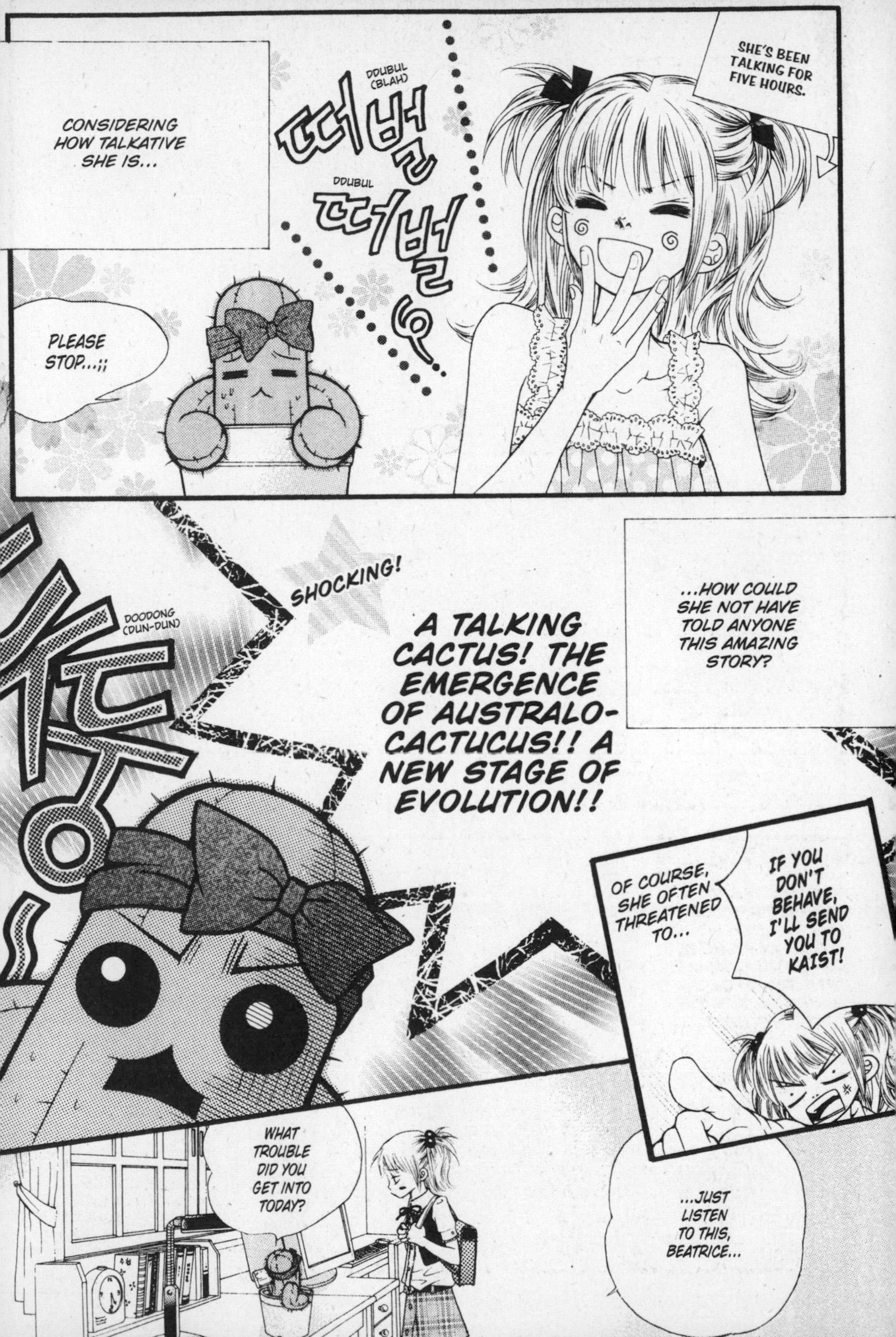
CONSIDERING HOW TALKATIVE SHE IS...
DDUBUL (BLAH)
떠벌
DDUBUL
떠벌
PLEASE STOP...;;
SHE'S BEEN TALKING FOR FIVE HOURS.
DOODONG (DUN-DUN)
SHOCKING!
A TALKING CACTUS! THE EMERGENCE OF AUSTRALO-CACTUCUS!! A NEW STAGE OF EVOLUTION!!
...HOW COULD SHE NOT HAVE TOLD ANYONE THIS AMAZING STORY?
OF COURSE, SHE OFTEN THREATENED TO...
IF YOU DON'T BEHAVE, I'LL SEND YOU TO KAIST!
WHAT TROUBLE DID YOU GET INTO TODAY?
...JUST LISTEN TO THIS, BEATRICE...

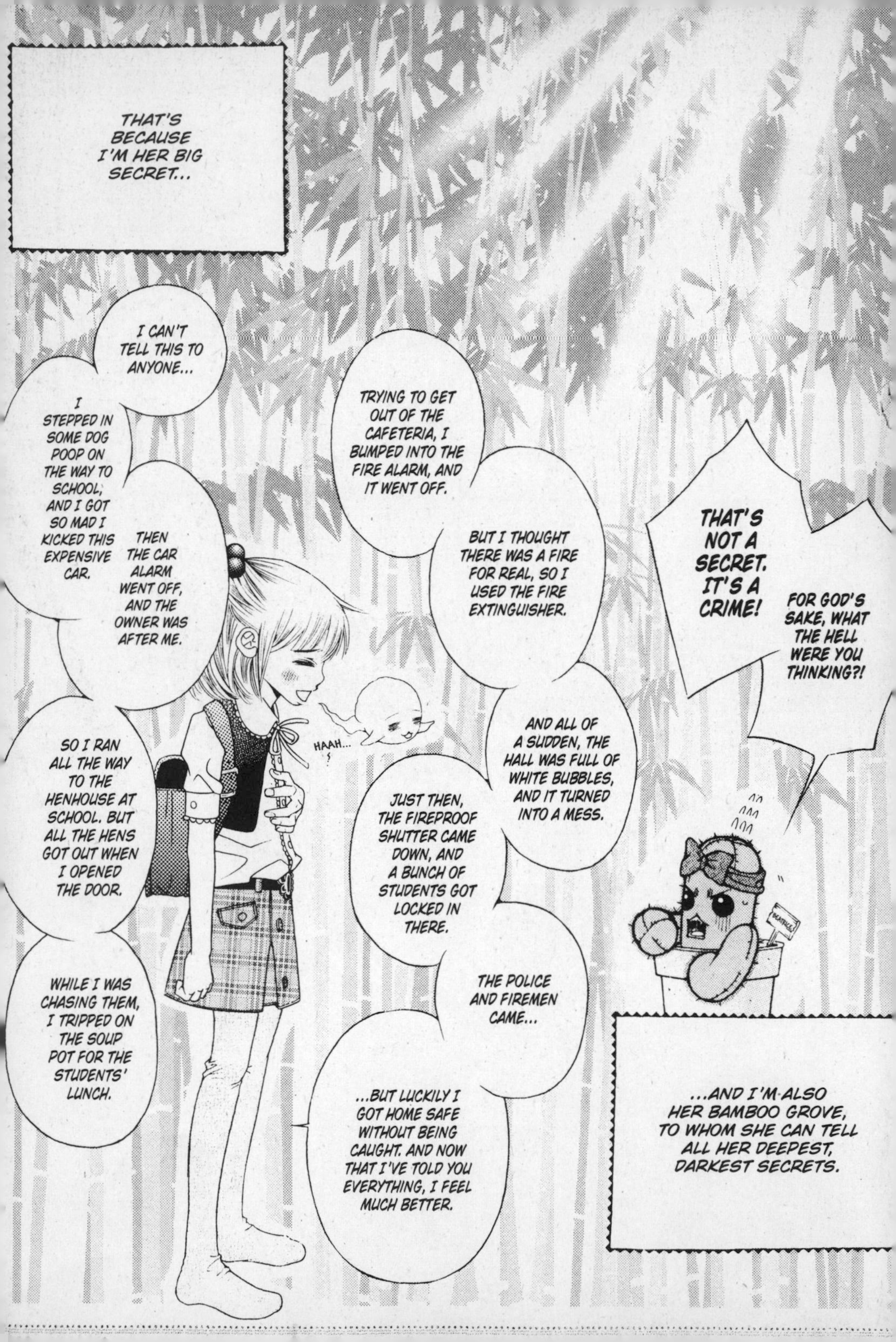
THAT'S BECAUSE I'M HER BIG SECRET...
I CAN'T TELL THIS TO ANYONE...
I STEPPED IN SOME DOG POOP ON THE WAY TO SCHOOL, AND I GOT SO MAD I KICKED THIS EXPENSIVE CAR.
THEN THE CAR ALARM WENT OFF, AND THE OWNER WAS AFTER ME.
SO I RAN ALL THE WAY TO THE HENHOUSE AT SCHOOL. BUT ALL THE HENS GOT OUT WHEN I OPENED THE DOOR.
WHILE I WAS CHASING THEM, I TRIPPED ON THE SOUP POT FOR THE STUDENTS' LUNCH.
HAAH...
TRYING TO GET OUT OF THE CAFETERIA, I BUMPED INTO THE FIRE ALARM, AND IT WENT OFF.
BUT I THOUGHT THERE WAS A FIRE FOR REAL, SO I USED THE FIRE EXTINGUISHER.
AND ALL OF A SUDDEN, THE HALL WAS FULL OF WHITE BUBBLES, AND IT TURNED INTO A MESS.
JUST THEN, THE FIREPROOF SHUTTER CAME DOWN, AND A BUNCH OF STUDENTS GOT LOCKED IN THERE.
THE POLICE AND FIREMEN CAME...
...BUT LUCKILY I GOT HOME SAFE WITHOUT BEING CAUGHT. AND NOW THAT I'VE TOLD YOU EVERYTHING, I FEEL MUCH BETTER.
THAT'S NOT A SECRET. IT'S A CRIME!
FOR GOD'S SAKE, WHAT THE HELL WERE YOU THINKING?!
BEATRICE
...AND I'M ALSO HER BAMBOO GROVE, TO WHOM SHE CAN TELL ALL HER DEEPEST, DARKEST SECRETS.

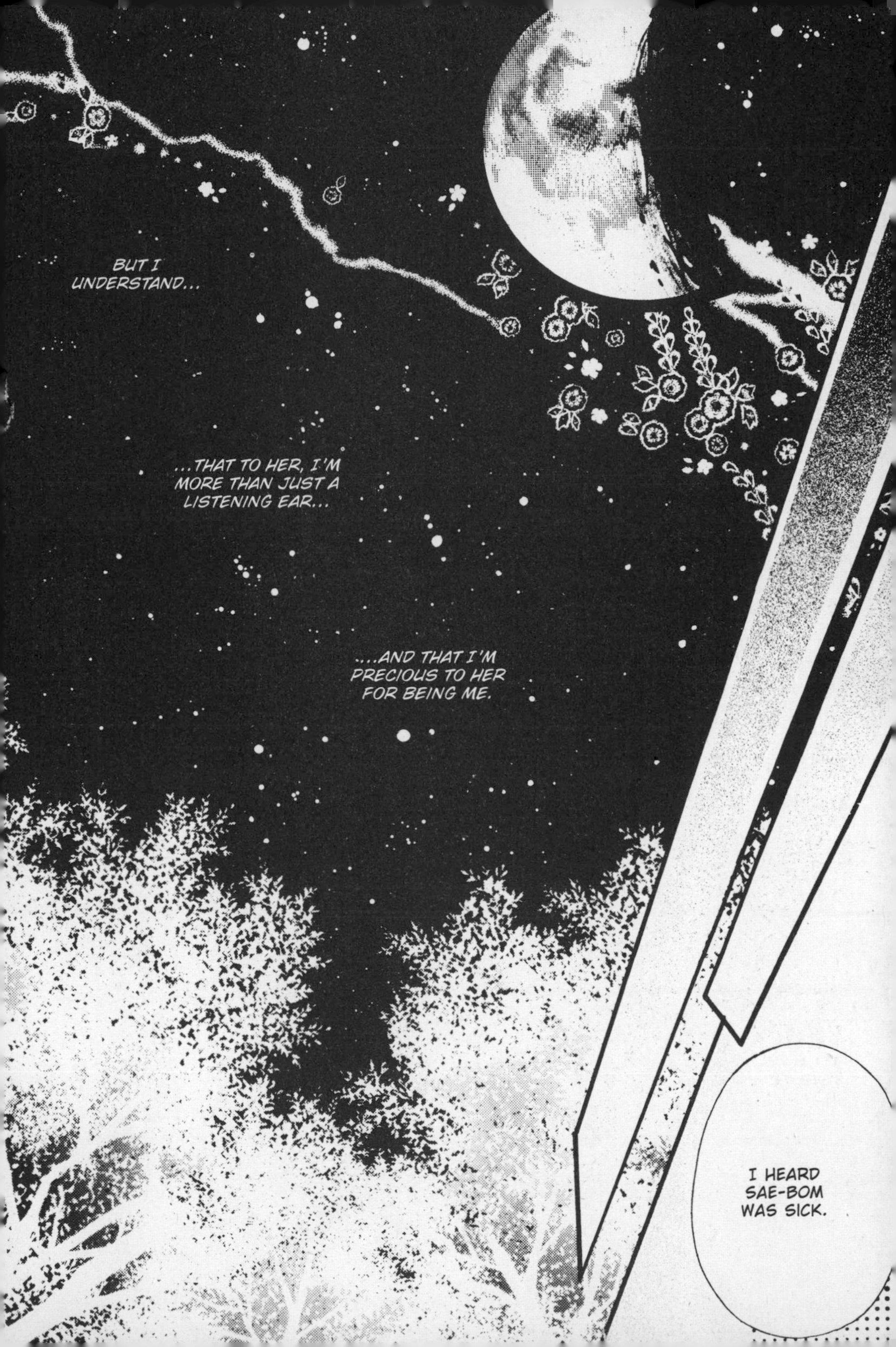

BUT I UNDERSTAND...
...THAT TO HER, I'M MORE THAN JUST A LISTENING EAR...
....AND THAT I'M PRECIOUS TO HER FOR BEING ME.
I HEARD SAE-BOM WAS SICK.

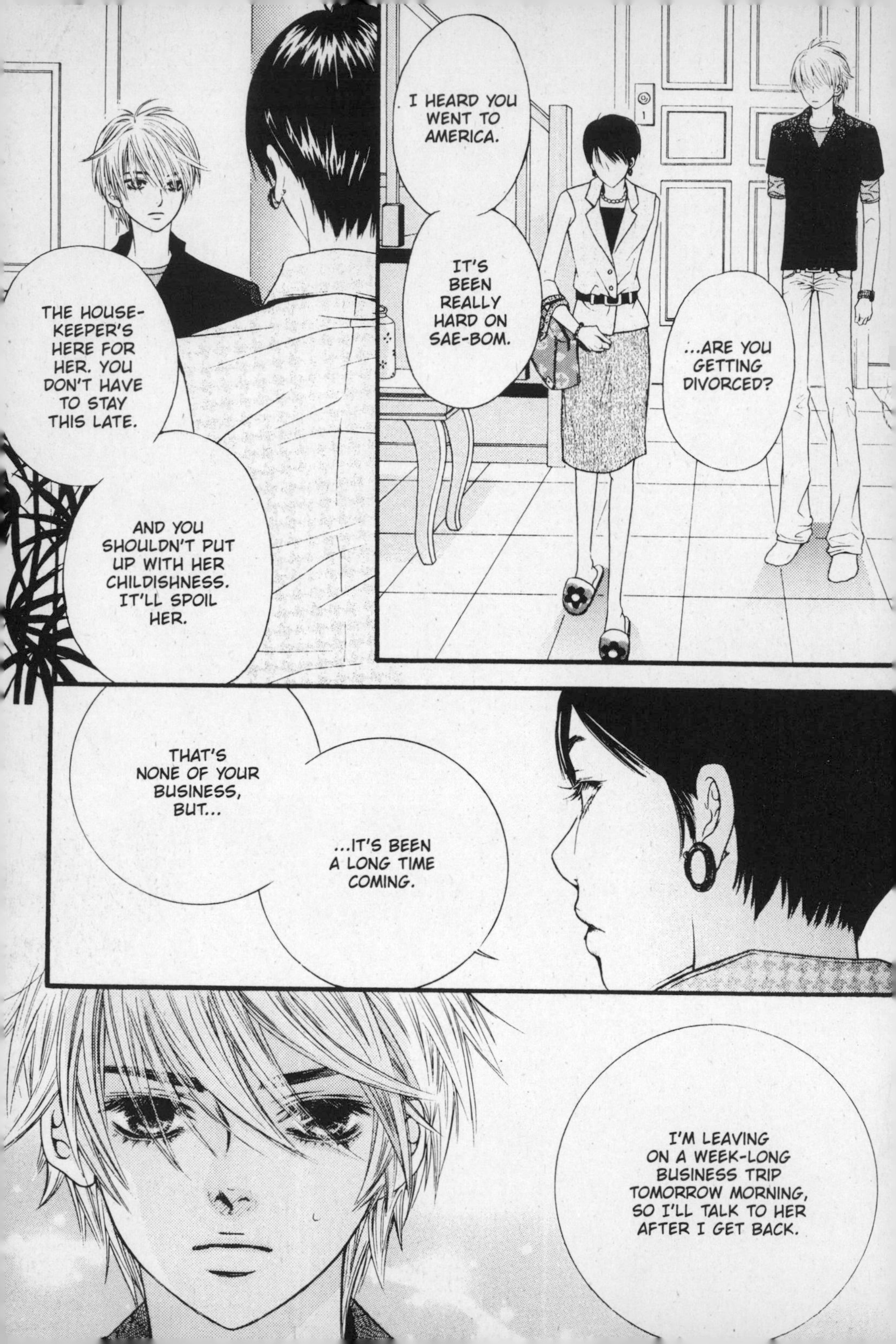
THE HOUSE-KEEPER'S HERE FOR HER. YOU DON'T HAVE TO STAY THIS LATE.
AND YOU SHOULDN'T PUT UP WITH HER CHILDISHNESS. IT'LL SPOIL HER.
I HEARD YOU WENT TO AMERICA.
IT'S BEEN REALLY HARD ON SAE-BOM.
...ARE YOU GETTING DIVORCED?
THAT'S NONE OF YOUR BUSINESS, BUT...
...IT'S BEEN A LONG TIME COMING.
I'M LEAVING ON A WEEK-LONG BUSINESS TRIP TOMORROW MORNING, SO I'LL TALK TO HER AFTER I GET BACK.

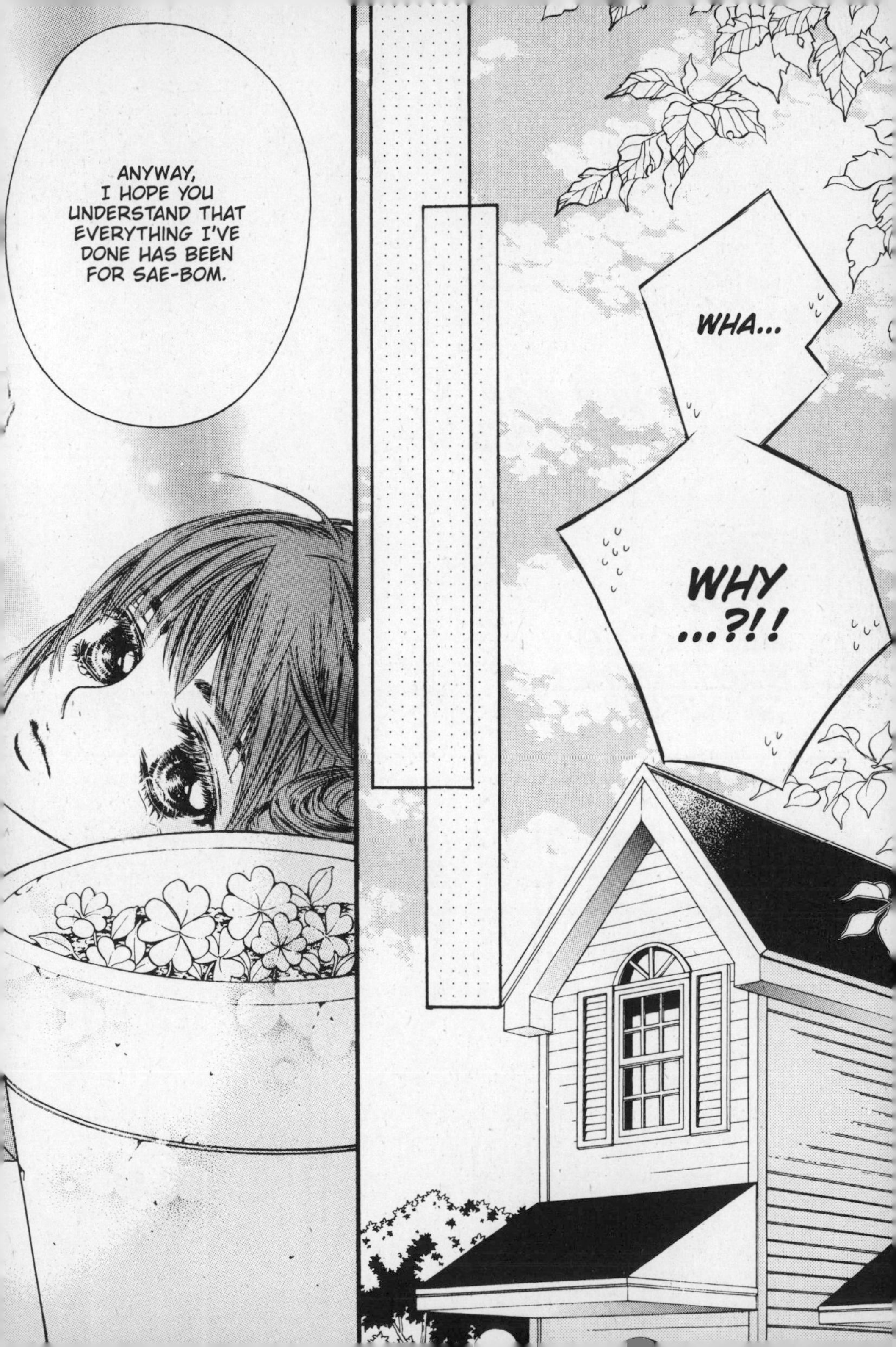
ANYWAY, I HOPE YOU UNDERSTAND THAT EVERYTHING I'VE DONE HAS BEEN FOR SAE-BOM.
WHA...
WHY ...?!!

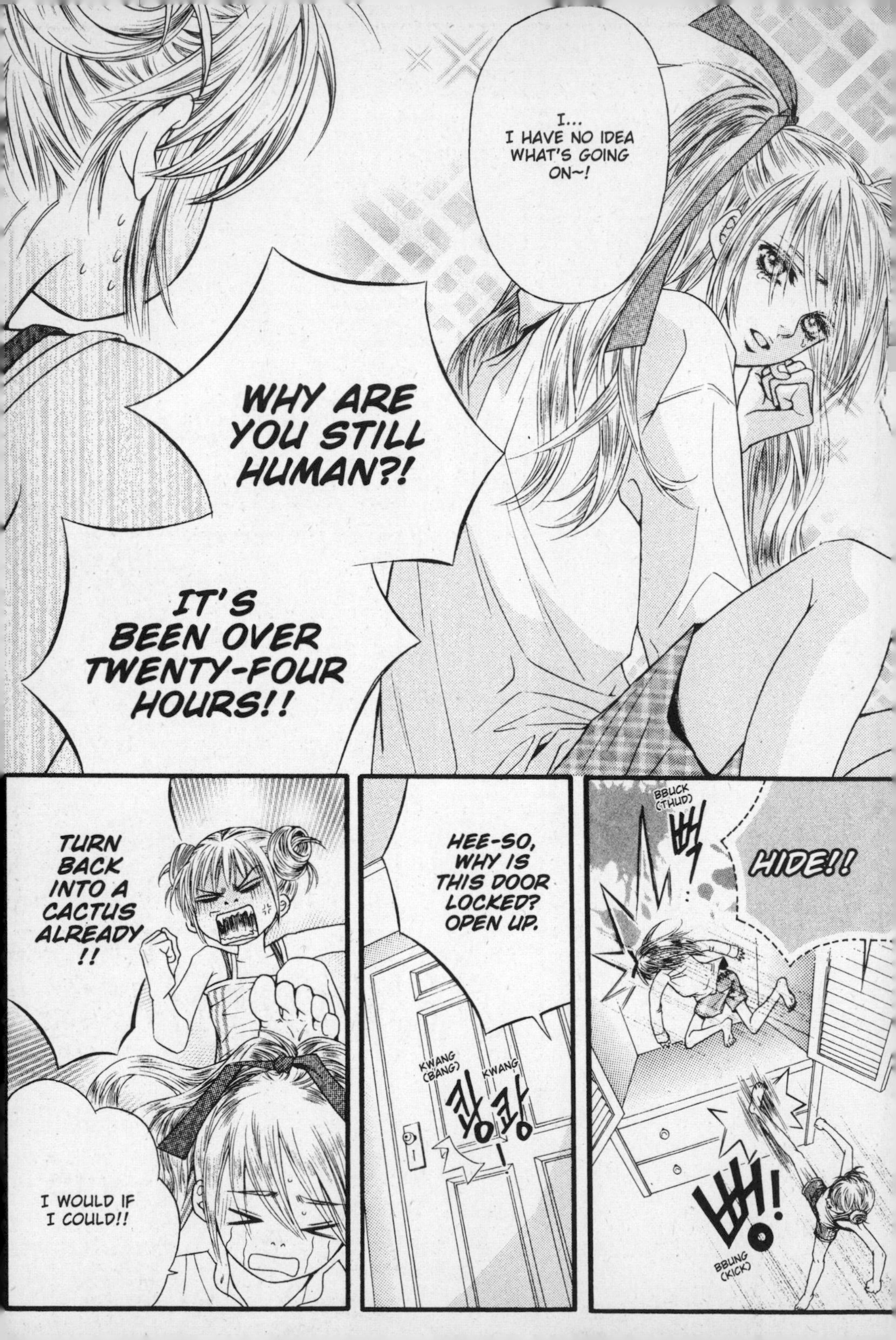
I... I HAVE NO IDEA WHAT'S GOING ON~!
WHY ARE YOU STILL HUMAN?!
IT'S BEEN OVER TWENTY-FOUR HOURS!!
TURN BACK INTO A CACTUS ALREADY !!
I WOULD IF I COULD!!
HEE-SO, WHY IS THIS DOOR LOCKED? OPEN UP.
KWANG (BANG) KWANG
쾅쾅!
BBUCK (THUD)
뻑
HIDE!!
뻥!
BBUNG (KICK)

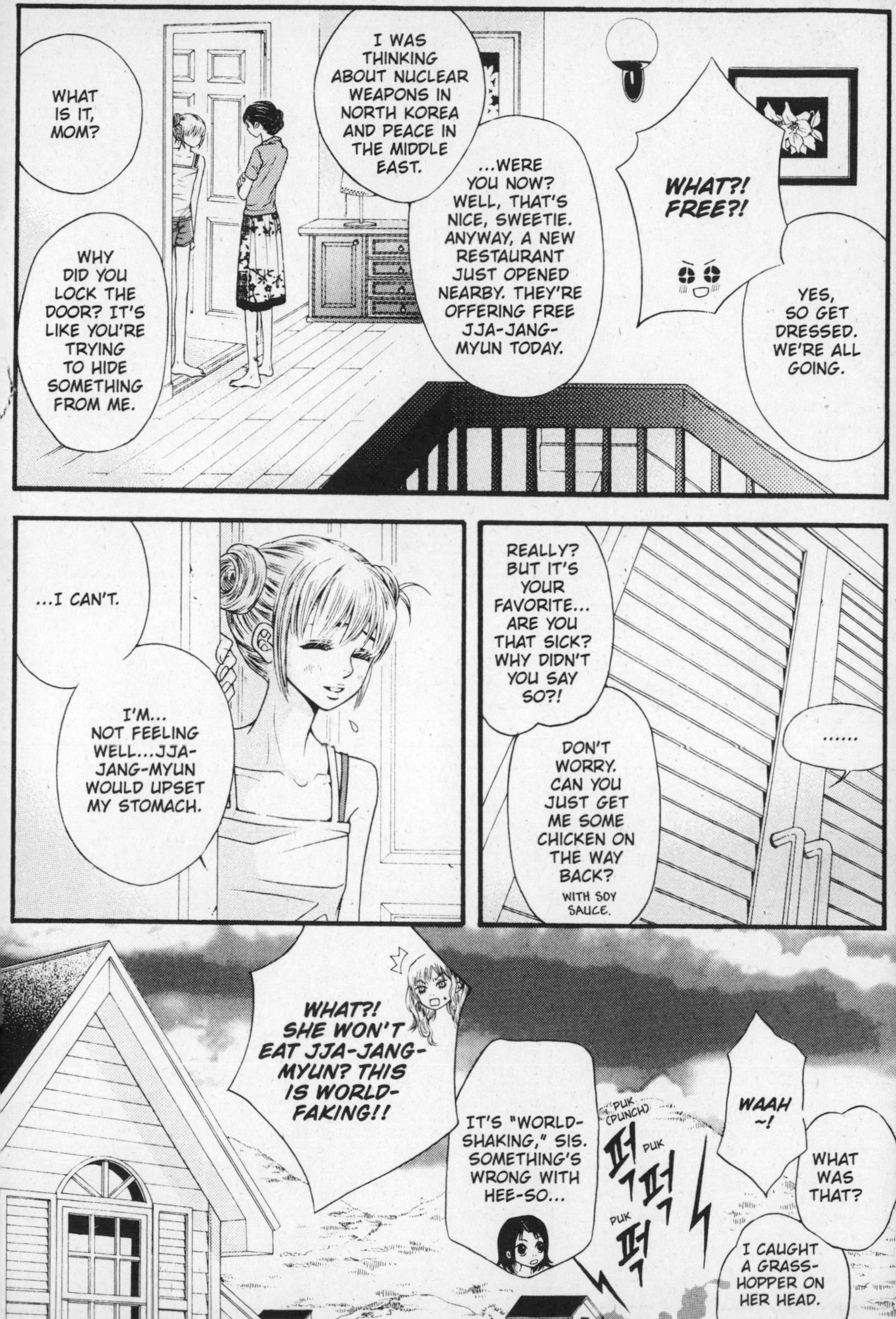
WHAT IS IT, MOM?
WHY DID YOU LOCK THE DOOR? IT'S LIKE YOU'RE TRYING TO HIDE SOMETHING FROM ME.
I WAS THINKING ABOUT NUCLEAR WEAPONS IN NORTH KOREA AND PEACE IN THE MIDDLE EAST.
...WERE YOU NOW? WELL, THAT'S NICE, SWEETIE. ANYWAY, A NEW RESTAURANT JUST OPENED NEARBY. THEY'RE OFFERING FREE JJA-JANG-MYUN TODAY.
WHAT?! FREE?!
YES, SO GET DRESSED. WE'RE ALL GOING.
...I CAN'T.
I'M... NOT FEELING WELL...JJA-JANG-MYUN WOULD UPSET MY STOMACH.
REALLY? BUT IT'S YOUR FAVORITE... ARE YOU THAT SICK? WHY DIDN'T YOU SAY SO?!
DON'T WORRY. CAN YOU JUST GET ME SOME CHICKEN ON THE WAY BACK? WITH SOY SAUCE.
......
WHAT?! SHE WON'T EAT JJA-JANG-MYUN? THIS IS WORLD-FAKING!!
IT'S "WORLD-SHAKING," SIS. SOMETHING'S WRONG WITH HEE-SO...
PUK (PUNCH) 퍽
PUK 퍽
PUK 퍽
WAAH ~!
WHAT WAS THAT?
I CAUGHT A GRASSHOPPER ON HER HEAD.

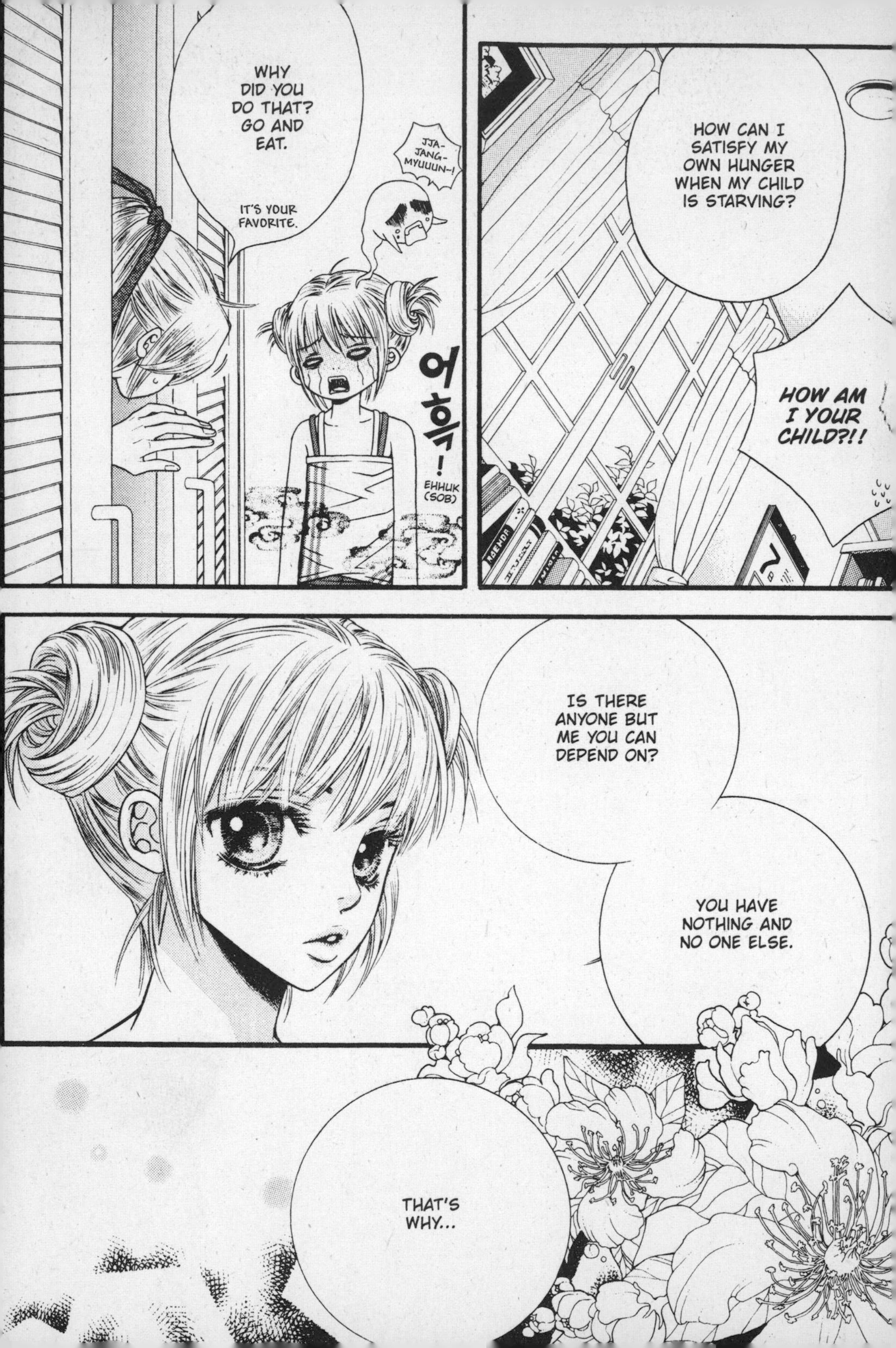
WHY DID YOU DO THAT? GO AND EAT.
IT'S YOUR FAVORITE.
JJA-JANG-MYUUUN~!
어흑!
EHHUK (SOB)
HOW CAN I SATISFY MY OWN HUNGER WHEN MY CHILD IS STARVING?
HOW AM I YOUR CHILD?!!
IS THERE ANYONE BUT ME YOU CAN DEPEND ON?
YOU HAVE NOTHING AND NO ONE ELSE.
THAT'S WHY...

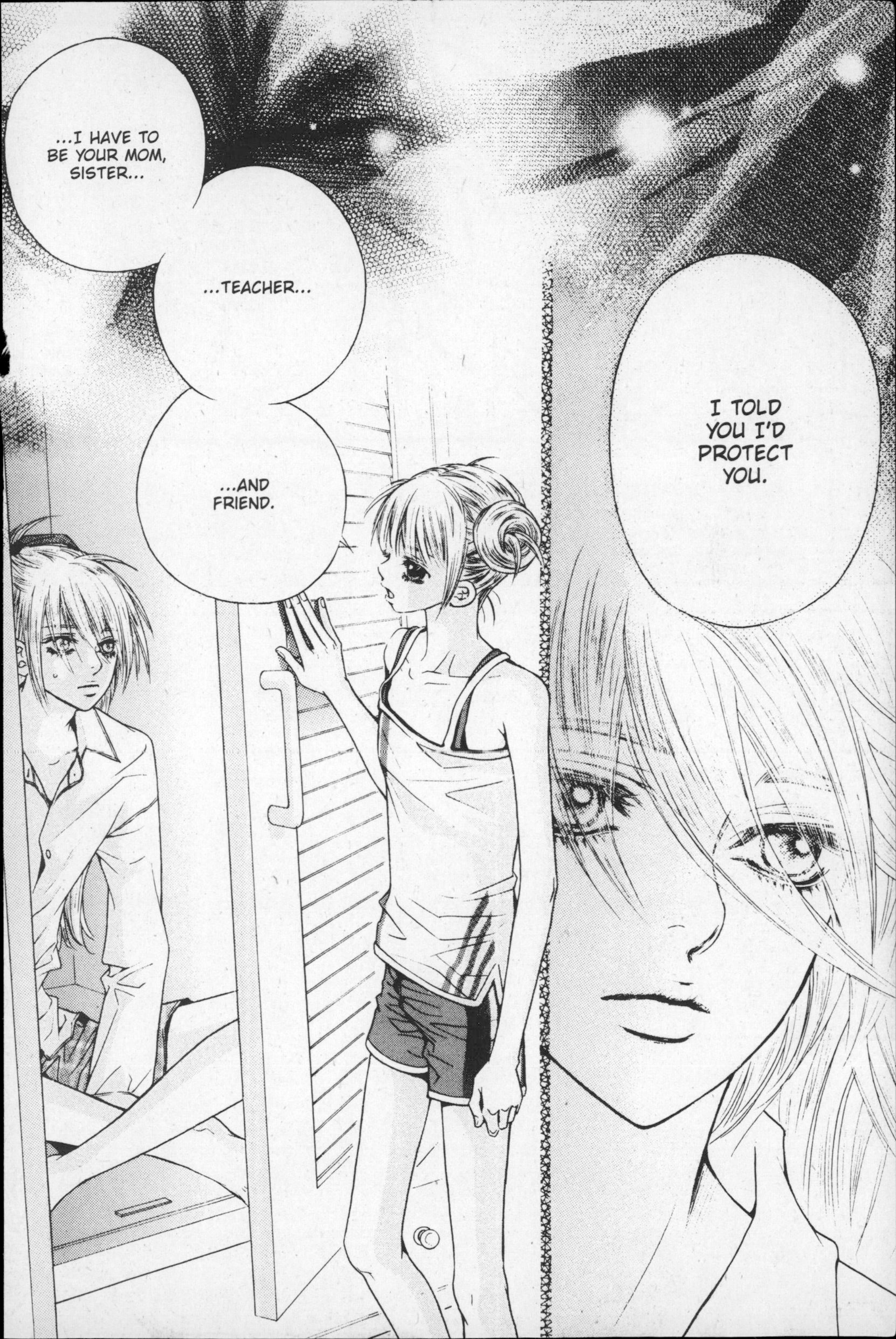
...I HAVE TO BE YOUR MOM, SISTER...
...TEACHER...
...AND FRIEND.
I TOLD YOU I'D PROTECT YOU.

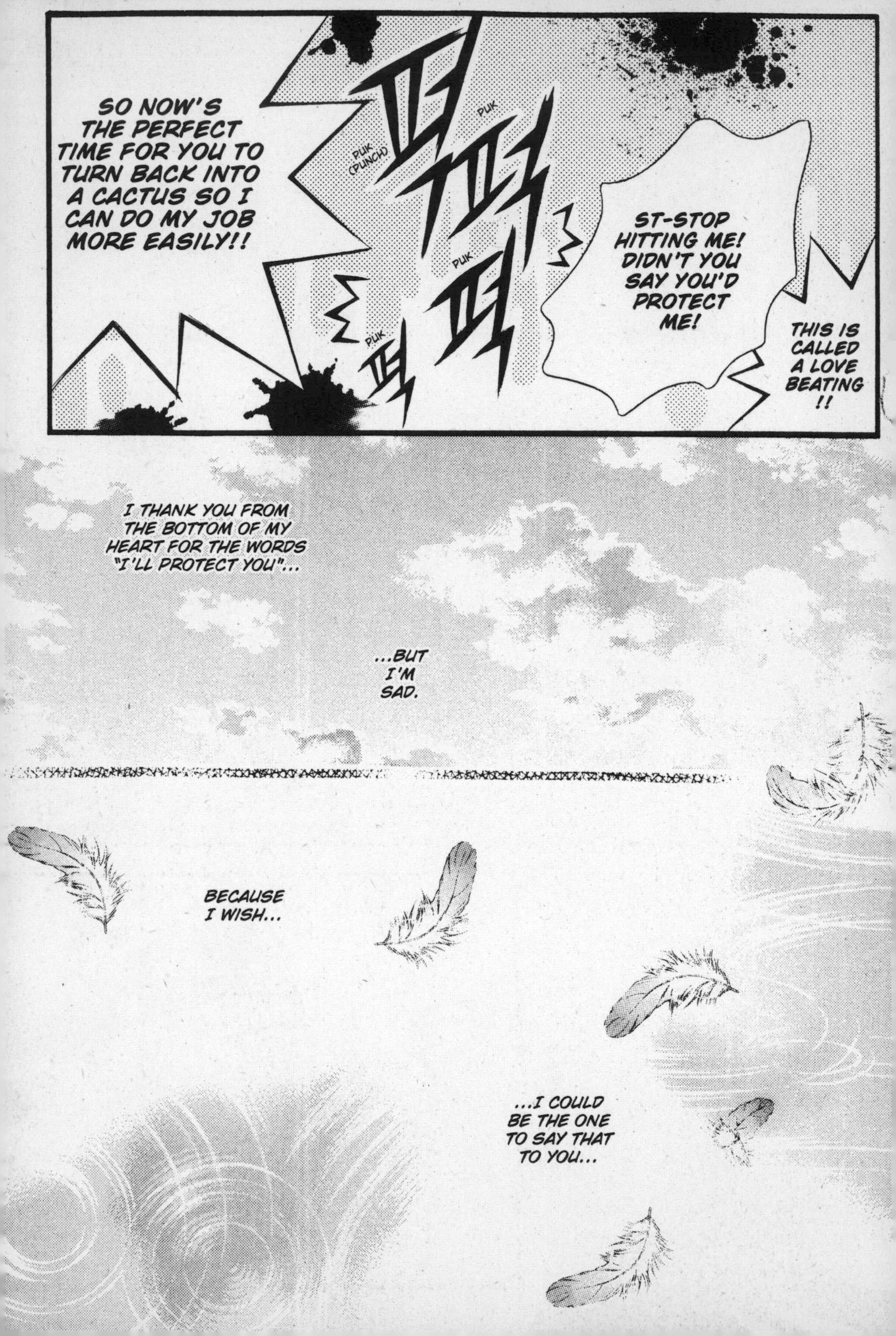
SO NOW'S THE PERFECT TIME FOR YOU TO TURN BACK INTO A CACTUS SO I CAN DO MY JOB MORE EASILY!!
PUK (PUNCH)
PUK
PUK
PUK
ST-STOP HITTING ME! DIDN'T YOU SAY YOU'D PROTECT ME!
THIS IS CALLED A LOVE BEATING !!
I THANK YOU FROM THE BOTTOM OF MY HEART FOR THE WORDS "I'LL PROTECT YOU"...
...BUT I'M SAD.
BECAUSE I WISH...
...I COULD BE THE ONE TO SAY THAT TO YOU...

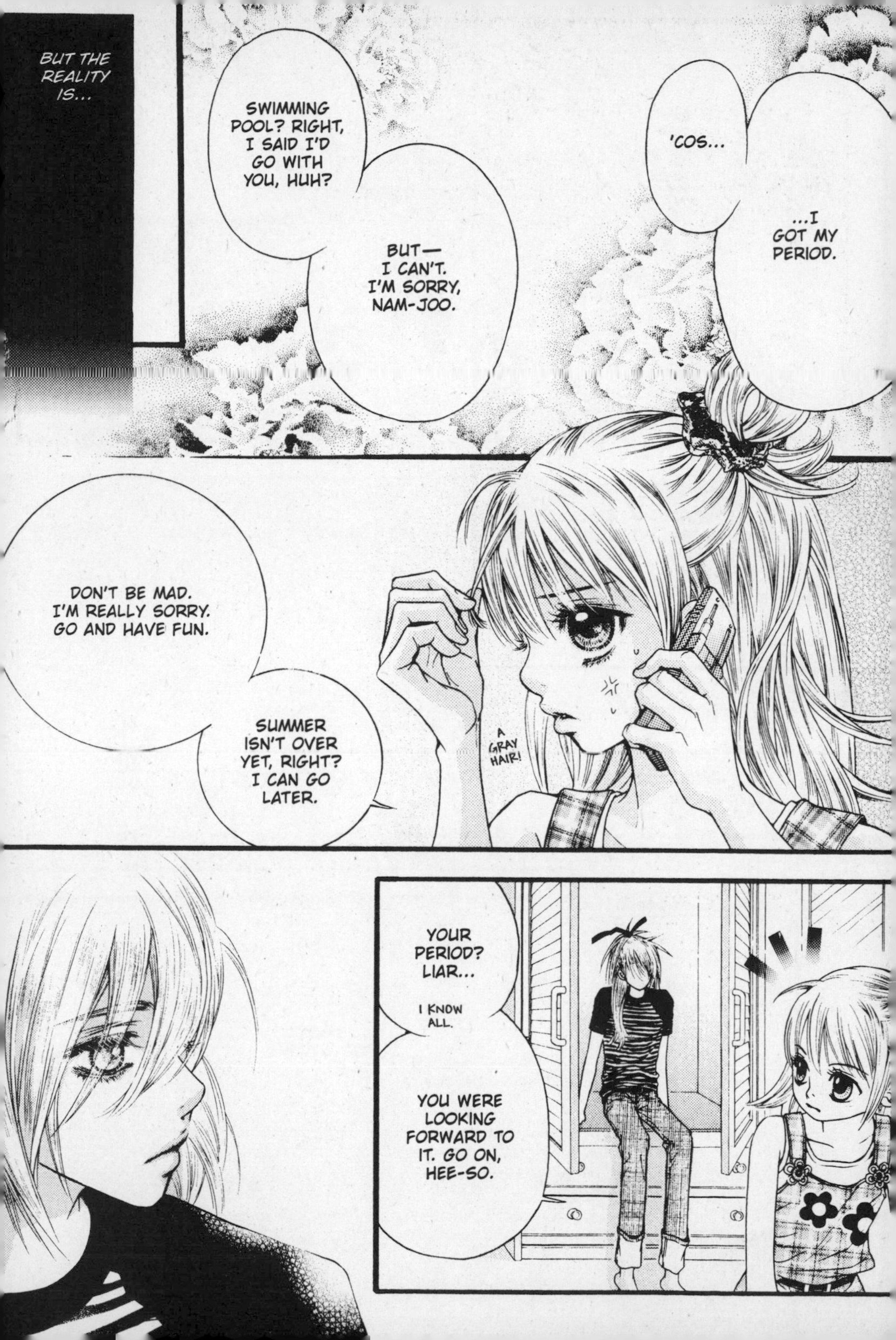

BUT THE REALITY IS...
SWIMMING POOL? RIGHT, I SAID I'D GO WITH YOU, HUH?
BUT— I CAN'T. I'M SORRY, NAM-JOO.
'COS...
...I GOT MY PERIOD.
DON'T BE MAD. I'M REALLY SORRY. GO AND HAVE FUN.
SUMMER ISN'T OVER YET, RIGHT? I CAN GO LATER.
A GRAY HAIR!
YOUR PERIOD? LIAR...
I KNOW ALL.
YOU WERE LOOKING FORWARD TO IT. GO ON, HEE-SO.

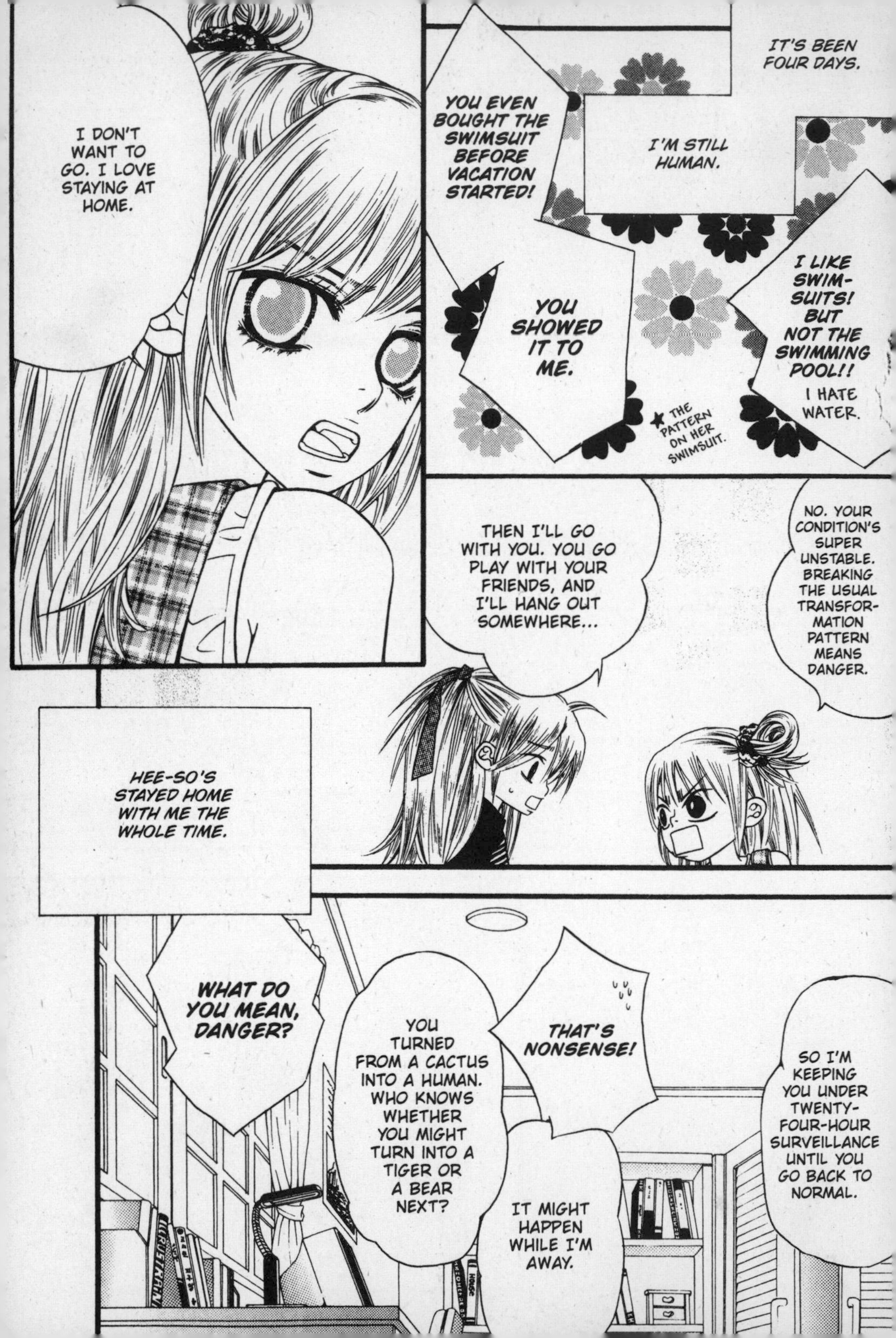

I DON'T WANT TO GO. I LOVE STAYING AT HOME.
YOU EVEN BOUGHT THE SWIMSUIT BEFORE VACATION STARTED!
IT'S BEEN FOUR DAYS.
I'M STILL HUMAN.
YOU SHOWED IT TO ME.
★ THE PATTERN ON HER SWIMSUIT.
I LIKE SWIM-SUITS! BUT NOT THE SWIMMING POOL!!
I HATE WATER.
THEN I'LL GO WITH YOU. YOU GO PLAY WITH YOUR FRIENDS, AND I'LL HANG OUT SOMEWHERE...
NO. YOUR CONDITION'S SUPER UNSTABLE. BREAKING THE USUAL TRANSFOR-MATION PATTERN MEANS DANGER.
HEE-SO'S STAYED HOME WITH ME THE WHOLE TIME.
WHAT DO YOU MEAN, DANGER?
YOU TURNED FROM A CACTUS INTO A HUMAN. WHO KNOWS WHETHER YOU MIGHT TURN INTO A TIGER OR A BEAR NEXT?
THAT'S NONSENSE!
IT MIGHT HAPPEN WHILE I'M AWAY.
SO I'M KEEPING YOU UNDER TWENTY-FOUR-HOUR SURVEILLANCE UNTIL YOU GO BACK TO NORMAL.

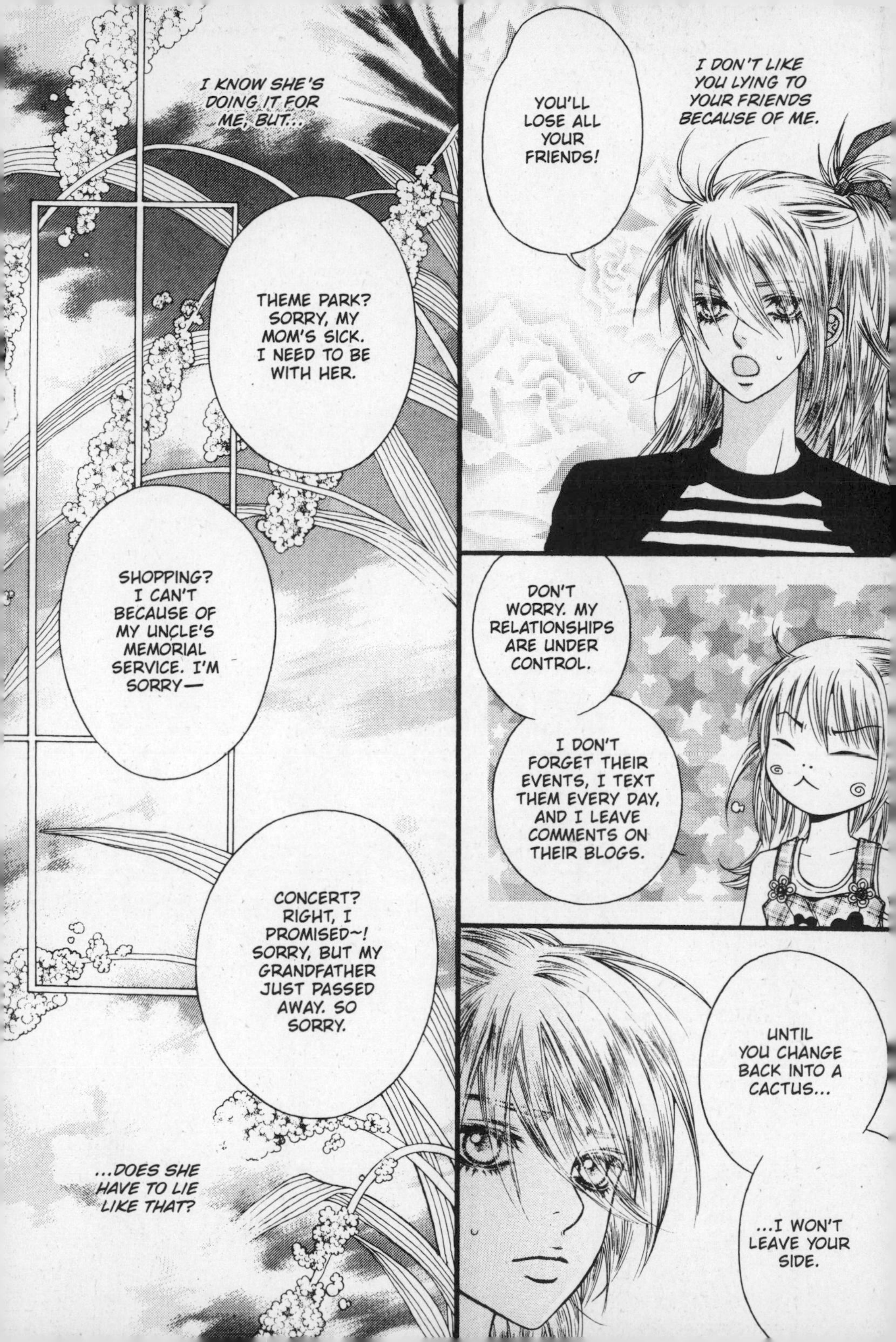
I KNOW SHE'S DOING IT FOR ME, BUT...
THEME PARK? SORRY, MY MOM'S SICK. I NEED TO BE WITH HER.
SHOPPING? I CAN'T BECAUSE OF MY UNCLE'S MEMORIAL SERVICE. I'M SORRY—
CONCERT? RIGHT, I PROMISED~! SORRY, BUT MY GRANDFATHER JUST PASSED AWAY. SO SORRY.
...DOES SHE HAVE TO LIE LIKE THAT?
YOU'LL LOSE ALL YOUR FRIENDS!
I DON'T LIKE YOU LYING TO YOUR FRIENDS BECAUSE OF ME.
DON'T WORRY. MY RELATIONSHIPS ARE UNDER CONTROL.
I DON'T FORGET THEIR EVENTS, I TEXT THEM EVERY DAY, AND I LEAVE COMMENTS ON THEIR BLOGS.
UNTIL YOU CHANGE BACK INTO A CACTUS...
...I WON'T LEAVE YOUR SIDE.

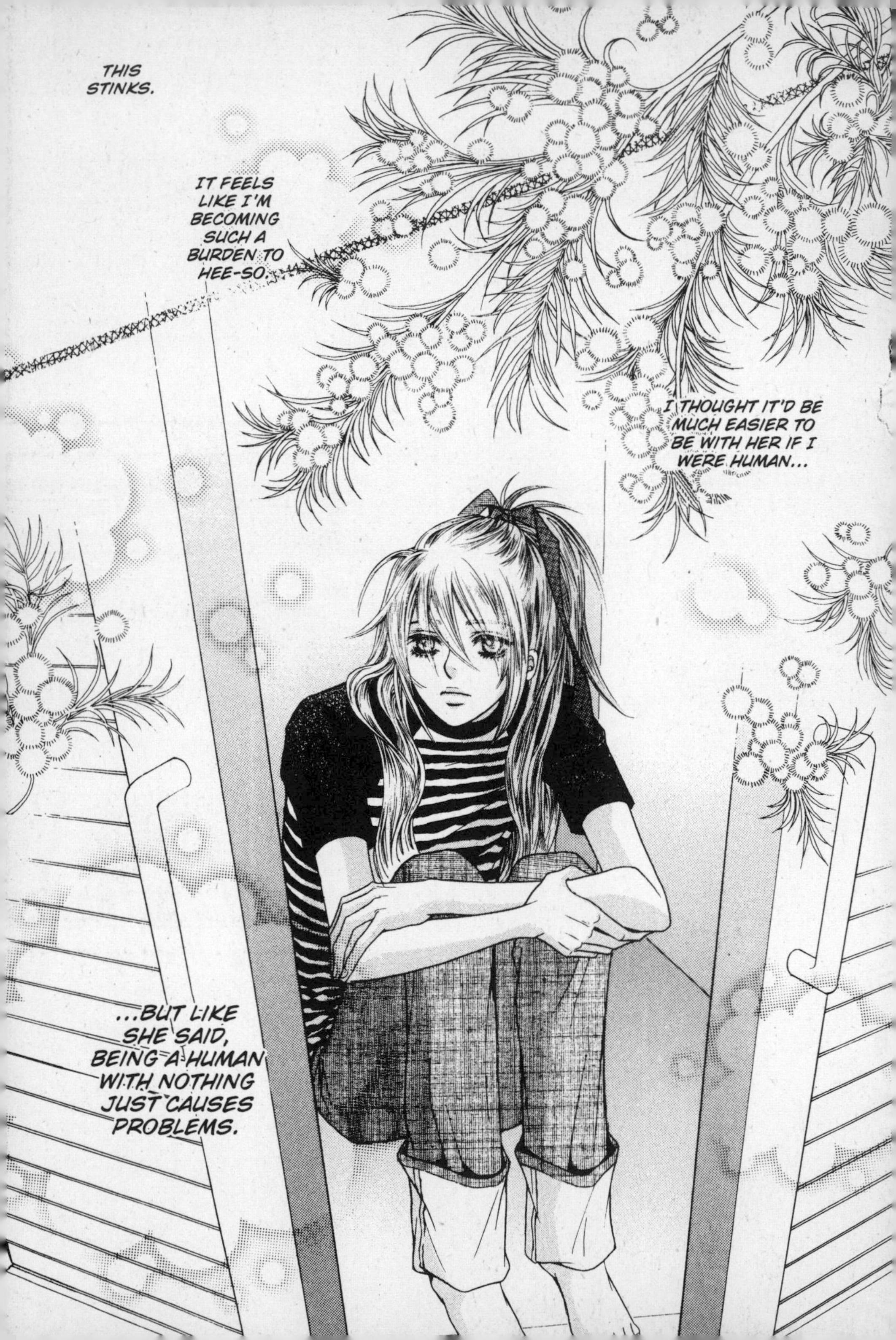
THIS STINKS.
IT FEELS LIKE I'M BECOMING SUCH A BURDEN TO HEE-SO.
I THOUGHT IT'D BE MUCH EASIER TO BE WITH HER IF I WERE HUMAN...
...BUT LIKE SHE SAID, BEING A HUMAN WITH NOTHING JUST CAUSES PROBLEMS.

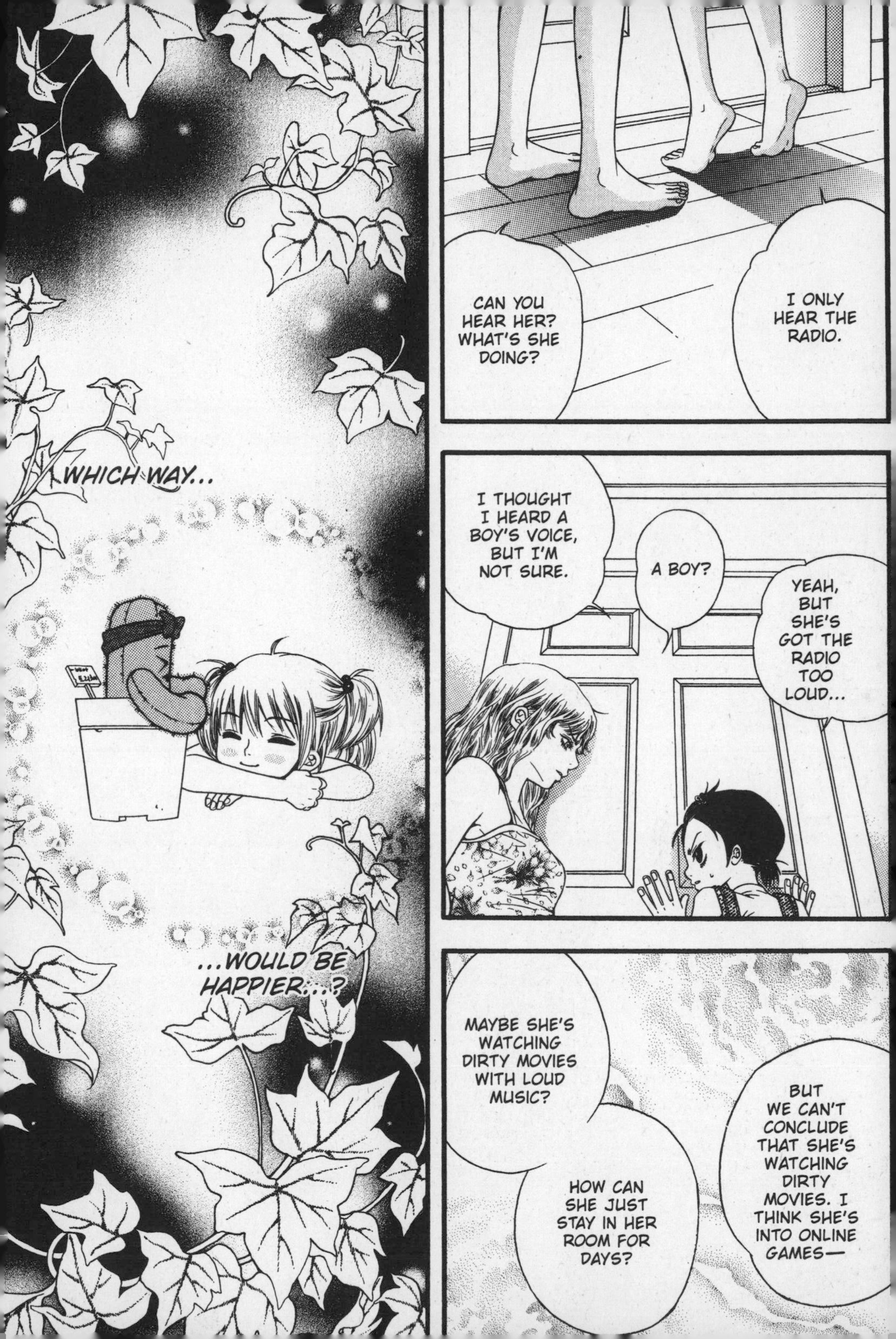
WHICH WAY...
...WOULD BE HAPPIER...?
CAN YOU HEAR HER? WHAT'S SHE DOING?
I ONLY HEAR THE RADIO.
I THOUGHT I HEARD A BOY'S VOICE, BUT I'M NOT SURE.
A BOY?
YEAH, BUT SHE'S GOT THE RADIO TOO LOUD...
MAYBE SHE'S WATCHING DIRTY MOVIES WITH LOUD MUSIC?
HOW CAN SHE JUST STAY IN HER ROOM FOR DAYS?
BUT WE CAN'T CONCLUDE THAT SHE'S WATCHING DIRTY MOVIES. I THINK SHE'S INTO ONLINE GAMES—

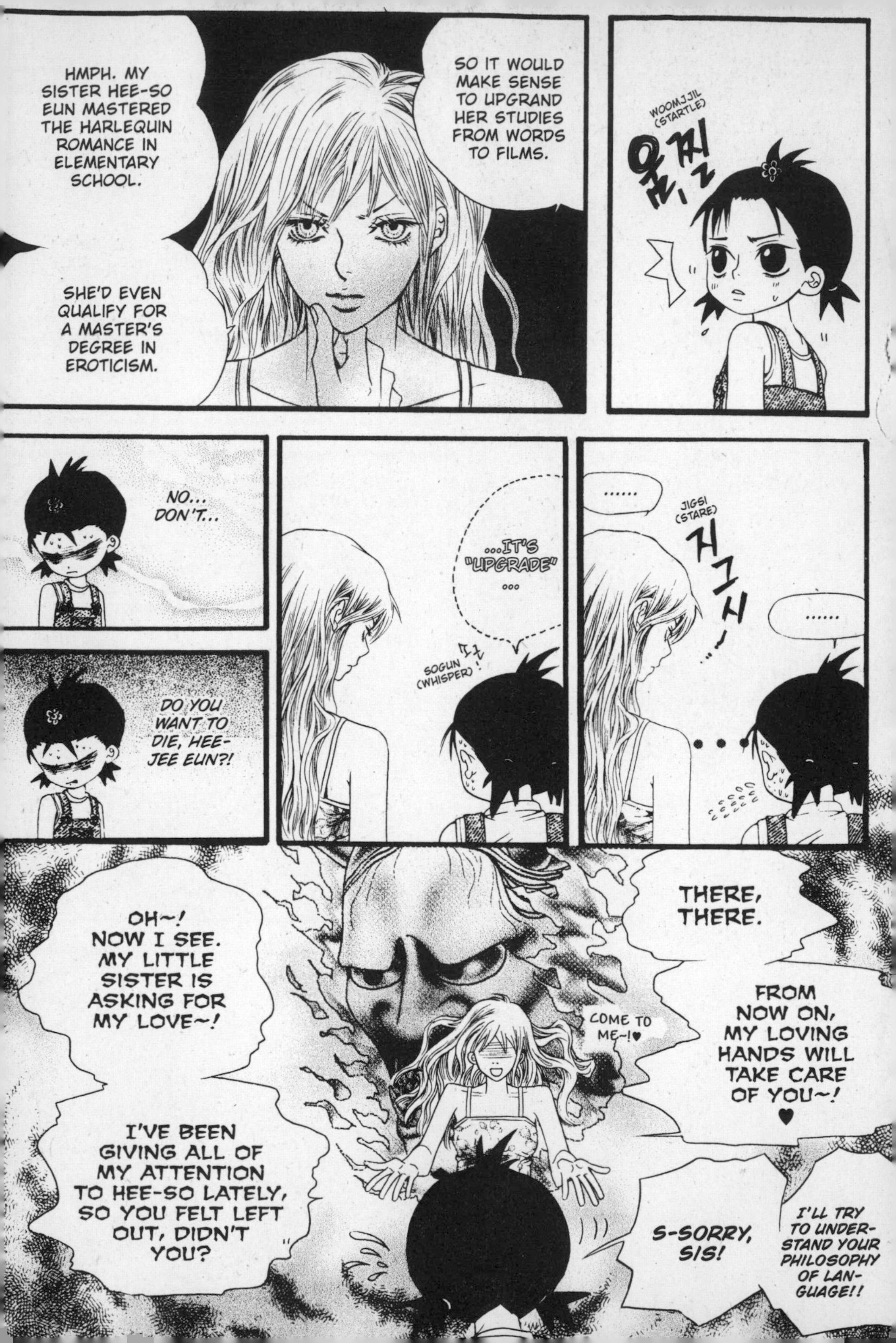
HMPH. MY SISTER HEE-SO EUN MASTERED THE HARLEQUIN ROMANCE IN ELEMENTARY SCHOOL.
SHE'D EVEN QUALIFY FOR A MASTER'S DEGREE IN EROTICISM.
SO IT WOULD MAKE SENSE TO UPGRAND HER STUDIES FROM WORDS TO FILMS.
WOOMJIL (STARTLE)
움찔
NO... DON'T...
DO YOU WANT TO DIE, HEE-JEE EUN?!
...IT'S "UPGRADE"...
SOGUN (WHISPER)
소근
......
JIGSI (STARE)
지그시
......
OH~! NOW I SEE. MY LITTLE SISTER IS ASKING FOR MY LOVE~!
I'VE BEEN GIVING ALL OF MY ATTENTION TO HEE-SO LATELY, SO YOU FELT LEFT OUT, DIDN'T YOU?
THERE, THERE.
FROM NOW ON, MY LOVING HANDS WILL TAKE CARE OF YOU~! ♥
COME TO ME~!♥
S-SORRY, SIS!
I'LL TRY TO UNDERSTAND YOUR PHILOSOPHY OF LANGUAGE!!

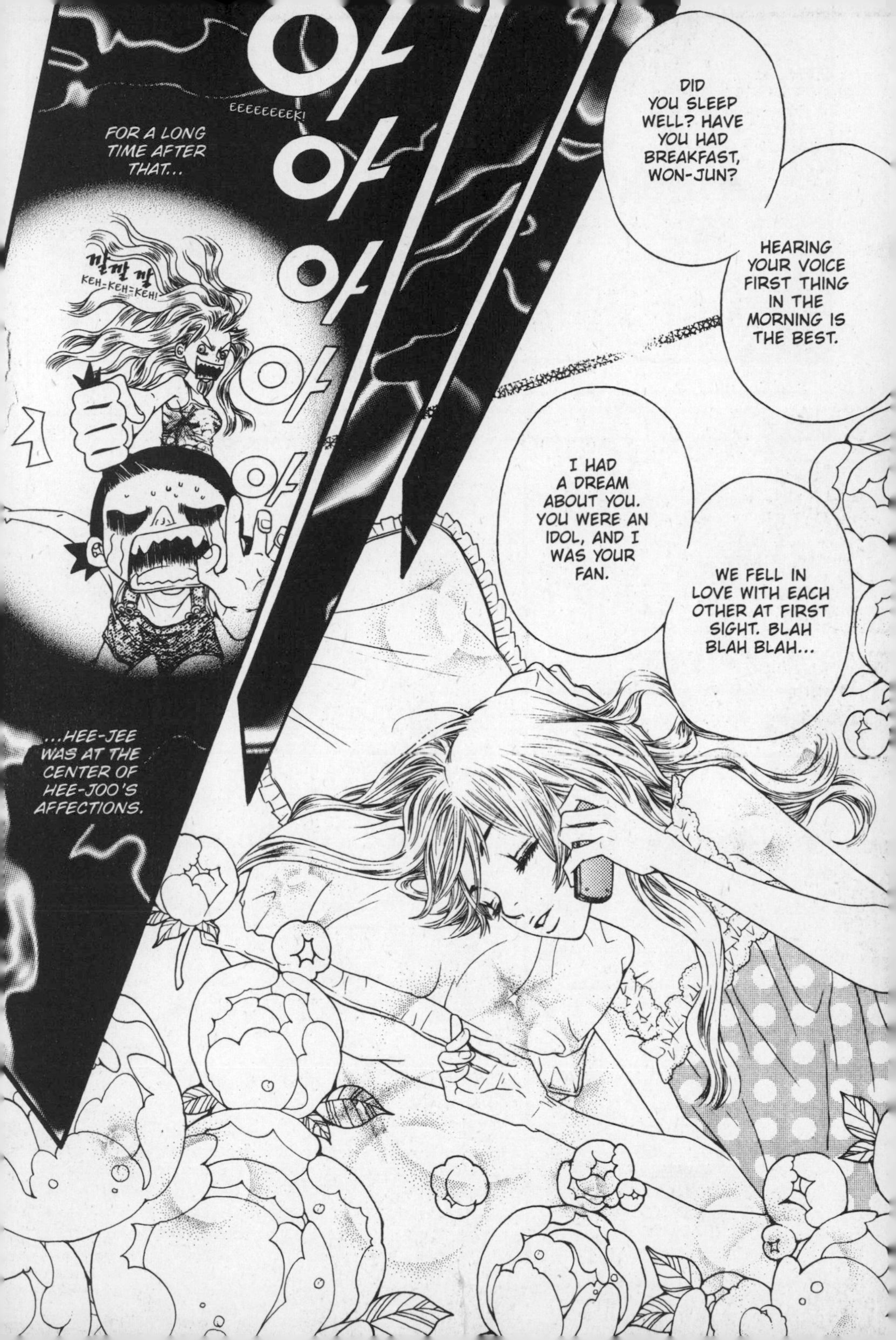
FOR A LONG TIME AFTER THAT...
아아아아아
EEEEEEEEK!
깔깔 깔
KEH-KEH-KEH!
...HEE-JEE WAS AT THE CENTER OF HEE-JOO'S AFFECTIONS.
DID YOU SLEEP WELL? HAVE YOU HAD BREAKFAST, WON-JUN?
HEARING YOUR VOICE FIRST THING IN THE MORNING IS THE BEST.
I HAD A DREAM ABOUT YOU. YOU WERE AN IDOL, AND I WAS YOUR FAN.
WE FELL IN LOVE WITH EACH OTHER AT FIRST SIGHT. BLAH BLAH BLAH...

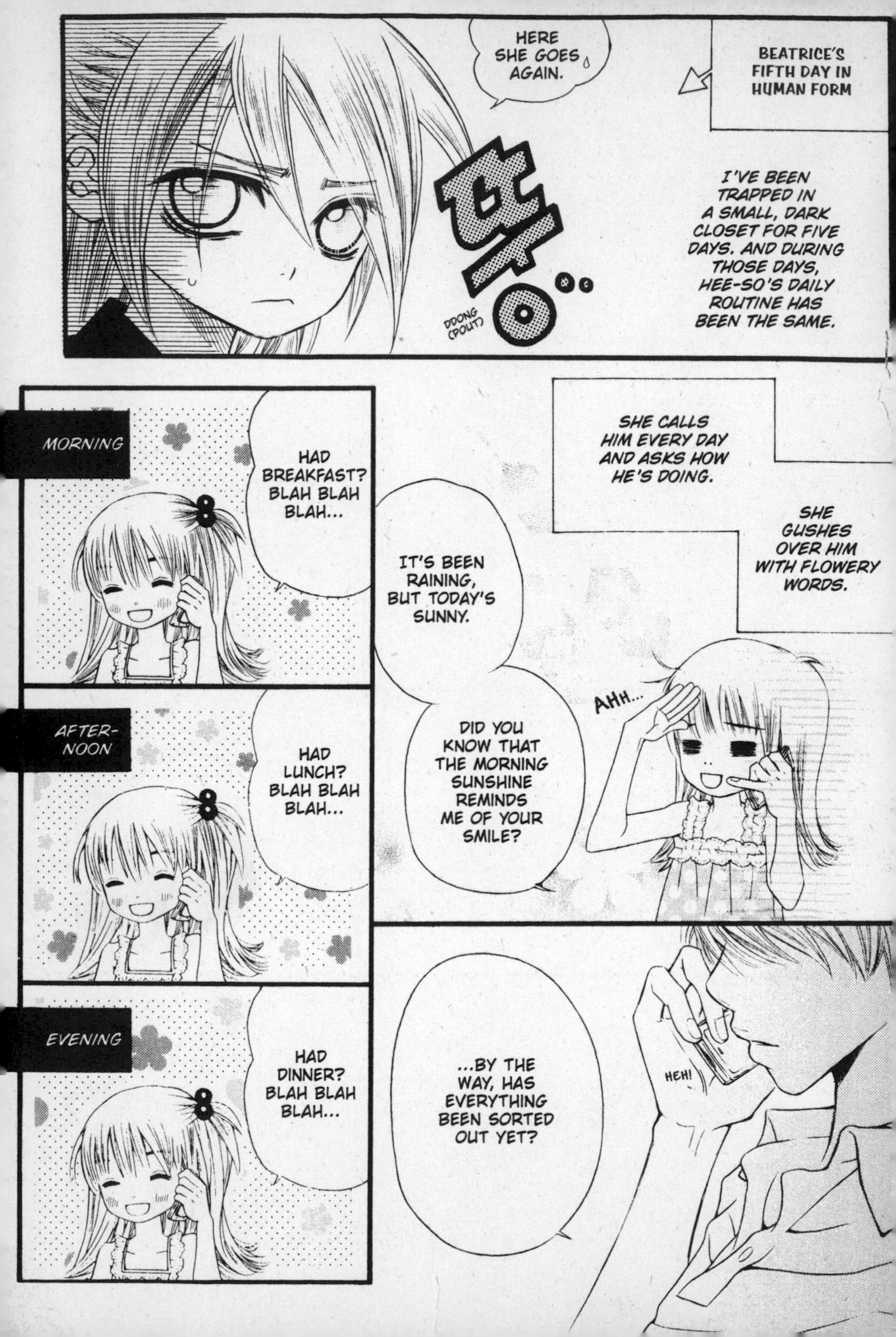
HERE SHE GOES AGAIN.
BEATRICE'S FIFTH DAY IN HUMAN FORM
DDONG (POUT)
I'VE BEEN TRAPPED IN A SMALL, DARK CLOSET FOR FIVE DAYS. AND DURING THOSE DAYS, HEE-SO'S DAILY ROUTINE HAS BEEN THE SAME.
MORNING
HAD BREAKFAST? BLAH BLAH BLAH...
AFTER-NOON
HAD LUNCH? BLAH BLAH BLAH...
EVENING
HAD DINNER? BLAH BLAH BLAH...
SHE CALLS HIM EVERY DAY AND ASKS HOW HE'S DOING.
SHE GUSHES OVER HIM WITH FLOWERY WORDS.
IT'S BEEN RAINING, BUT TODAY'S SUNNY.
DID YOU KNOW THAT THE MORNING SUNSHINE REMINDS ME OF YOUR SMILE?
AHH...
...BY THE WAY, HAS EVERYTHING BEEN SORTED OUT YET?
HEH!

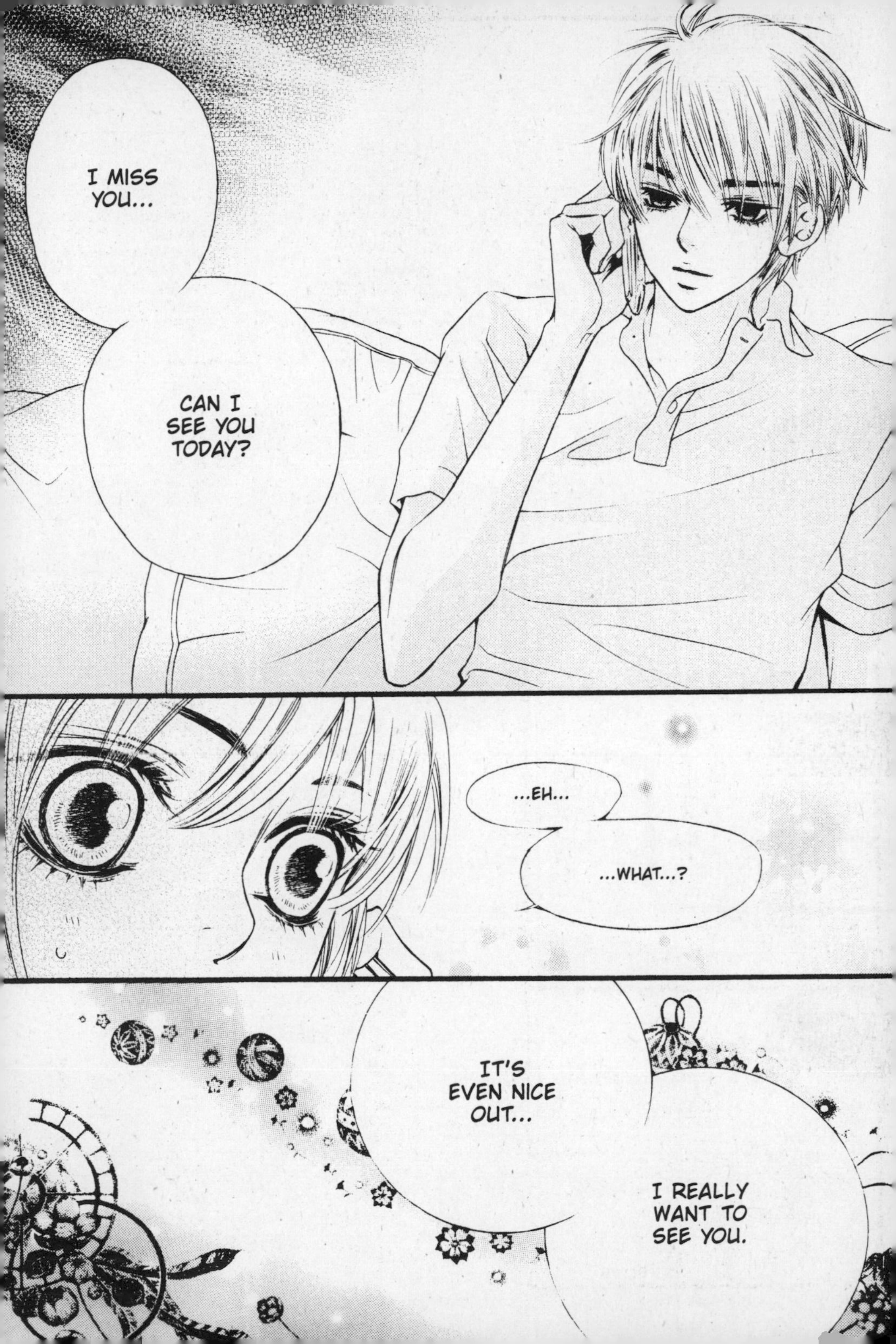
I MISS YOU...
CAN I SEE YOU TODAY?
...EH...
...WHAT...?
IT'S EVEN NICE OUT...
I REALLY WANT TO SEE YOU.

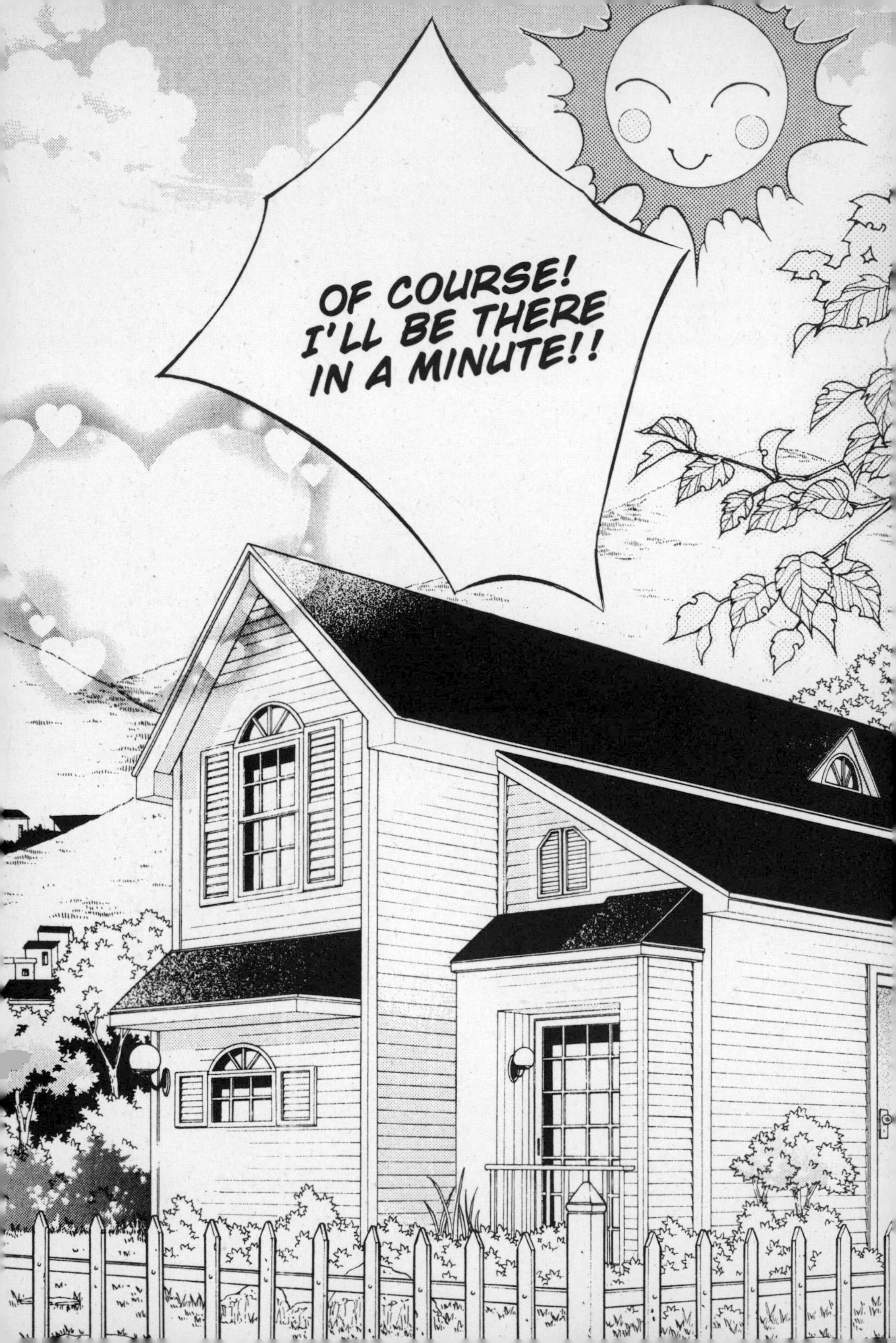
OF COURSE! I'LL BE THERE IN A MINUTE!!

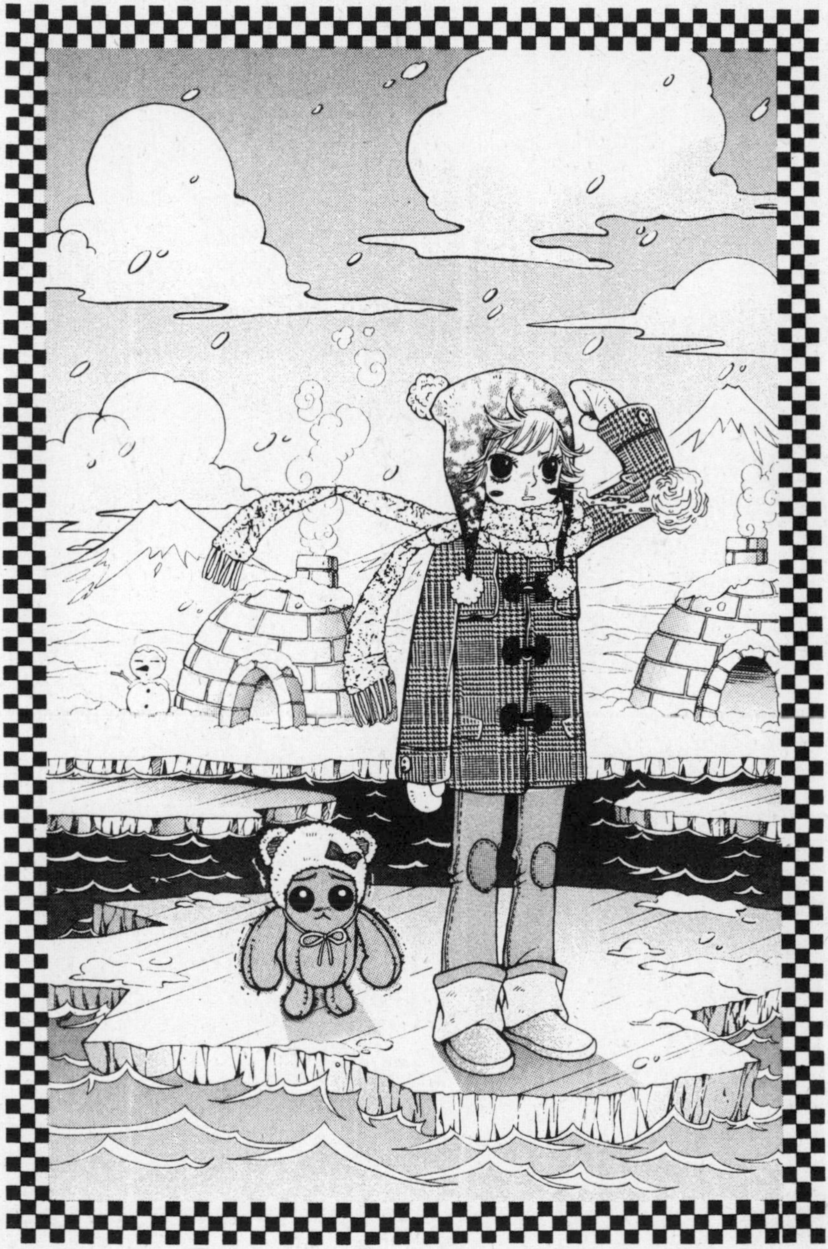

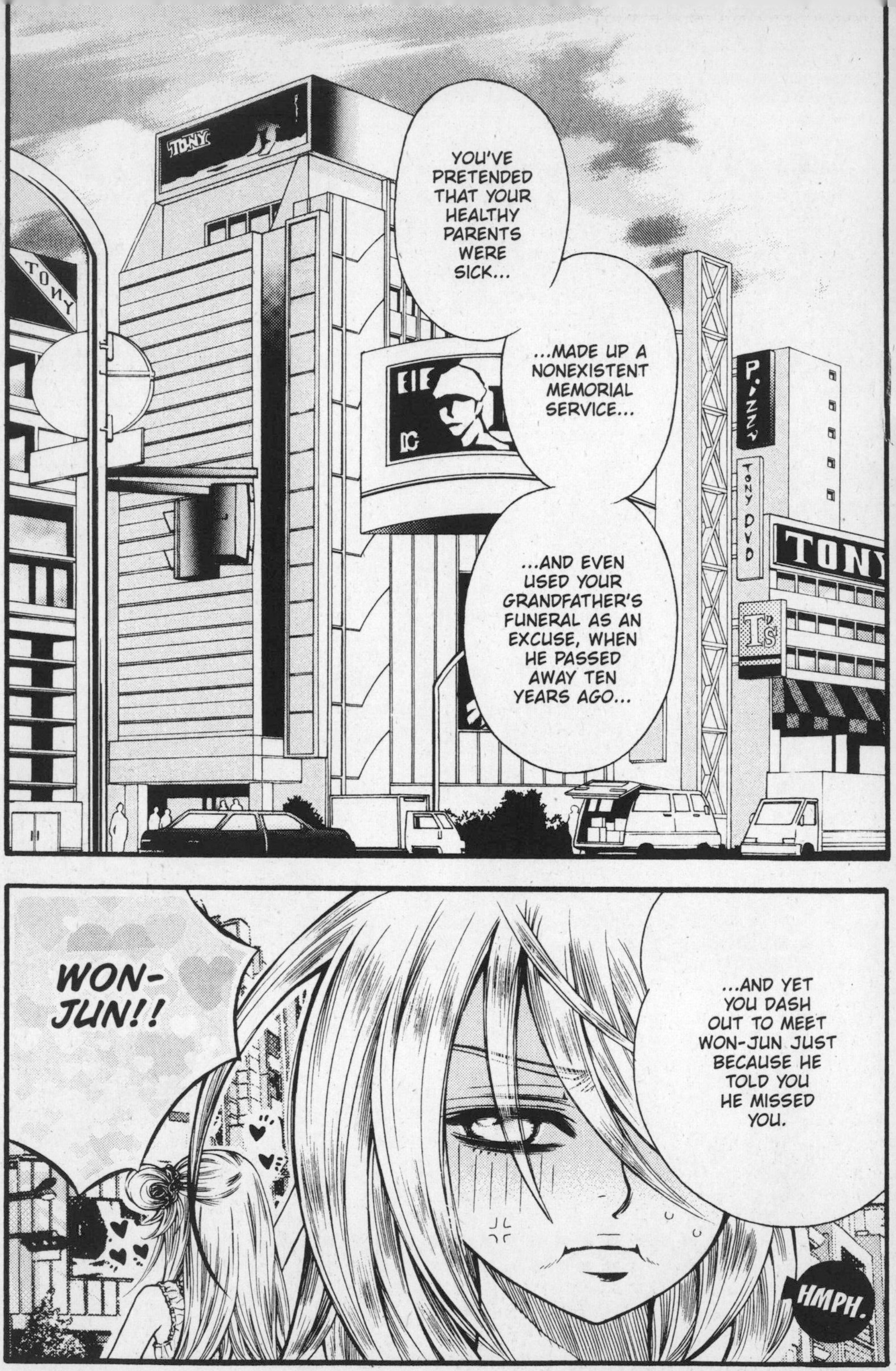
YOU'VE PRETENDED THAT YOUR HEALTHY PARENTS WERE SICK...
...MADE UP A NONEXISTENT MEMORIAL SERVICE...
...AND EVEN USED YOUR GRANDFATHER'S FUNERAL AS AN EXCUSE, WHEN HE PASSED AWAY TEN YEARS AGO...
WON-JUN!!
...AND YET YOU DASH OUT TO MEET WON-JUN JUST BECAUSE HE TOLD YOU HE MISSED YOU.
HMPH.

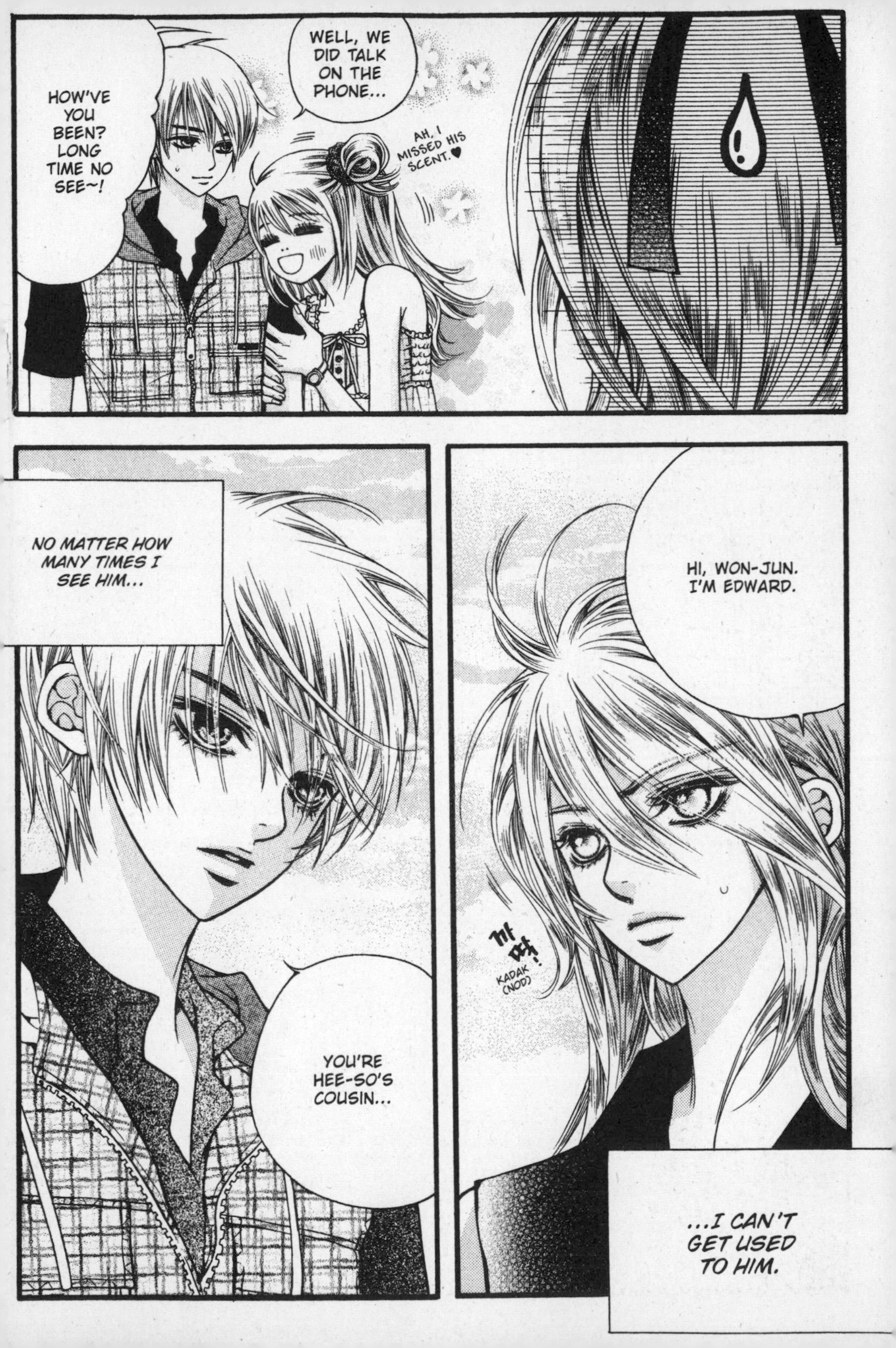
HOW'VE YOU BEEN? LONG TIME NO SEE~!
WELL, WE DID TALK ON THE PHONE...
AH, I MISSED HIS SCENT.♥
NO MATTER HOW MANY TIMES I SEE HIM...
YOU'RE HEE-SO'S COUSIN...
HI, WON-JUN. I'M EDWARD.
까딱!
KADAK (NOD)
...I CAN'T GET USED TO HIM.

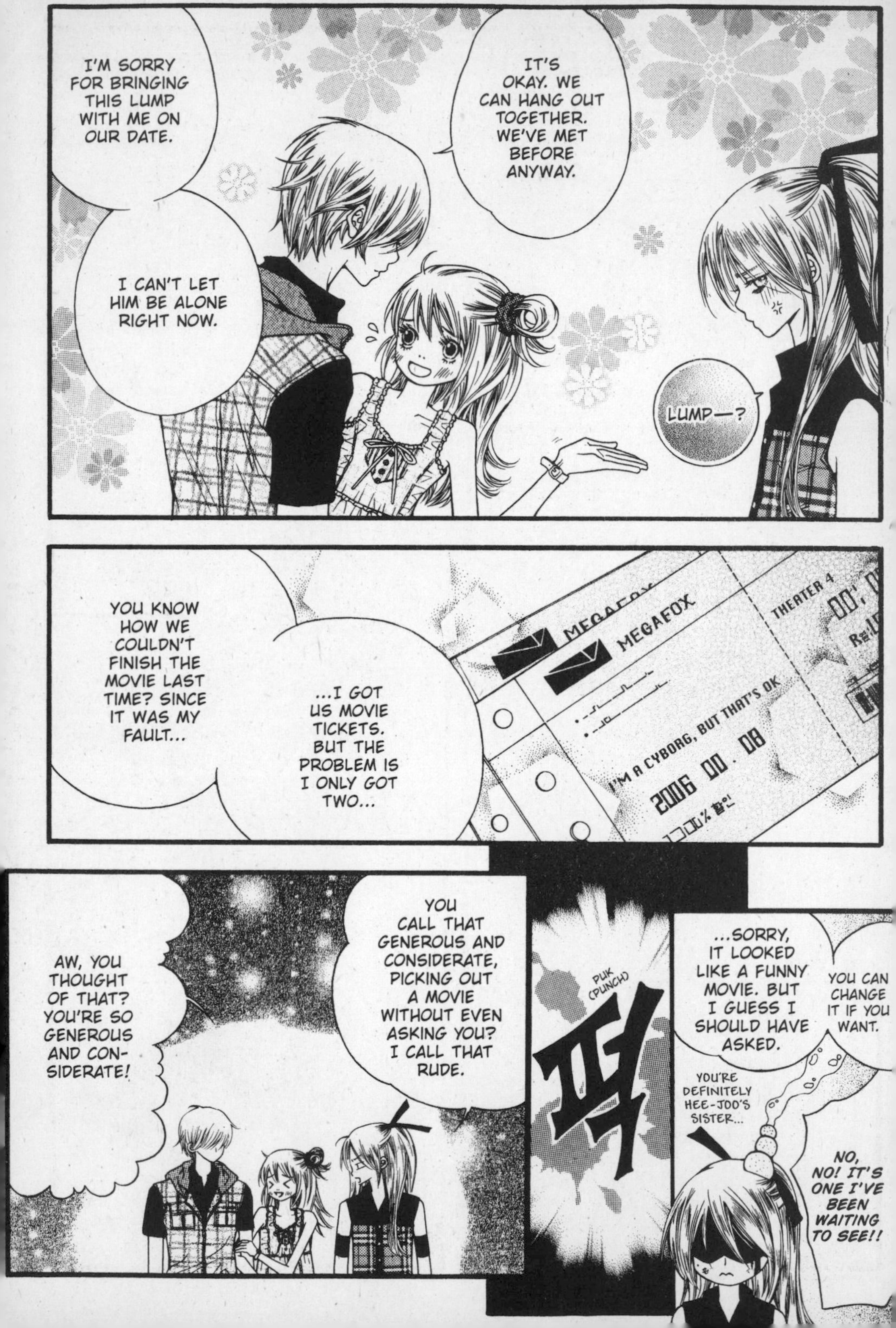
I'M SORRY FOR BRINGING THIS LUMP WITH ME ON OUR DATE.
I CAN'T LET HIM BE ALONE RIGHT NOW.
IT'S OKAY. WE CAN HANG OUT TOGETHER. WE'VE MET BEFORE ANYWAY.
LUMP—?
YOU KNOW HOW WE COULDN'T FINISH THE MOVIE LAST TIME? SINCE IT WAS MY FAULT...
...I GOT US MOVIE TICKETS. BUT THE PROBLEM IS I ONLY GOT TWO...
MEGAFOX
MEGAFOX
THEATER 4
I'M A CYBORG, BUT THAT'S OK
2006 00. 08
AW, YOU THOUGHT OF THAT? YOU'RE SO GENEROUS AND CON-SIDERATE!
YOU CALL THAT GENEROUS AND CONSIDERATE, PICKING OUT A MOVIE WITHOUT EVEN ASKING YOU? I CALL THAT RUDE.
PUK (PUNCH)
퍽
...SORRY, IT LOOKED LIKE A FUNNY MOVIE. BUT I GUESS I SHOULD HAVE ASKED.
YOU CAN CHANGE IT IF YOU WANT.
YOU'RE DEFINITELY HEE-JOO'S SISTER...
NO, NO! IT'S ONE I'VE BEEN WAITING TO SEE!!

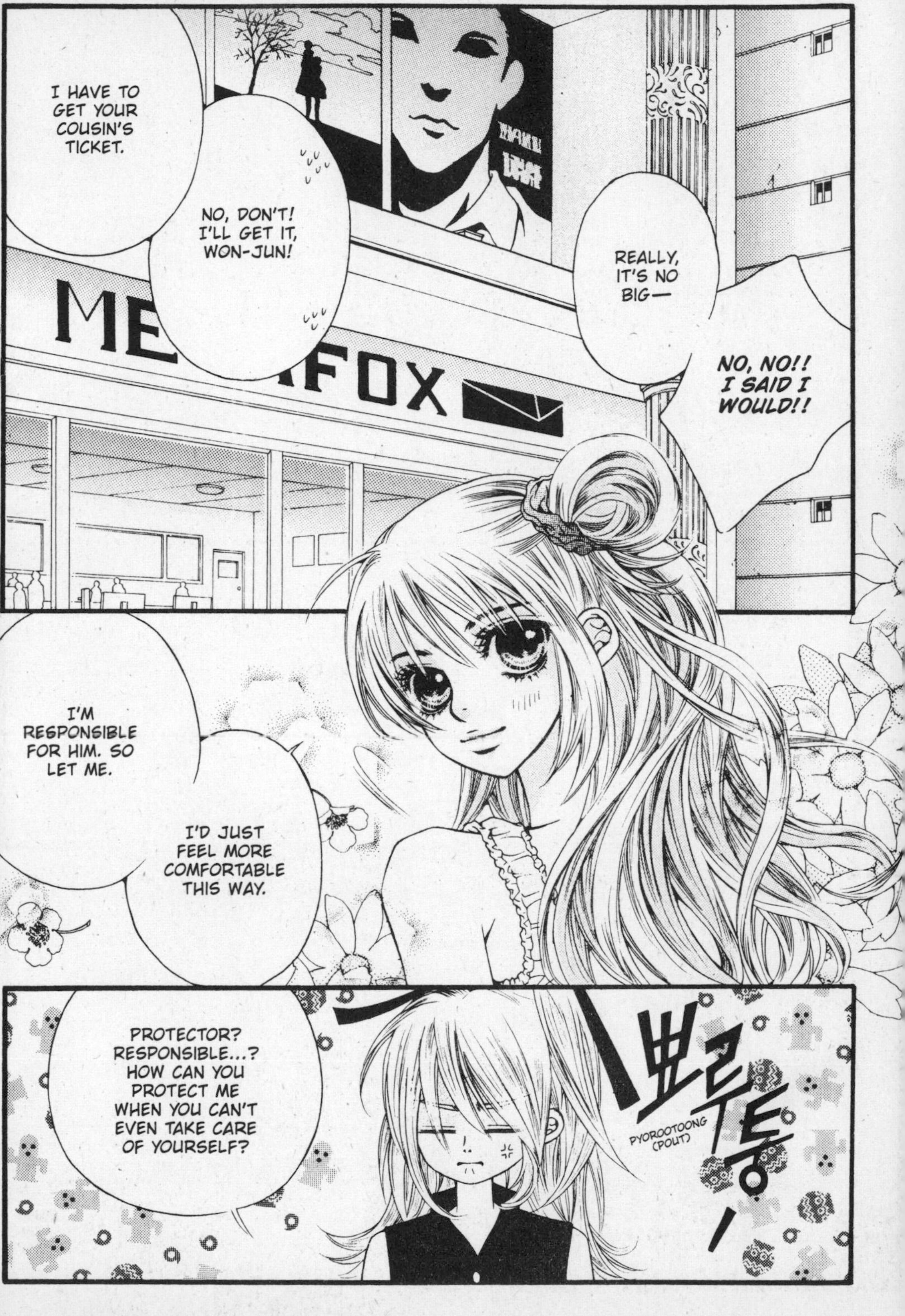
I HAVE TO GET YOUR COUSIN'S TICKET.
NO, DON'T! I'LL GET IT, WON-JUN!
REALLY, IT'S NO BIG—
NO, NO!! I SAID I WOULD!!
I'M RESPONSIBLE FOR HIM. SO LET ME.
I'D JUST FEEL MORE COMFORTABLE THIS WAY.
PROTECTOR? RESPONSIBLE...? HOW CAN YOU PROTECT ME WHEN YOU CAN'T EVEN TAKE CARE OF YOURSELF?
뾰루퉁
PYOROOTOONG (POUT)

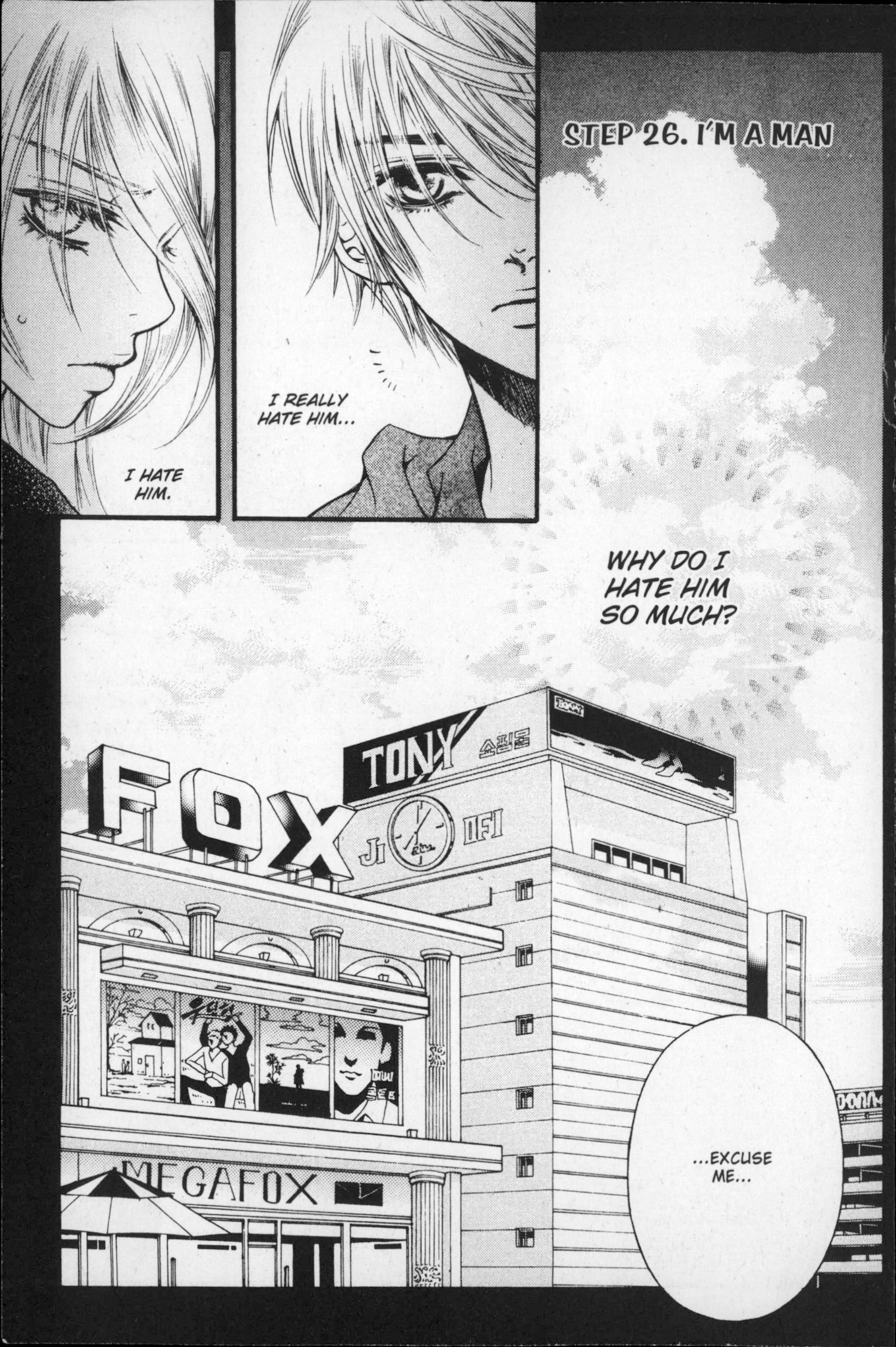
I HATE HIM.
I REALLY HATE HIM...
STEP 26. I'M A MAN
WHY DO I HATE HIM SO MUCH?
FOX
TONY
MEGAFOX
...EXCUSE ME...

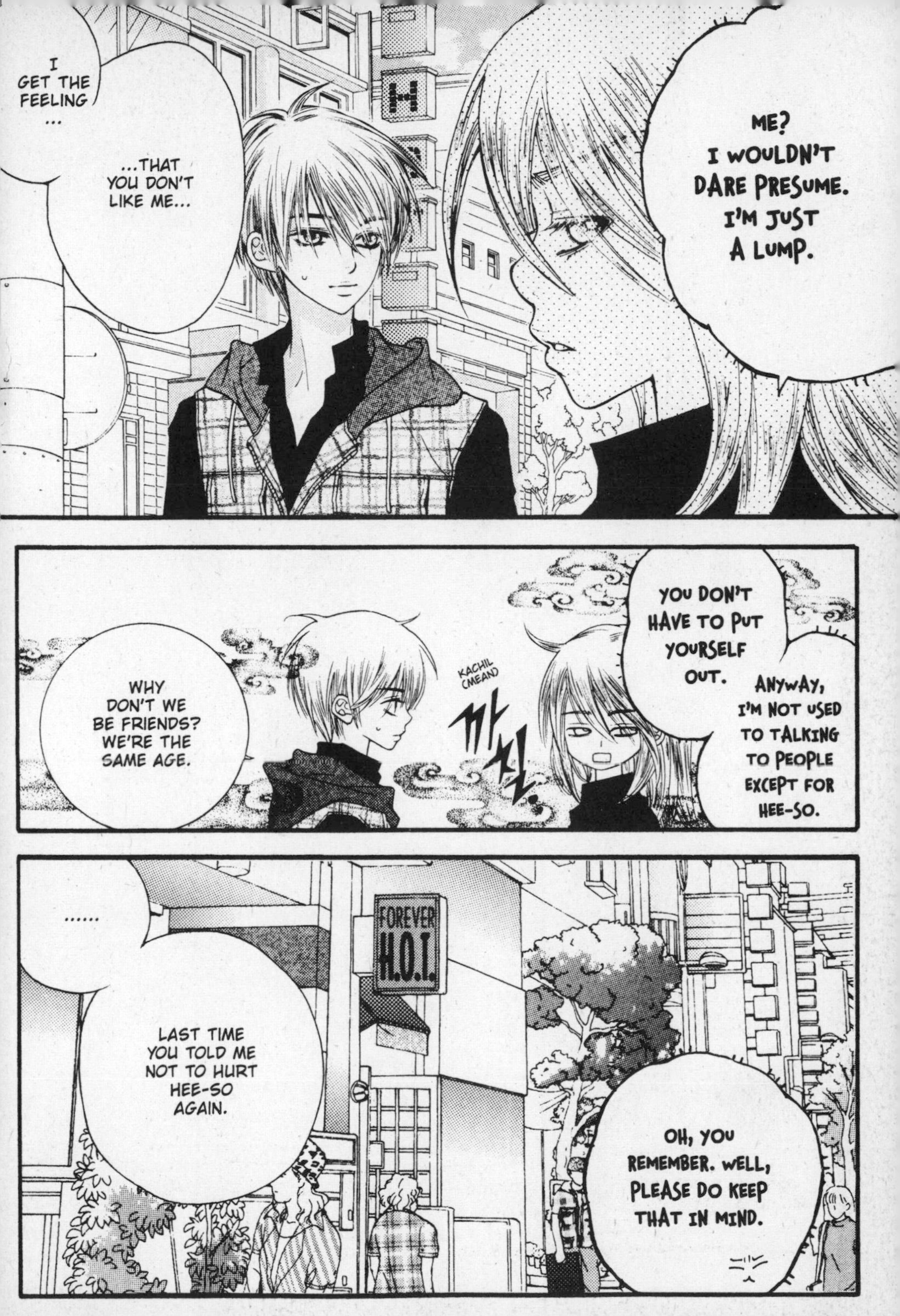
I GET THE FEELING ...
...THAT YOU DON'T LIKE ME...
ME? I WOULDN'T DARE PRESUME. I'M JUST A LUMP.
WHY DON'T WE BE FRIENDS? WE'RE THE SAME AGE.
까칠
KACHIL (MEAN)
YOU DON'T HAVE TO PUT YOURSELF OUT.
ANYWAY, I'M NOT USED TO TALKING TO PEOPLE EXCEPT FOR HEE-SO.
......
FOREVER H.O.T.
LAST TIME YOU TOLD ME NOT TO HURT HEE-SO AGAIN.
OH, YOU REMEMBER. WELL, PLEASE DO KEEP THAT IN MIND.

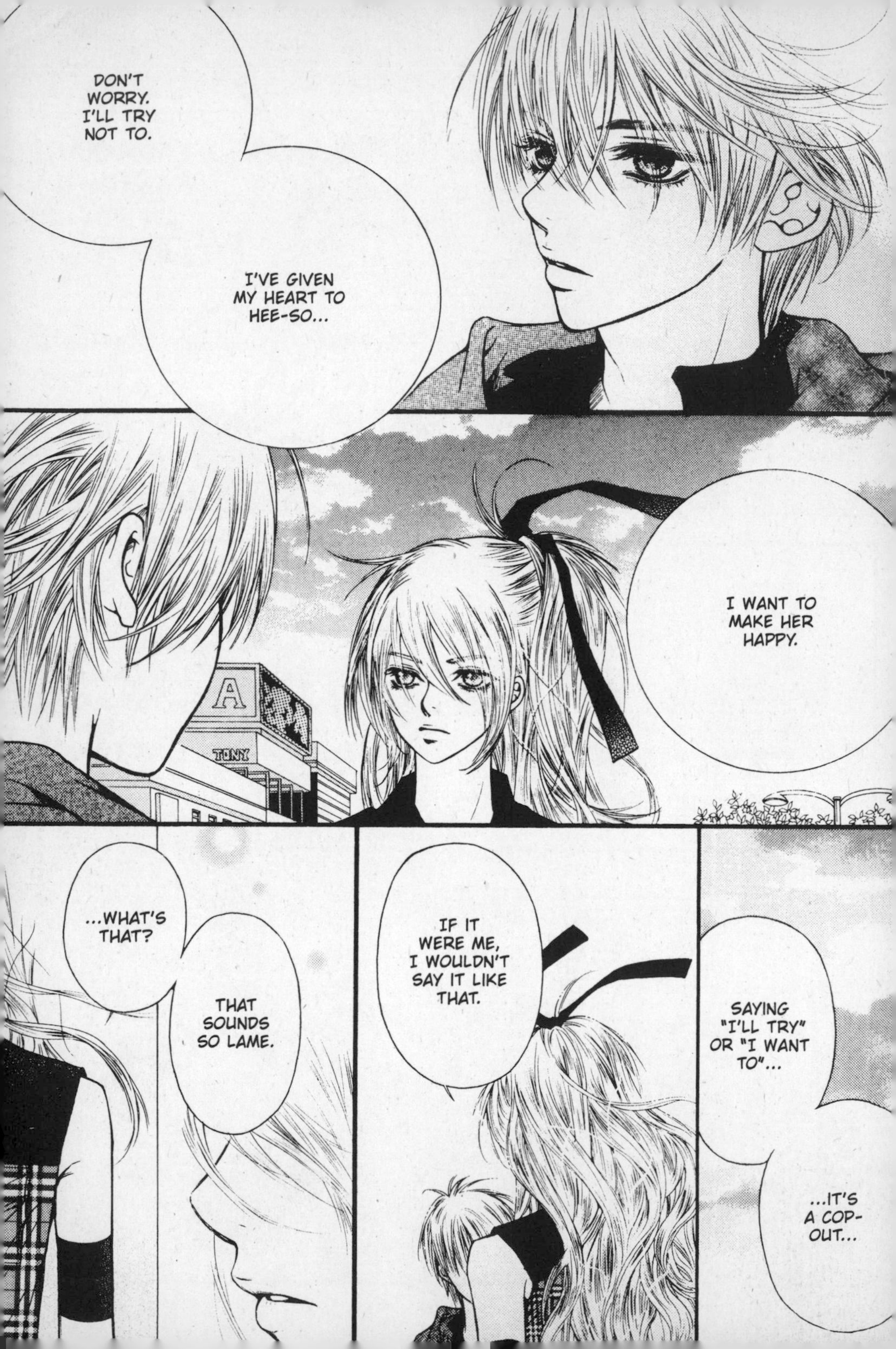
DON'T WORRY. I'LL TRY NOT TO.
I'VE GIVEN MY HEART TO HEE-SO...
A
TONY
I WANT TO MAKE HER HAPPY.
...WHAT'S THAT?
THAT SOUNDS SO LAME.
IF IT WERE ME, I WOULDN'T SAY IT LIKE THAT.
SAYING "I'LL TRY" OR "I WANT TO"...
...IT'S A COP-OUT...

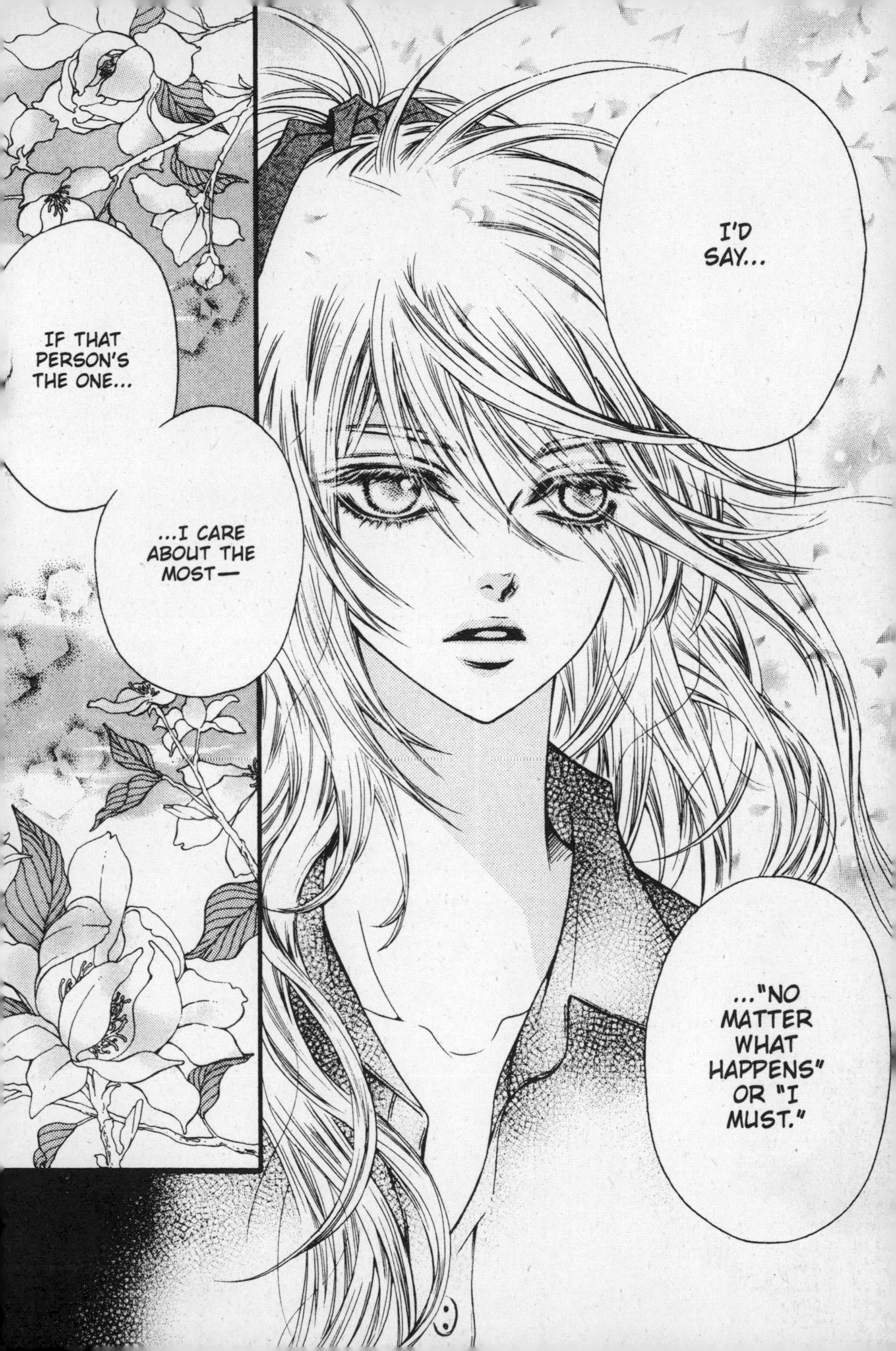
IF THAT PERSON'S THE ONE...
...I CARE ABOUT THE MOST—
I'D SAY...
..."NO MATTER WHAT HAPPENS" OR "I MUST."

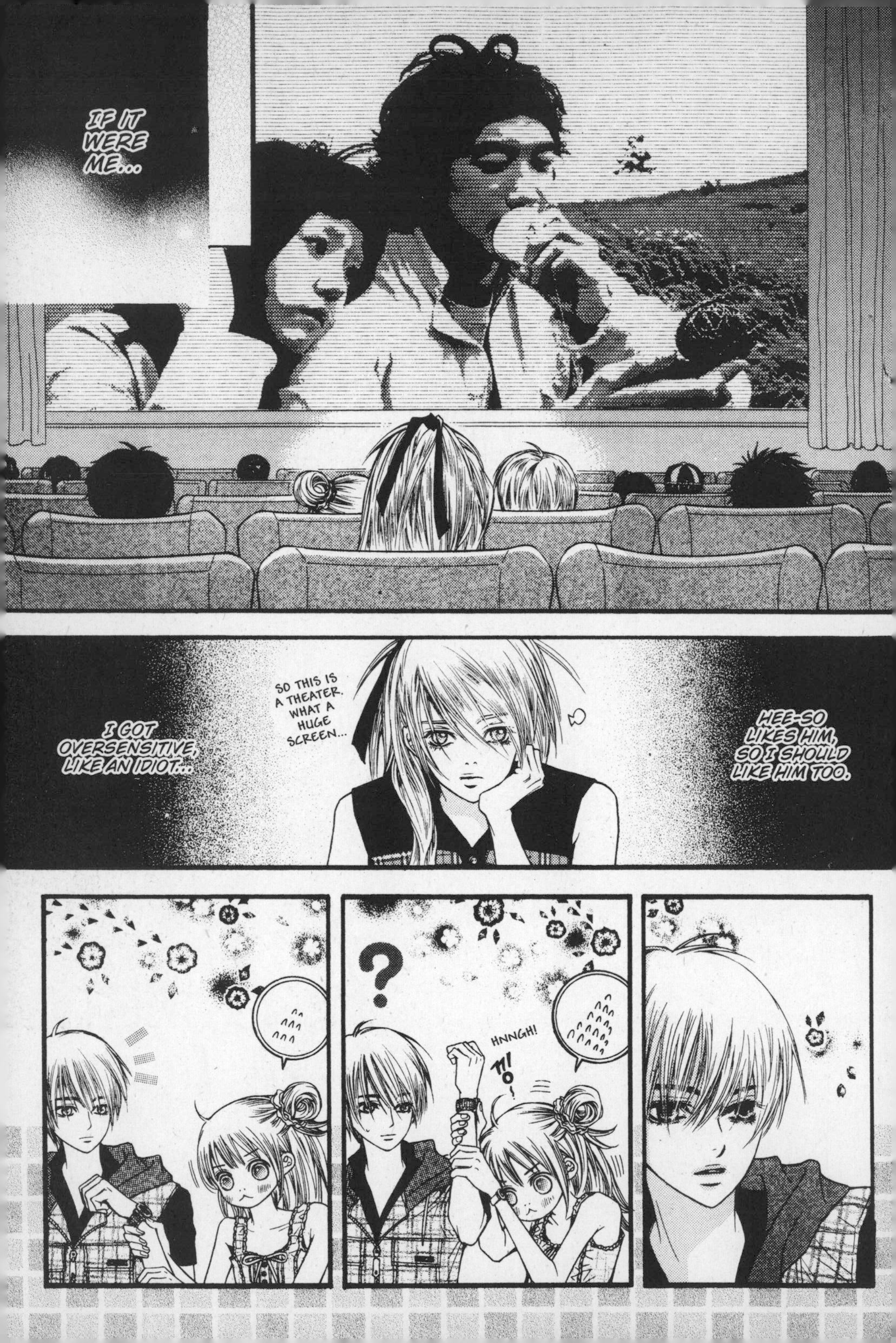
IF IT WERE ME...
I GOT OVERSENSITIVE, LIKE AN IDIOT...
SO THIS IS A THEATER. WHAT A HUGE SCREEN...
HEE-SO LIKES HIM, SO I SHOULD LIKE HIM TOO.
HNNGH!

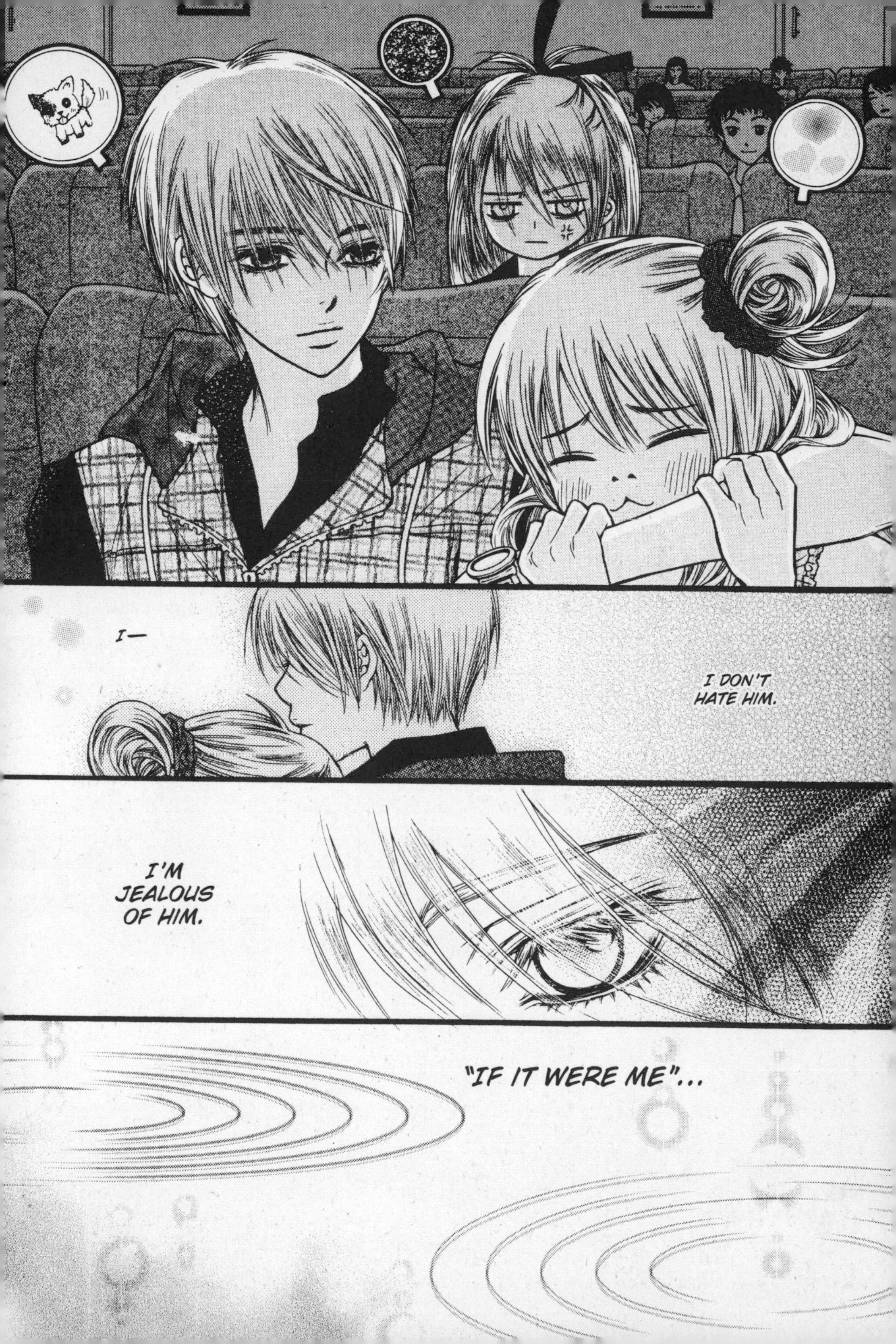
I—
I DON'T HATE HIM.
I'M JEALOUS OF HIM.
"IF IT WERE ME"...

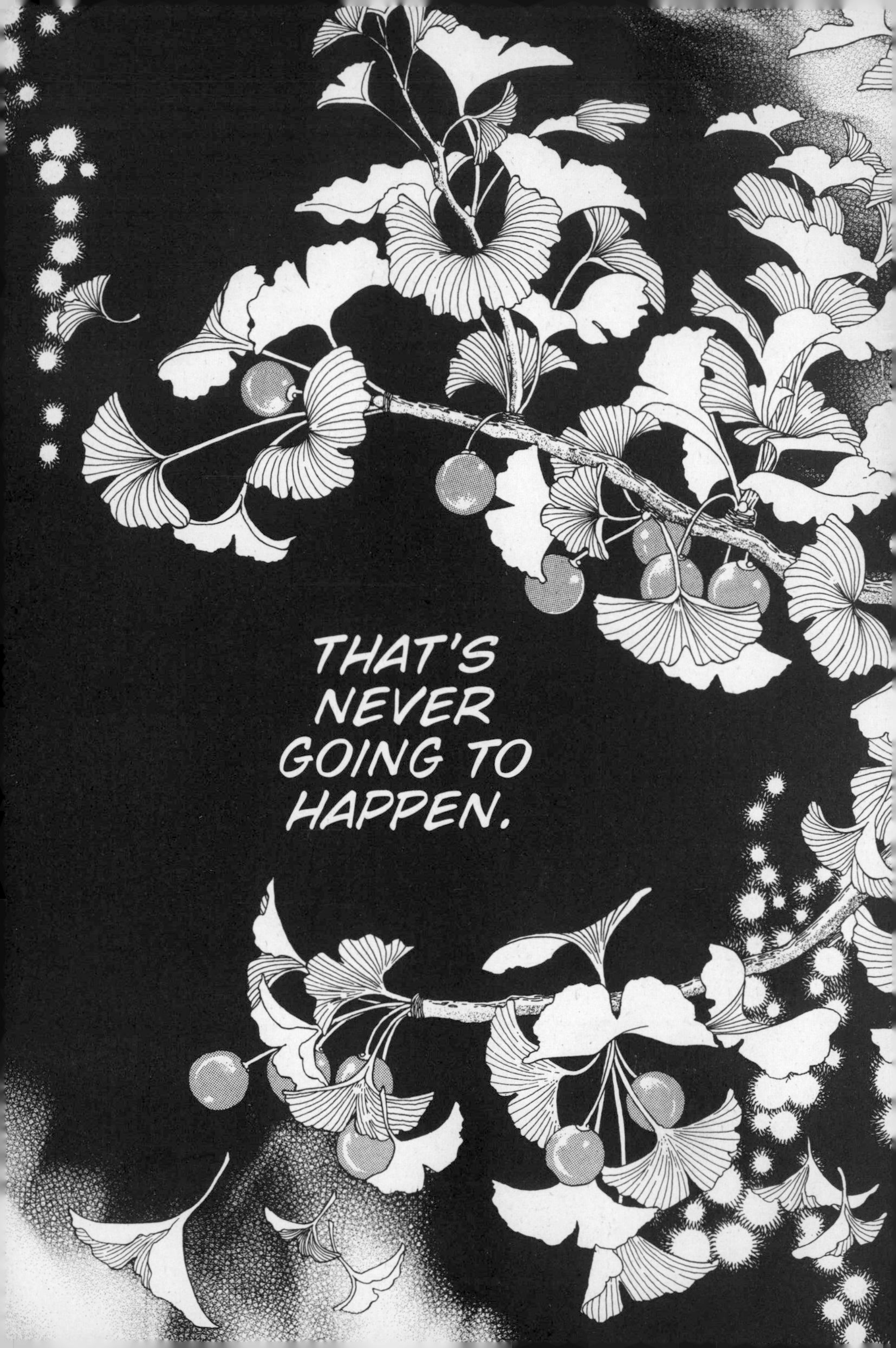
THAT'S NEVER GOING TO HAPPEN.

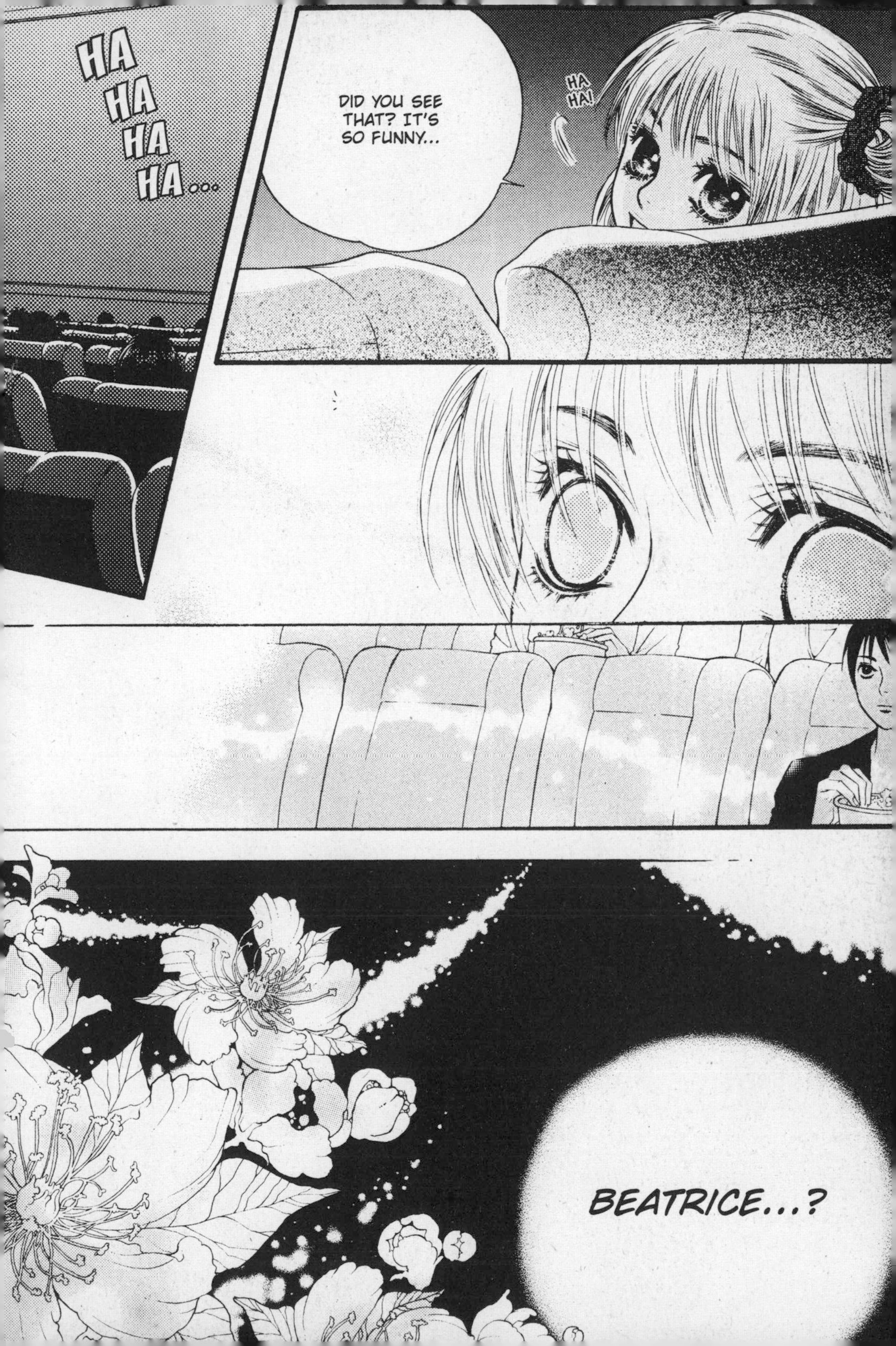
HA HA HA HA...
DID YOU SEE THAT? IT'S SO FUNNY...
HA HA!
BEATRICE...?

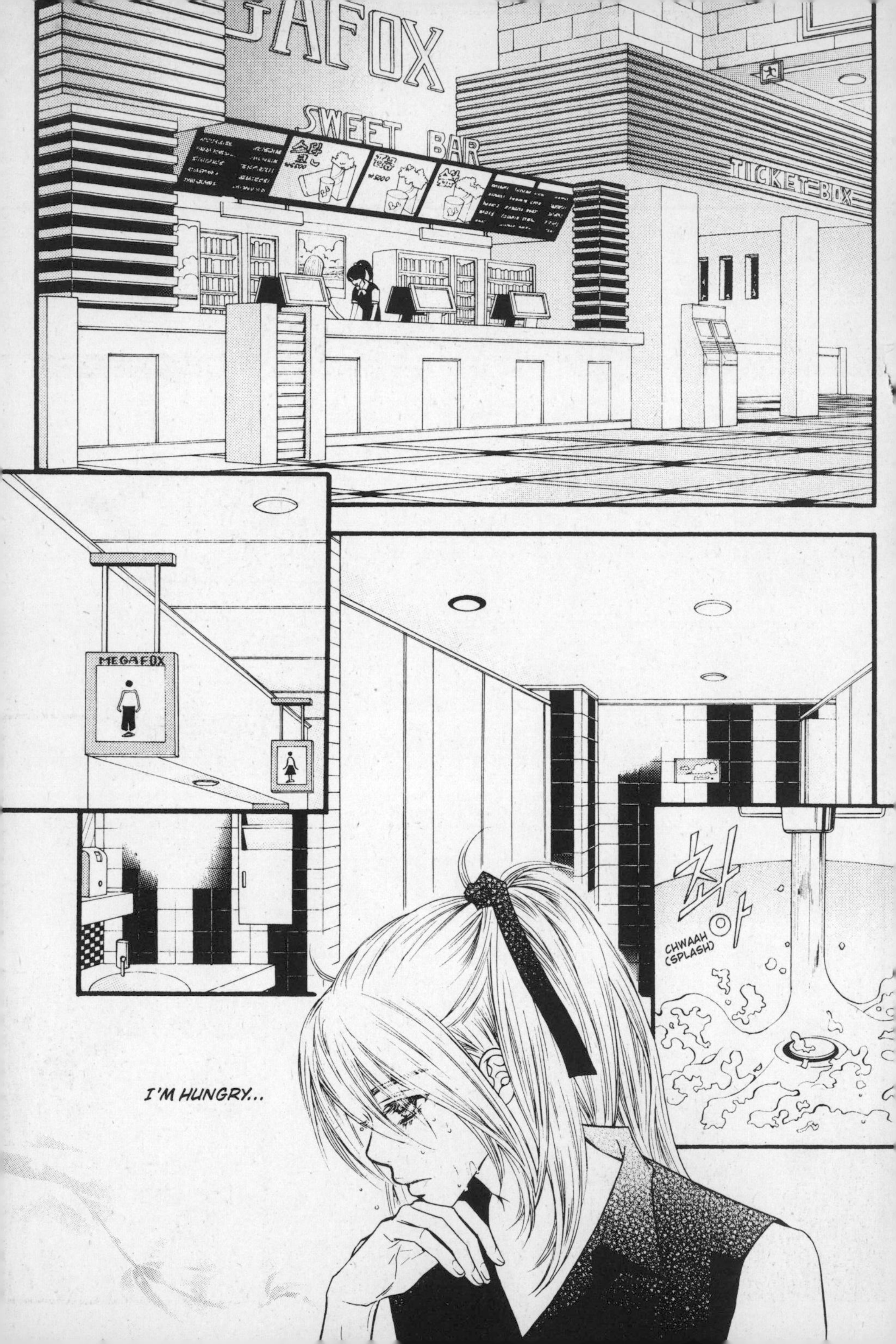
GAFOX
SWEET BAR
TICKET BOX
MEGAFOX
촤아
CHWAAH (SPLASH)
I'M HUNGRY...

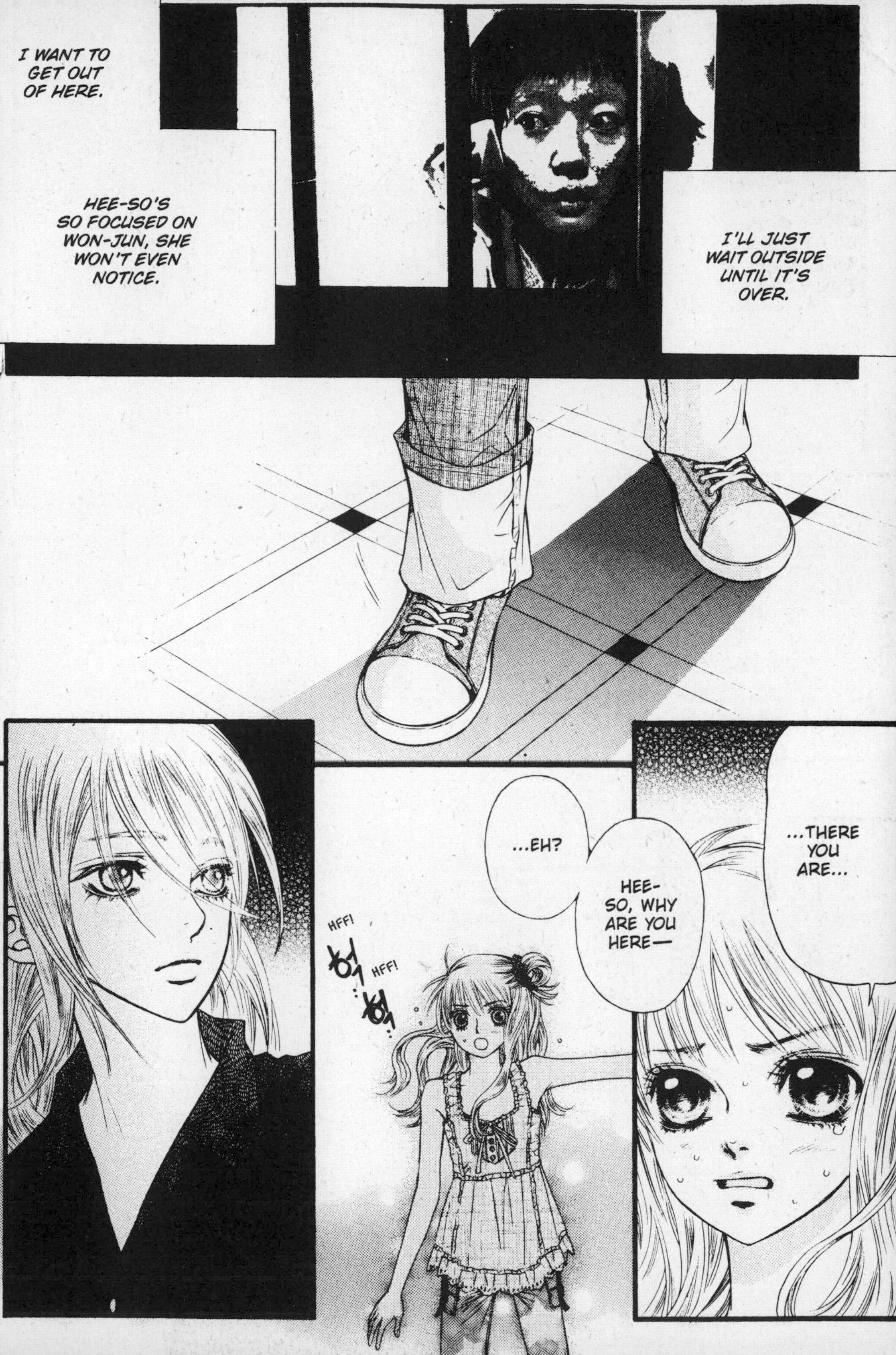
I WANT TO GET OUT OF HERE.
HEE-SO'S SO FOCUSED ON WON-JUN, SHE WON'T EVEN NOTICE.
I'LL JUST WAIT OUTSIDE UNTIL IT'S OVER.
HFF!
HFF!
...EH?
HEE-SO, WHY ARE YOU HERE—
...THERE YOU ARE...

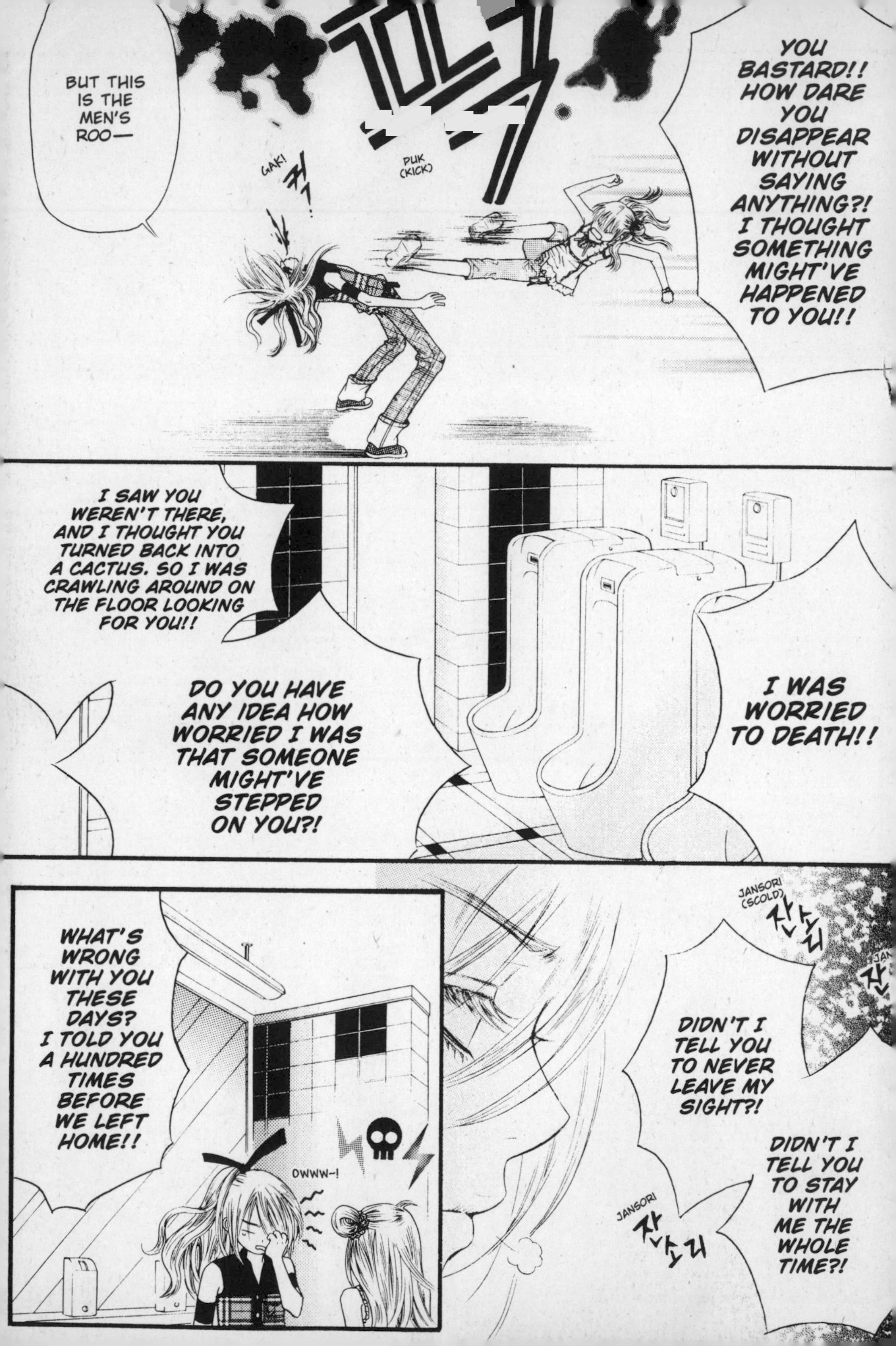
BUT THIS IS THE MEN'S ROO—
GAK!
PUK (KICK)
YOU BASTARD!! HOW DARE YOU DISAPPEAR WITHOUT SAYING ANYTHING?! I THOUGHT SOMETHING MIGHT'VE HAPPENED TO YOU!!
I SAW YOU WEREN'T THERE, AND I THOUGHT YOU TURNED BACK INTO A CACTUS. SO I WAS CRAWLING AROUND ON THE FLOOR LOOKING FOR YOU!!
DO YOU HAVE ANY IDEA HOW WORRIED I WAS THAT SOMEONE MIGHT'VE STEPPED ON YOU?!
I WAS WORRIED TO DEATH!!
WHAT'S WRONG WITH YOU THESE DAYS? I TOLD YOU A HUNDRED TIMES BEFORE WE LEFT HOME!!
OWWW-!
JANSORI (SCOLD)
잔소리
DIDN'T I TELL YOU TO NEVER LEAVE MY SIGHT?!
DIDN'T I TELL YOU TO STAY WITH ME THE WHOLE TIME?!
JANSORI
잔소리

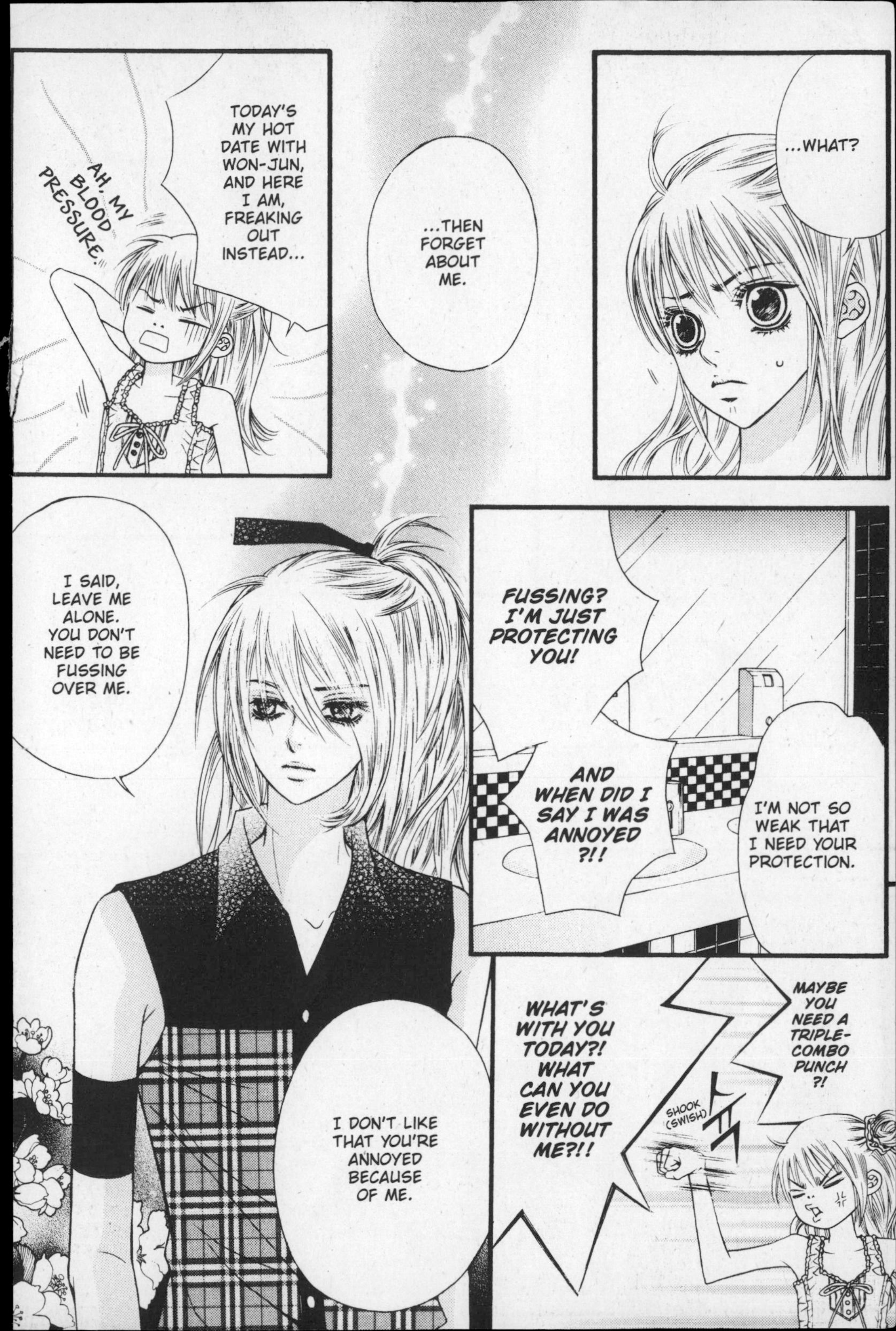
TODAY'S MY HOT DATE WITH WON-JUN, AND HERE I AM, FREAKING OUT INSTEAD...
AH, MY BLOOD PRESSURE.
...THEN FORGET ABOUT ME.
...WHAT?
I SAID, LEAVE ME ALONE. YOU DON'T NEED TO BE FUSSING OVER ME.
FUSSING? I'M JUST PROTECTING YOU!
AND WHEN DID I SAY I WAS ANNOYED ?!!
I'M NOT SO WEAK THAT I NEED YOUR PROTECTION.
I DON'T LIKE THAT YOU'RE ANNOYED BECAUSE OF ME.
WHAT'S WITH YOU TODAY?! WHAT CAN YOU EVEN DO WITHOUT ME?!!
SHOOK (SWISH)
MAYBE YOU NEED A TRIPLE-COMBO PUNCH ?!

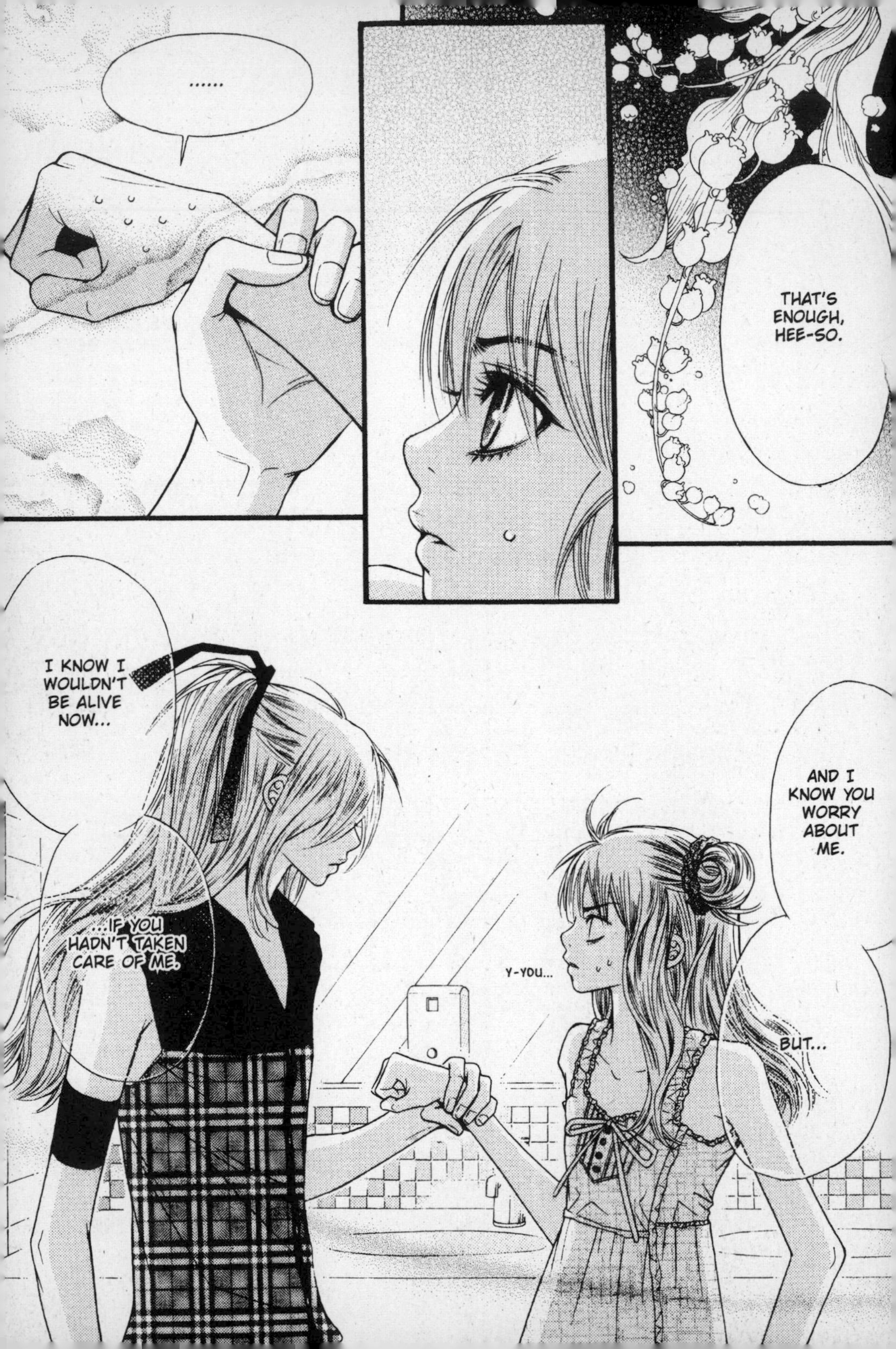
......
THAT'S ENOUGH, HEE-SO.
I KNOW I WOULDN'T BE ALIVE NOW...
...IF YOU HADN'T TAKEN CARE OF ME.
Y-YOU...
AND I KNOW YOU WORRY ABOUT ME.
BUT...

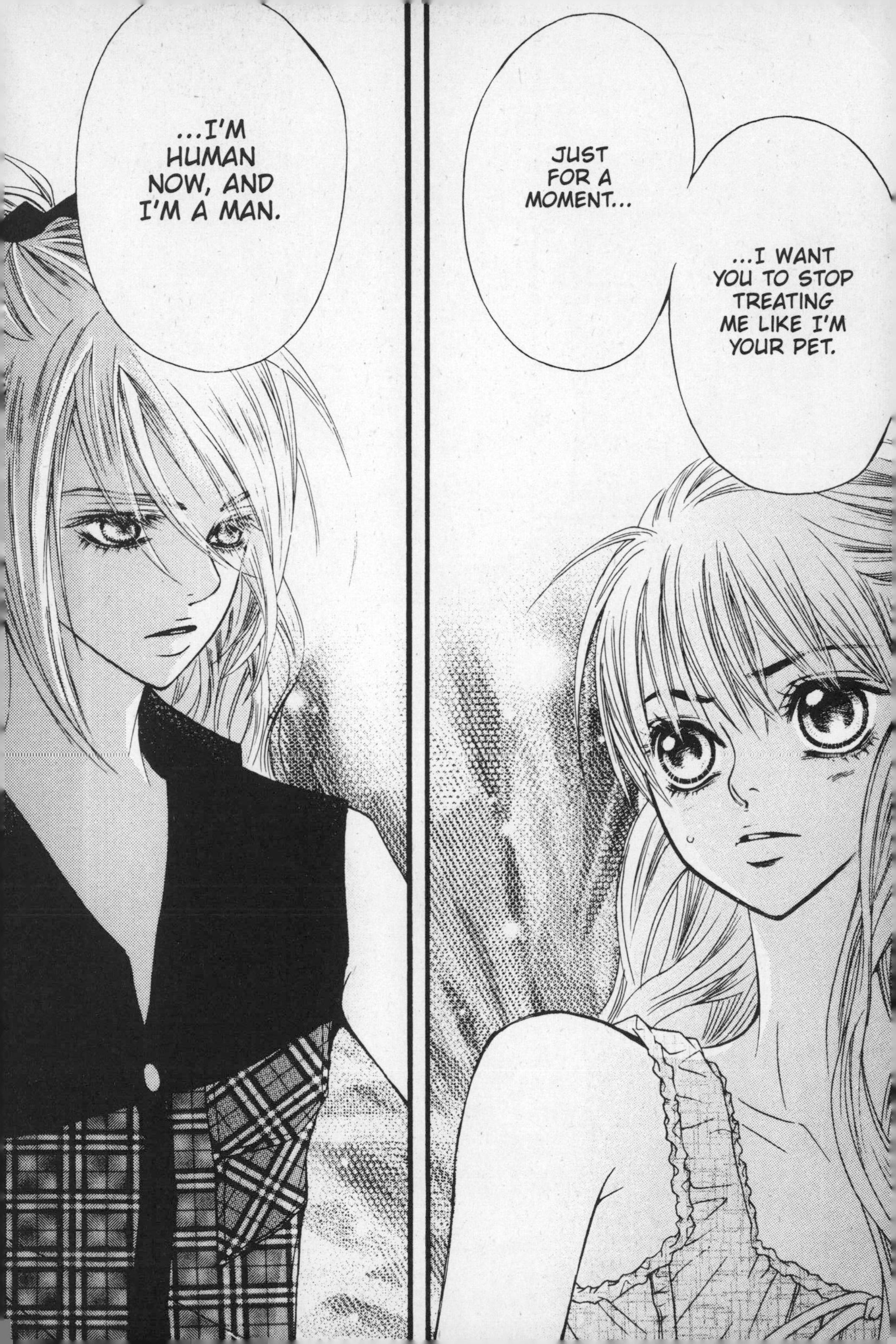
...I'M HUMAN NOW, AND I'M A MAN.
JUST FOR A MOMENT...
...I WANT YOU TO STOP TREATING ME LIKE I'M YOUR PET.

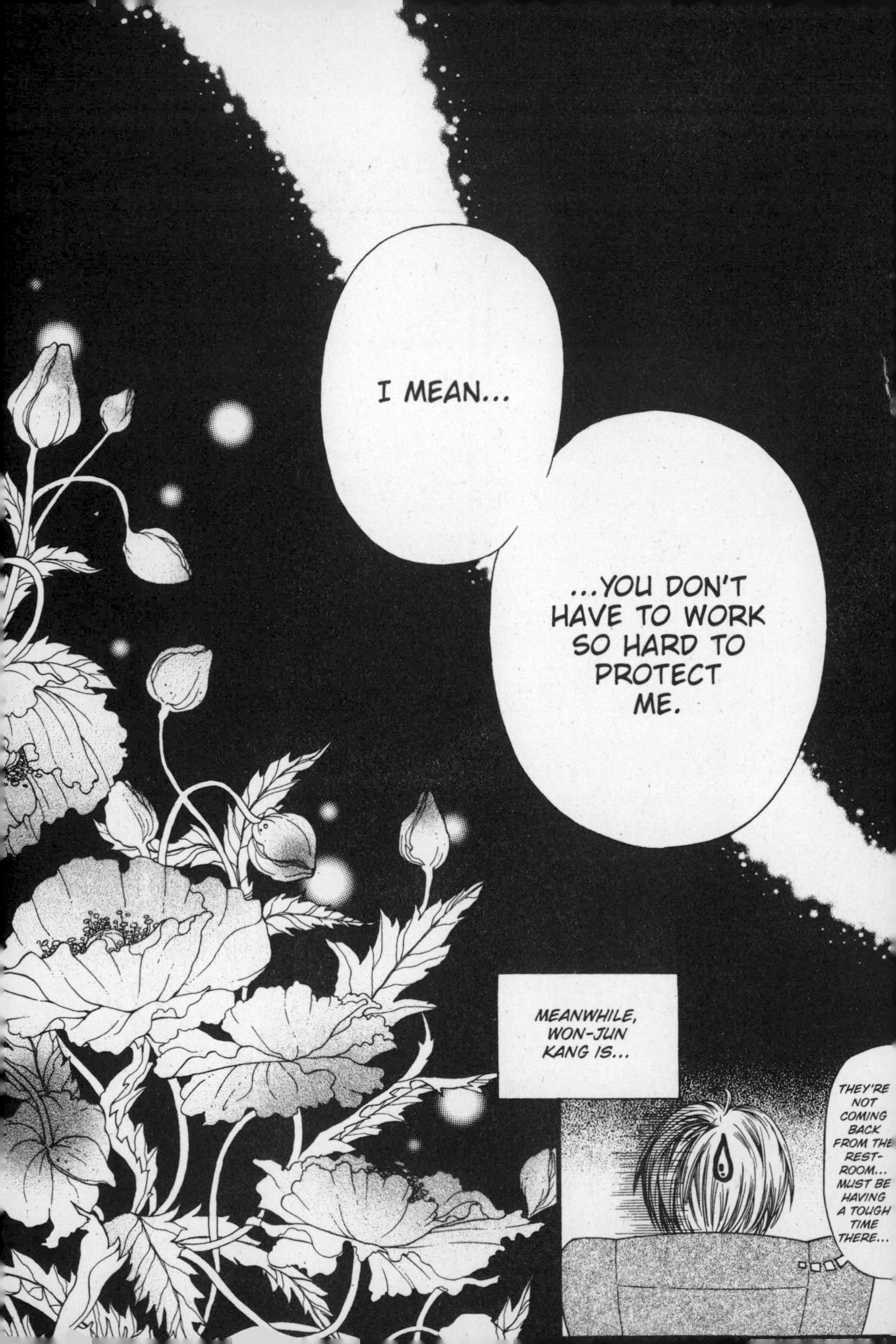
I MEAN...
...YOU DON'T HAVE TO WORK SO HARD TO PROTECT ME.
MEANWHILE, WON-JUN KANG IS...
THEY'RE NOT COMING BACK FROM THE REST-ROOM... MUST BE HAVING A TOUGH TIME THERE...

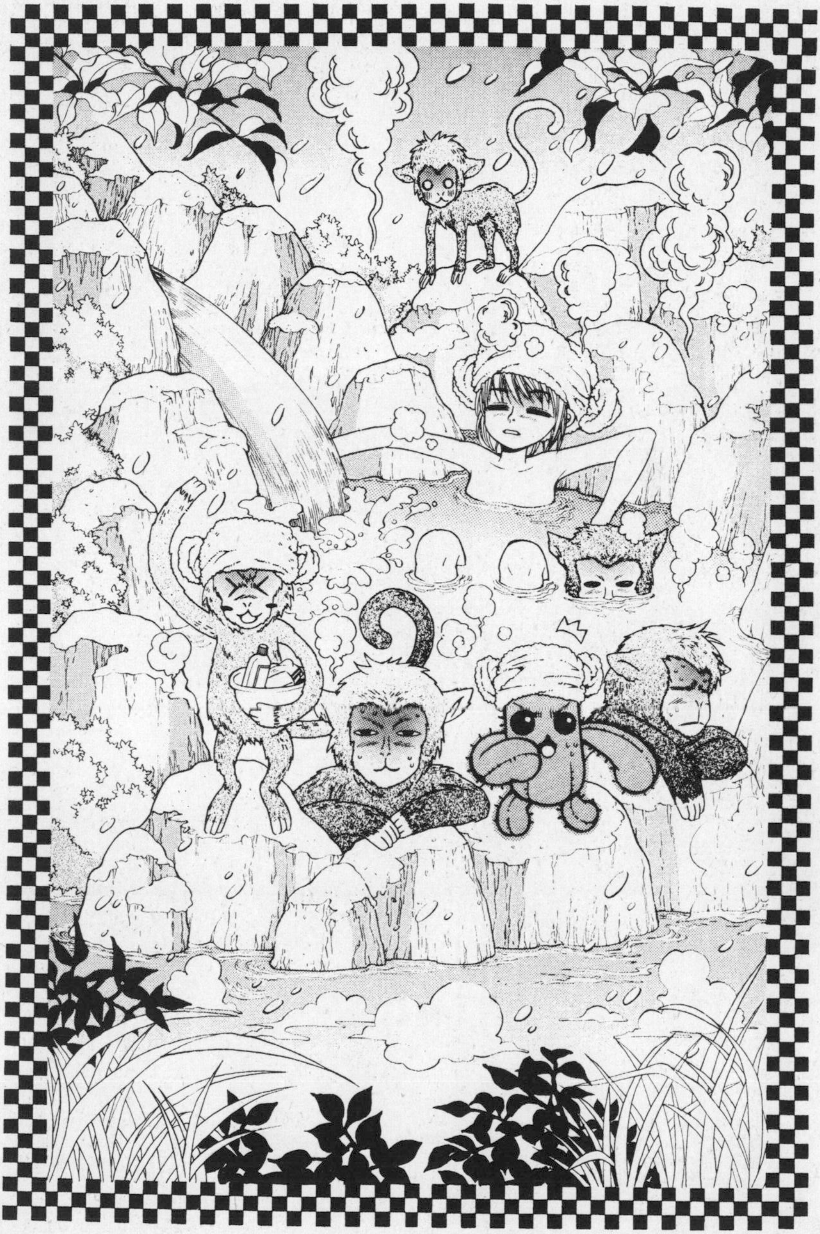

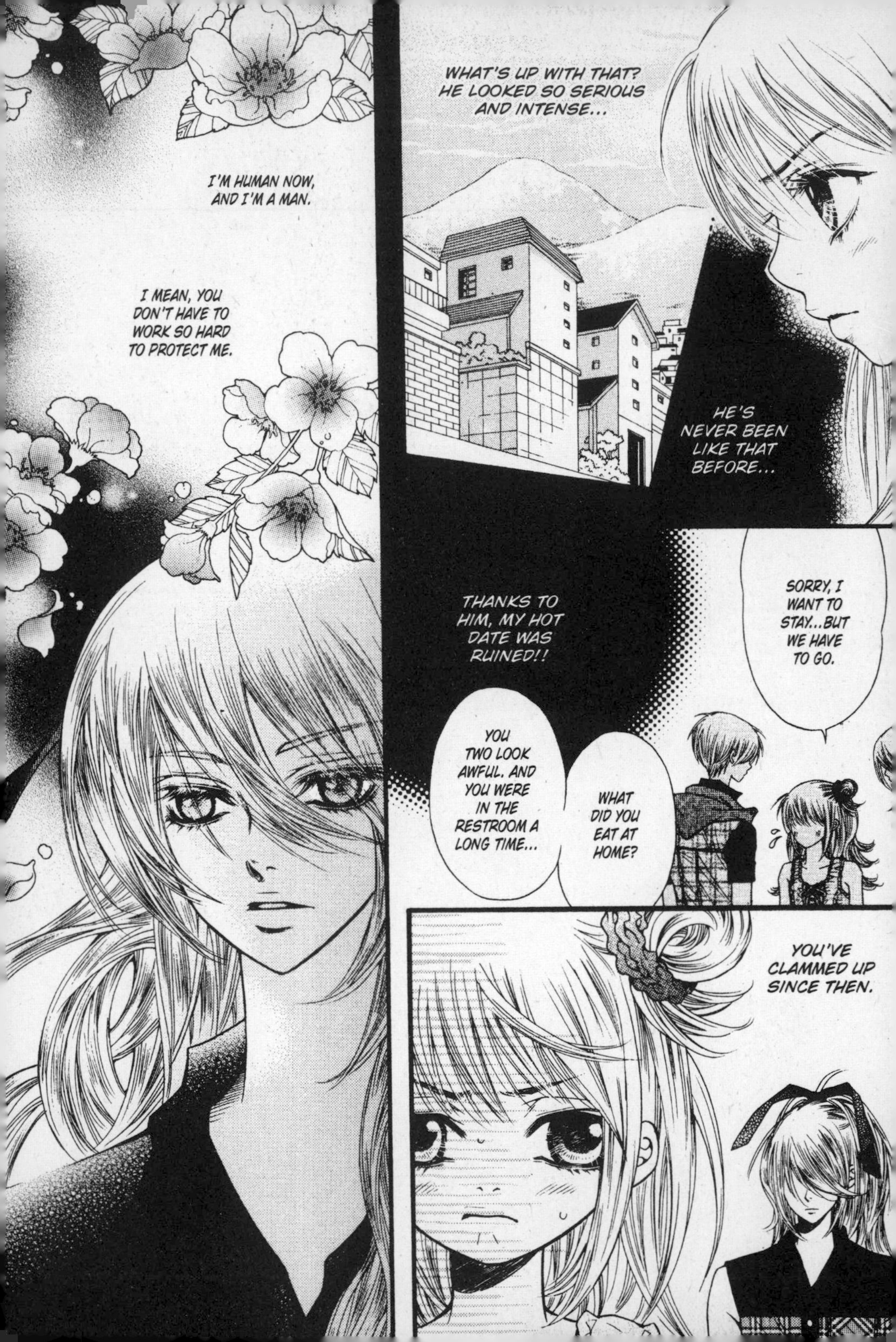
I'M HUMAN NOW, AND I'M A MAN.
I MEAN, YOU DON'T HAVE TO WORK SO HARD TO PROTECT ME.
WHAT'S UP WITH THAT? HE LOOKED SO SERIOUS AND INTENSE...
HE'S NEVER BEEN LIKE THAT BEFORE...
THANKS TO HIM, MY HOT DATE WAS RUINED!!
YOU TWO LOOK AWFUL. AND YOU WERE IN THE RESTROOM A LONG TIME...
WHAT DID YOU EAT AT HOME?
SORRY, I WANT TO STAY...BUT WE HAVE TO GO.
YOU'VE CLAMMED UP SINCE THEN.

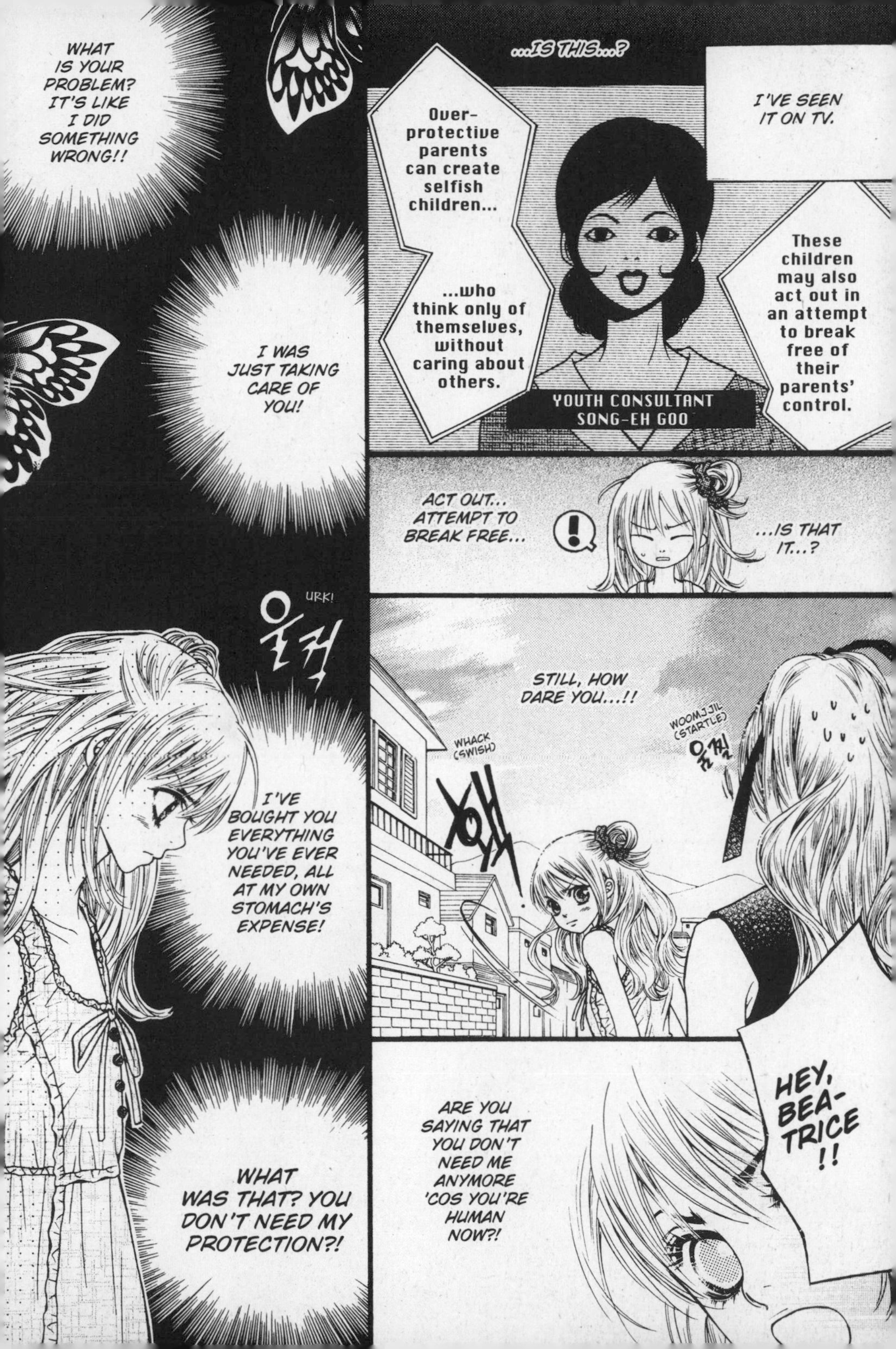
WHAT IS YOUR PROBLEM? IT'S LIKE I DID SOMETHING WRONG!!
I WAS JUST TAKING CARE OF YOU!
URK!
I'VE BOUGHT YOU EVERYTHING YOU'VE EVER NEEDED, ALL AT MY OWN STOMACH'S EXPENSE!
WHAT WAS THAT? YOU DON'T NEED MY PROTECTION?!
...IS THIS...?
Over-protective parents can create selfish children...
...who think only of themselves, without caring about others.
YOUTH CONSULTANT SONG-EH GOO
I'VE SEEN IT ON TV.
These children may also act out in an attempt to break free of their parents' control.
ACT OUT... ATTEMPT TO BREAK FREE...
...IS THAT IT...?
STILL, HOW DARE YOU...!!
WHACK (SWISH)
WOOMJJIL (STARTLE)
ARE YOU SAYING THAT YOU DON'T NEED ME ANYMORE 'COS YOU'RE HUMAN NOW?!
HEY, BEA-TRICE!!

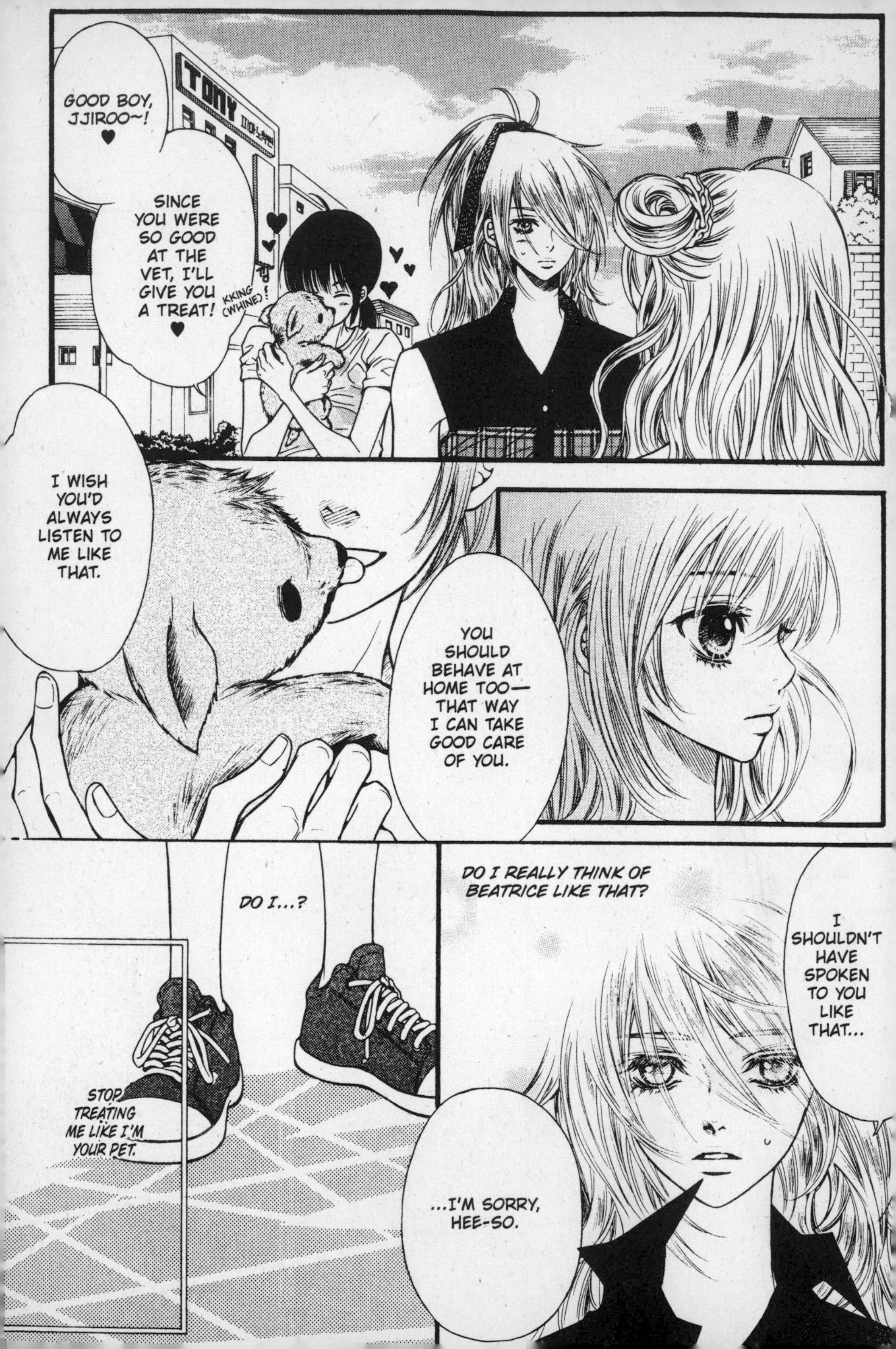
TONY
GOOD BOY, JJIROO~! ♥
SINCE YOU WERE SO GOOD AT THE VET, I'LL GIVE YOU A TREAT! ♥
KKING (WHINE)!
I WISH YOU'D ALWAYS LISTEN TO ME LIKE THAT.
YOU SHOULD BEHAVE AT HOME TOO—THAT WAY I CAN TAKE GOOD CARE OF YOU.
DO I...?
STOP TREATING ME LIKE I'M YOUR PET.
DO I REALLY THINK OF BEATRICE LIKE THAT?
I SHOULDN'T HAVE SPOKEN TO YOU LIKE THAT...
...I'M SORRY, HEE-SO.

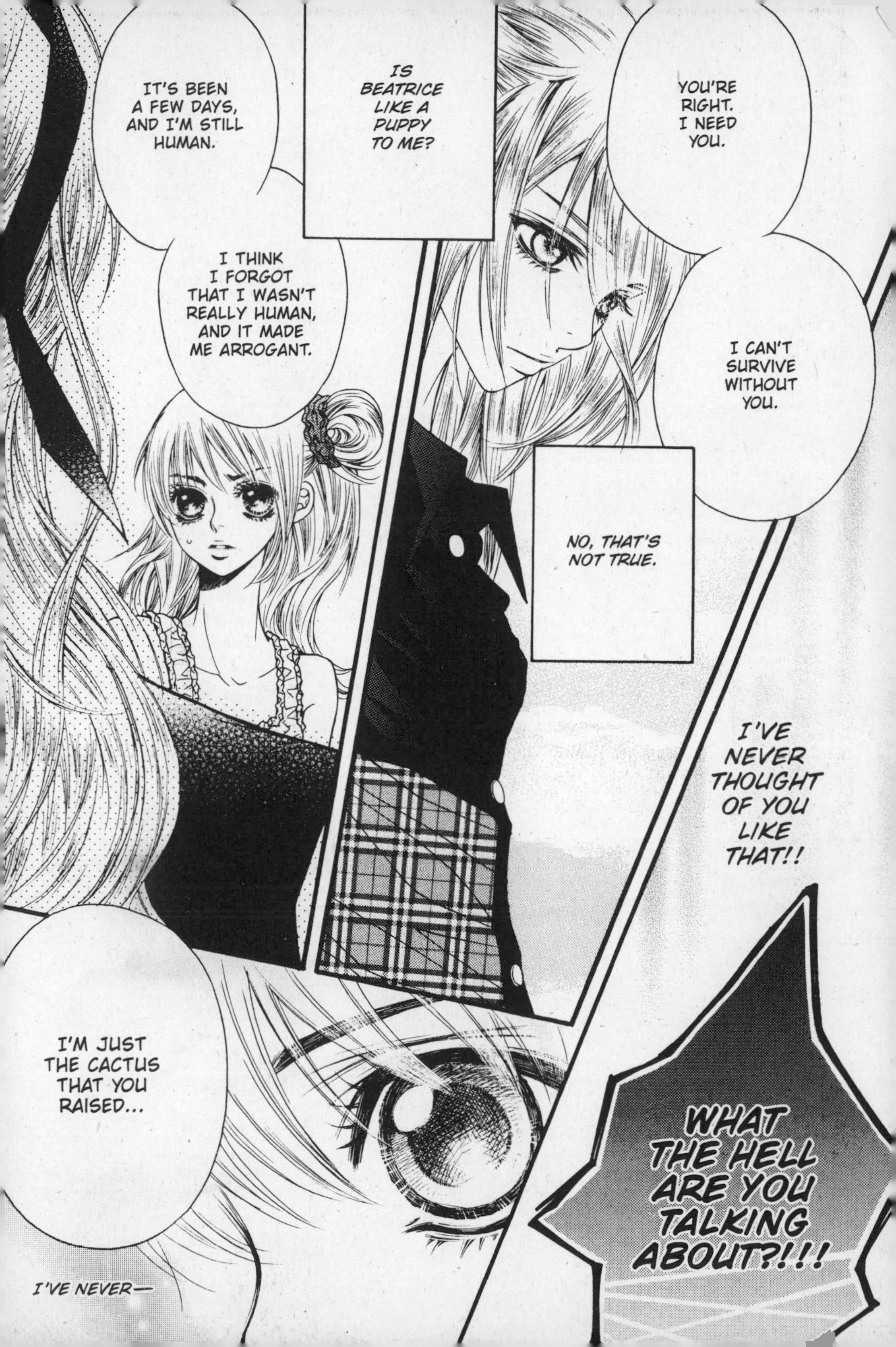

IT'S BEEN A FEW DAYS, AND I'M STILL HUMAN.
I THINK I FORGOT THAT I WASN'T REALLY HUMAN, AND IT MADE ME ARROGANT.
IS BEATRICE LIKE A PUPPY TO ME?
YOU'RE RIGHT. I NEED YOU.
I CAN'T SURVIVE WITHOUT YOU.
NO, THAT'S NOT TRUE.
I'VE NEVER THOUGHT OF YOU LIKE THAT!!
I'M JUST THE CACTUS THAT YOU RAISED...
I'VE NEVER—
WHAT THE HELL ARE YOU TALKING ABOUT?!!!

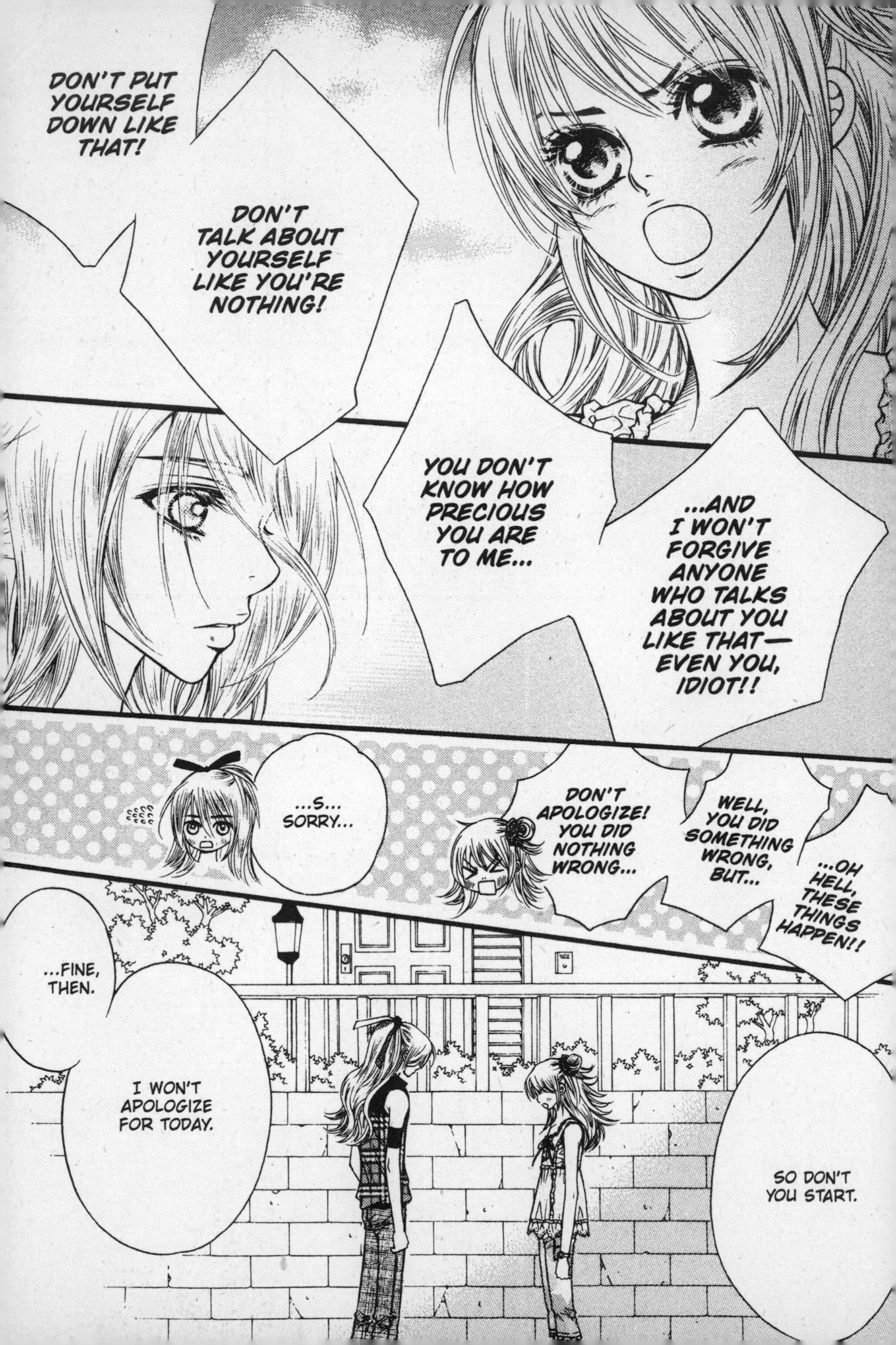
DON'T PUT YOURSELF DOWN LIKE THAT!
DON'T TALK ABOUT YOURSELF LIKE YOU'RE NOTHING!
YOU DON'T KNOW HOW PRECIOUS YOU ARE TO ME...
...AND I WON'T FORGIVE ANYONE WHO TALKS ABOUT YOU LIKE THAT— EVEN YOU, IDIOT!!
...S... SORRY...
DON'T APOLOGIZE! YOU DID NOTHING WRONG...
WELL, YOU DID SOMETHING WRONG, BUT...
...OH HELL, THESE THINGS HAPPEN!!
...FINE, THEN.
I WON'T APOLOGIZE FOR TODAY.
SO DON'T YOU START.

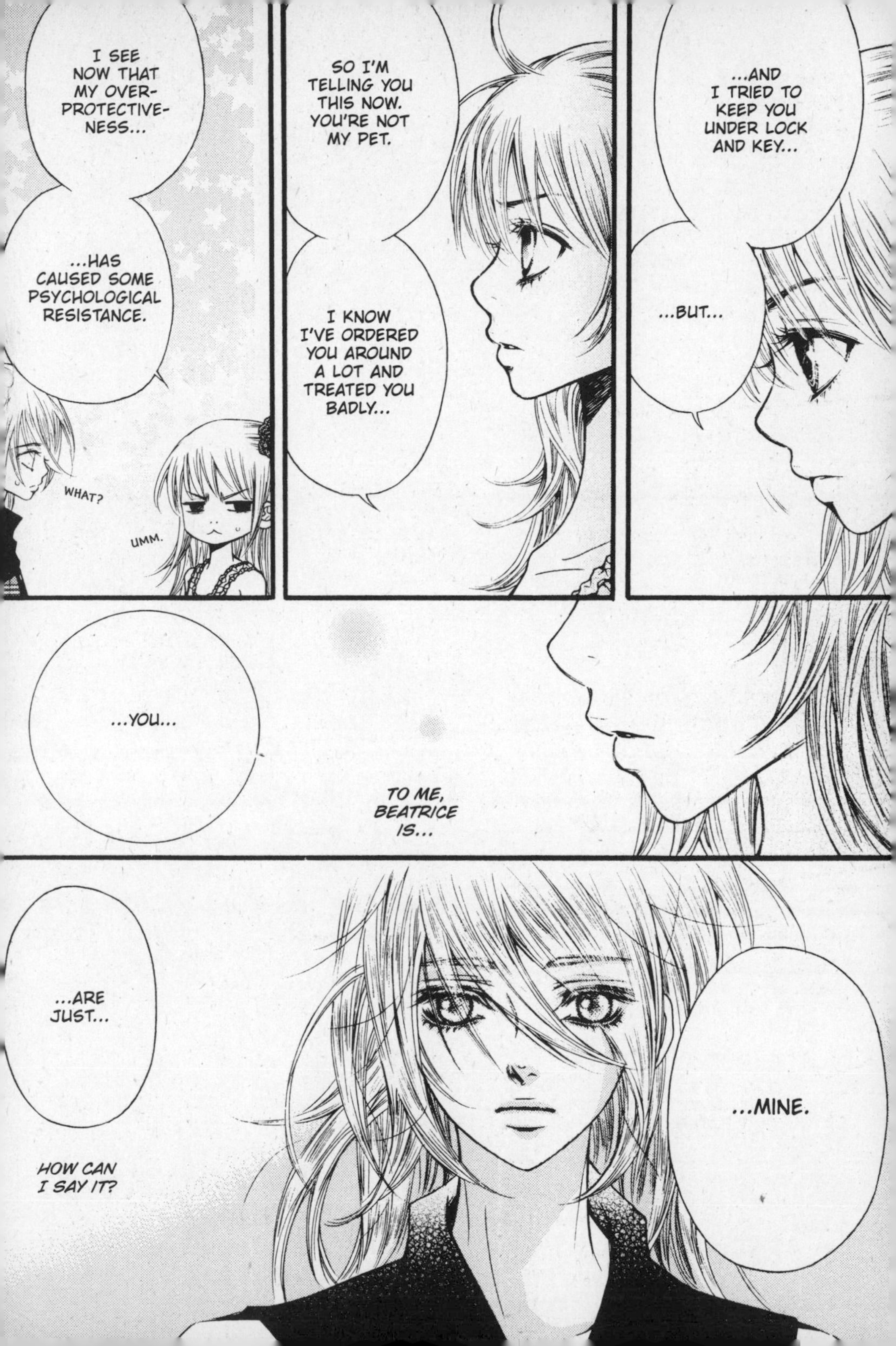
I SEE NOW THAT MY OVER-PROTECTIVE-NESS...
...HAS CAUSED SOME PSYCHOLOGICAL RESISTANCE.
WHAT?
UMM.
SO I'M TELLING YOU THIS NOW. YOU'RE NOT MY PET.
I KNOW I'VE ORDERED YOU AROUND A LOT AND TREATED YOU BADLY...
...AND I TRIED TO KEEP YOU UNDER LOCK AND KEY...
...BUT...
...YOU...
TO ME, BEATRICE IS...
...ARE JUST...
HOW CAN I SAY IT?
...MINE.

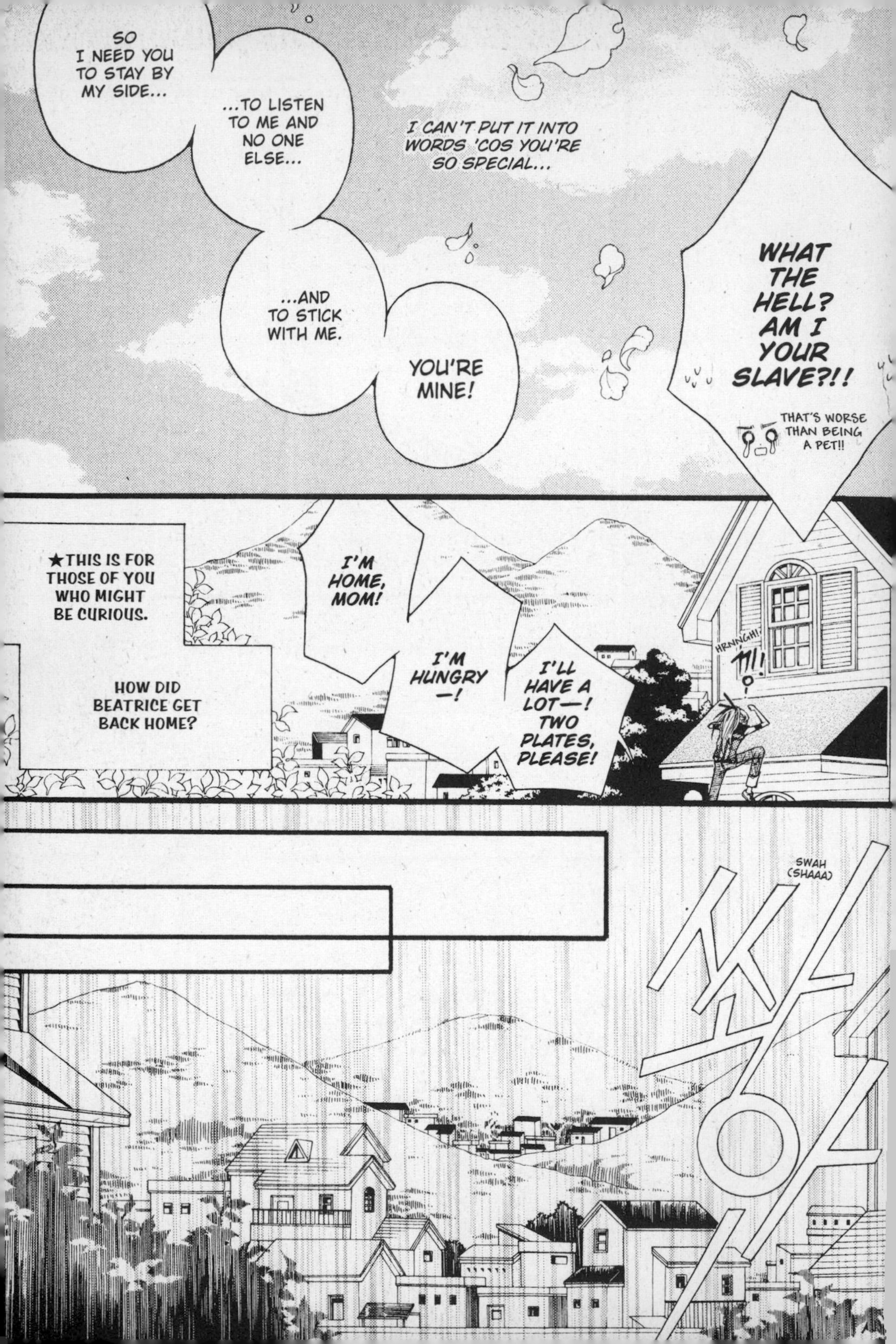
SO I NEED YOU TO STAY BY MY SIDE...
...TO LISTEN TO ME AND NO ONE ELSE...
...AND TO STICK WITH ME.
YOU'RE MINE!
I CAN'T PUT IT INTO WORDS 'COS YOU'RE SO SPECIAL...
WHAT THE HELL? AM I YOUR SLAVE?!!
THAT'S WORSE THAN BEING A PET!!
★THIS IS FOR THOSE OF YOU WHO MIGHT BE CURIOUS.
HOW DID BEATRICE GET BACK HOME?
I'M HOME, MOM!
I'M HUNGRY—!
I'LL HAVE A LOT—! TWO PLATES, PLEASE!
HRNNGH!
SWAH (SHAAA)

STEP 27. LOVE IS LIKE RAINDROPS OUTSIDE THE WINDOW~! ♬

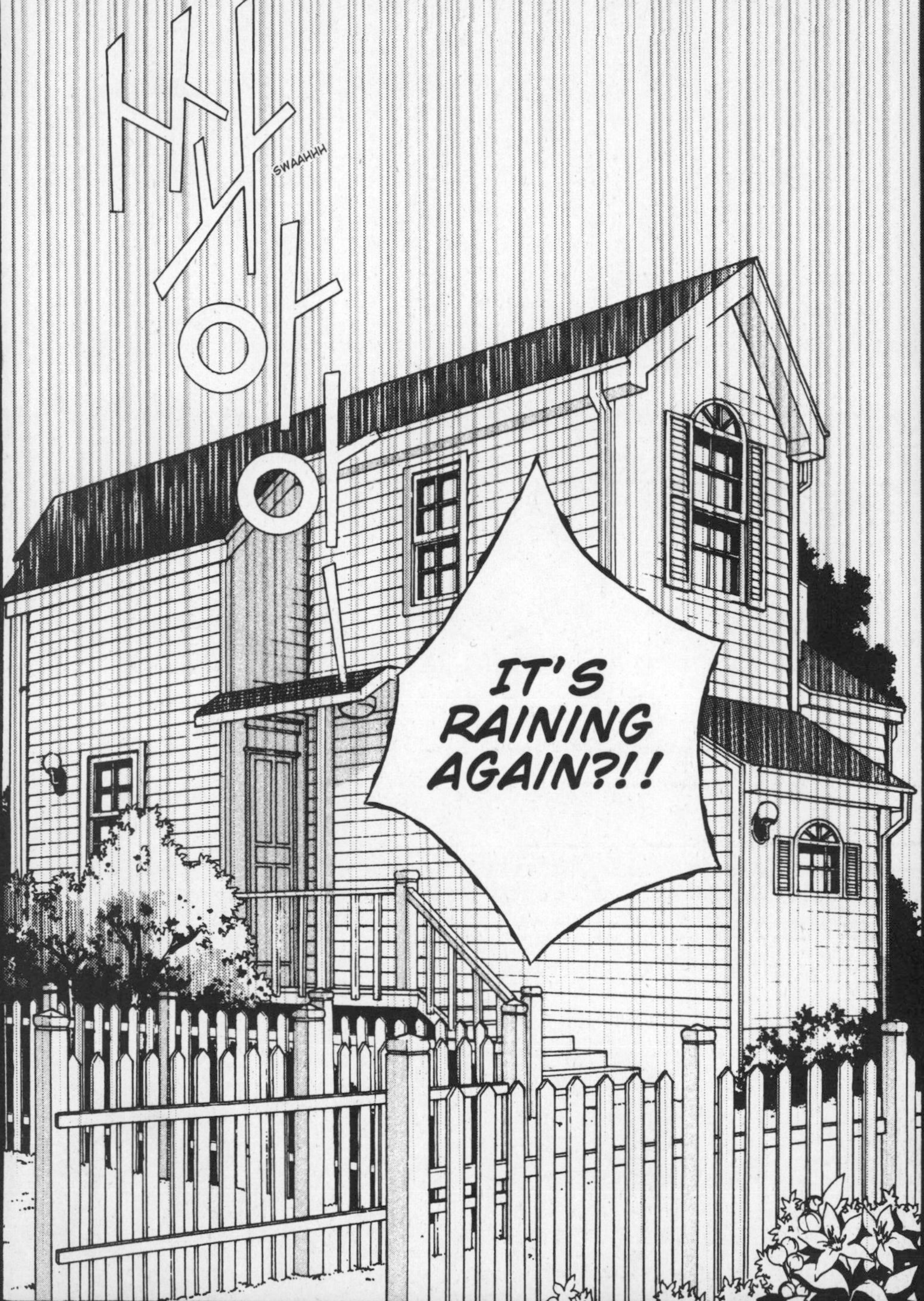
SWAAHHH
IT'S RAINING AGAIN?!!

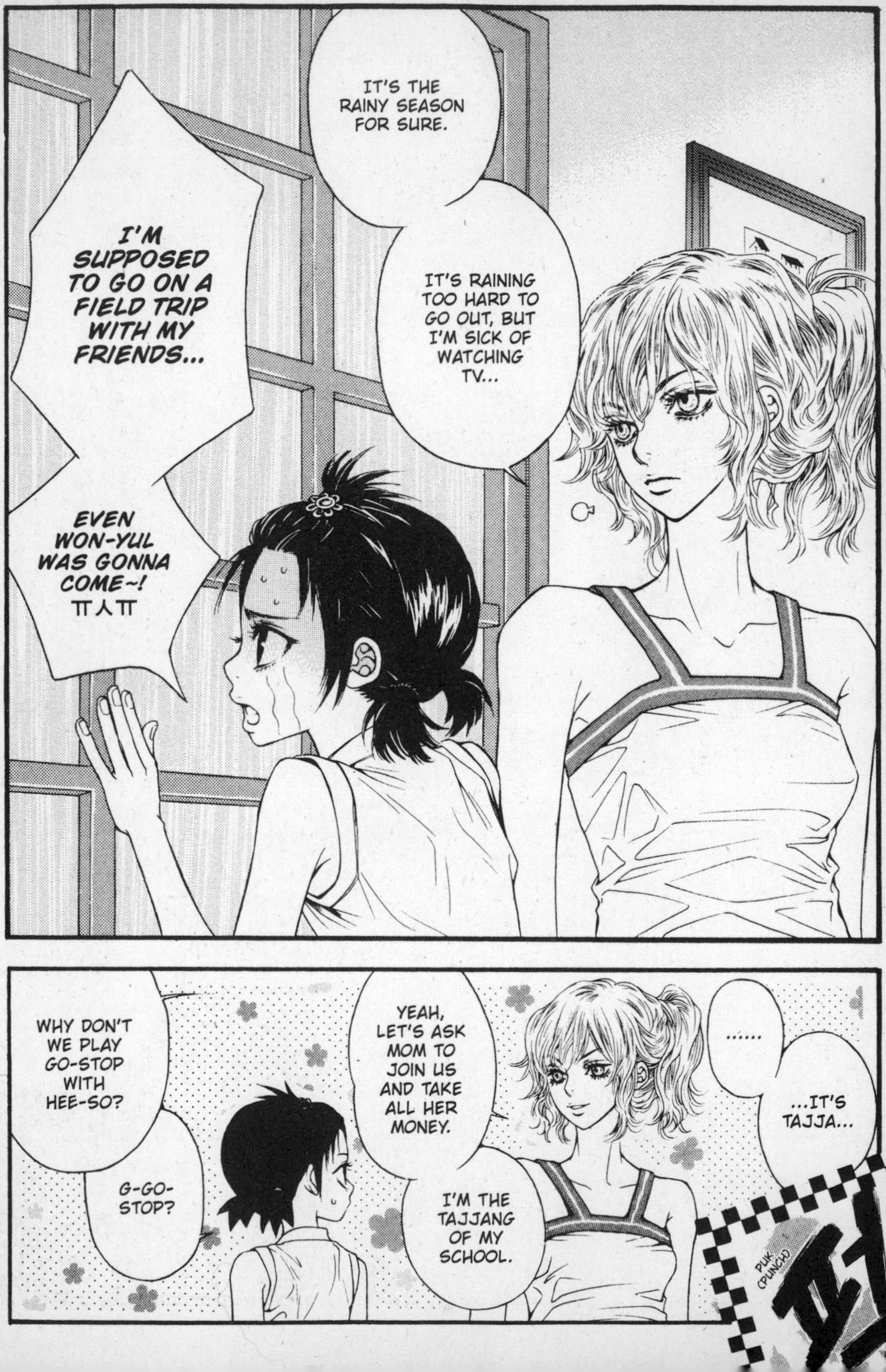
I'M SUPPOSED TO GO ON A FIELD TRIP WITH MY FRIENDS...
EVEN WON-YUL WAS GONNA COME~! ㅠ人ㅠ
IT'S THE RAINY SEASON FOR SURE.
IT'S RAINING TOO HARD TO GO OUT, BUT I'M SICK OF WATCHING TV...
WHY DON'T WE PLAY GO-STOP WITH HEE-SO?
G-GO-STOP?
YEAH, LET'S ASK MOM TO JOIN US AND TAKE ALL HER MONEY.
I'M THE TAJJANG OF MY SCHOOL.
......
...IT'S TAJJA...
PUK (PUNCH)

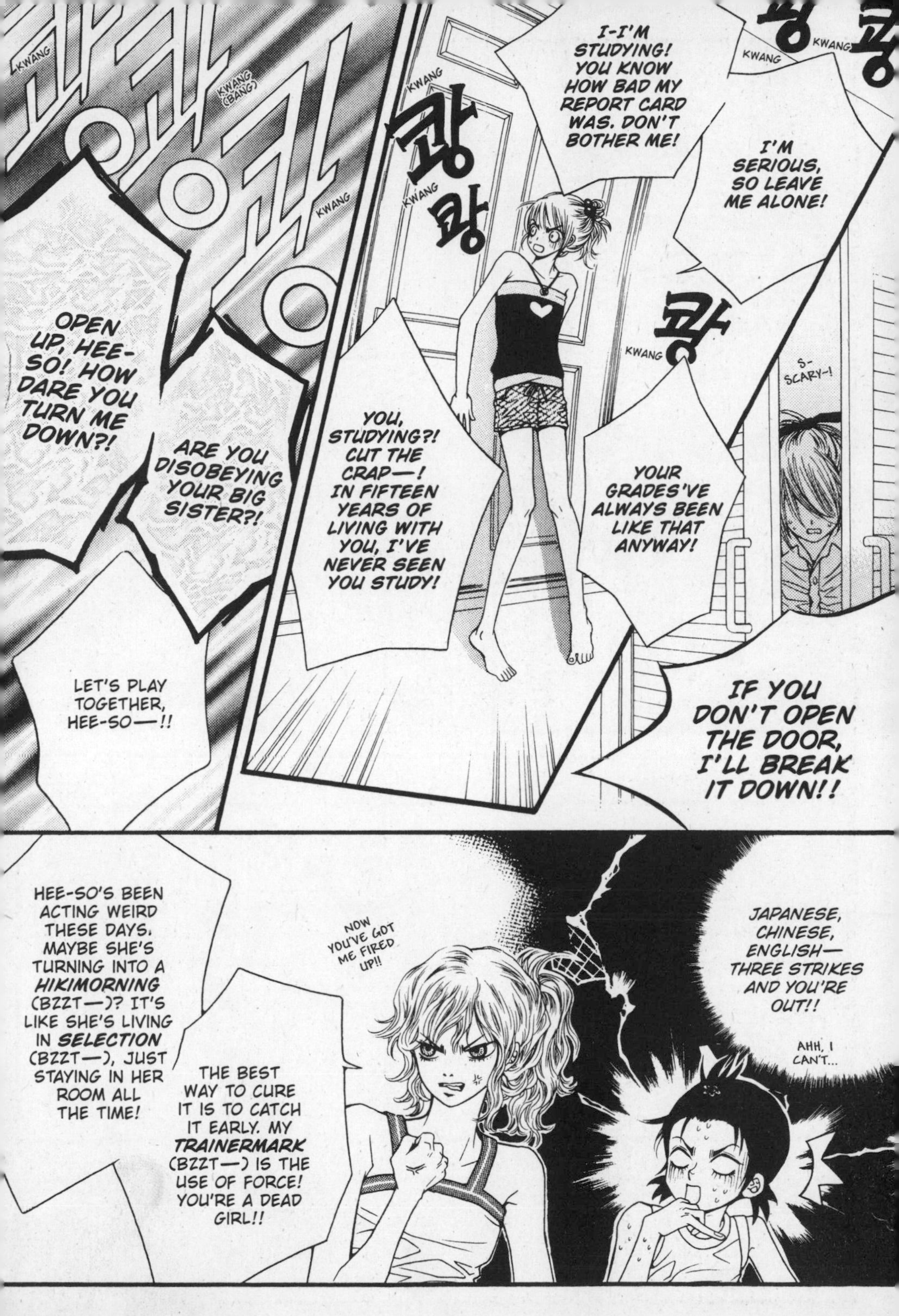

콰광광
KWANG
KWANG (BANG)
KWANG
OPEN UP, HEE-SO! HOW DARE YOU TURN ME DOWN?!
ARE YOU DISOBEYING YOUR BIG SISTER?!
LET'S PLAY TOGETHER, HEE-SO—!!
광
KWANG
광
KWANG
I-I'M STUDYING! YOU KNOW HOW BAD MY REPORT CARD WAS. DON'T BOTHER ME!
YOU, STUDYING?! CUT THE CRAP—! IN FIFTEEN YEARS OF LIVING WITH YOU, I'VE NEVER SEEN YOU STUDY!
광
KWANG
YOUR GRADES'VE ALWAYS BEEN LIKE THAT ANYWAY!
광
KWANG
광
KWANG
I'M SERIOUS, SO LEAVE ME ALONE!
S-SCARY-!
IF YOU DON'T OPEN THE DOOR, I'LL BREAK IT DOWN!!
HEE-SO'S BEEN ACTING WEIRD THESE DAYS. MAYBE SHE'S TURNING INTO A HIKIMORNING (BZZT—)? IT'S LIKE SHE'S LIVING IN SELECTION (BZZT—), JUST STAYING IN HER ROOM ALL THE TIME!
THE BEST WAY TO CURE IT IS TO CATCH IT EARLY. MY TRAINERMARK (BZZT—) IS THE USE OF FORCE! YOU'RE A DEAD GIRL!!
NOW YOU'VE GOT ME FIRED UP!!
JAPANESE, CHINESE, ENGLISH— THREE STRIKES AND YOU'RE OUT!!
AHH, I CAN'T...

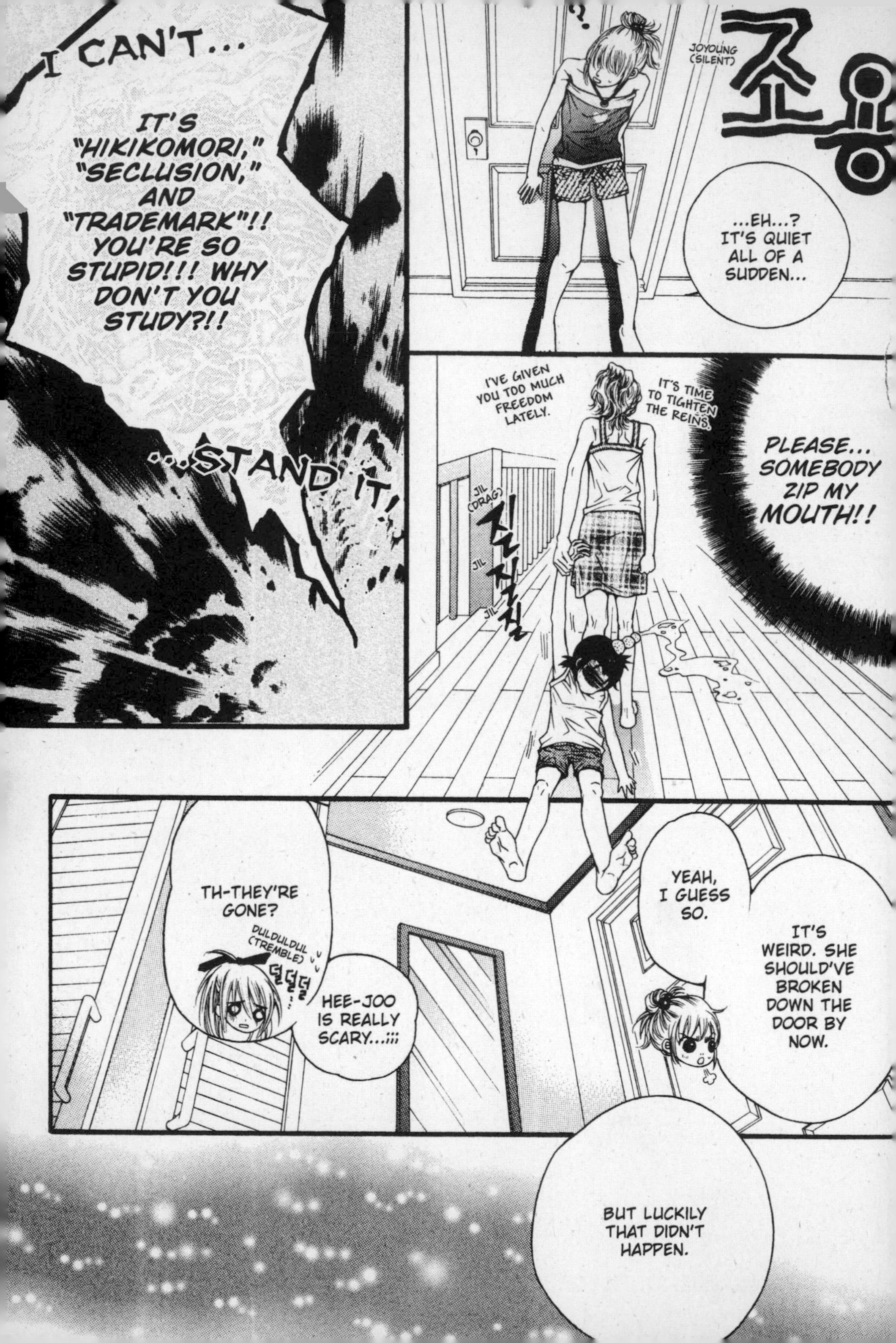

I CAN'T...
IT'S "HIKIKOMORI," "SECLUSION," AND "TRADEMARK"!! YOU'RE SO STUPID!!! WHY DON'T YOU STUDY?!!
...STAND IT!
?
JOYOUNG (SILENT)
조용
...EH...? IT'S QUIET ALL OF A SUDDEN...
I'VE GIVEN YOU TOO MUCH FREEDOM LATELY.
IT'S TIME TO TIGHTEN THE REINS.
PLEASE... SOMEBODY ZIP MY MOUTH!!
JIL (DRAG)
JIL
JIL
질질질
TH-THEY'RE GONE?
DULDULDUL (TREMBLE)
덜덜덜
HEE-JOO IS REALLY SCARY...;;;
YEAH, I GUESS SO.
IT'S WEIRD. SHE SHOULD'VE BROKEN DOWN THE DOOR BY NOW.
BUT LUCKILY THAT DIDN'T HAPPEN.

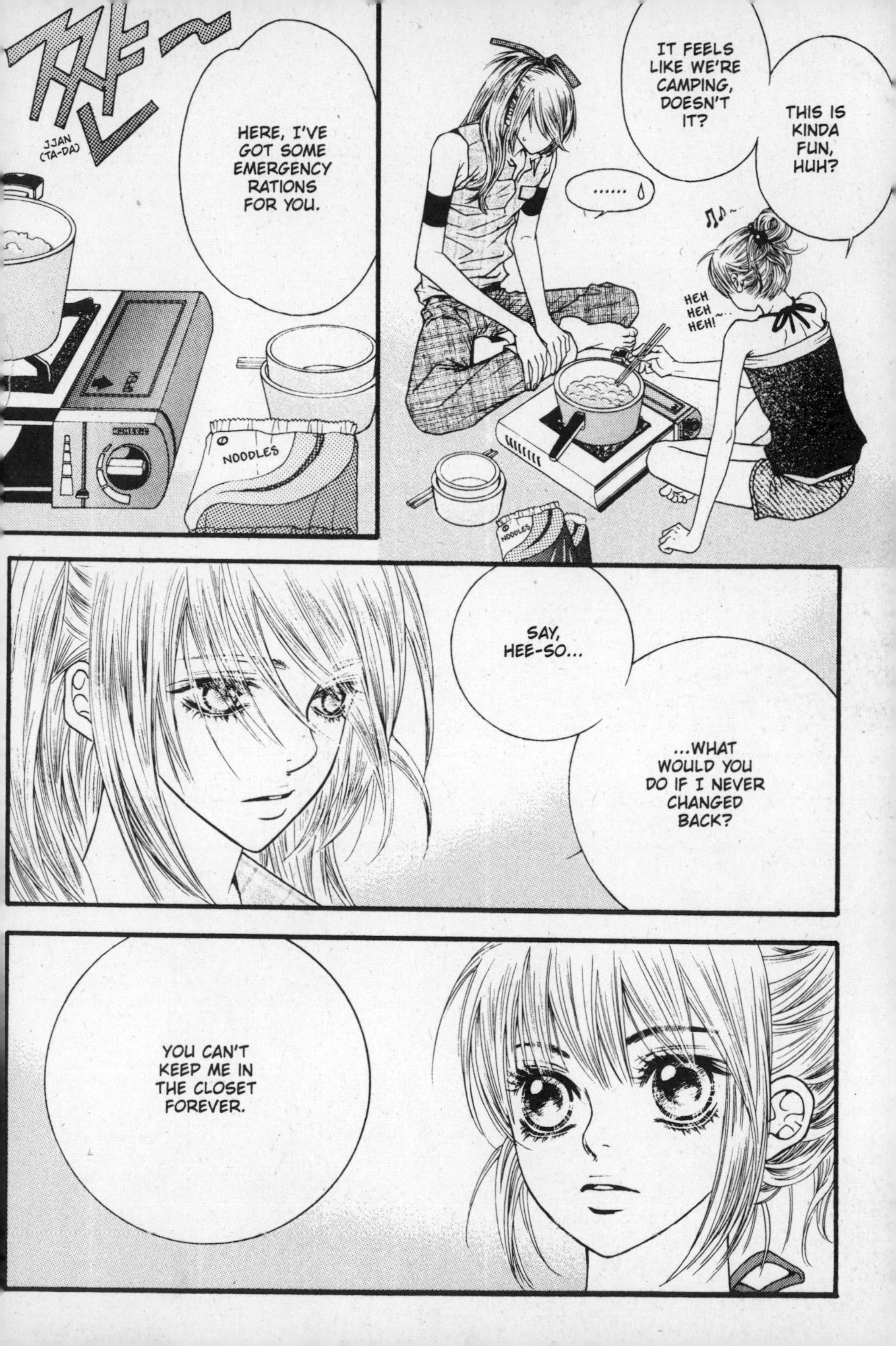
JJAN (TA-DA)
HERE, I'VE GOT SOME EMERGENCY RATIONS FOR YOU.
NOODLES
IT FEELS LIKE WE'RE CAMPING, DOESN'T IT?
THIS IS KINDA FUN, HUH?
......
HEH HEH HEH!~
NOODLES
SAY, HEE-SO...
...WHAT WOULD YOU DO IF I NEVER CHANGED BACK?
YOU CAN'T KEEP ME IN THE CLOSET FOREVER.

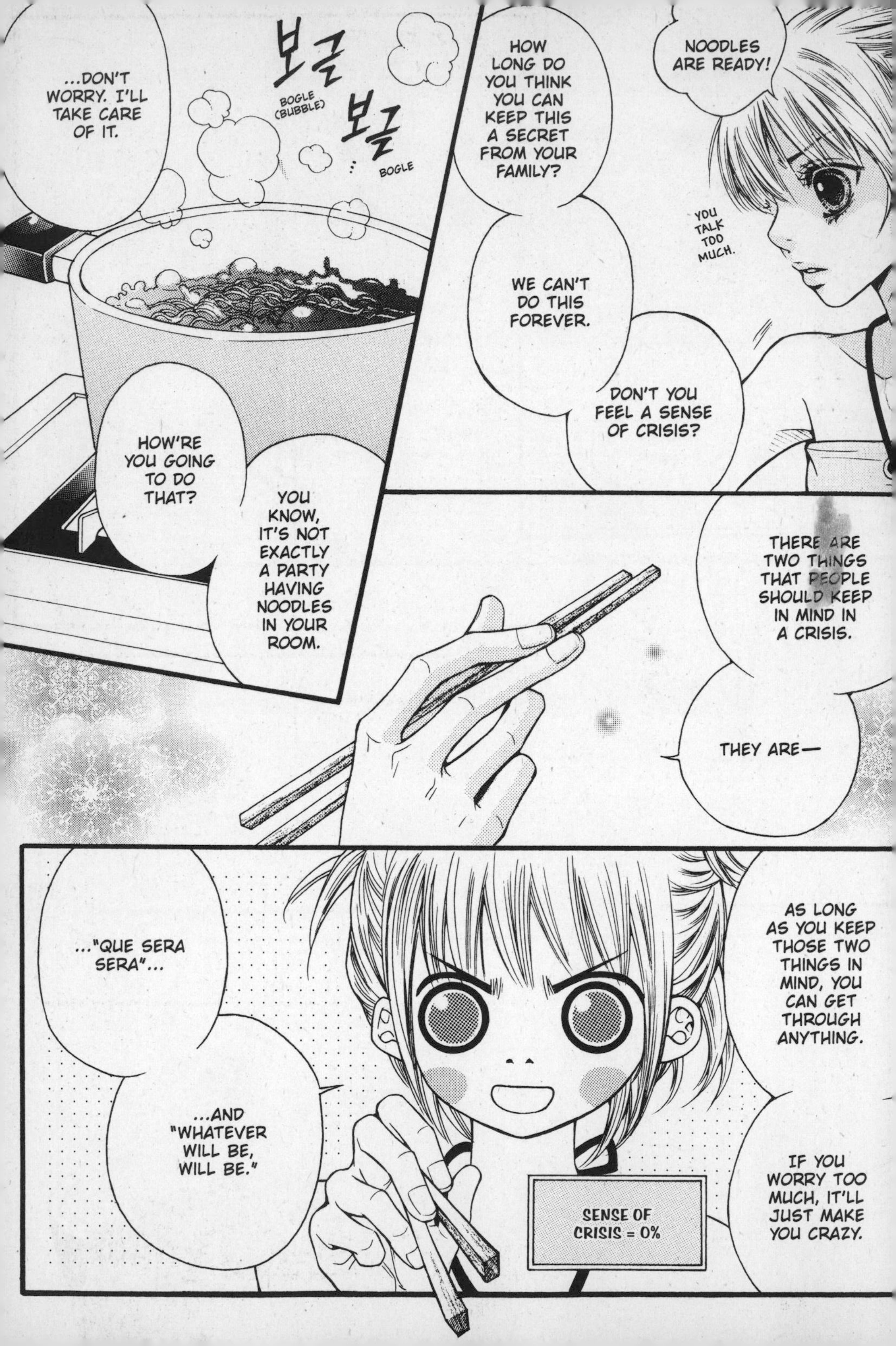
...DON'T WORRY. I'LL TAKE CARE OF IT.
보글
BOGLE (BUBBLE)
보글
BOGLE
HOW'RE YOU GOING TO DO THAT?
YOU KNOW, IT'S NOT EXACTLY A PARTY HAVING NOODLES IN YOUR ROOM.
HOW LONG DO YOU THINK YOU CAN KEEP THIS A SECRET FROM YOUR FAMILY?
WE CAN'T DO THIS FOREVER.
DON'T YOU FEEL A SENSE OF CRISIS?
NOODLES ARE READY!
YOU TALK TOO MUCH.
THERE ARE TWO THINGS THAT PEOPLE SHOULD KEEP IN MIND IN A CRISIS.
THEY ARE—
..."QUE SERA SERA"...
...AND "WHATEVER WILL BE, WILL BE."
SENSE OF CRISIS = 0%
AS LONG AS YOU KEEP THOSE TWO THINGS IN MIND, YOU CAN GET THROUGH ANYTHING.
IF YOU WORRY TOO MUCH, IT'LL JUST MAKE YOU CRAZY.

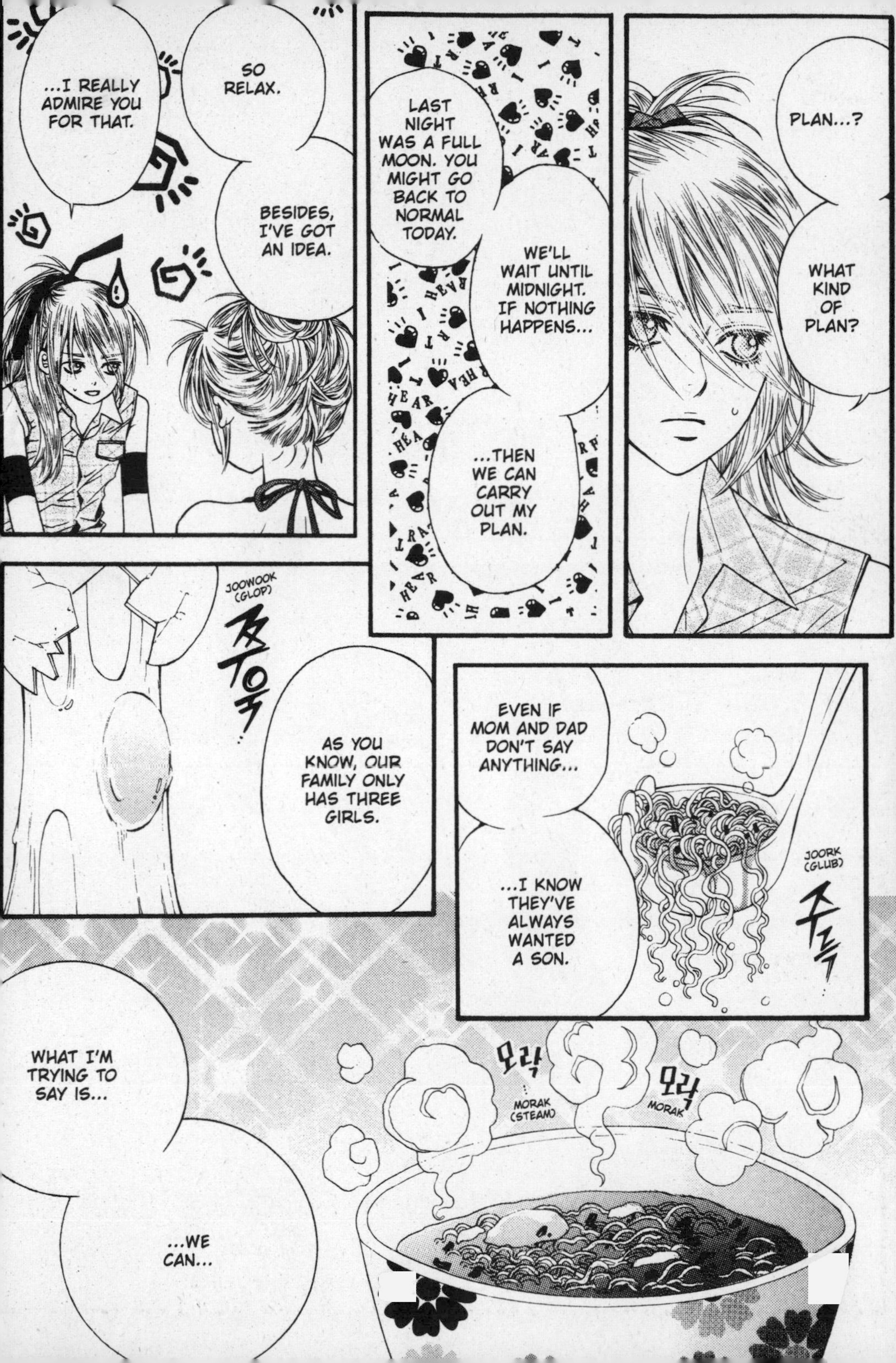
...I REALLY ADMIRE YOU FOR THAT.
SO RELAX.
BESIDES, I'VE GOT AN IDEA.
LAST NIGHT WAS A FULL MOON. YOU MIGHT GO BACK TO NORMAL TODAY.
WE'LL WAIT UNTIL MIDNIGHT. IF NOTHING HAPPENS...
...THEN WE CAN CARRY OUT MY PLAN.
PLAN...?
WHAT KIND OF PLAN?
JOOWOOK (GLOP)
AS YOU KNOW, OUR FAMILY ONLY HAS THREE GIRLS.
EVEN IF MOM AND DAD DON'T SAY ANYTHING...
...I KNOW THEY'VE ALWAYS WANTED A SON.
JOORK (GLUB)
WHAT I'M TRYING TO SAY IS...
...WE CAN...
모락
MORAK (STEAM)
모락
MORAK

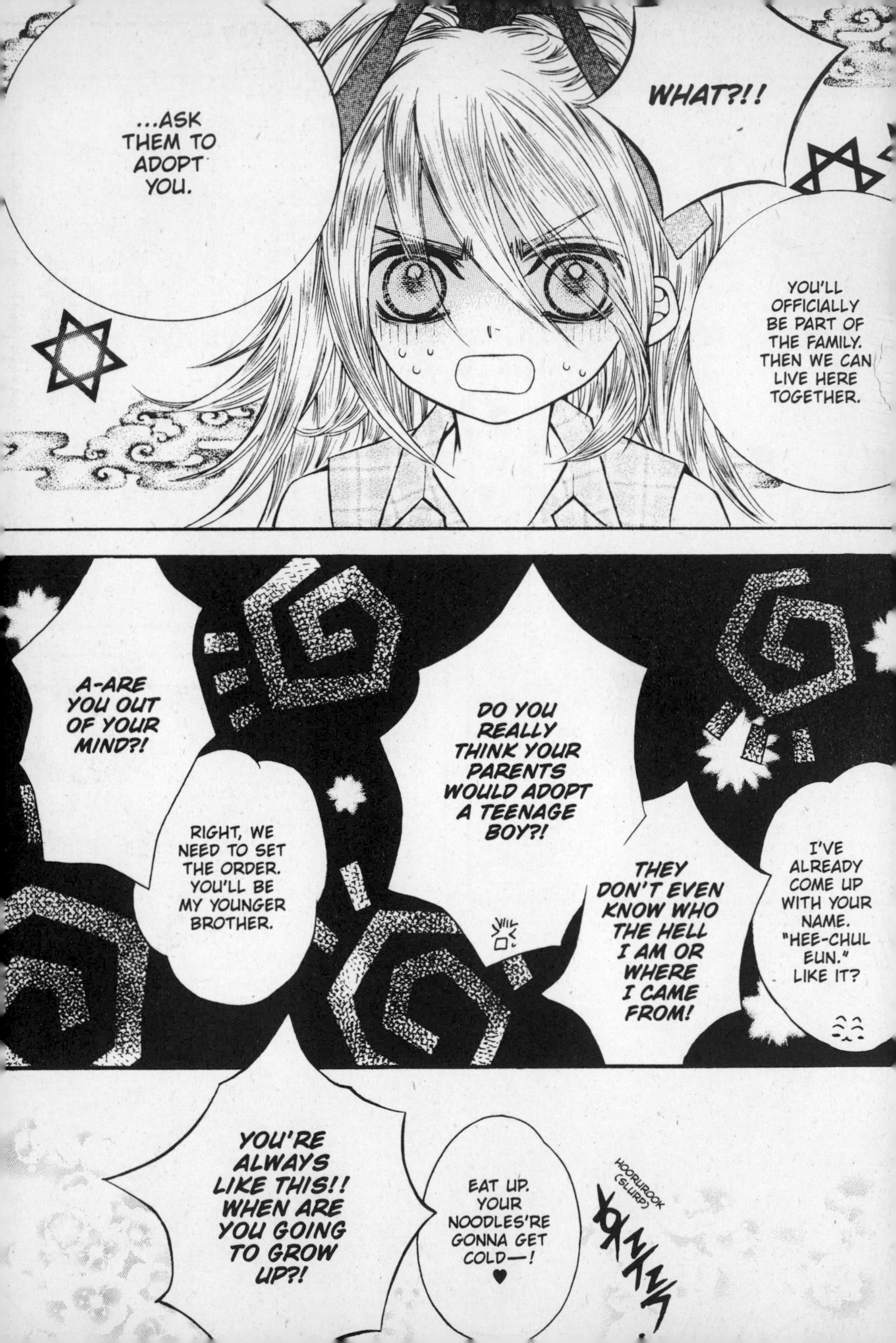
...ASK THEM TO ADOPT YOU.
WHAT?!!
YOU'LL OFFICIALLY BE PART OF THE FAMILY. THEN WE CAN LIVE HERE TOGETHER.
A-ARE YOU OUT OF YOUR MIND?!
RIGHT, WE NEED TO SET THE ORDER. YOU'LL BE MY YOUNGER BROTHER.
DO YOU REALLY THINK YOUR PARENTS WOULD ADOPT A TEENAGE BOY?!
THEY DON'T EVEN KNOW WHO THE HELL I AM OR WHERE I CAME FROM!
I'VE ALREADY COME UP WITH YOUR NAME. "HEE-CHUL EUN." LIKE IT?
YOU'RE ALWAYS LIKE THIS!! WHEN ARE YOU GOING TO GROW UP?!
EAT UP. YOUR NOODLES'RE GONNA GET COLD—! ♥
HOORUROOK (SLURP)

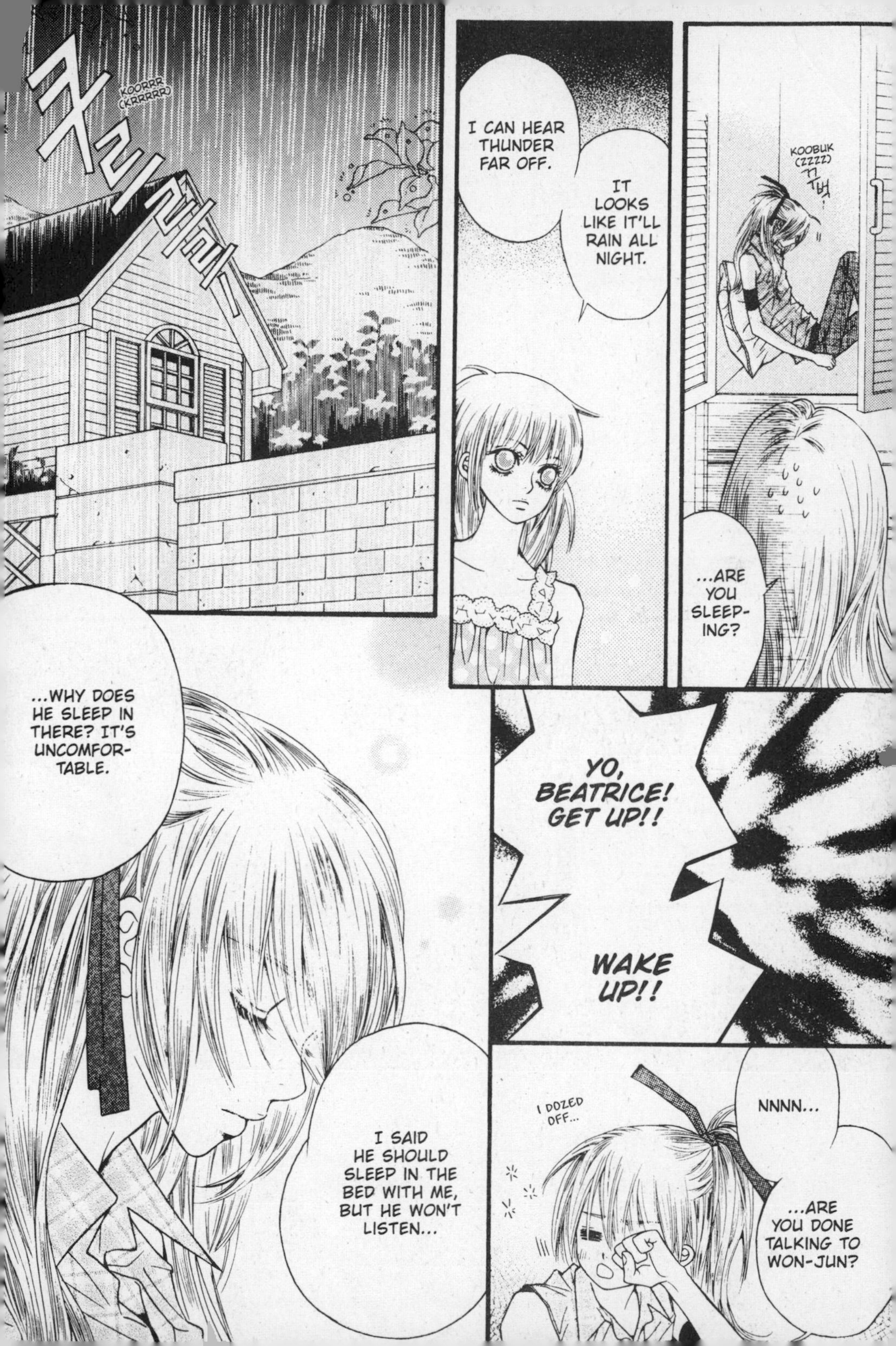
KOORRR (KRRRRR)
I CAN HEAR THUNDER FAR OFF.
IT LOOKS LIKE IT'LL RAIN ALL NIGHT.
KOOBUK (ZZZZ)
...ARE YOU SLEEP-ING?
...WHY DOES HE SLEEP IN THERE? IT'S UNCOMFOR-TABLE.
I SAID HE SHOULD SLEEP IN THE BED WITH ME, BUT HE WON'T LISTEN...
YO, BEATRICE! GET UP!!
WAKE UP!!
I DOZED OFF...
NNNN...
...ARE YOU DONE TALKING TO WON-JUN?

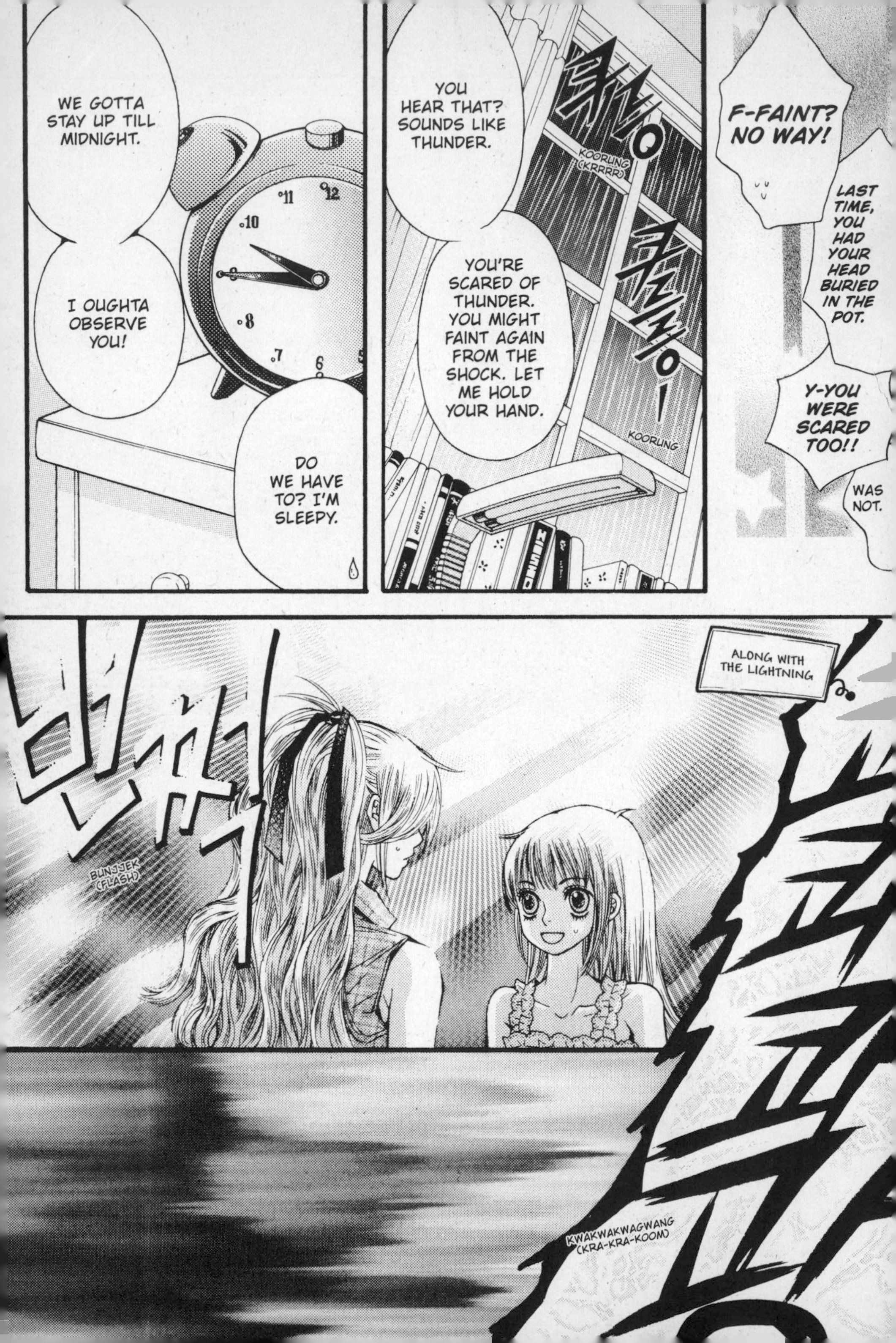
WE GOTTA STAY UP TILL MIDNIGHT.
I OUGHTA OBSERVE YOU!
DO WE HAVE TO? I'M SLEEPY.
YOU HEAR THAT? SOUNDS LIKE THUNDER.
KOORUNG (KRRRR)
YOU'RE SCARED OF THUNDER. YOU MIGHT FAINT AGAIN FROM THE SHOCK. LET ME HOLD YOUR HAND.
KOORUNG
F-FAINT? NO WAY!
LAST TIME, YOU HAD YOUR HEAD BURIED IN THE POT.
Y-YOU WERE SCARED TOO!!
WAS NOT.
ALONG WITH THE LIGHTNING
BUNJJEK (FLASH)
KWAKWAKWAGWANG (KRA-KRA-KOOM)

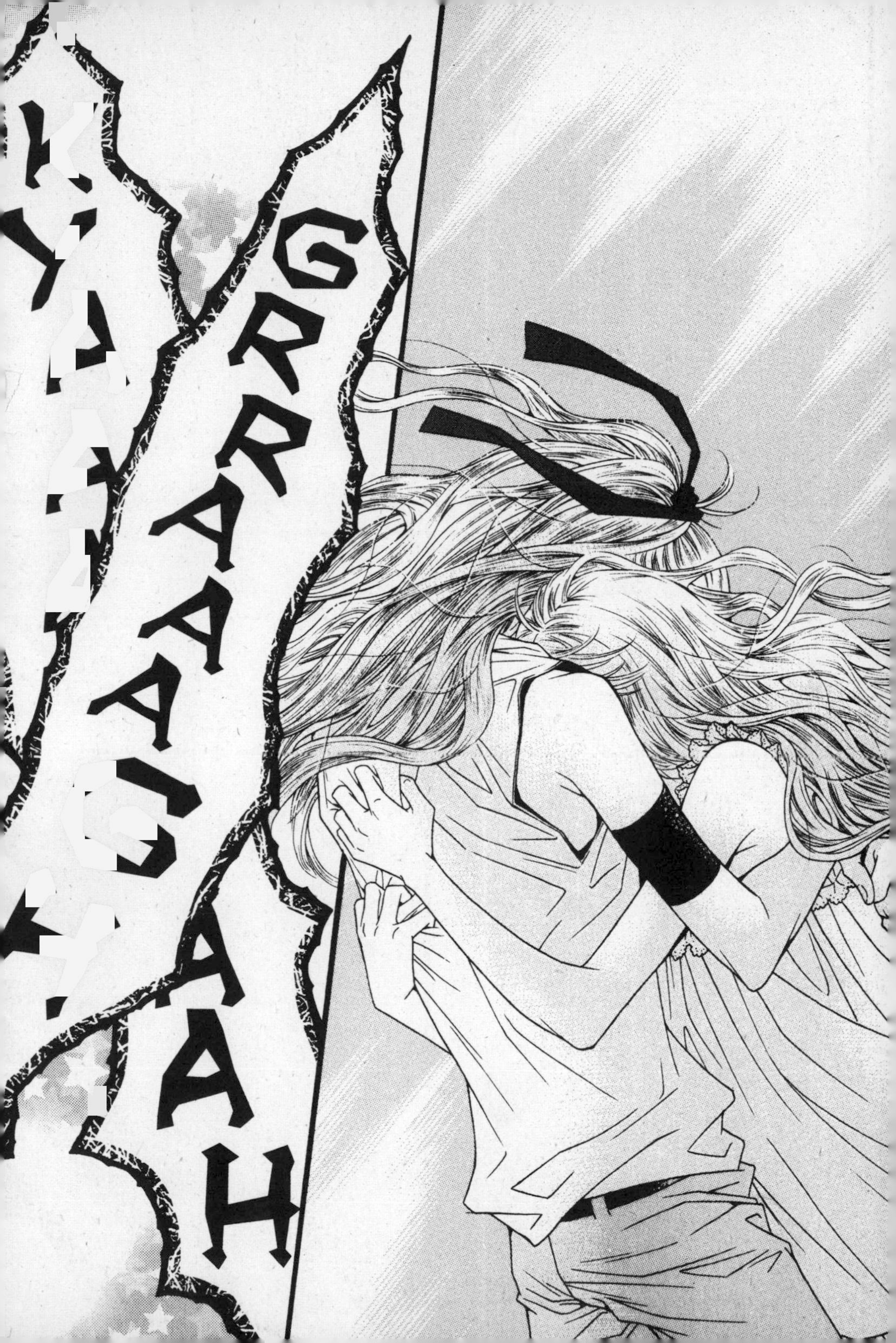
GRRAAAA
AAH

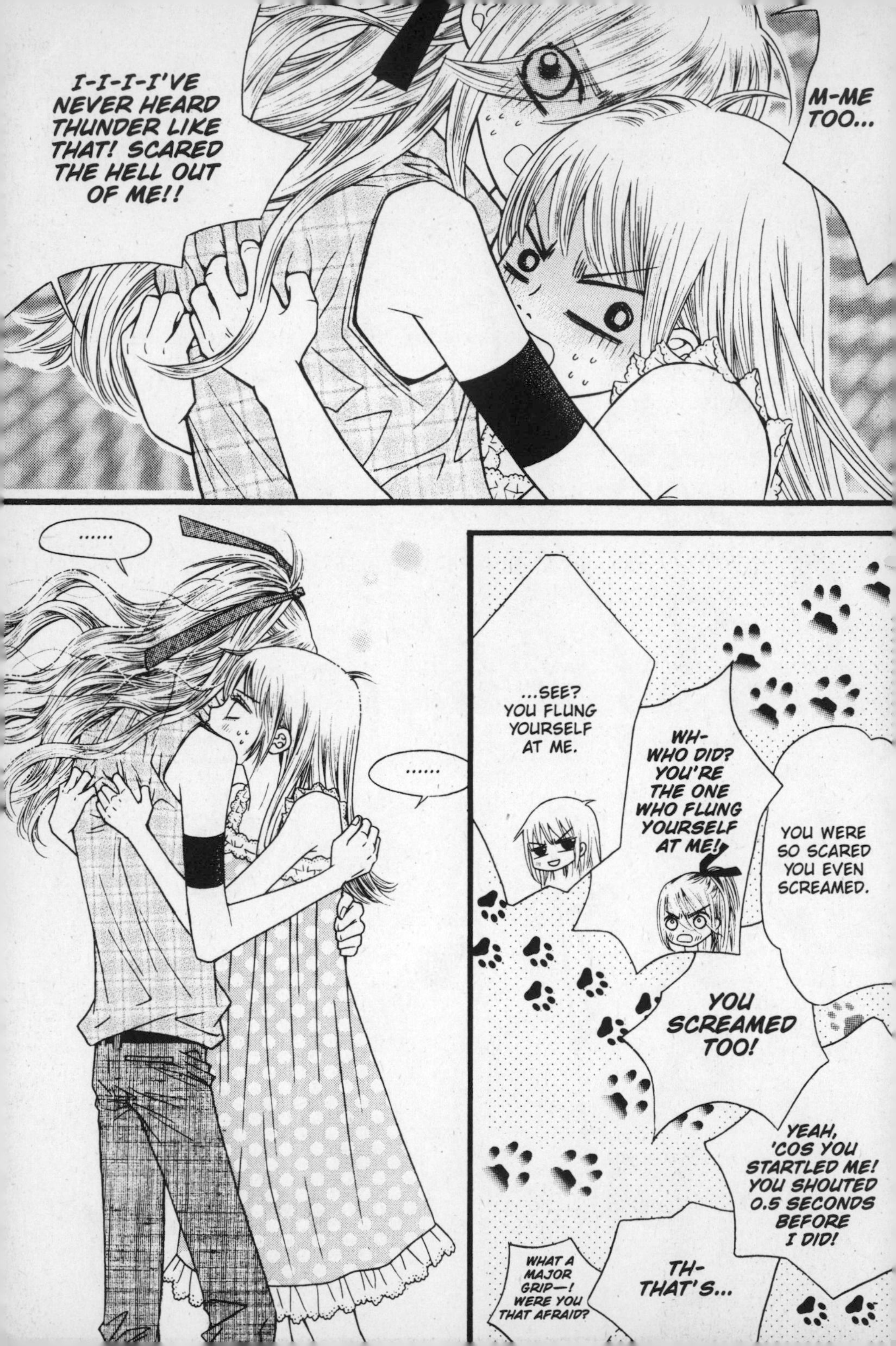
I-I-I-I'VE NEVER HEARD THUNDER LIKE THAT! SCARED THE HELL OUT OF ME!!
M-ME TOO...
......
......
...SEE? YOU FLUNG YOURSELF AT ME.
WH- WHO DID? YOU'RE THE ONE WHO FLUNG YOURSELF AT ME!
YOU WERE SO SCARED YOU EVEN SCREAMED.
YOU SCREAMED TOO!
YEAH, 'COS YOU STARTLED ME! YOU SHOUTED 0.5 SECONDS BEFORE I DID!
WHAT A MAJOR GRIP—! WERE YOU THAT AFRAID?
TH- THAT'S...

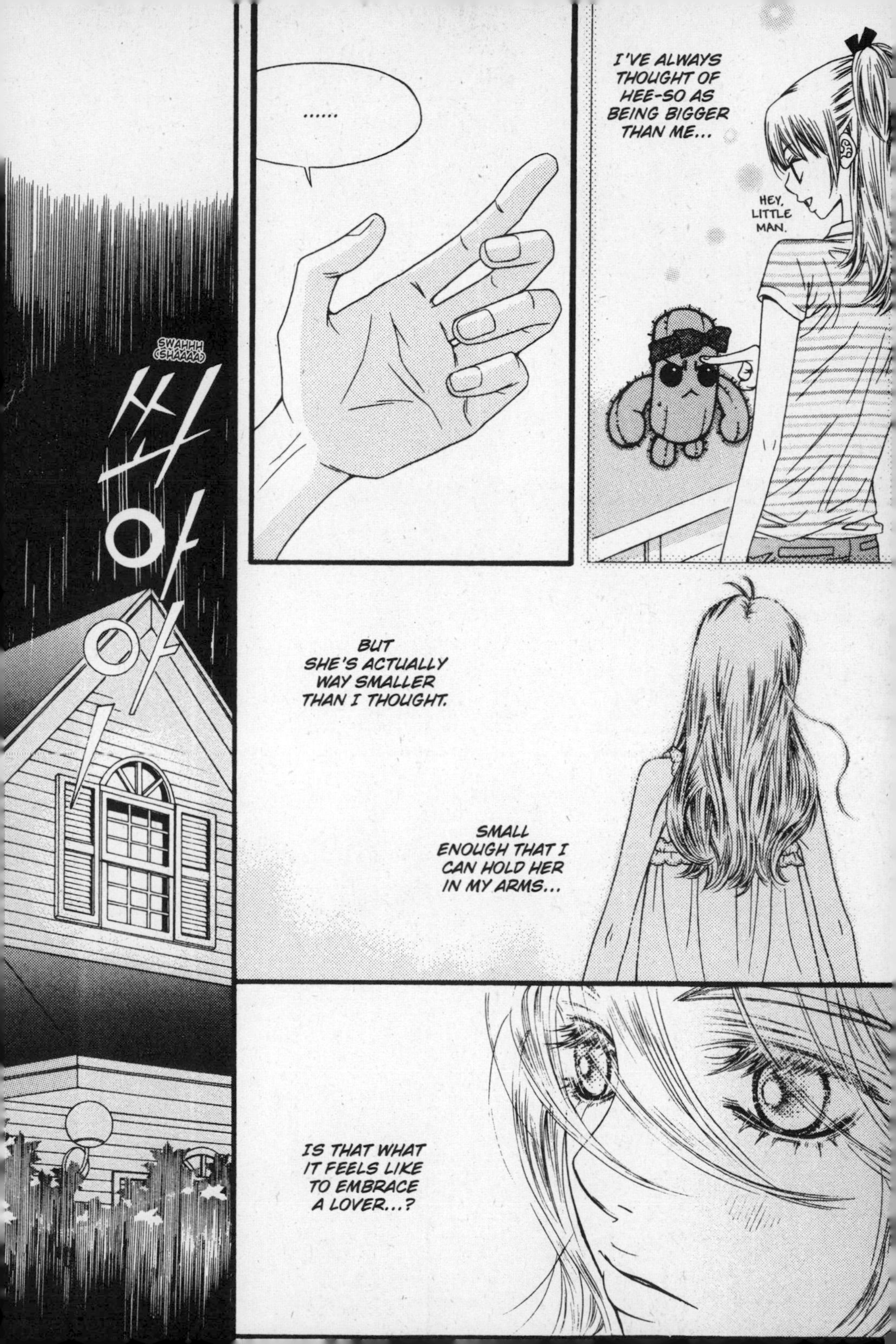
SWAHHH (SHAAAA)
쏴아아
......
I'VE ALWAYS THOUGHT OF HEE-SO AS BEING BIGGER THAN ME...
HEY, LITTLE MAN.
BUT SHE'S ACTUALLY WAY SMALLER THAN I THOUGHT.
SMALL ENOUGH THAT I CAN HOLD HER IN MY ARMS...
IS THAT WHAT IT FEELS LIKE TO EMBRACE A LOVER...?

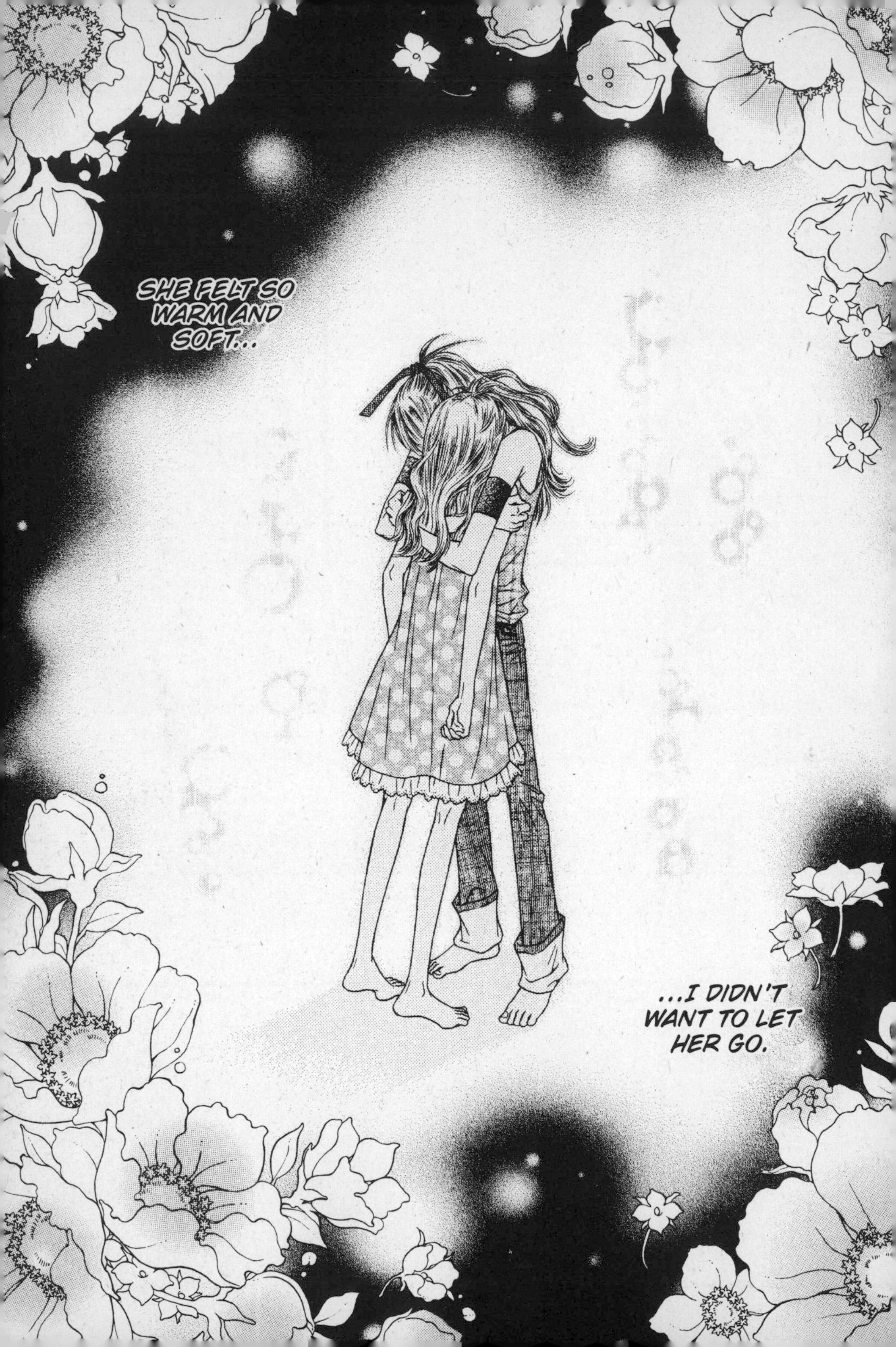
SHE FELT SO WARM AND SOFT...
...I DIDN'T WANT TO LET HER GO.

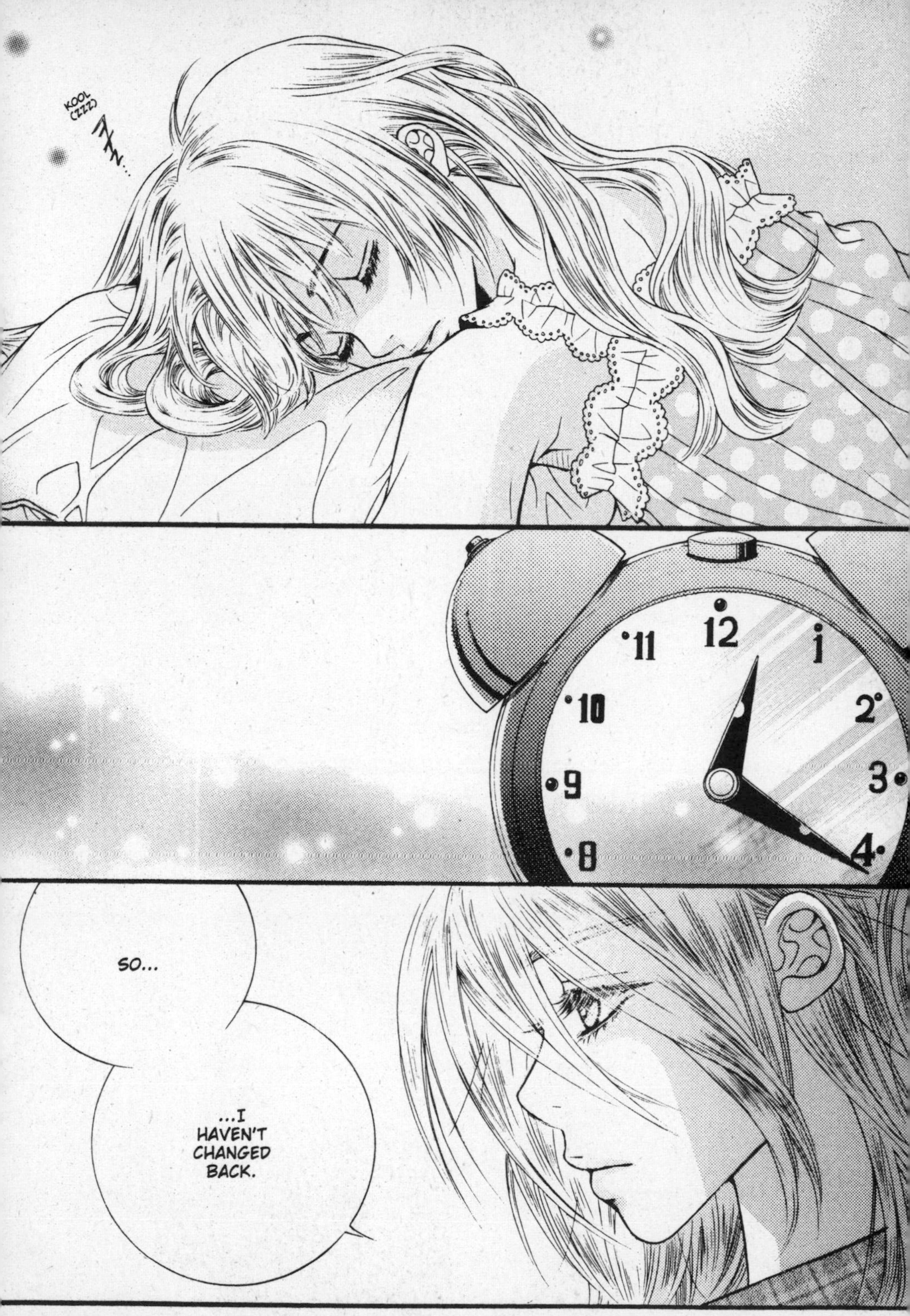
KOOL (ZZZZ)
ZZZ...
12
1
2
3
4
8
9
10
11
SO...
...I HAVEN'T CHANGED BACK.

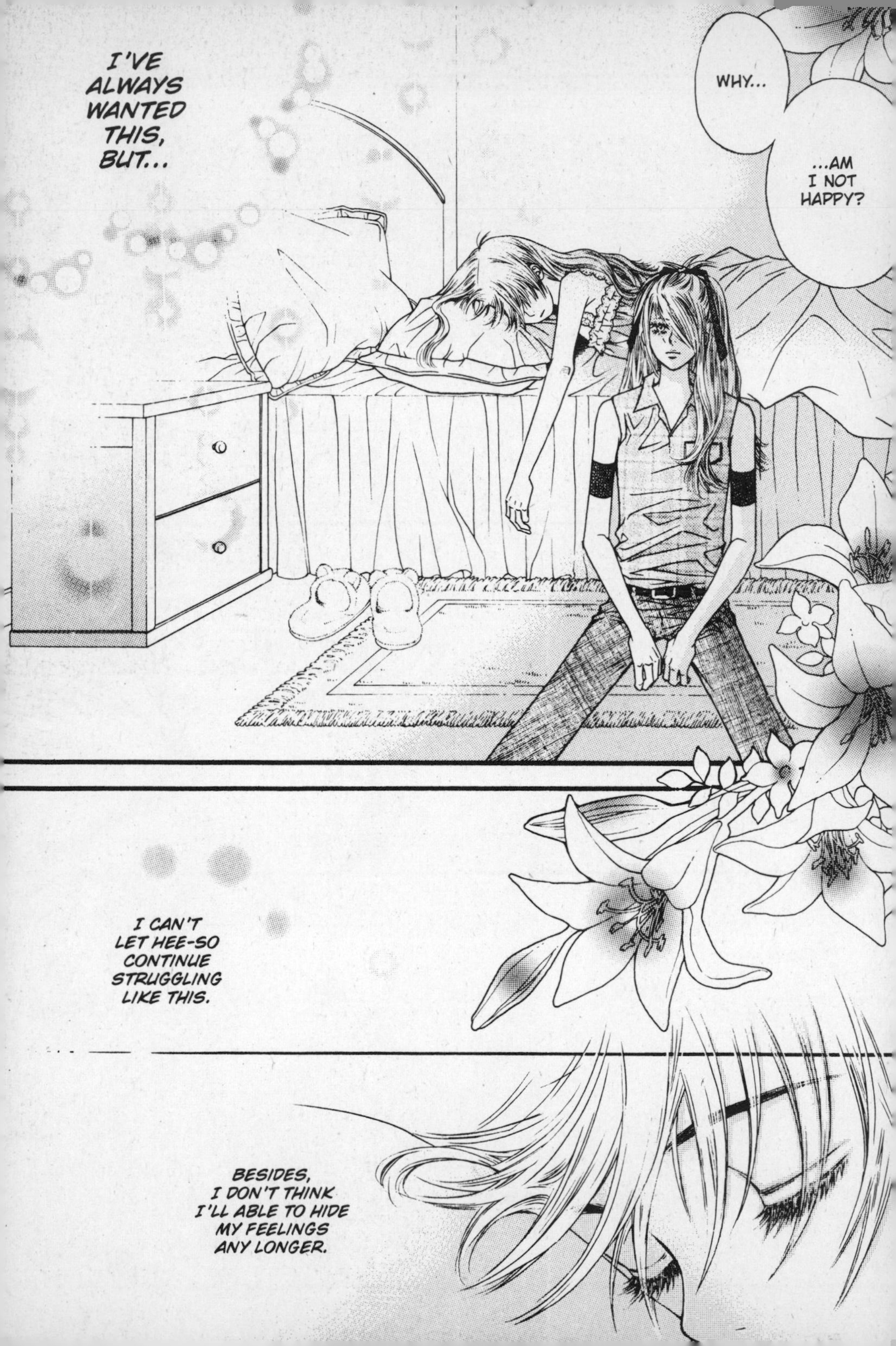
I'VE ALWAYS WANTED THIS, BUT...
WHY...
...AM I NOT HAPPY?
I CAN'T LET HEE-SO CONTINUE STRUGGLING LIKE THIS.
BESIDES, I DON'T THINK I'LL ABLE TO HIDE MY FEELINGS ANY LONGER.

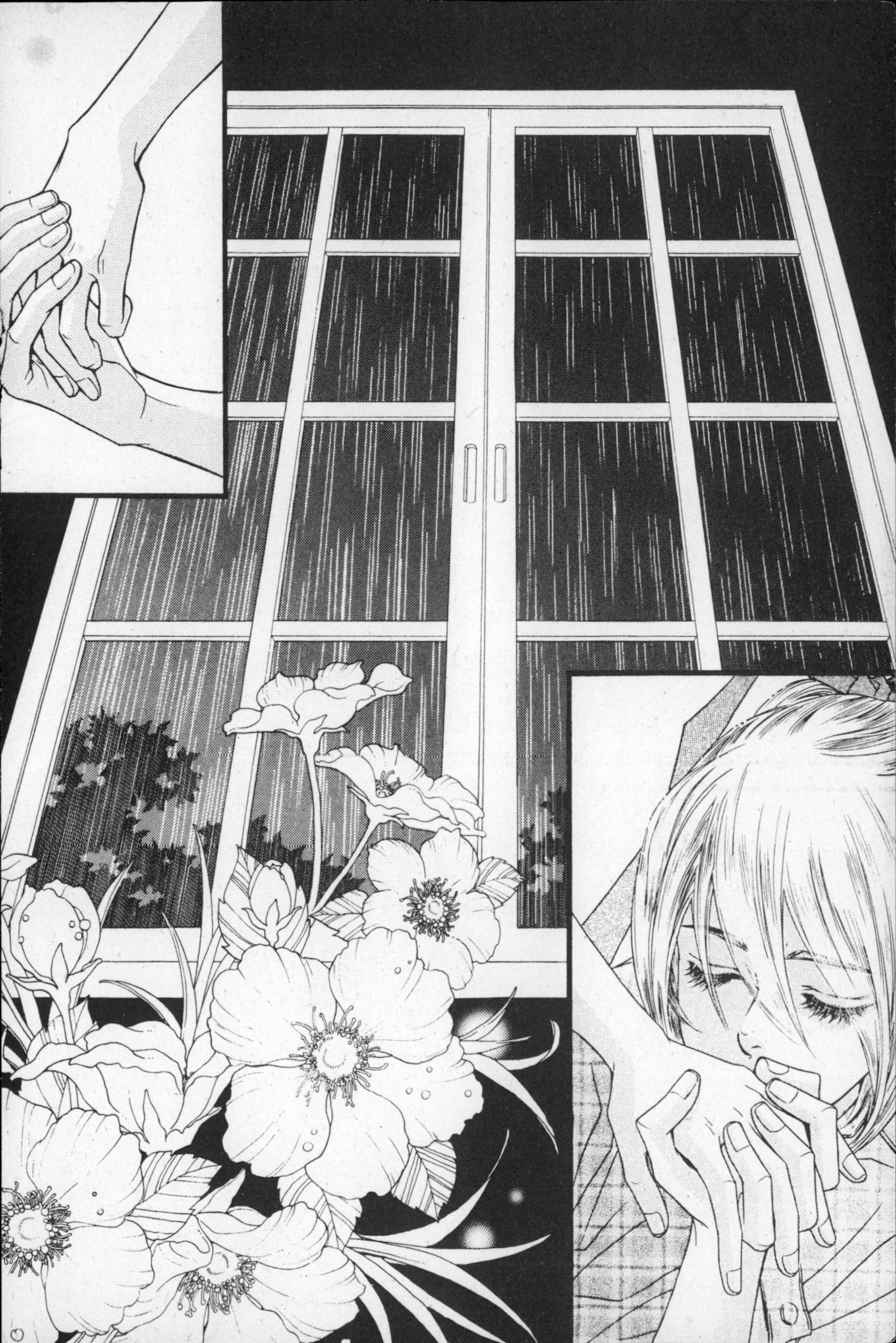

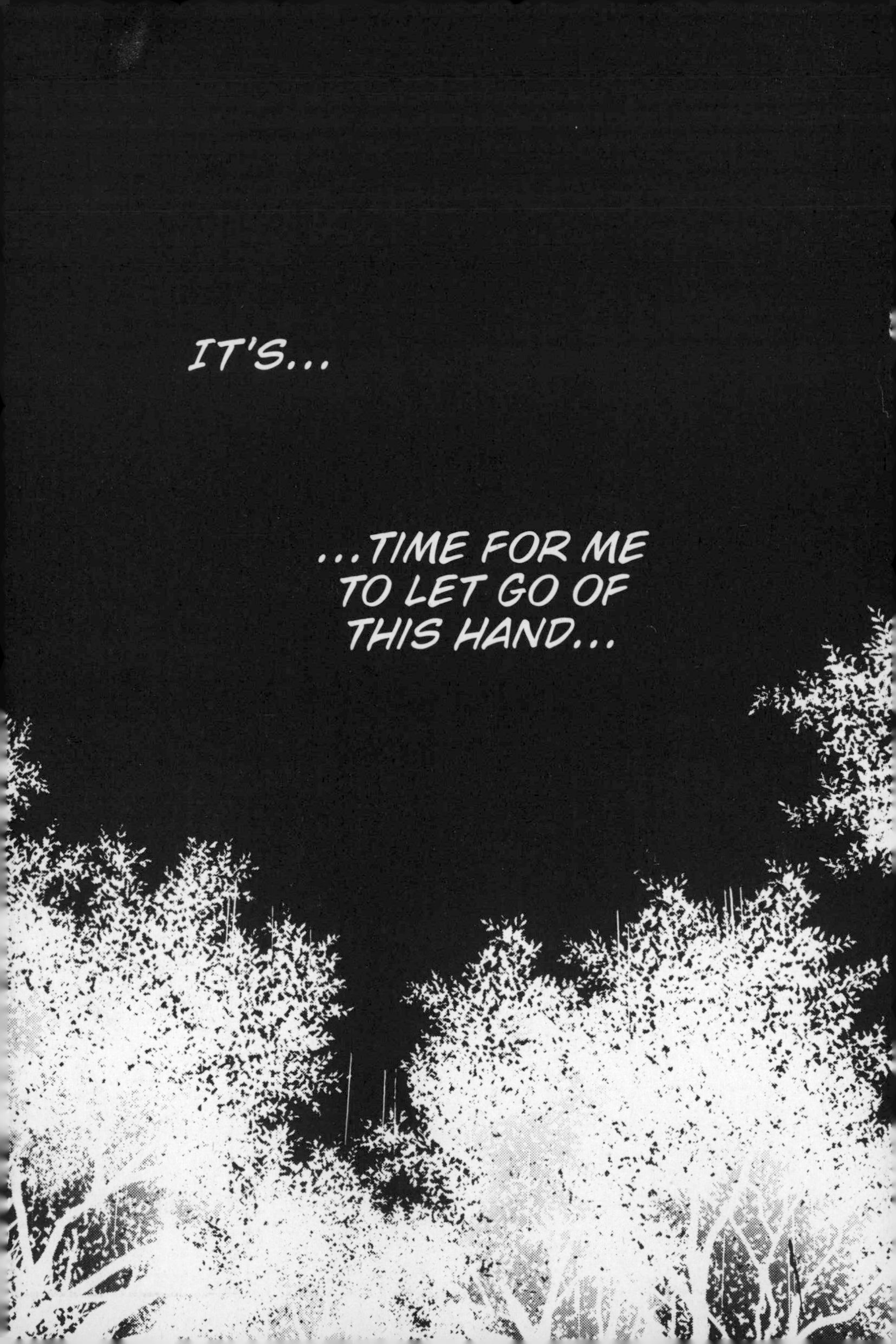
IT'S...
...TIME FOR ME TO LET GO OF THIS HAND...

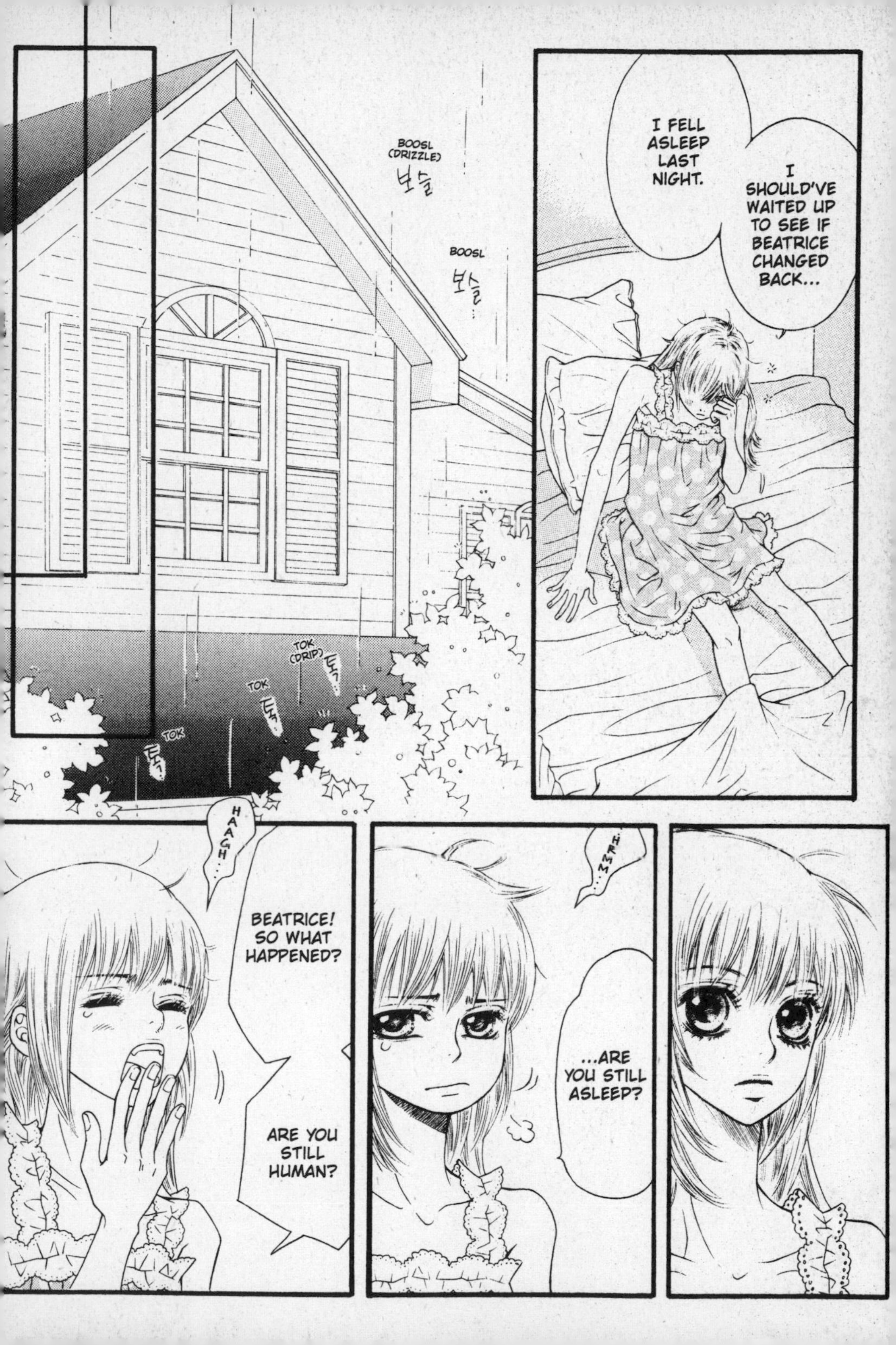

BOOSL (DRIZZLE)
보슬
BOOSL
보슬
TOK (DRIP)
톡
TOK
톡
TOK
톡
I FELL ASLEEP LAST NIGHT.
I SHOULD'VE WAITED UP TO SEE IF BEATRICE CHANGED BACK...
HAAGH...
BEATRICE! SO WHAT HAPPENED?
ARE YOU STILL HUMAN?
HRMM...
...ARE YOU STILL ASLEEP?

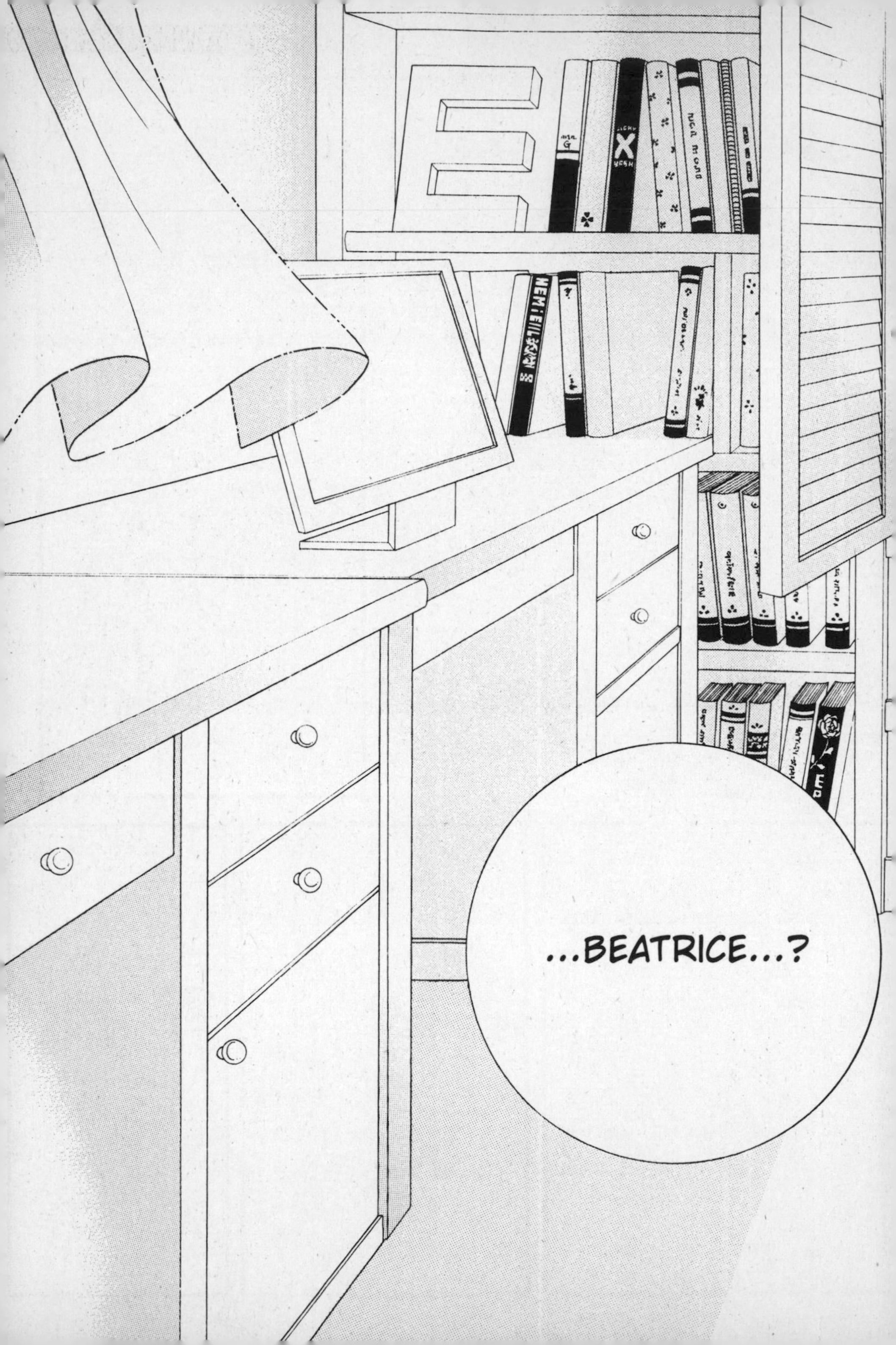
...BEATRICE...?

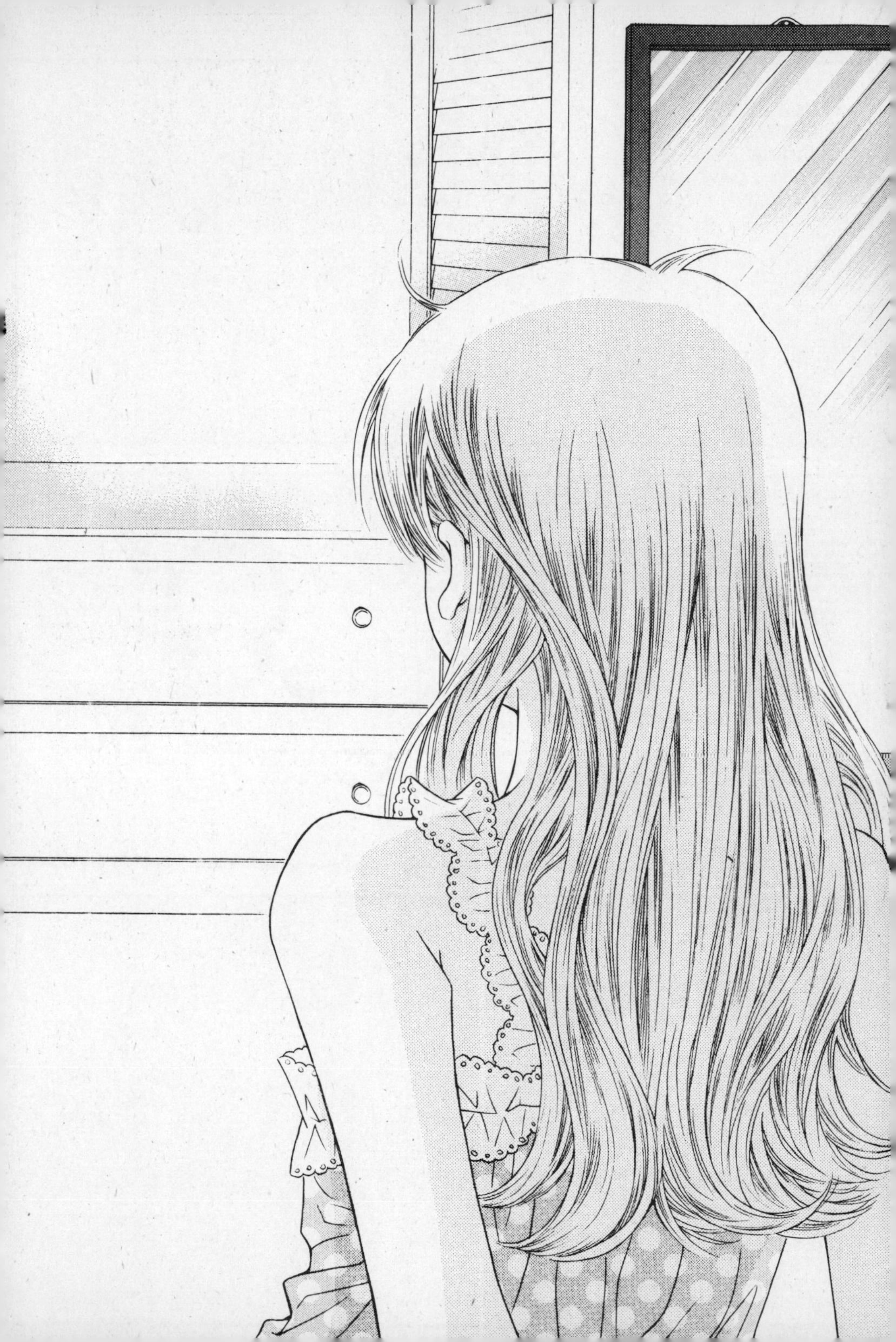

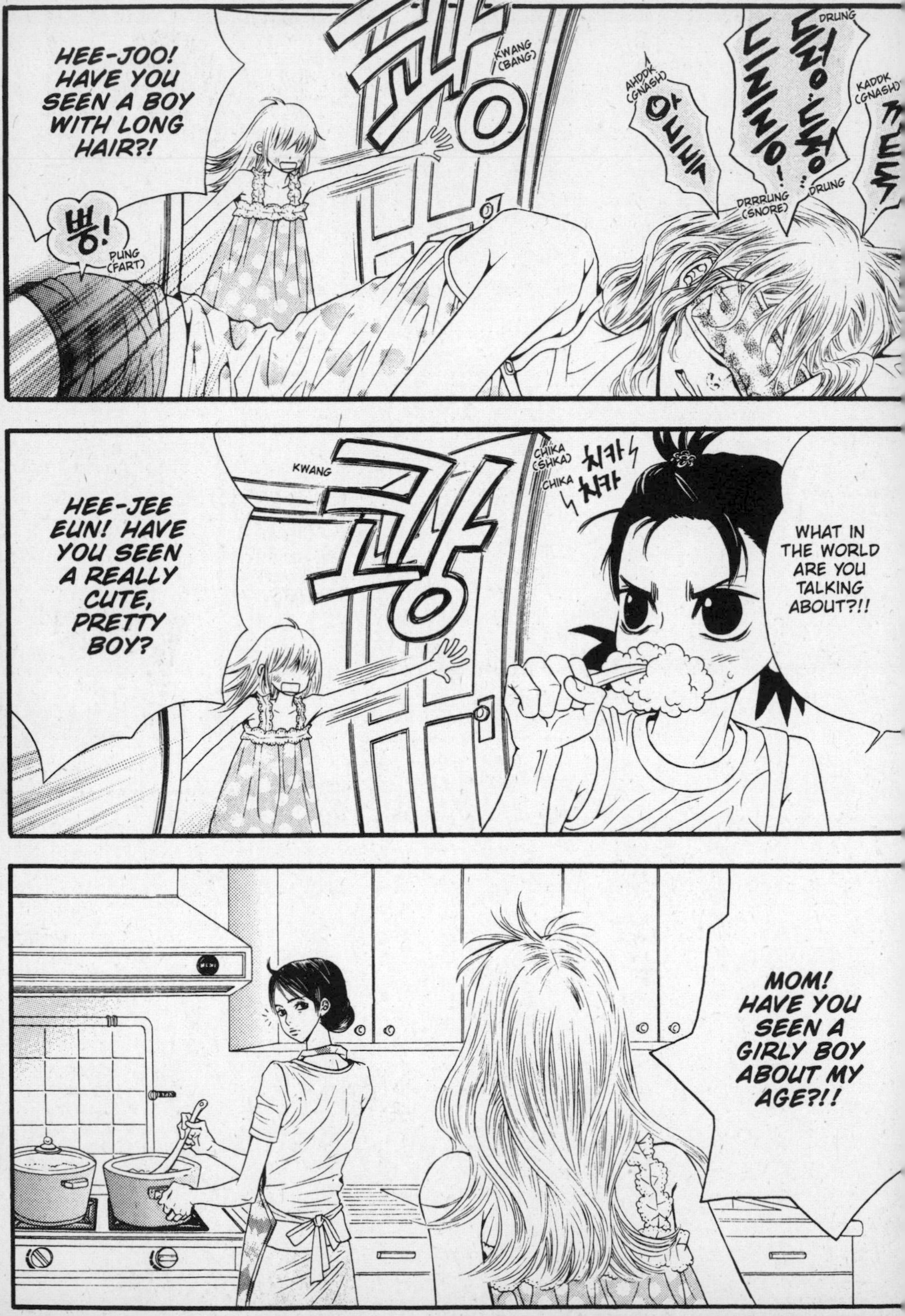
HEE-JOO! HAVE YOU SEEN A BOY WITH LONG HAIR?!
뿡!
PUNG (FART)
쾅
KWANG (BANG)
AHDDK (GNASH)
DRRRUNG (SNORE)
DRUNG
DRUNG
KADDK (GNASH)
KWANG
쾅
HEE-JEE EUN! HAVE YOU SEEN A REALLY CUTE, PRETTY BOY?
CHIKA (SHIKA)
CHIKA
치카
치카
WHAT IN THE WORLD ARE YOU TALKING ABOUT?!!
MOM! HAVE YOU SEEN A GIRLY BOY ABOUT MY AGE?!!

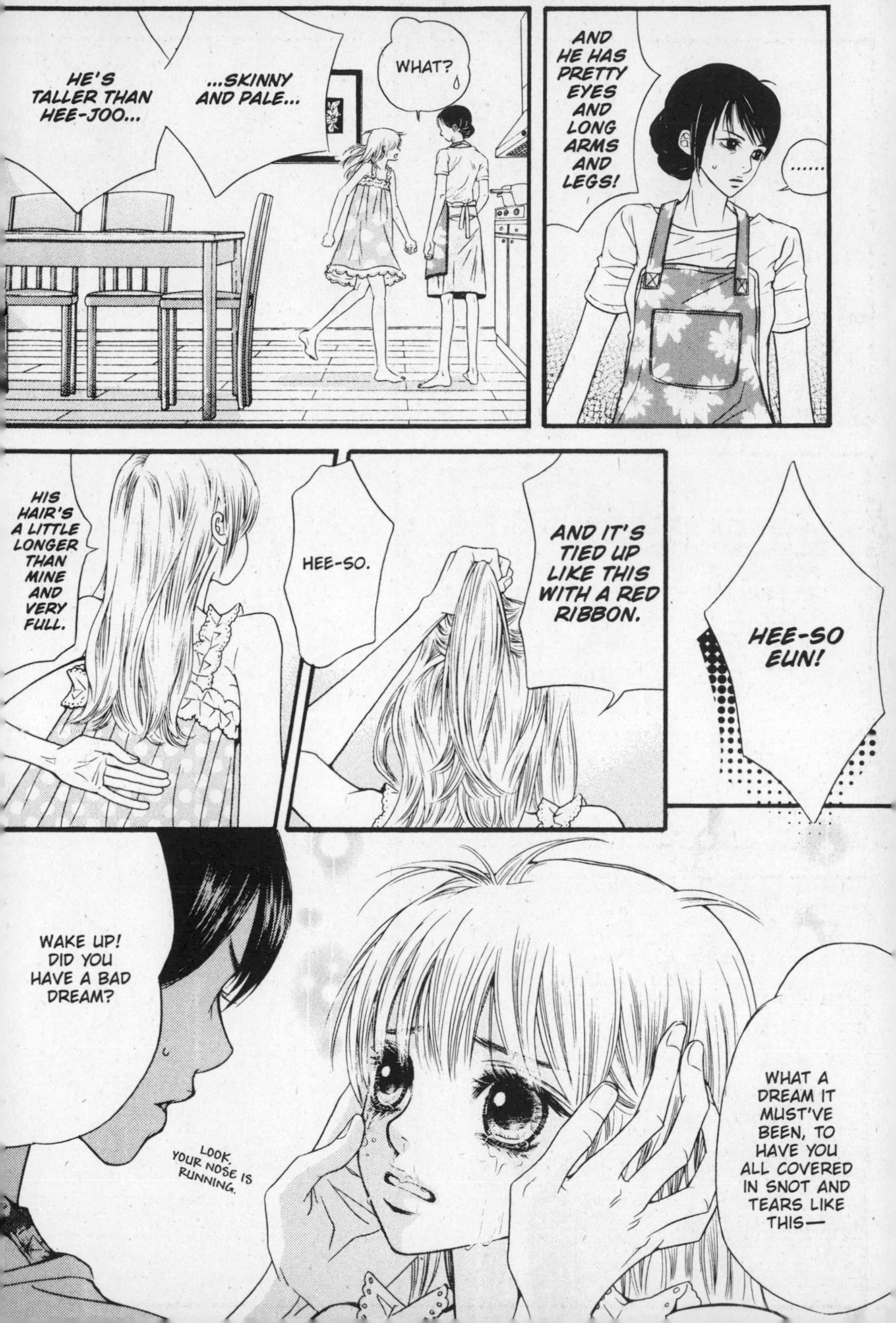
HE'S TALLER THAN HEE-JOO...
...SKINNY AND PALE...
WHAT?
AND HE HAS PRETTY EYES AND LONG ARMS AND LEGS!
......
HIS HAIR'S A LITTLE LONGER THAN MINE AND VERY FULL.
HEE-SO.
AND IT'S TIED UP LIKE THIS WITH A RED RIBBON.
HEE-SO EUN!
WAKE UP! DID YOU HAVE A BAD DREAM?
LOOK, YOUR NOSE IS RUNNING.
WHAT A DREAM IT MUST'VE BEEN, TO HAVE YOU ALL COVERED IN SNOT AND TEARS LIKE THIS—

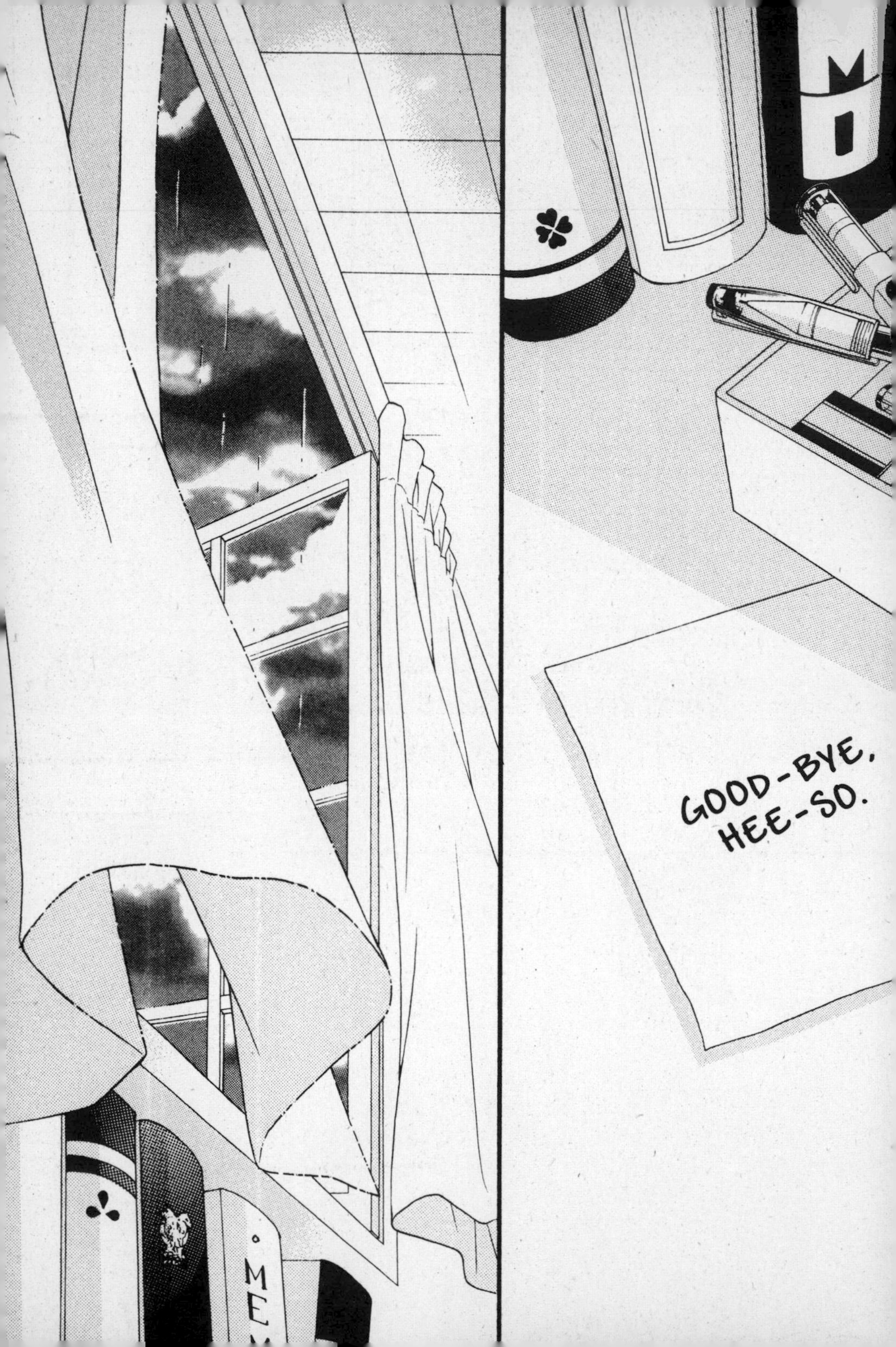
GOOD-BYE,
HEE-SO.

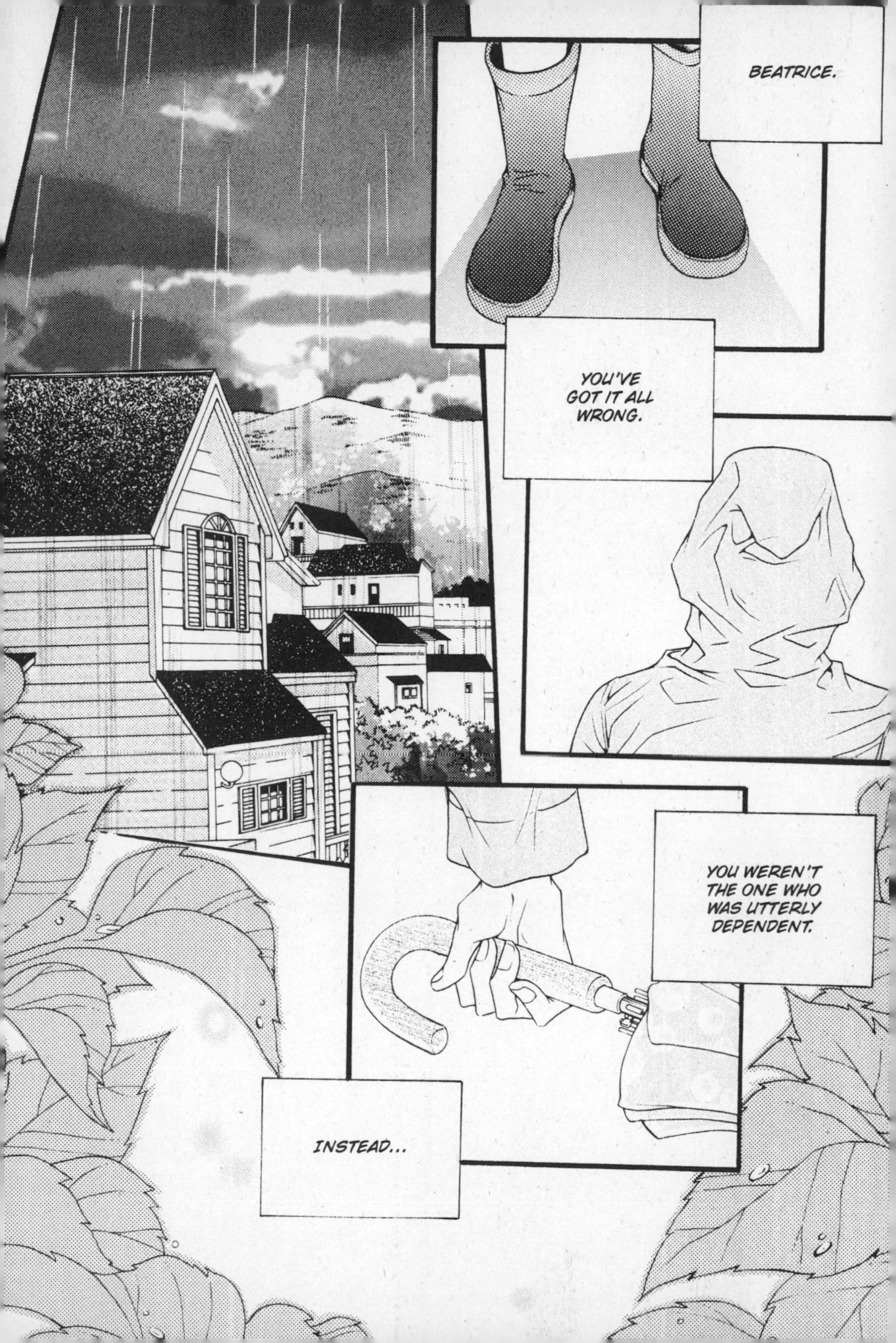
BEATRICE.
YOU'VE GOT IT ALL WRONG.
YOU WEREN'T THE ONE WHO WAS UTTERLY DEPENDENT.
INSTEAD...

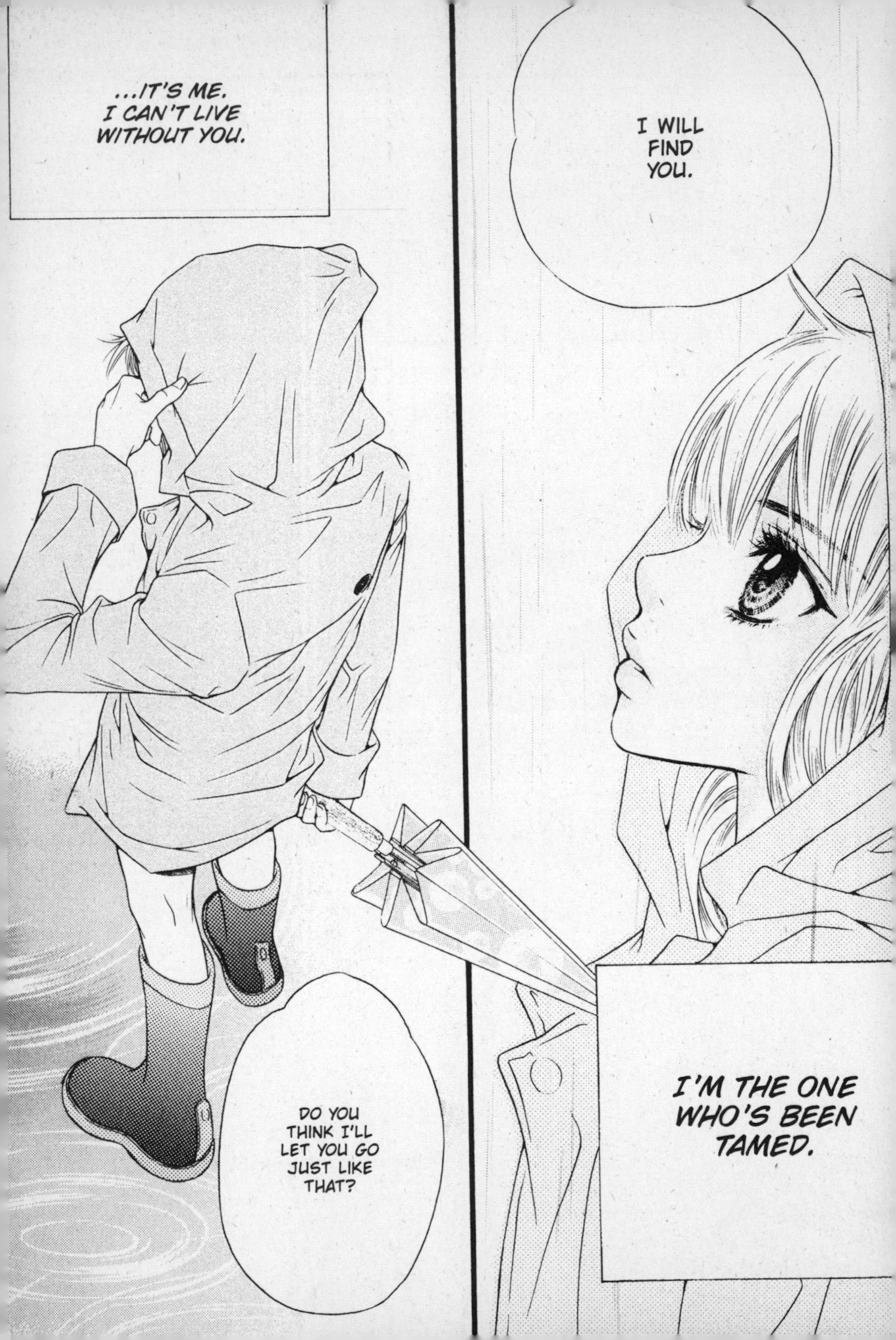
...IT'S ME. I CAN'T LIVE WITHOUT YOU.
DO YOU THINK I'LL LET YOU GO JUST LIKE THAT?
I WILL FIND YOU.
I'M THE ONE WHO'S BEEN TAMED.

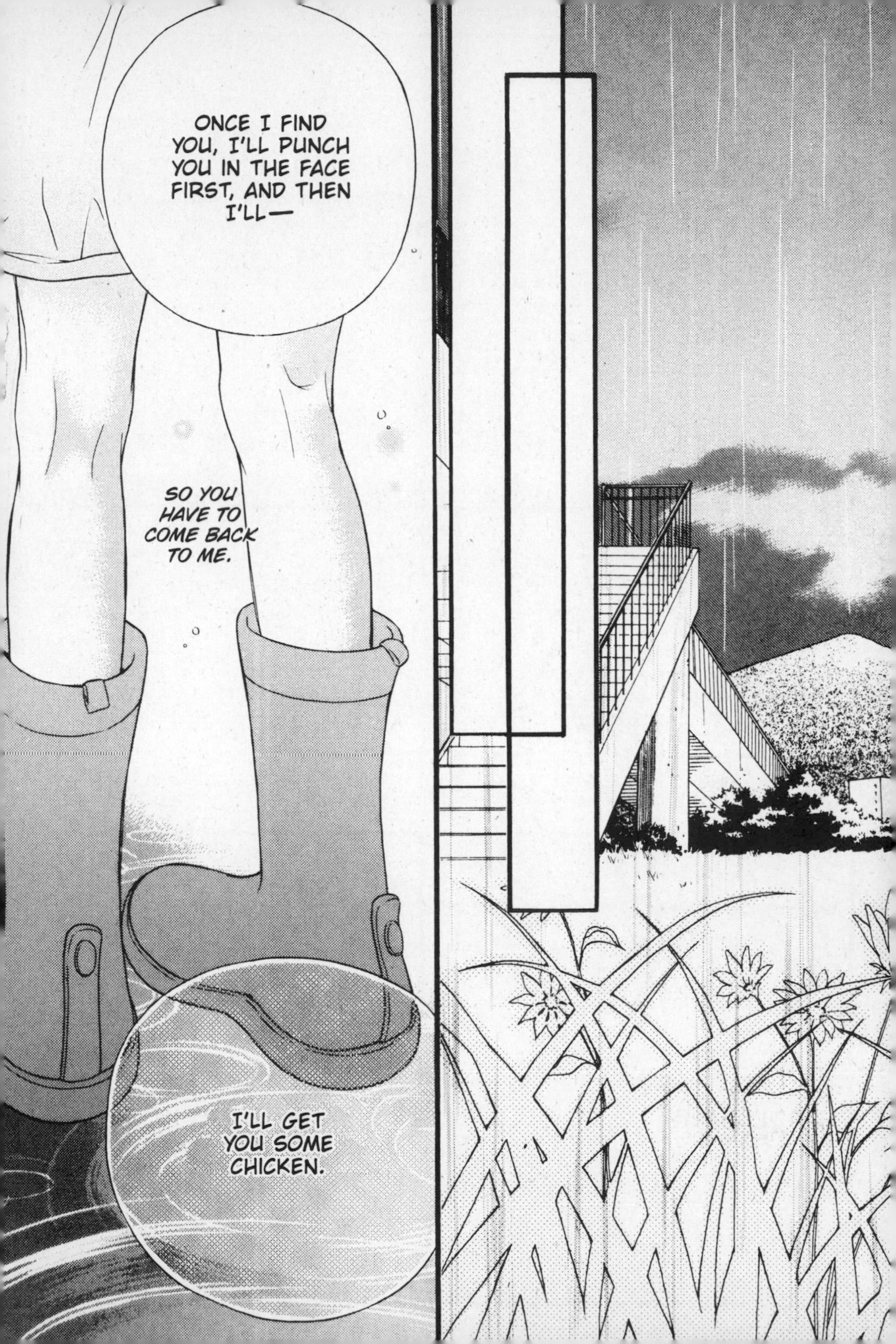
ONCE I FIND YOU, I'LL PUNCH YOU IN THE FACE FIRST, AND THEN I'LL—
SO YOU HAVE TO COME BACK TO ME.
I'LL GET YOU SOME CHICKEN.

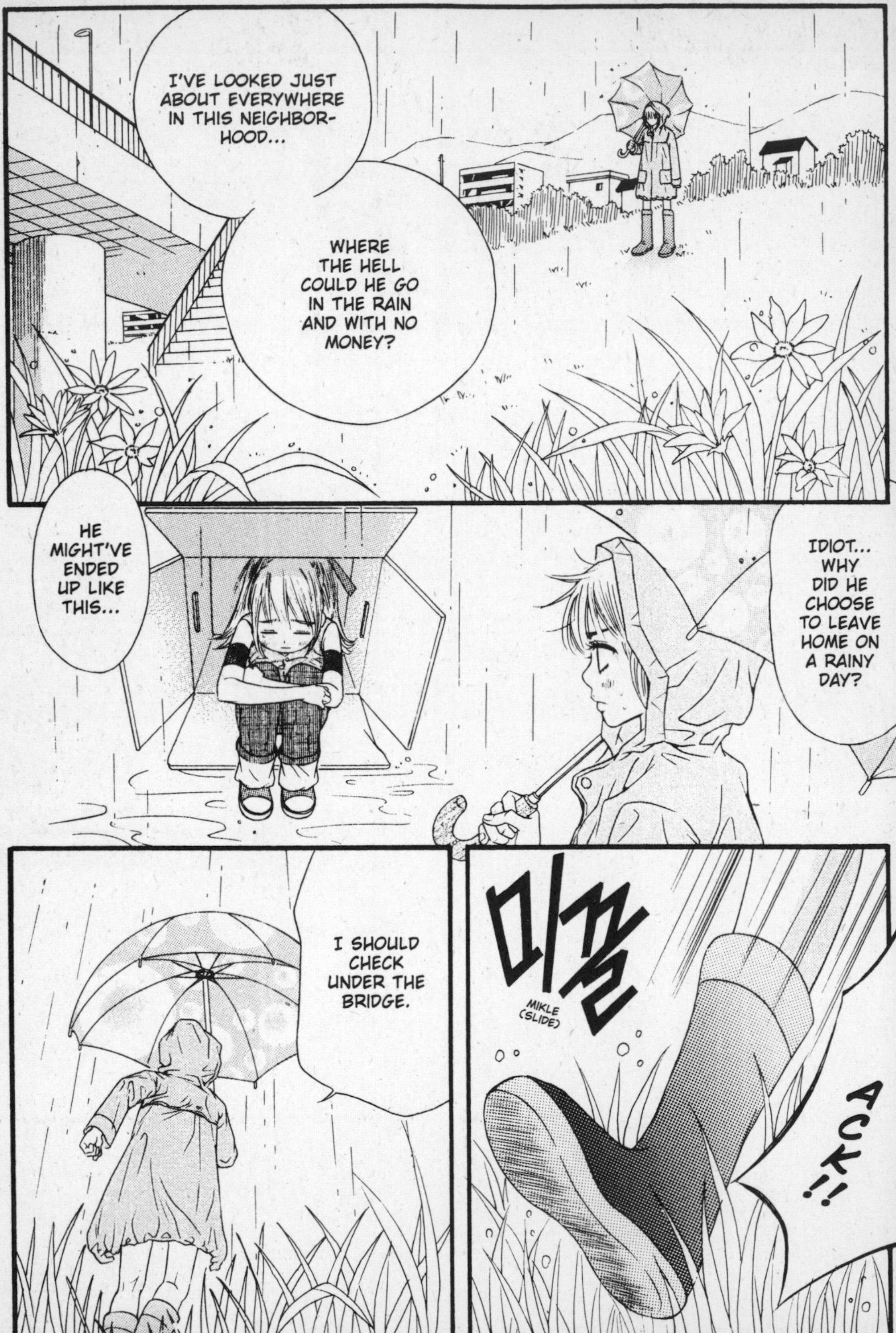
I'VE LOOKED JUST ABOUT EVERYWHERE IN THIS NEIGHBOR-HOOD...
WHERE THE HELL COULD HE GO IN THE RAIN AND WITH NO MONEY?
HE MIGHT'VE ENDED UP LIKE THIS...
IDIOT... WHY DID HE CHOOSE TO LEAVE HOME ON A RAINY DAY?
I SHOULD CHECK UNDER THE BRIDGE.
미끌
MIKLE (SLIDE)
ACK!!

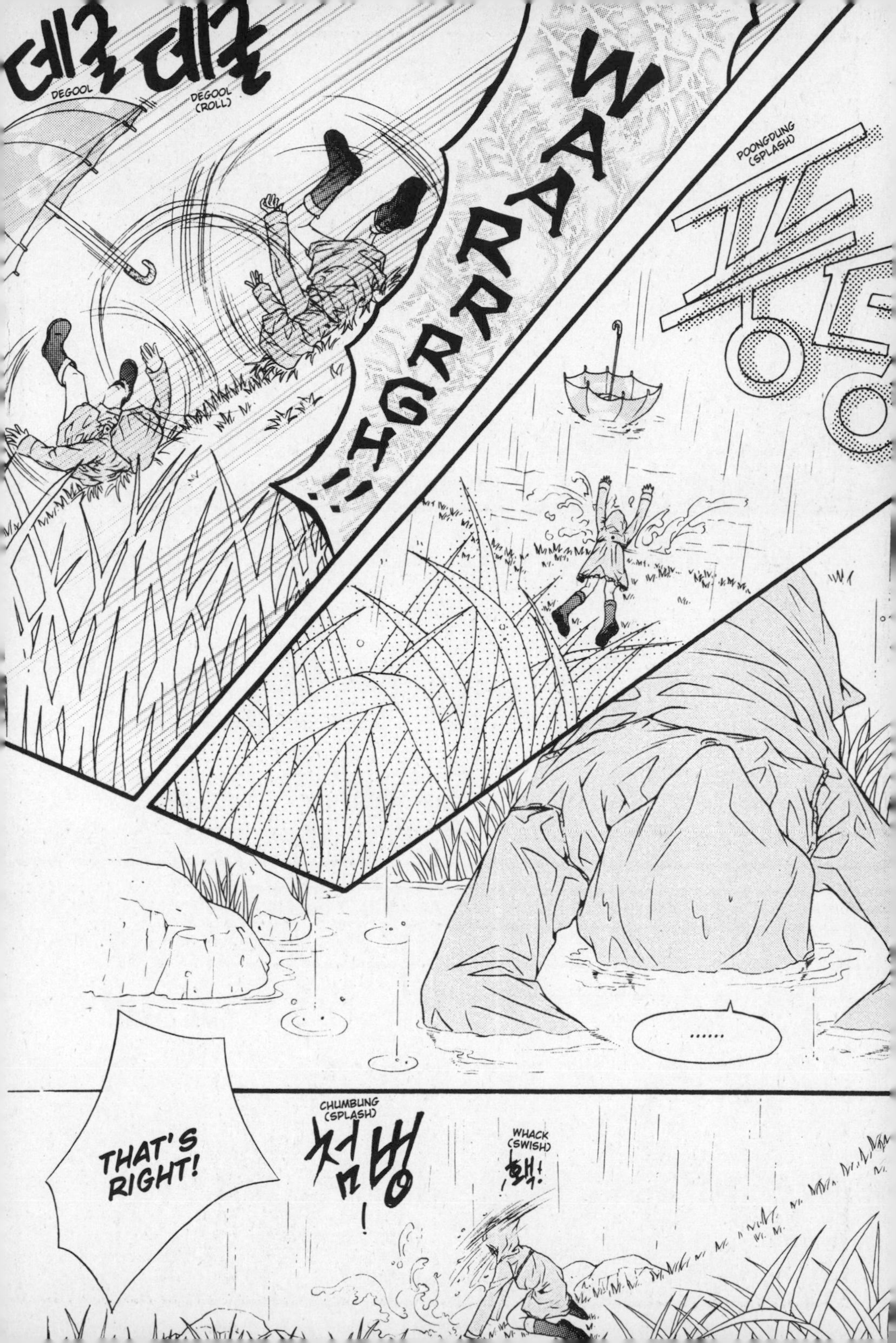

데굴 데굴
DEGOOL
DEGOOL (ROLL)
WAARRGH!!!
POONGDUNG (SPLASH)
......
THAT'S RIGHT!
CHUMBUNG (SPLASH)
첨벙!
WHACK (SWISH)
홱!

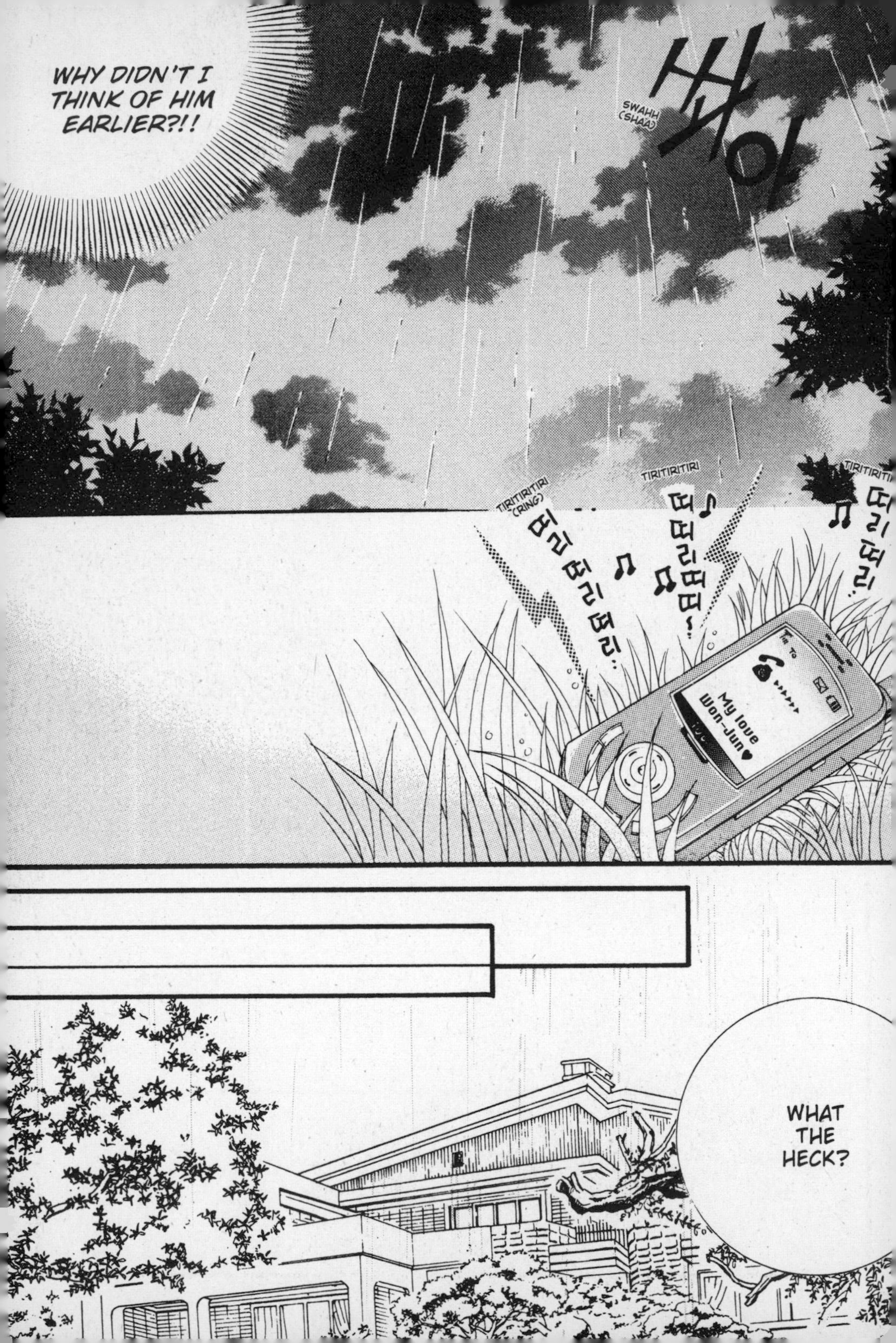
WHY DIDN'T I THINK OF HIM EARLIER?!!
SWAHH (SHAA)
TIRITIRITIRI (RING)
TIRITIRITIRI
TIRITIRITIRI
My love Won-Jun♥
WHAT THE HECK?

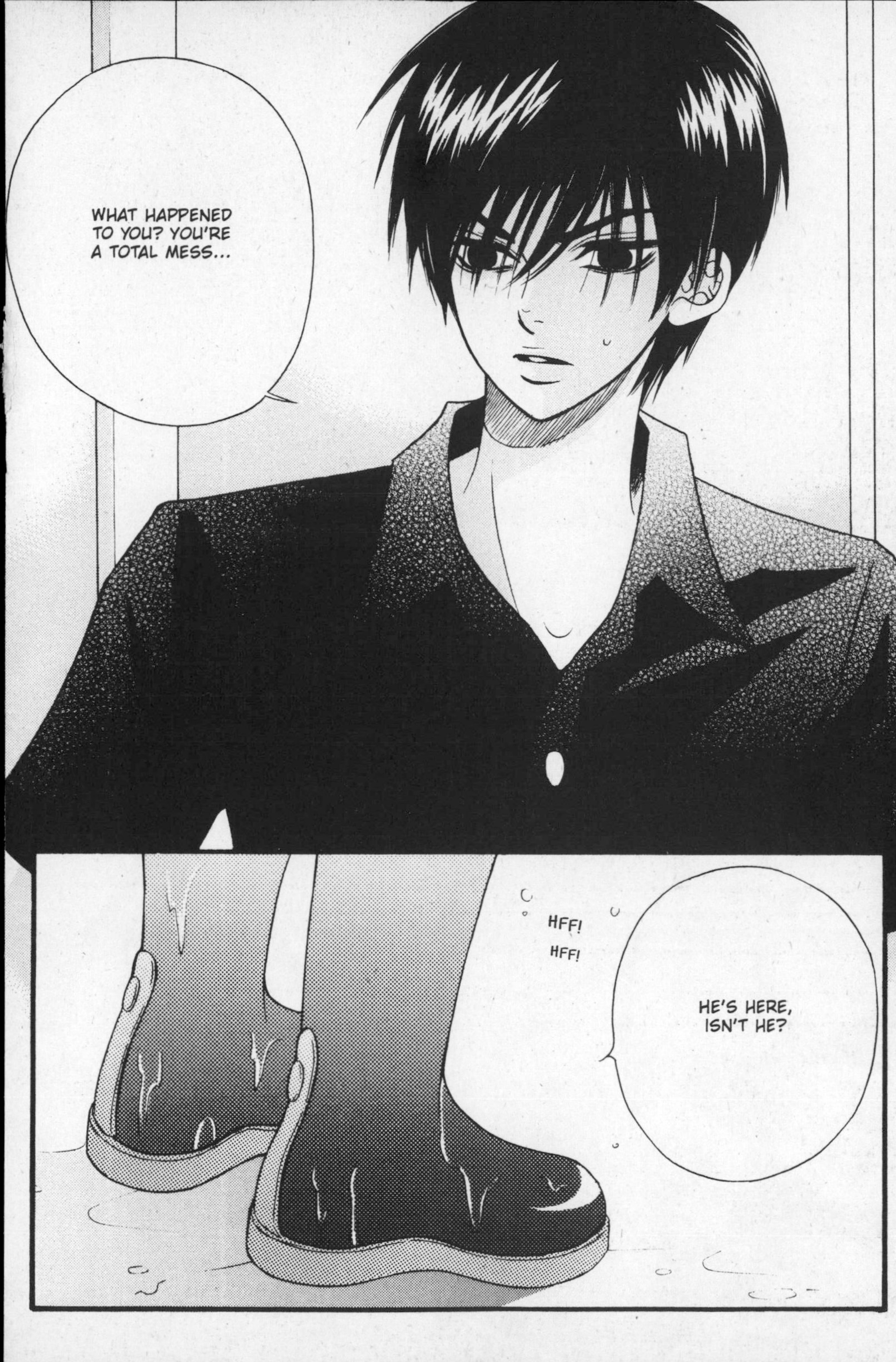
WHAT HAPPENED TO YOU? YOU'RE A TOTAL MESS...
HFF!
HFF!
HE'S HERE, ISN'T HE?

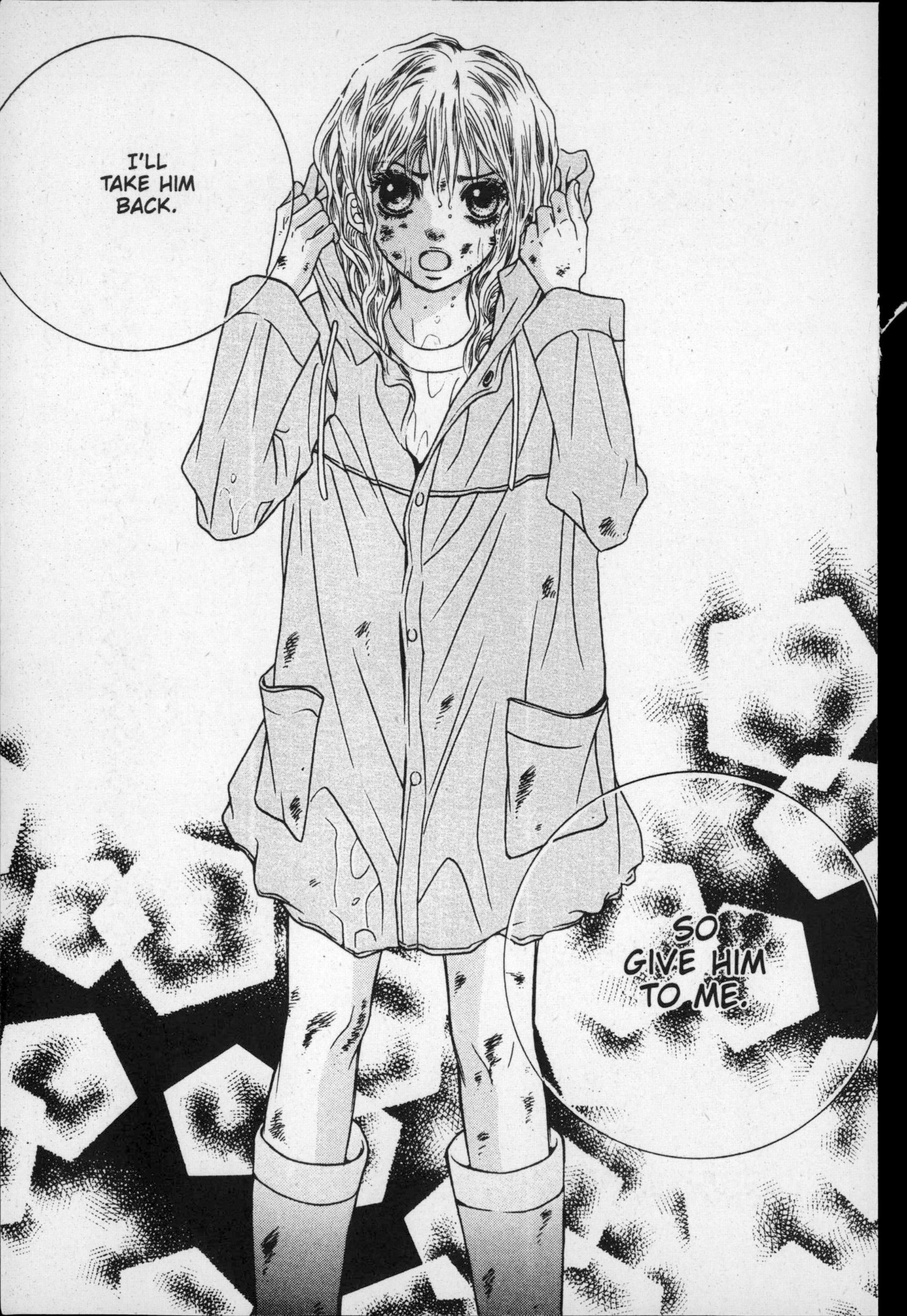
I'LL TAKE HIM BACK.
SO GIVE HIM TO ME.

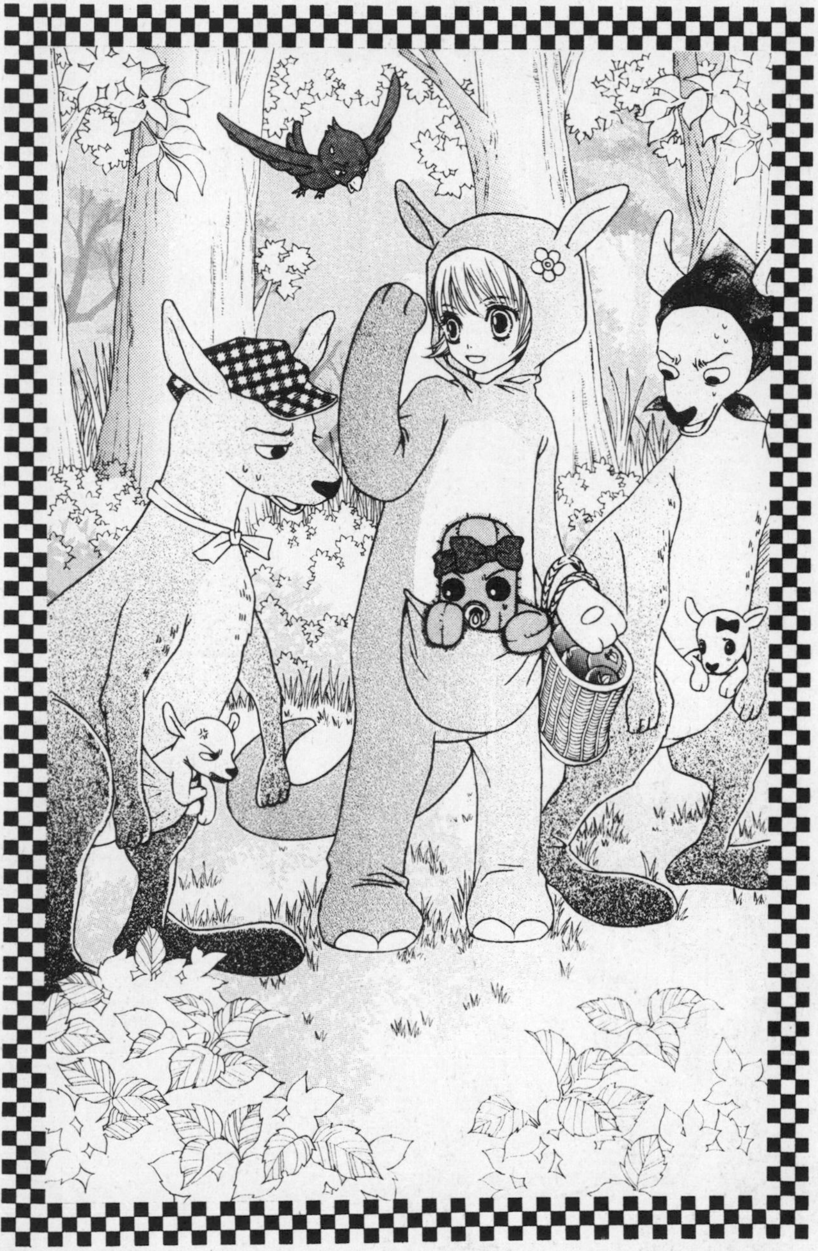

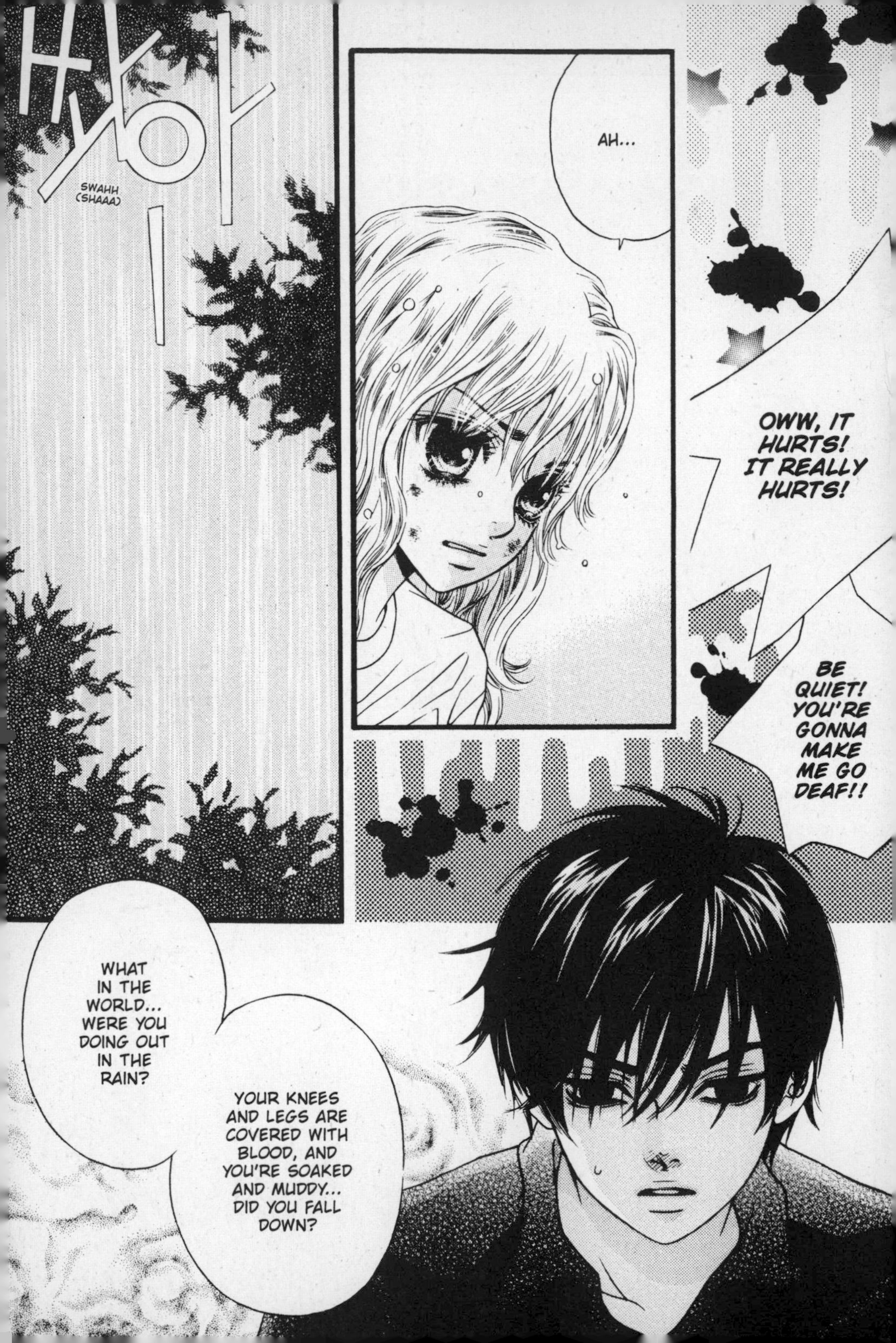
SWAHH (SHAAA)
AH...
OWW, IT HURTS! IT REALLY HURTS!
BE QUIET! YOU'RE GONNA MAKE ME GO DEAF!!
WHAT IN THE WORLD... WERE YOU DOING OUT IN THE RAIN?
YOUR KNEES AND LEGS ARE COVERED WITH BLOOD, AND YOU'RE SOAKED AND MUDDY... DID YOU FALL DOWN?

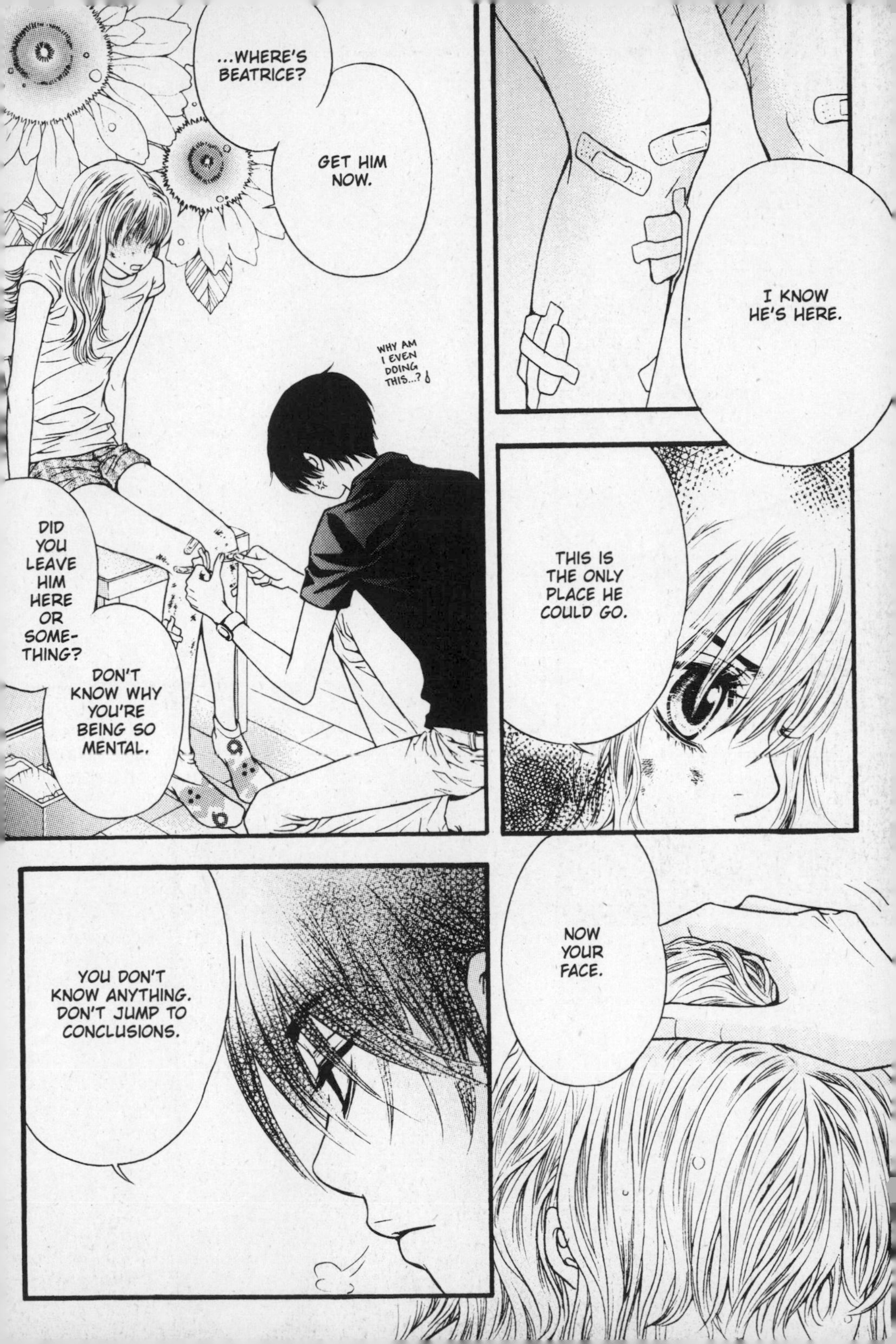
...WHERE'S BEATRICE?
GET HIM NOW.
WHY AM I EVEN DOING THIS...?
DID YOU LEAVE HIM HERE OR SOME-THING?
DON'T KNOW WHY YOU'RE BEING SO MENTAL.
I KNOW HE'S HERE.
THIS IS THE ONLY PLACE HE COULD GO.
YOU DON'T KNOW ANYTHING. DON'T JUMP TO CONCLUSIONS.
NOW YOUR FACE.

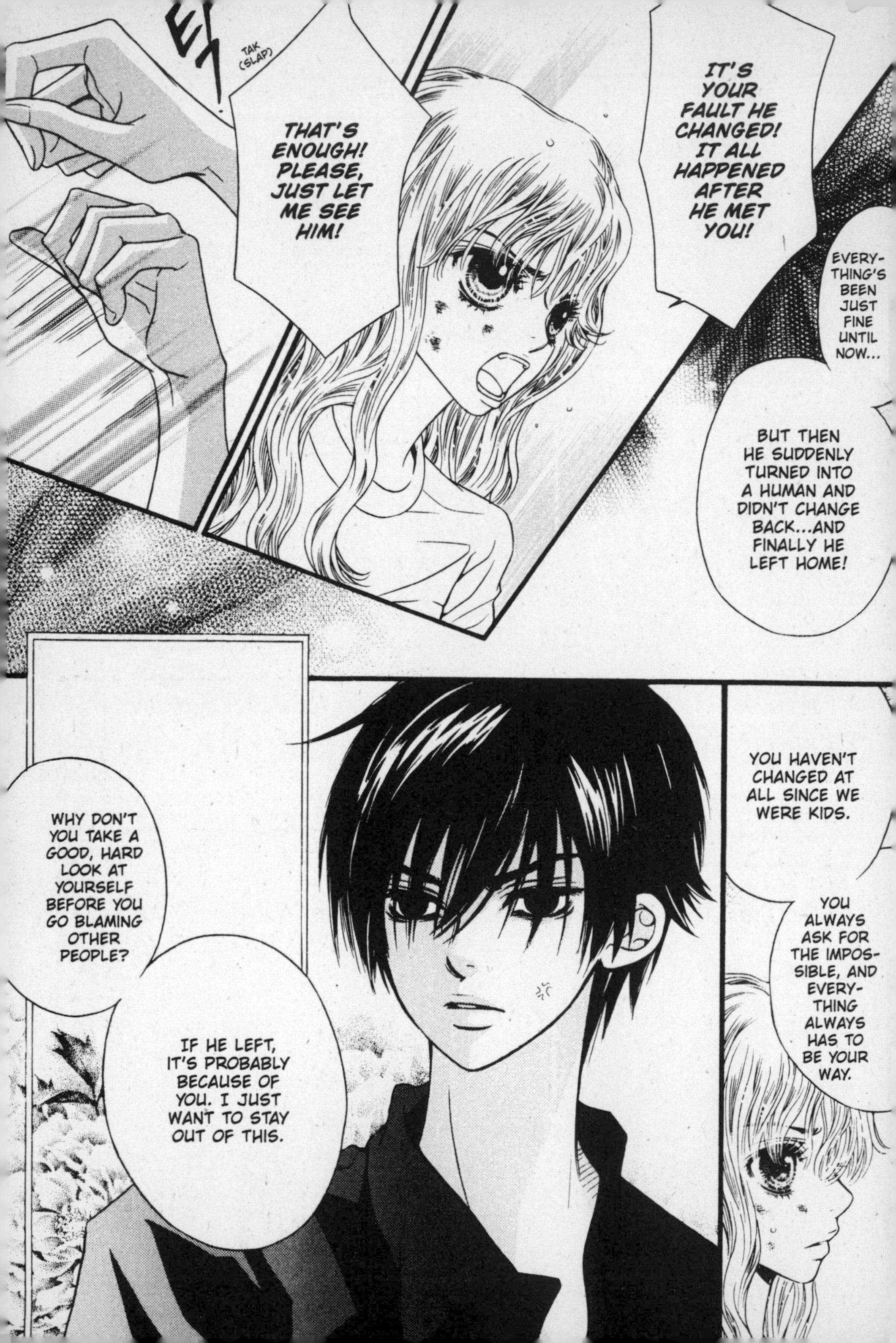
TAK (SLAP)
IT'S YOUR FAULT HE CHANGED! IT ALL HAPPENED AFTER HE MET YOU!
THAT'S ENOUGH! PLEASE, JUST LET ME SEE HIM!
EVERYTHING'S BEEN JUST FINE UNTIL NOW...
BUT THEN HE SUDDENLY TURNED INTO A HUMAN AND DIDN'T CHANGE BACK...AND FINALLY HE LEFT HOME!
YOU HAVEN'T CHANGED AT ALL SINCE WE WERE KIDS.
YOU ALWAYS ASK FOR THE IMPOSSIBLE, AND EVERYTHING ALWAYS HAS TO BE YOUR WAY.
WHY DON'T YOU TAKE A GOOD, HARD LOOK AT YOURSELF BEFORE YOU GO BLAMING OTHER PEOPLE?
IF HE LEFT, IT'S PROBABLY BECAUSE OF YOU. I JUST WANT TO STAY OUT OF THIS.

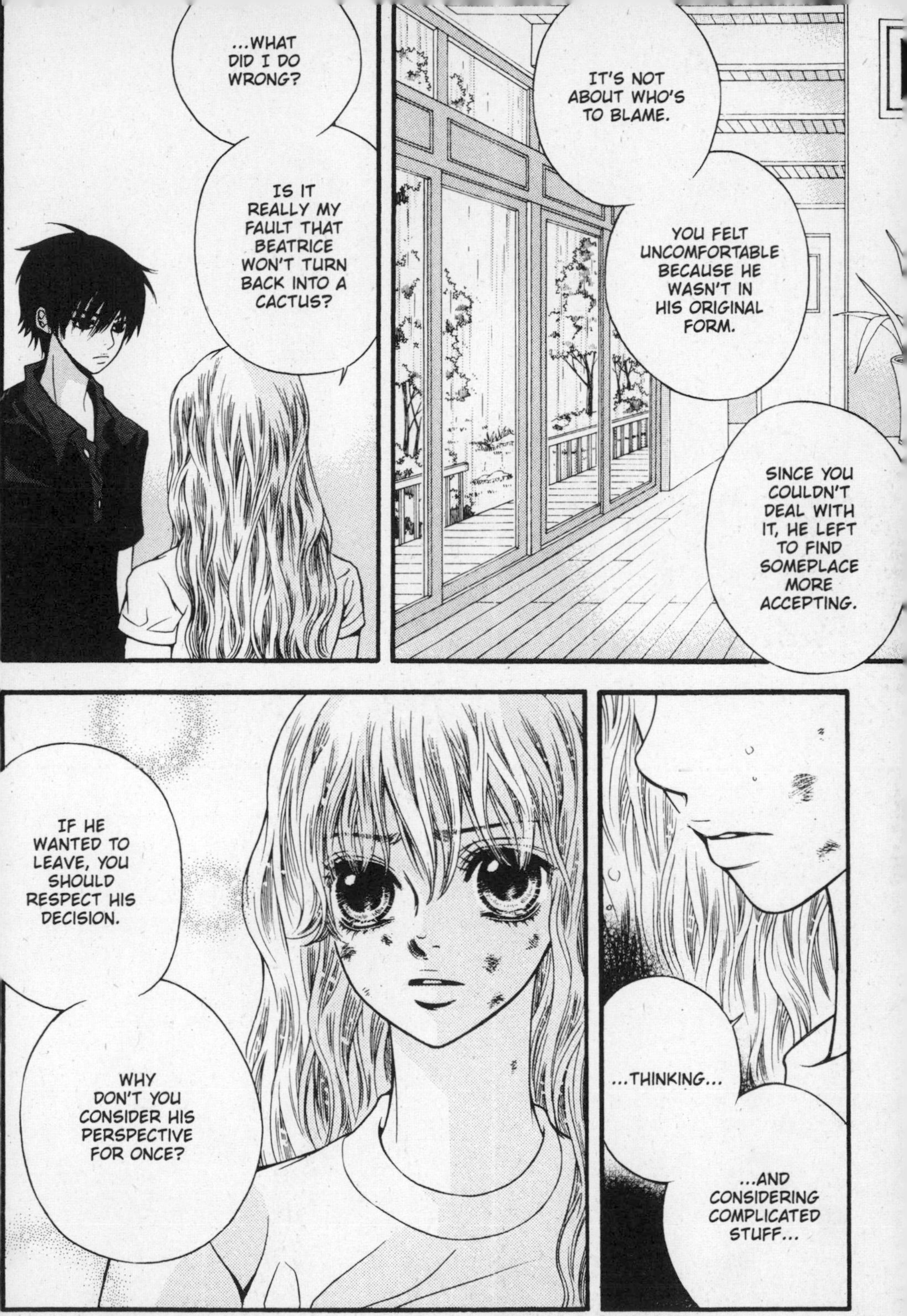
...WHAT DID I DO WRONG?
IS IT REALLY MY FAULT THAT BEATRICE WON'T TURN BACK INTO A CACTUS?
IT'S NOT ABOUT WHO'S TO BLAME.
YOU FELT UNCOMFORTABLE BECAUSE HE WASN'T IN HIS ORIGINAL FORM.
SINCE YOU COULDN'T DEAL WITH IT, HE LEFT TO FIND SOMEPLACE MORE ACCEPTING.
IF HE WANTED TO LEAVE, YOU SHOULD RESPECT HIS DECISION.
WHY DON'T YOU CONSIDER HIS PERSPECTIVE FOR ONCE?
...THINKING...
...AND CONSIDERING COMPLICATED STUFF...

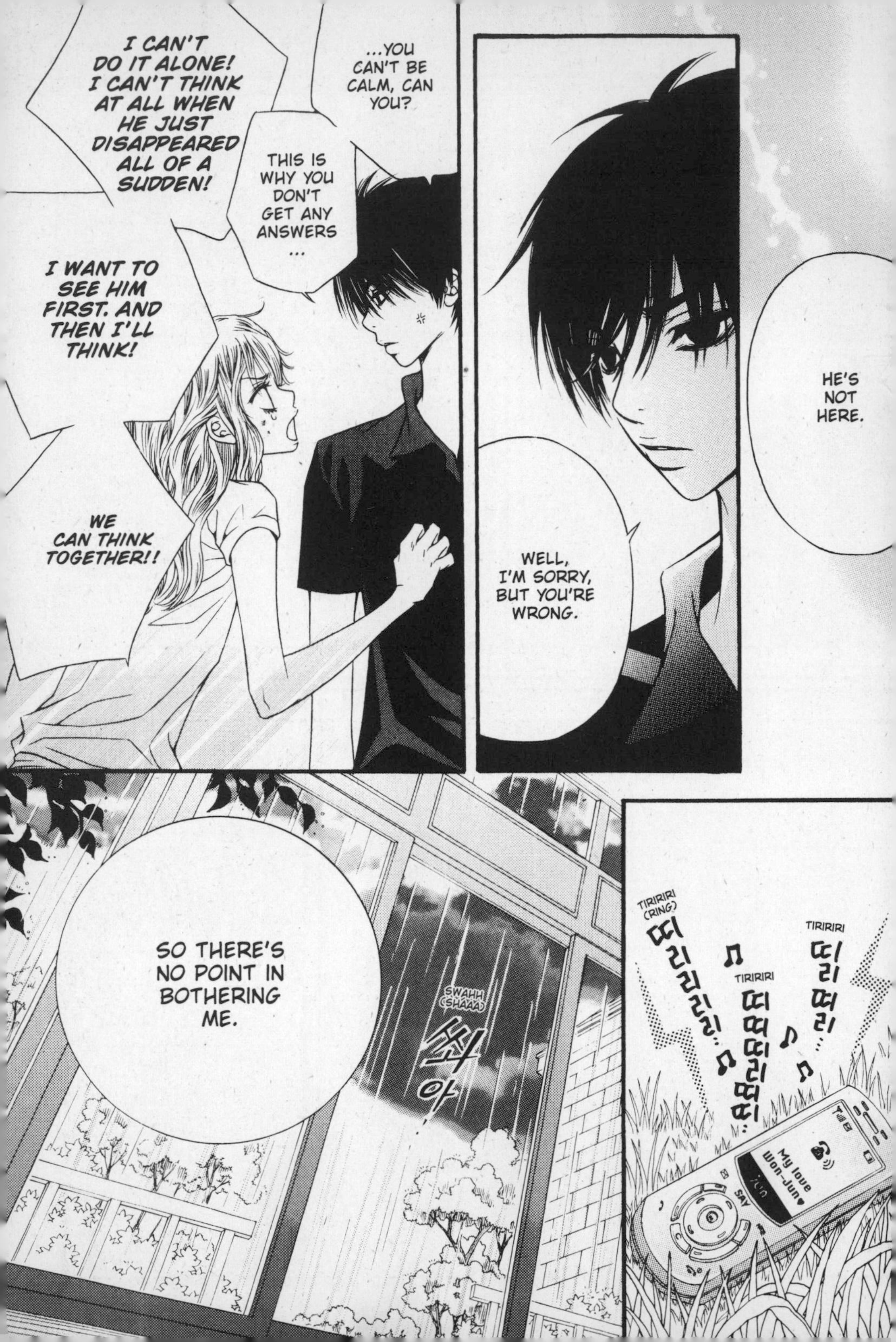
I CAN'T DO IT ALONE! I CAN'T THINK AT ALL WHEN HE JUST DISAPPEARED ALL OF A SUDDEN!
...YOU CAN'T BE CALM, CAN YOU?
THIS IS WHY YOU DON'T GET ANY ANSWERS ...
I WANT TO SEE HIM FIRST. AND THEN I'LL THINK!
WE CAN THINK TOGETHER!!
HE'S NOT HERE.
WELL, I'M SORRY, BUT YOU'RE WRONG.
SO THERE'S NO POINT IN BOTHERING ME.
SWAHH (SHAAA)
쏴아
TIRIRIRI (RING)
띠리리리…
TIRIRIRI
띠띠띠띠띠…
TIRIRIRI
띠리띠리…
My love Won-Jun♥

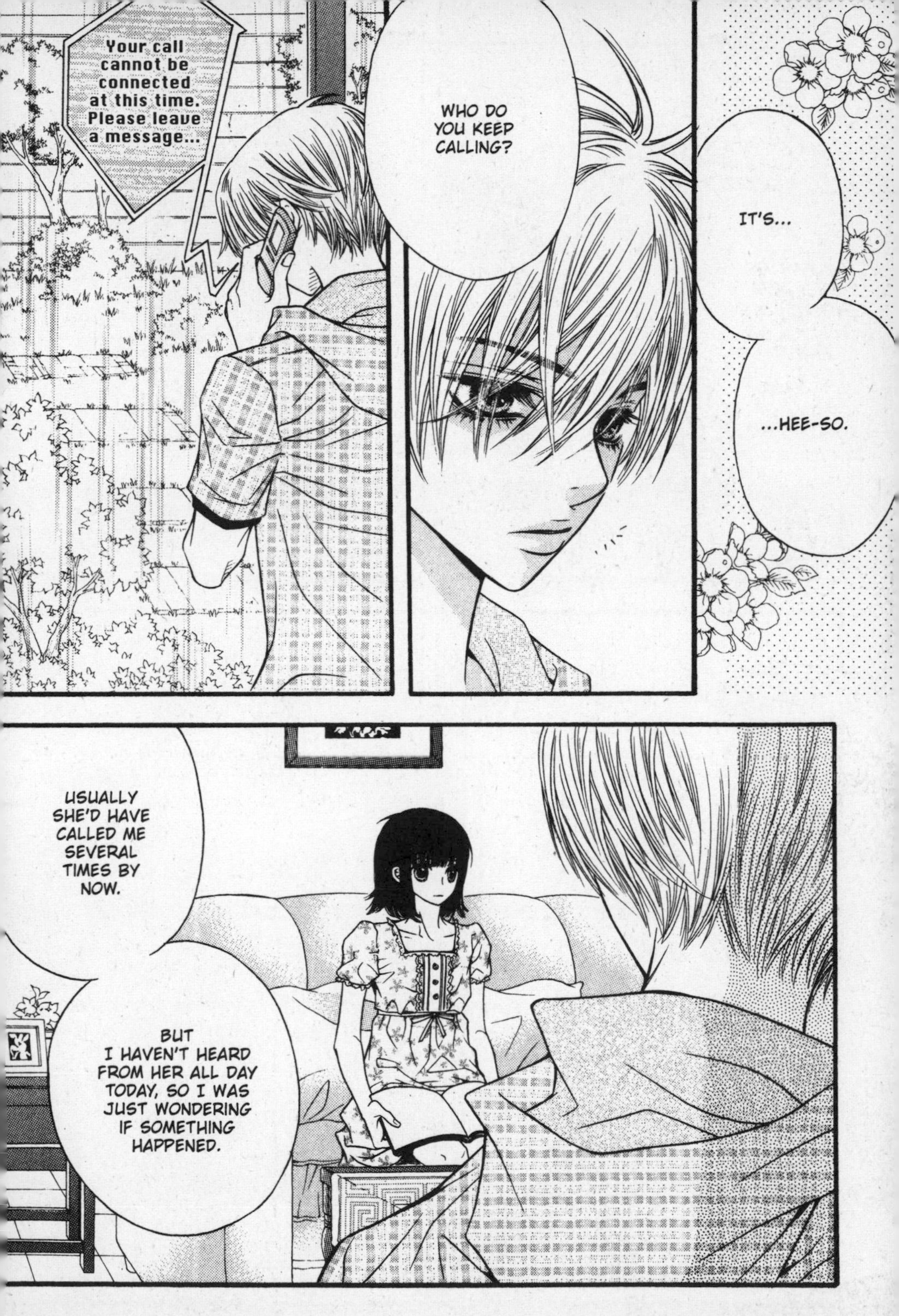
Your call cannot be connected at this time. Please leave a message...
WHO DO YOU KEEP CALLING?
IT'S...
...HEE-SO.
USUALLY SHE'D HAVE CALLED ME SEVERAL TIMES BY NOW.
BUT I HAVEN'T HEARD FROM HER ALL DAY TODAY, SO I WAS JUST WONDERING IF SOMETHING HAPPENED.

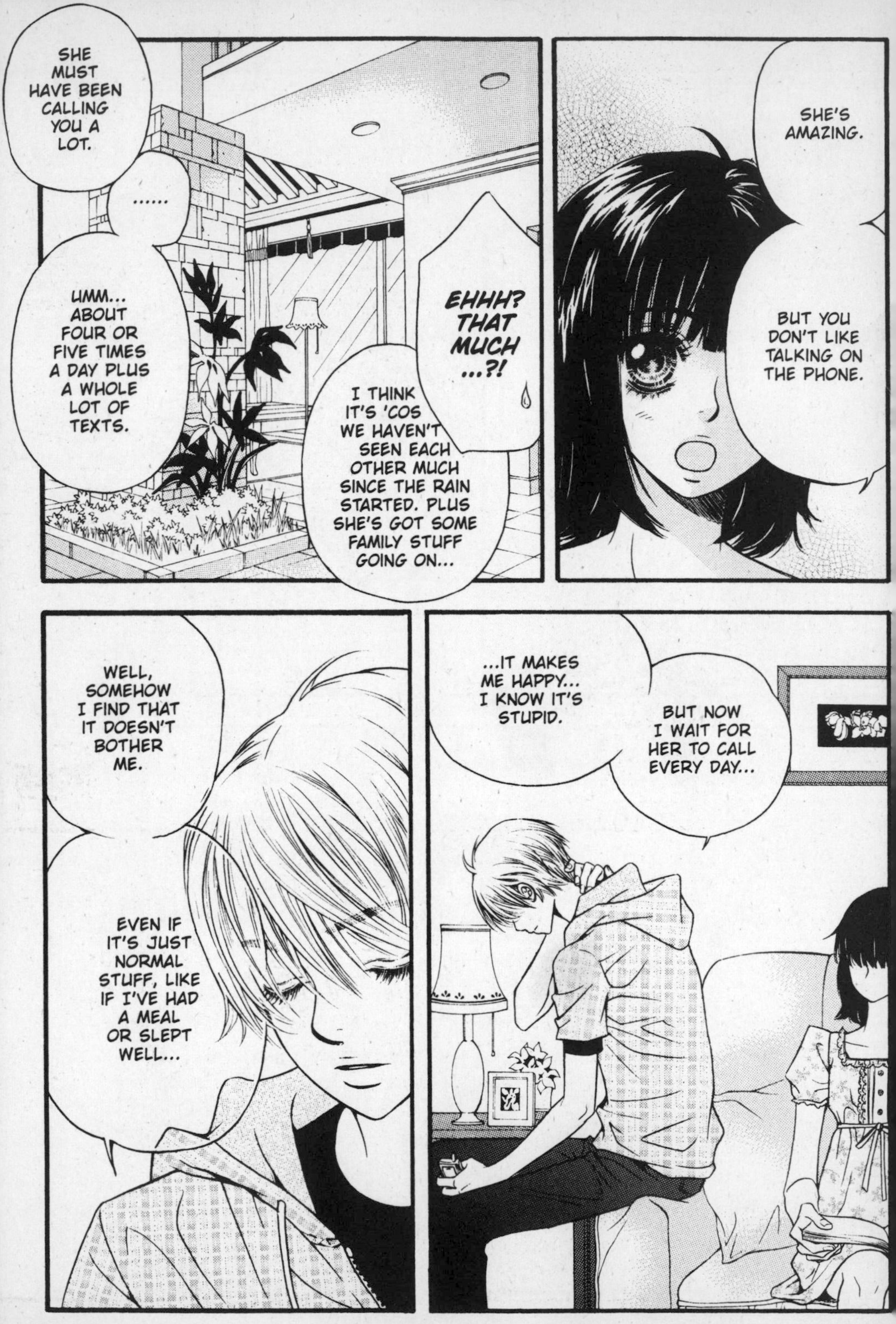
SHE MUST HAVE BEEN CALLING YOU A LOT.
......
UMM... ABOUT FOUR OR FIVE TIMES A DAY PLUS A WHOLE LOT OF TEXTS.
EHHH? THAT MUCH ...?!
I THINK IT'S 'COS WE HAVEN'T SEEN EACH OTHER MUCH SINCE THE RAIN STARTED. PLUS SHE'S GOT SOME FAMILY STUFF GOING ON...
SHE'S AMAZING.
BUT YOU DON'T LIKE TALKING ON THE PHONE.
WELL, SOMEHOW I FIND THAT IT DOESN'T BOTHER ME.
EVEN IF IT'S JUST NORMAL STUFF, LIKE IF I'VE HAD A MEAL OR SLEPT WELL...
...IT MAKES ME HAPPY... I KNOW IT'S STUPID.
BUT NOW I WAIT FOR HER TO CALL EVERY DAY...

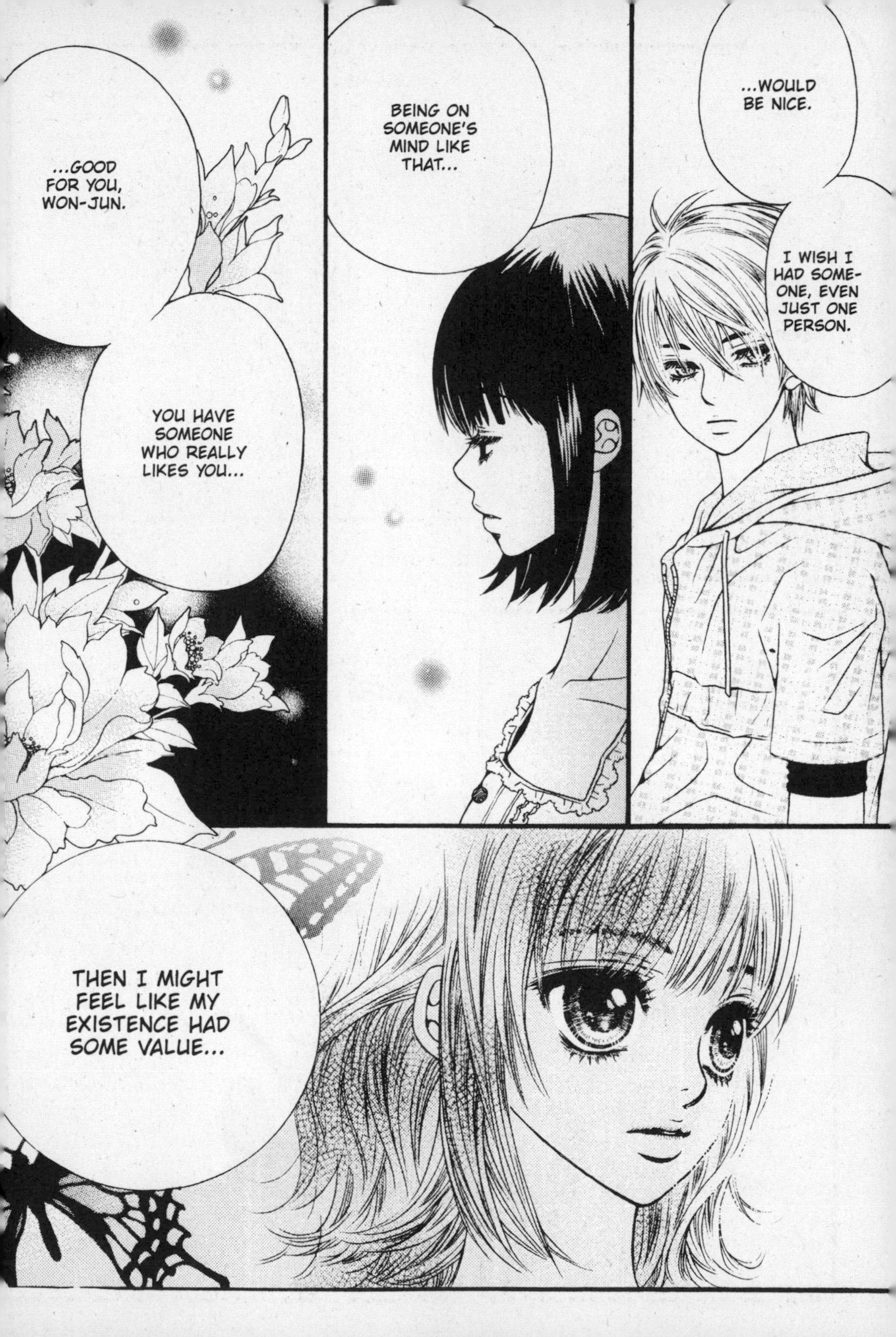
...GOOD FOR YOU, WON-JUN.
YOU HAVE SOMEONE WHO REALLY LIKES YOU...
BEING ON SOMEONE'S MIND LIKE THAT...
...WOULD BE NICE.
I WISH I HAD SOME-ONE, EVEN JUST ONE PERSON.
THEN I MIGHT FEEL LIKE MY EXISTENCE HAD SOME VALUE...

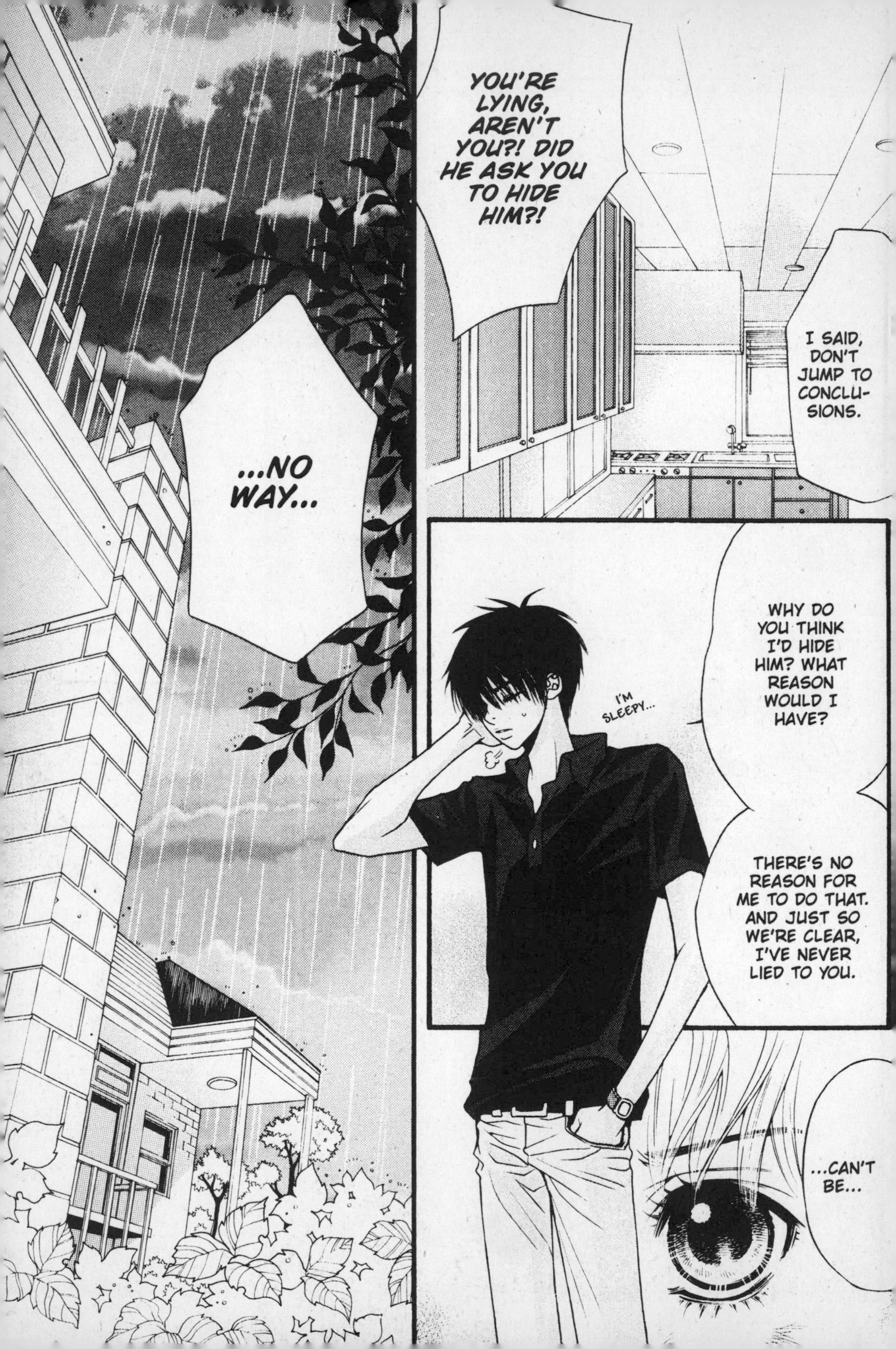
...NO WAY...
YOU'RE LYING, AREN'T YOU?! DID HE ASK YOU TO HIDE HIM?!
I SAID, DON'T JUMP TO CONCLU-SIONS.
WHY DO YOU THINK I'D HIDE HIM? WHAT REASON WOULD I HAVE?
I'M SLEEPY...
THERE'S NO REASON FOR ME TO DO THAT. AND JUST SO WE'RE CLEAR, I'VE NEVER LIED TO YOU.
...CAN'T BE...

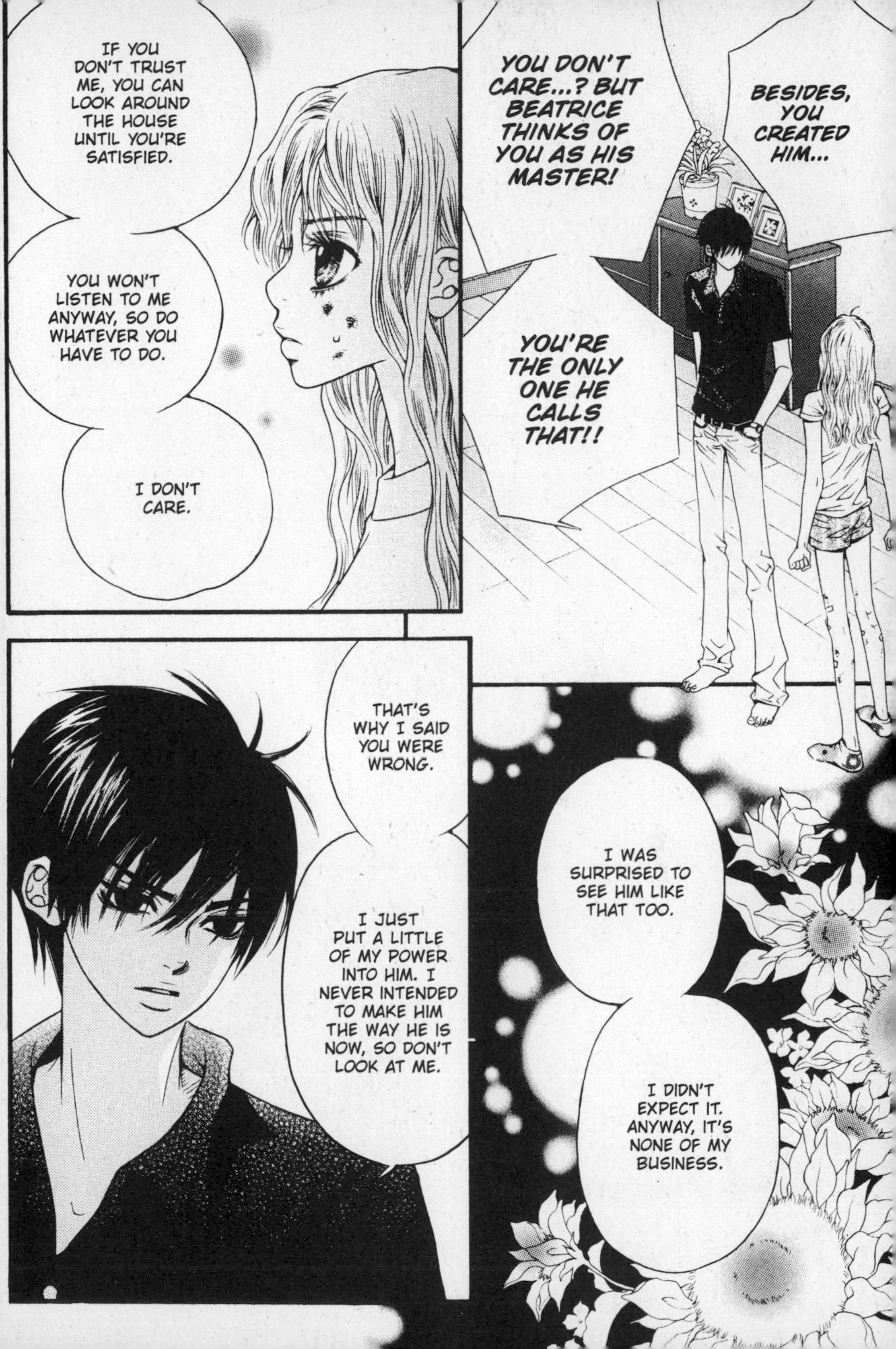

IF YOU DON'T TRUST ME, YOU CAN LOOK AROUND THE HOUSE UNTIL YOU'RE SATISFIED.
YOU WON'T LISTEN TO ME ANYWAY, SO DO WHATEVER YOU HAVE TO DO.
I DON'T CARE.
YOU DON'T CARE...? BUT BEATRICE THINKS OF YOU AS HIS MASTER!
YOU'RE THE ONLY ONE HE CALLS THAT!!
BESIDES, YOU CREATED HIM...
THAT'S WHY I SAID YOU WERE WRONG.
I JUST PUT A LITTLE OF MY POWER INTO HIM. I NEVER INTENDED TO MAKE HIM THE WAY HE IS NOW, SO DON'T LOOK AT ME.
I WAS SURPRISED TO SEE HIM LIKE THAT TOO.
I DIDN'T EXPECT IT. ANYWAY, IT'S NONE OF MY BUSINESS.

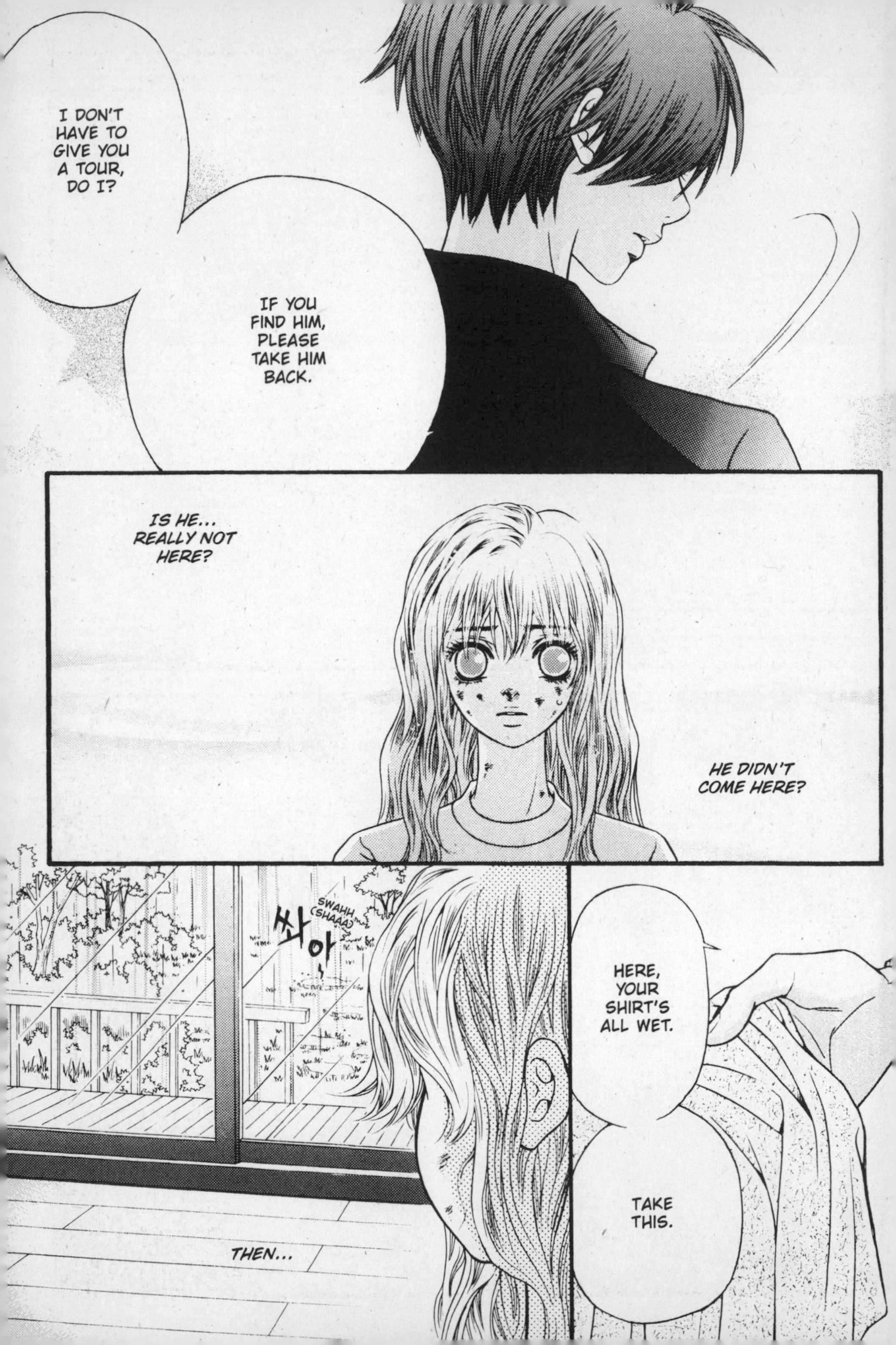

I DON'T HAVE TO GIVE YOU A TOUR, DO I?
IF YOU FIND HIM, PLEASE TAKE HIM BACK.
IS HE... REALLY NOT HERE?
HE DIDN'T COME HERE?
쏴아
SWAHH (SHAAA)
THEN...
HERE, YOUR SHIRT'S ALL WET.
TAKE THIS.

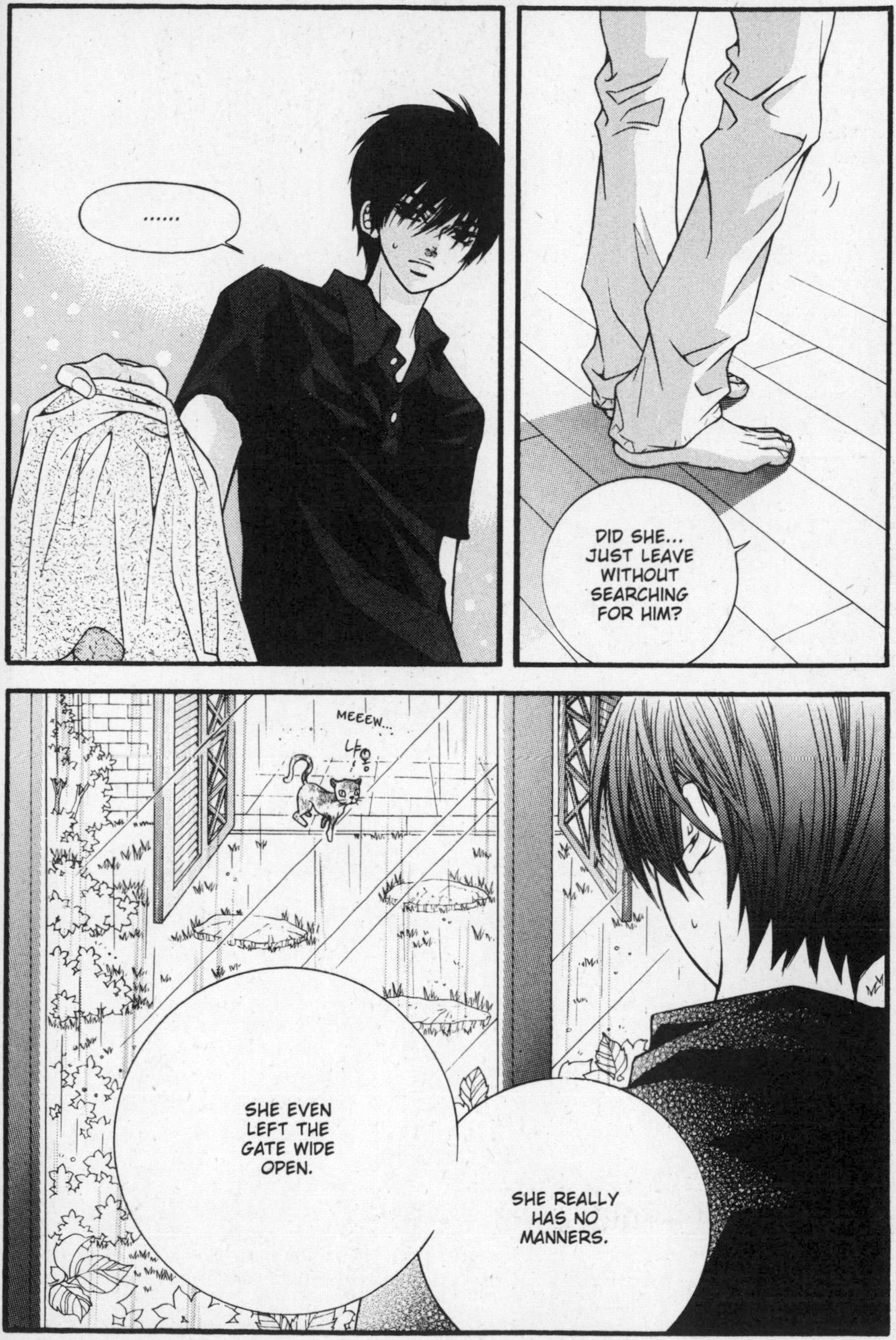
......
DID SHE... JUST LEAVE WITHOUT SEARCHING FOR HIM?
MEEEW...
SHE EVEN LEFT THE GATE WIDE OPEN.
SHE REALLY HAS NO MANNERS.

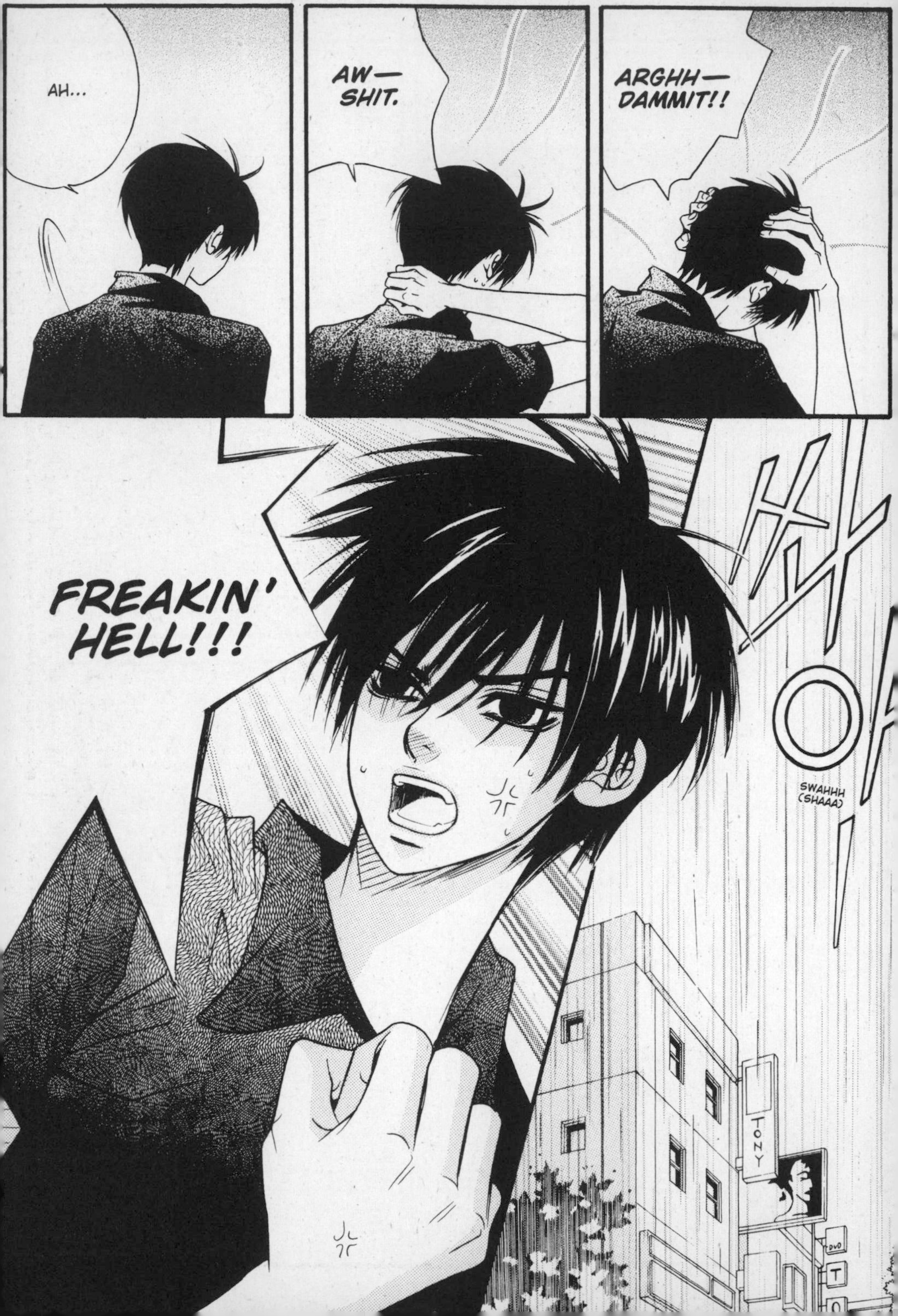
ARGHH— DAMMIT!!
AW— SHIT.
AH...
FREAKIN' HELL!!!
SWAHHH (SHAAA)
TONY

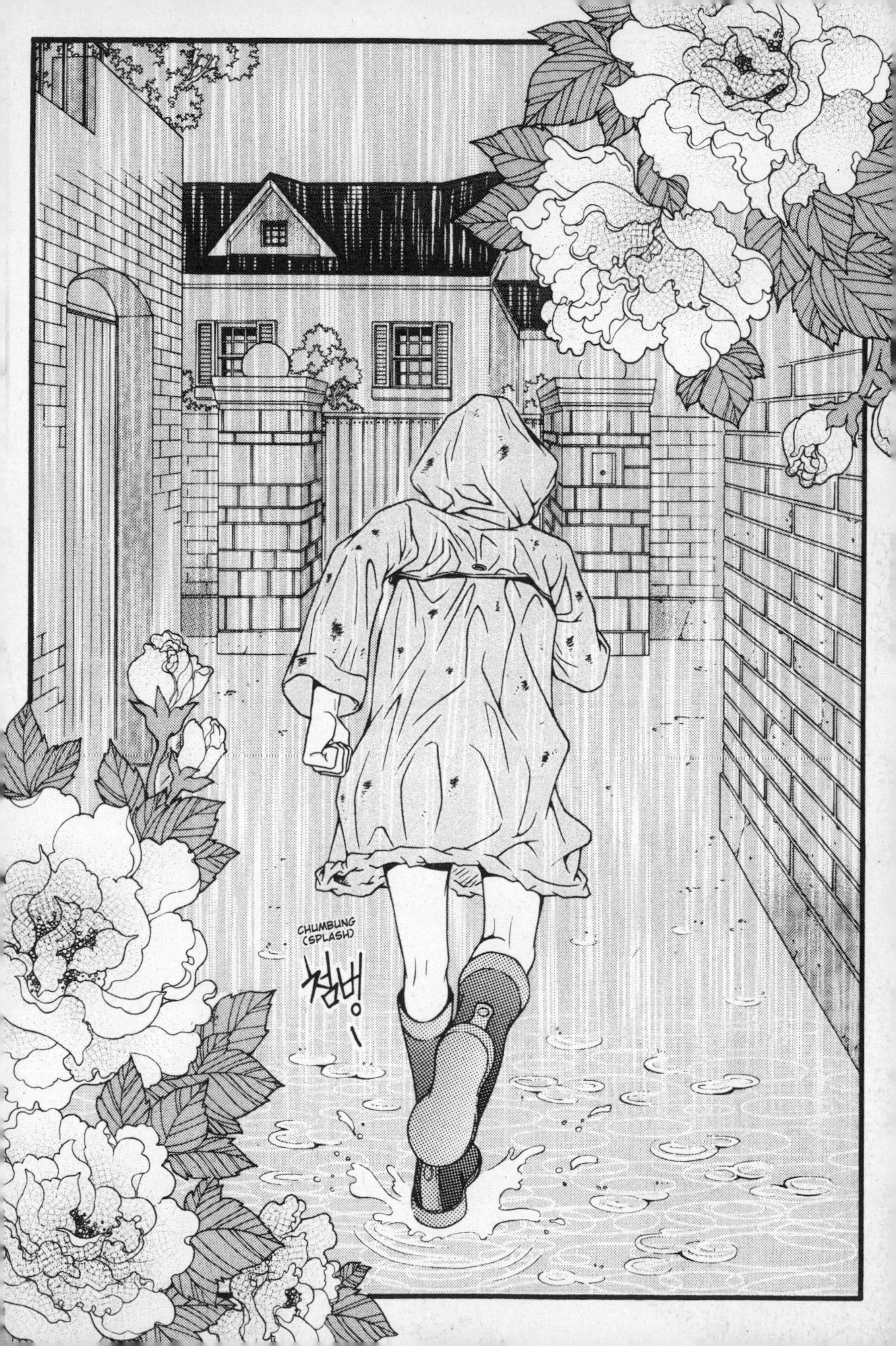
CHUMBUNG
(SPLASH)
첨벙!

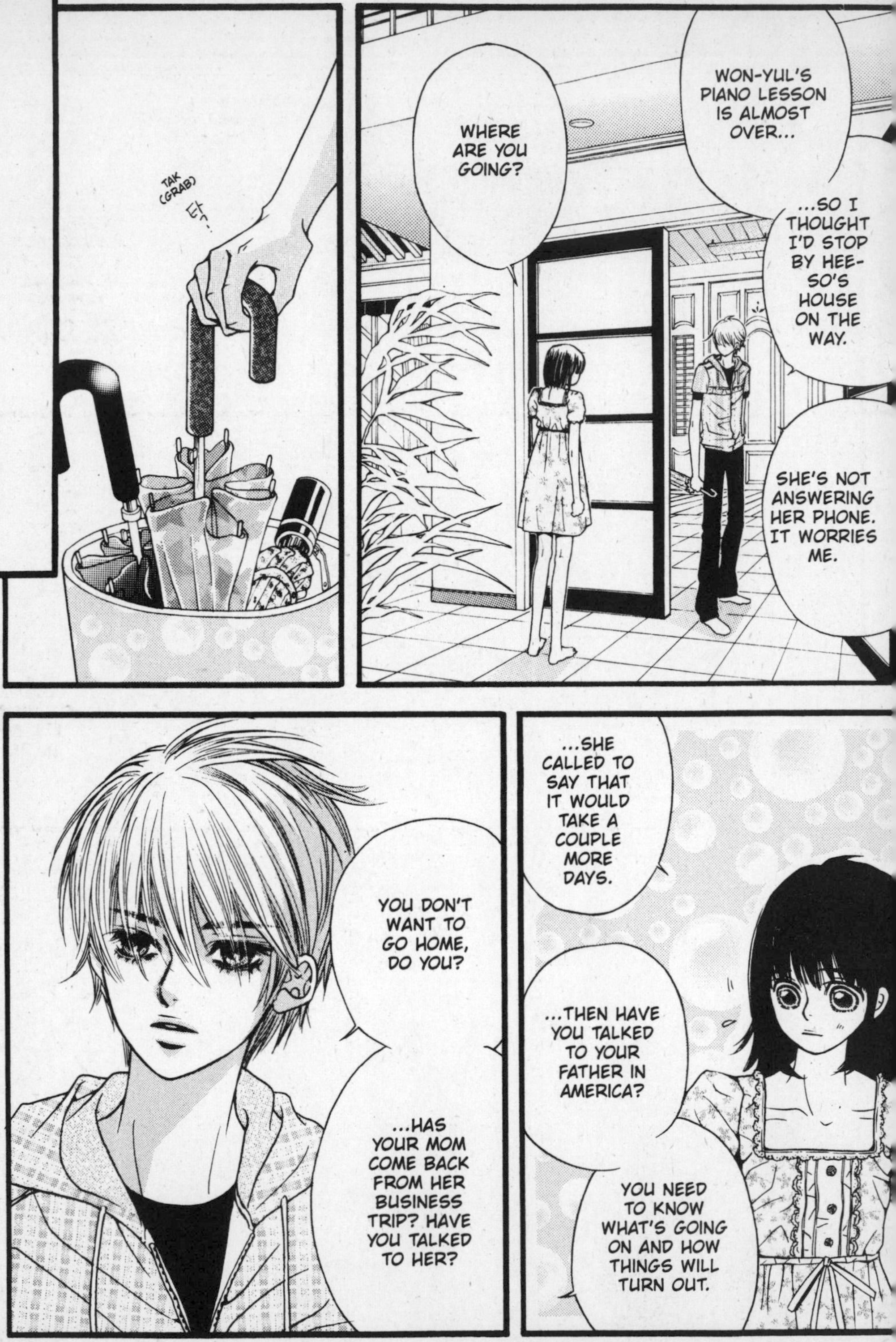

TAK (GRAB)
탁!
WHERE ARE YOU GOING?
WON-YUL'S PIANO LESSON IS ALMOST OVER...
...SO I THOUGHT I'D STOP BY HEE-SO'S HOUSE ON THE WAY.
SHE'S NOT ANSWERING HER PHONE. IT WORRIES ME.
YOU DON'T WANT TO GO HOME, DO YOU?
...HAS YOUR MOM COME BACK FROM HER BUSINESS TRIP? HAVE YOU TALKED TO HER?
...SHE CALLED TO SAY THAT IT WOULD TAKE A COUPLE MORE DAYS.
...THEN HAVE YOU TALKED TO YOUR FATHER IN AMERICA?
YOU NEED TO KNOW WHAT'S GOING ON AND HOW THINGS WILL TURN OUT.

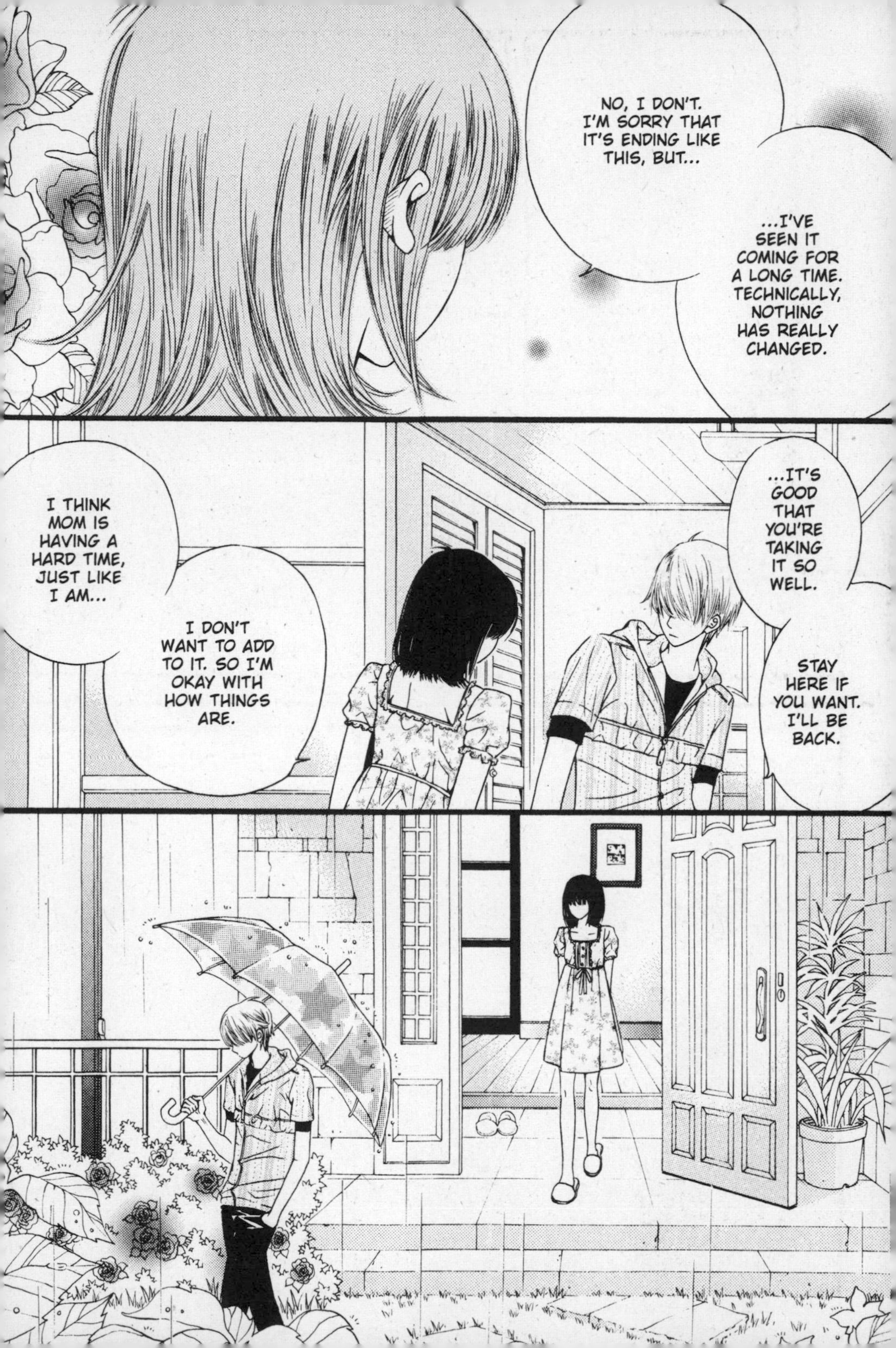
NO, I DON'T. I'M SORRY THAT IT'S ENDING LIKE THIS, BUT...
...I'VE SEEN IT COMING FOR A LONG TIME. TECHNICALLY, NOTHING HAS REALLY CHANGED.
I THINK MOM IS HAVING A HARD TIME, JUST LIKE I AM...
I DON'T WANT TO ADD TO IT. SO I'M OKAY WITH HOW THINGS ARE.
...IT'S GOOD THAT YOU'RE TAKING IT SO WELL.
STAY HERE IF YOU WANT. I'LL BE BACK.

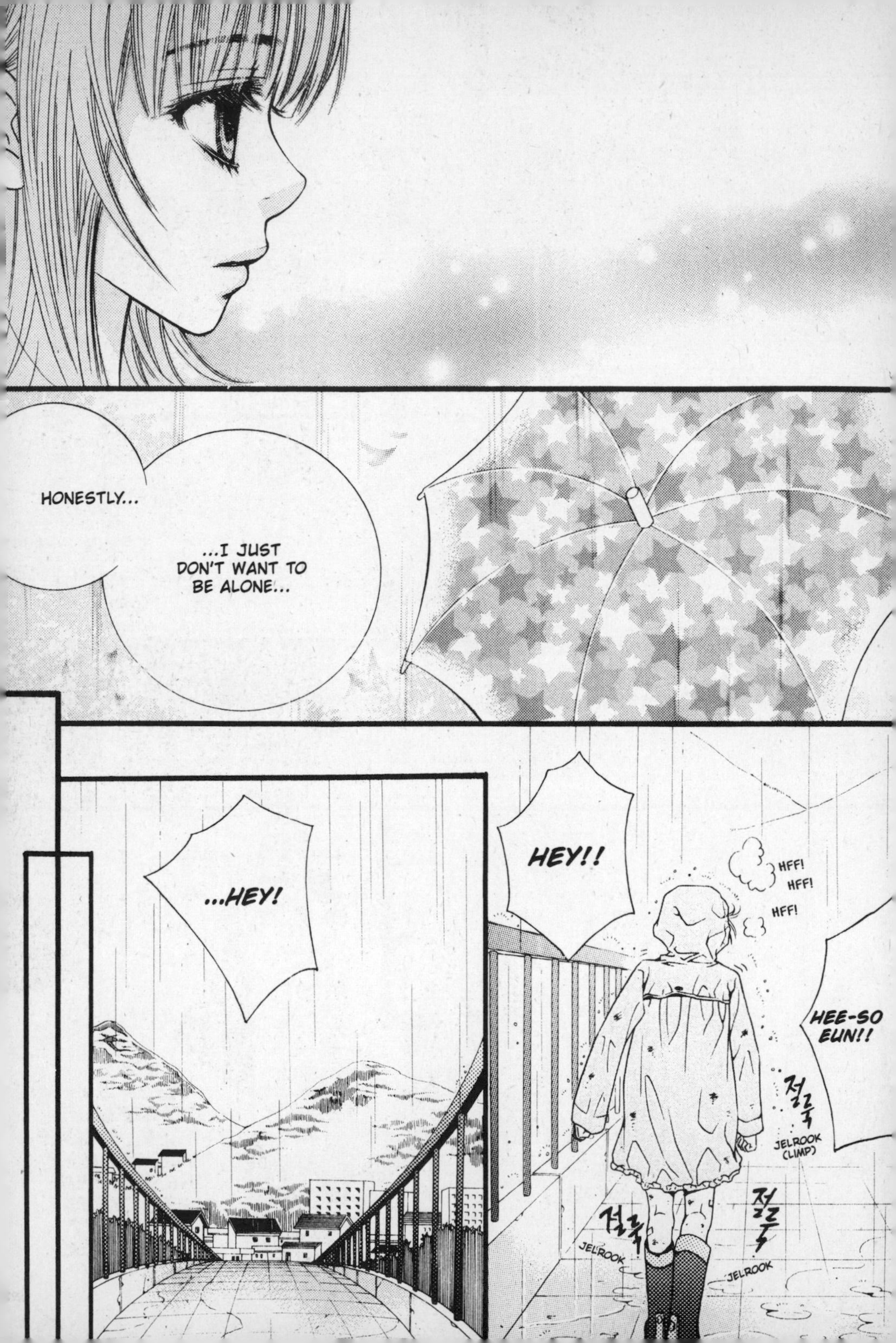
HONESTLY...
...I JUST DON'T WANT TO BE ALONE...
...HEY!
HEY!!
HFF! HFF! HFF!
HEE-SO EUN!!
절룩
JELROOK (LIMP)
절룩
JELROOK
절룩
JELROOK

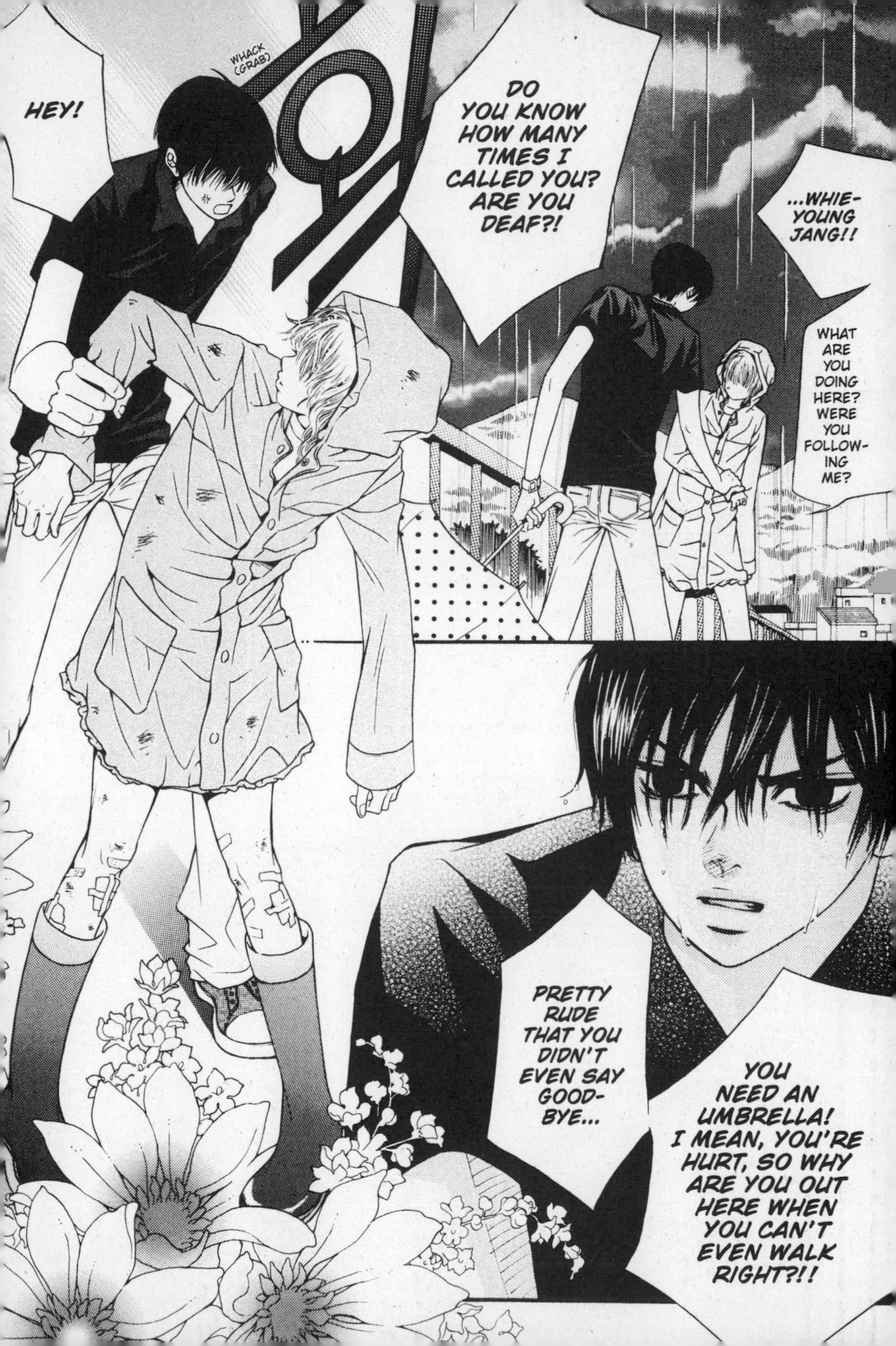
HEY!
WHACK (GRAB)
DO YOU KNOW HOW MANY TIMES I CALLED YOU? ARE YOU DEAF?!
...WHIE-YOUNG JANG!!
WHAT ARE YOU DOING HERE? WERE YOU FOLLOWING ME?
PRETTY RUDE THAT YOU DIDN'T EVEN SAY GOOD-BYE...
YOU NEED AN UMBRELLA! I MEAN, YOU'RE HURT, SO WHY ARE YOU OUT HERE WHEN YOU CAN'T EVEN WALK RIGHT?!!

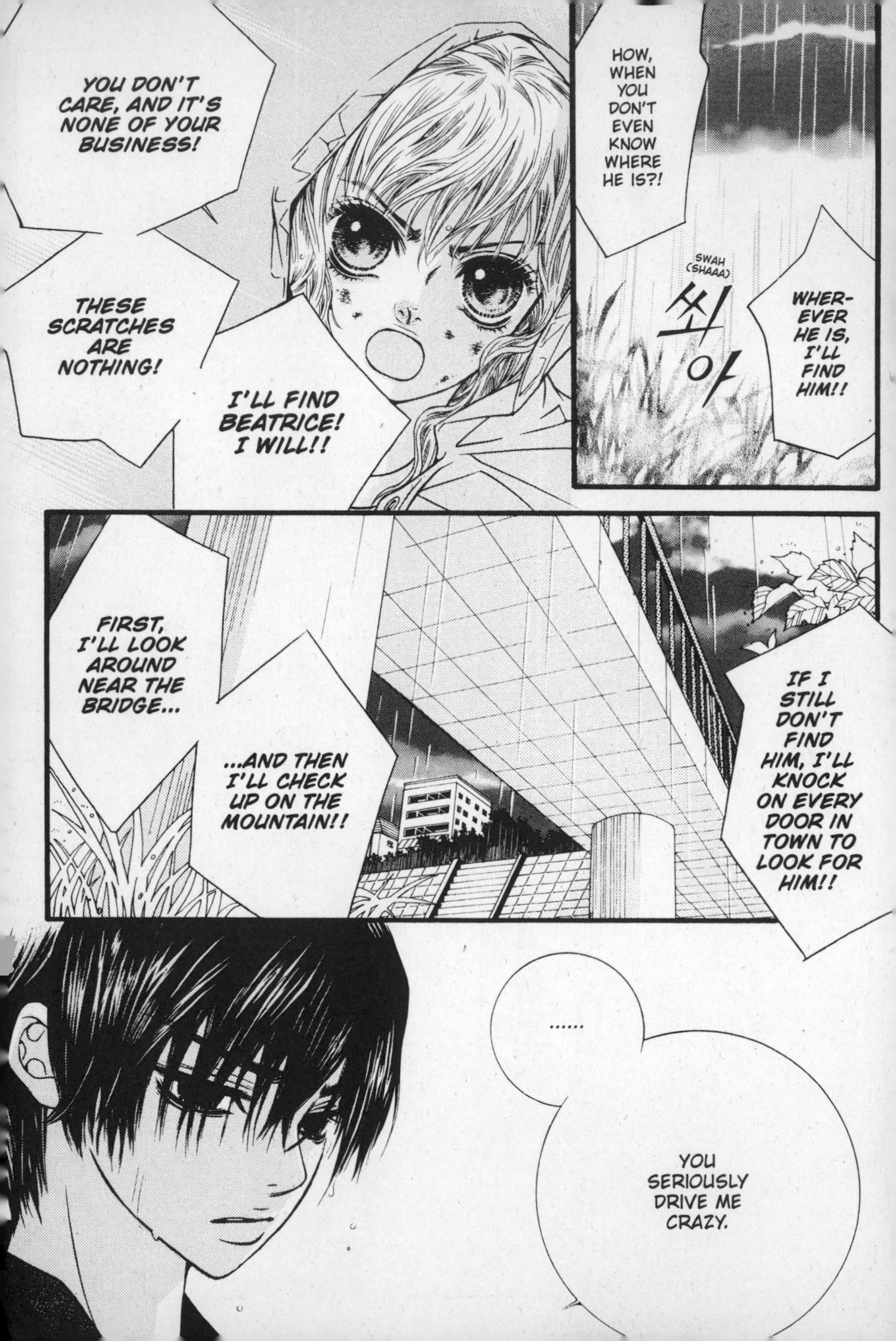
YOU DON'T CARE, AND IT'S NONE OF YOUR BUSINESS!
THESE SCRATCHES ARE NOTHING!
I'LL FIND BEATRICE! I WILL!!
HOW, WHEN YOU DON'T EVEN KNOW WHERE HE IS?!
SWAH (SHAAA)
솨아
WHER-EVER HE IS, I'LL FIND HIM!!
FIRST, I'LL LOOK AROUND NEAR THE BRIDGE...
...AND THEN I'LL CHECK UP ON THE MOUNTAIN!!
IF I STILL DON'T FIND HIM, I'LL KNOCK ON EVERY DOOR IN TOWN TO LOOK FOR HIM!!
......
YOU SERIOUSLY DRIVE ME CRAZY.

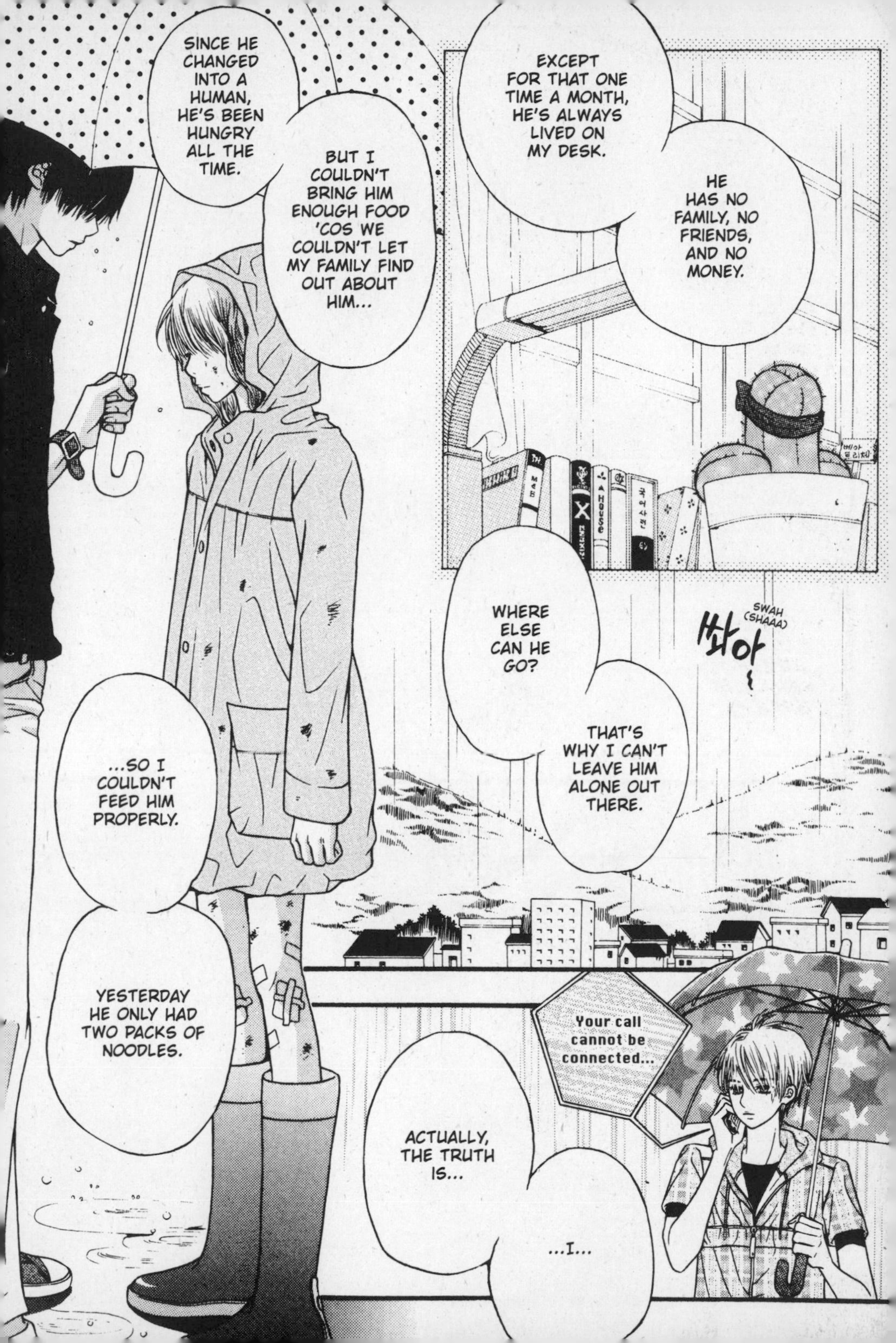
SINCE HE CHANGED INTO A HUMAN, HE'S BEEN HUNGRY ALL THE TIME.
BUT I COULDN'T BRING HIM ENOUGH FOOD 'COS WE COULDN'T LET MY FAMILY FIND OUT ABOUT HIM...
...SO I COULDN'T FEED HIM PROPERLY.
YESTERDAY HE ONLY HAD TWO PACKS OF NOODLES.
EXCEPT FOR THAT ONE TIME A MONTH, HE'S ALWAYS LIVED ON MY DESK.
HE HAS NO FAMILY, NO FRIENDS, AND NO MONEY.
WHERE ELSE CAN HE GO?
쏴아
SWAH (SHAAA)
THAT'S WHY I CAN'T LEAVE HIM ALONE OUT THERE.
Your call cannot be connected...
ACTUALLY, THE TRUTH IS...
...I...

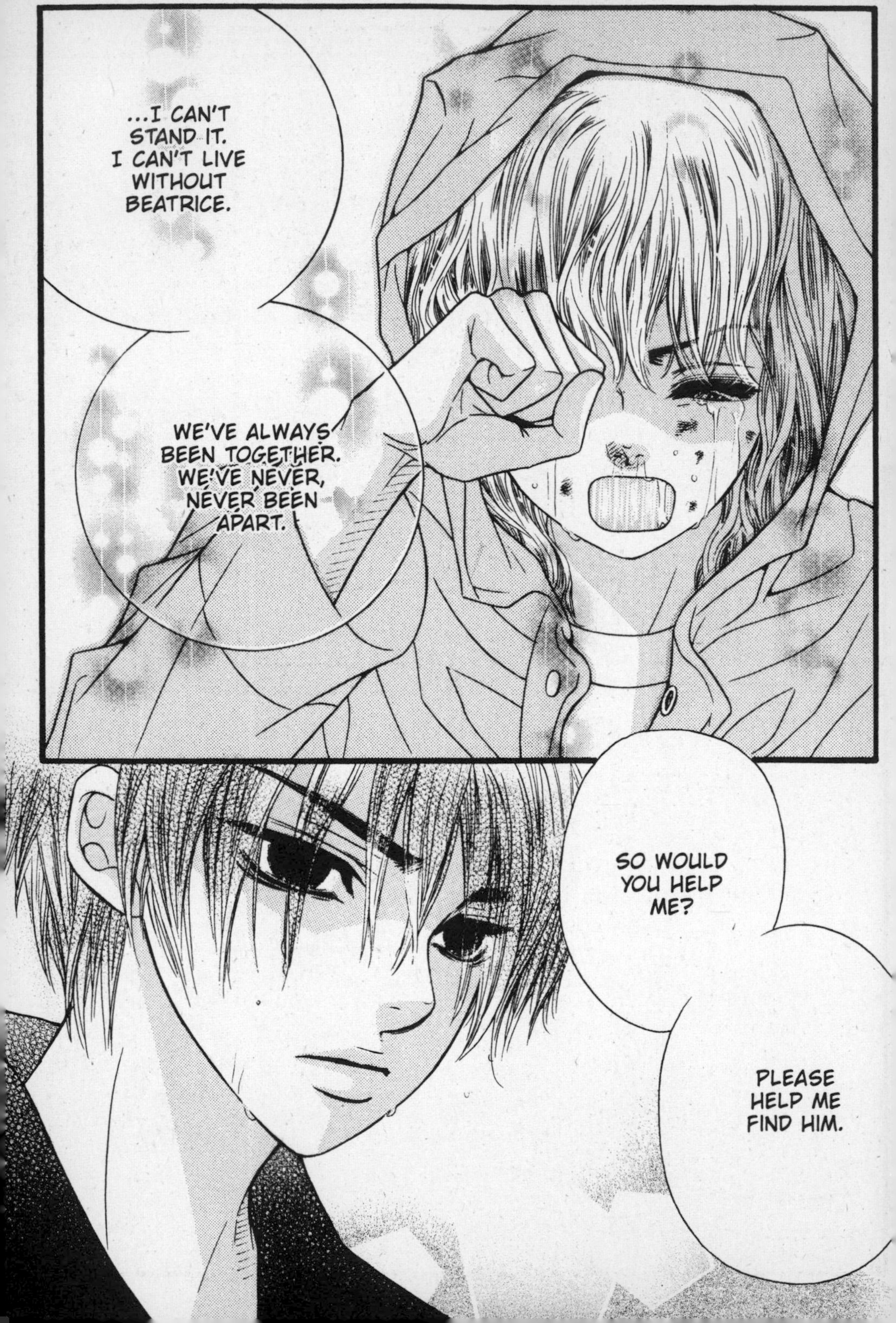
...I CAN'T STAND IT. I CAN'T LIVE WITHOUT BEATRICE.
WE'VE ALWAYS BEEN TOGETHER. WE'VE NEVER, NEVER BEEN APART.
SO WOULD YOU HELP ME?
PLEASE HELP ME FIND HIM.

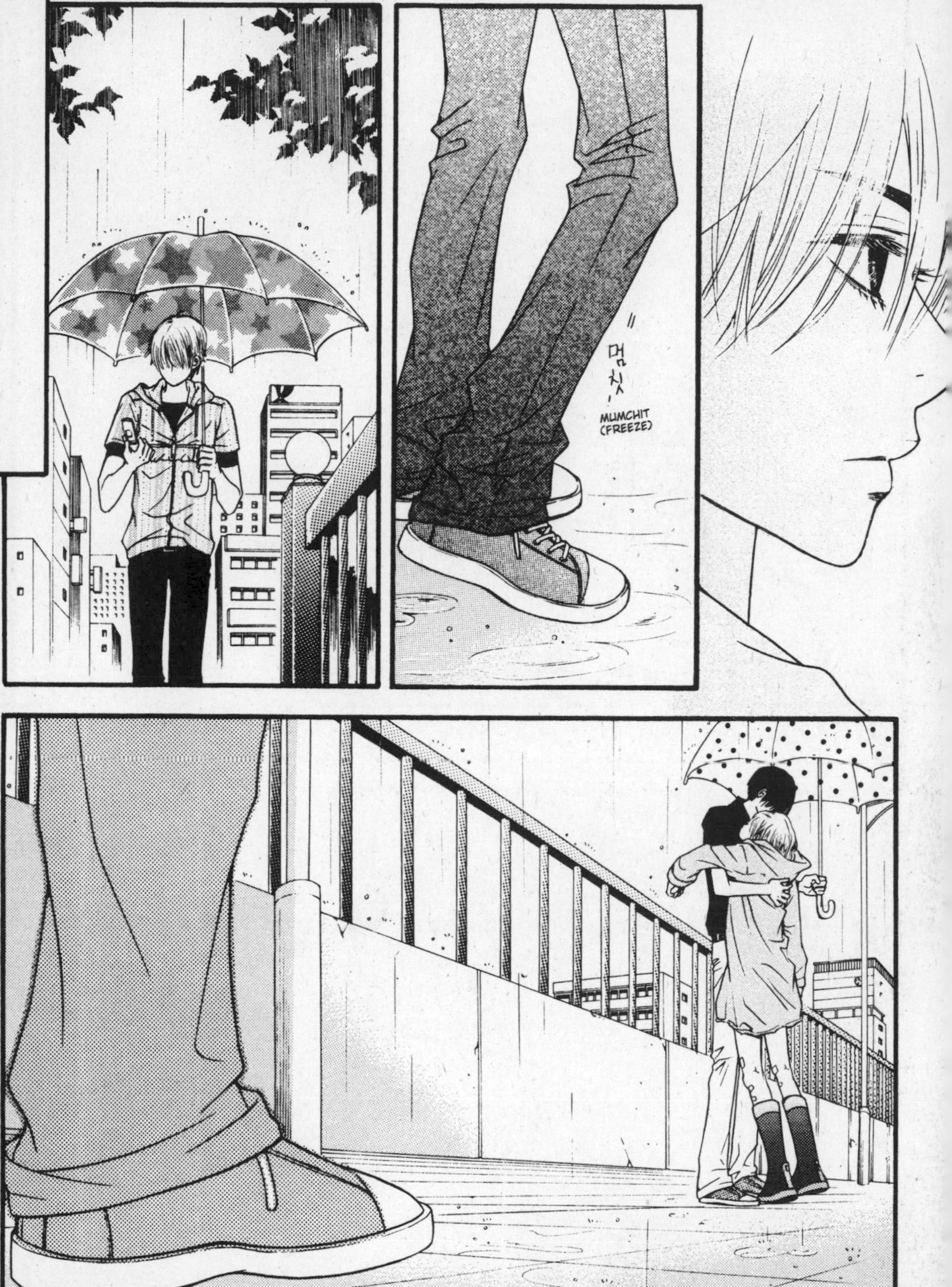
멈칫!
MUMCHIT
(FREEZE)

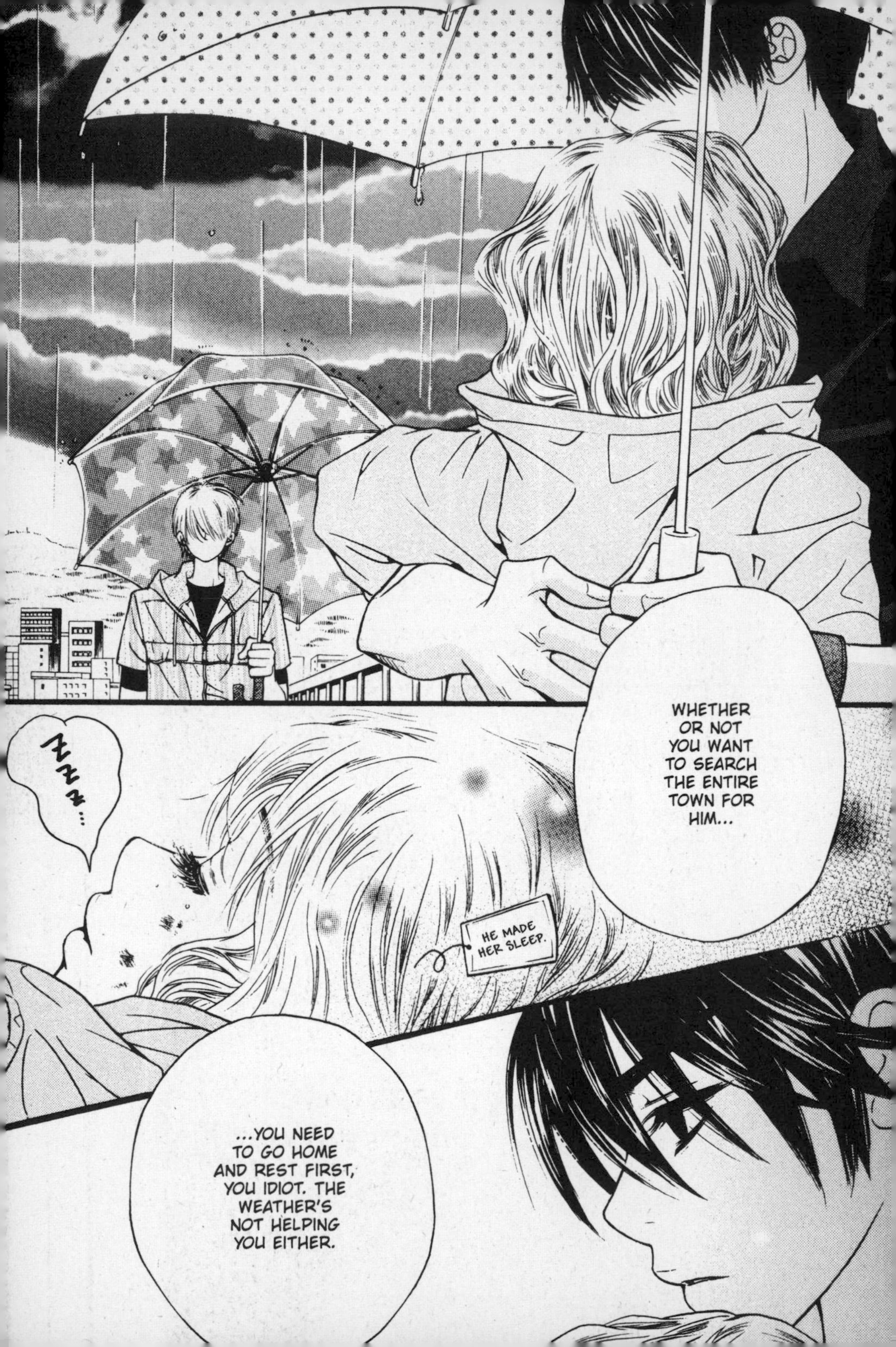
WHETHER OR NOT YOU WANT TO SEARCH THE ENTIRE TOWN FOR HIM...
ZZZ...
HE MADE HER SLEEP.
...YOU NEED TO GO HOME AND REST FIRST, YOU IDIOT. THE WEATHER'S NOT HELPING YOU EITHER.

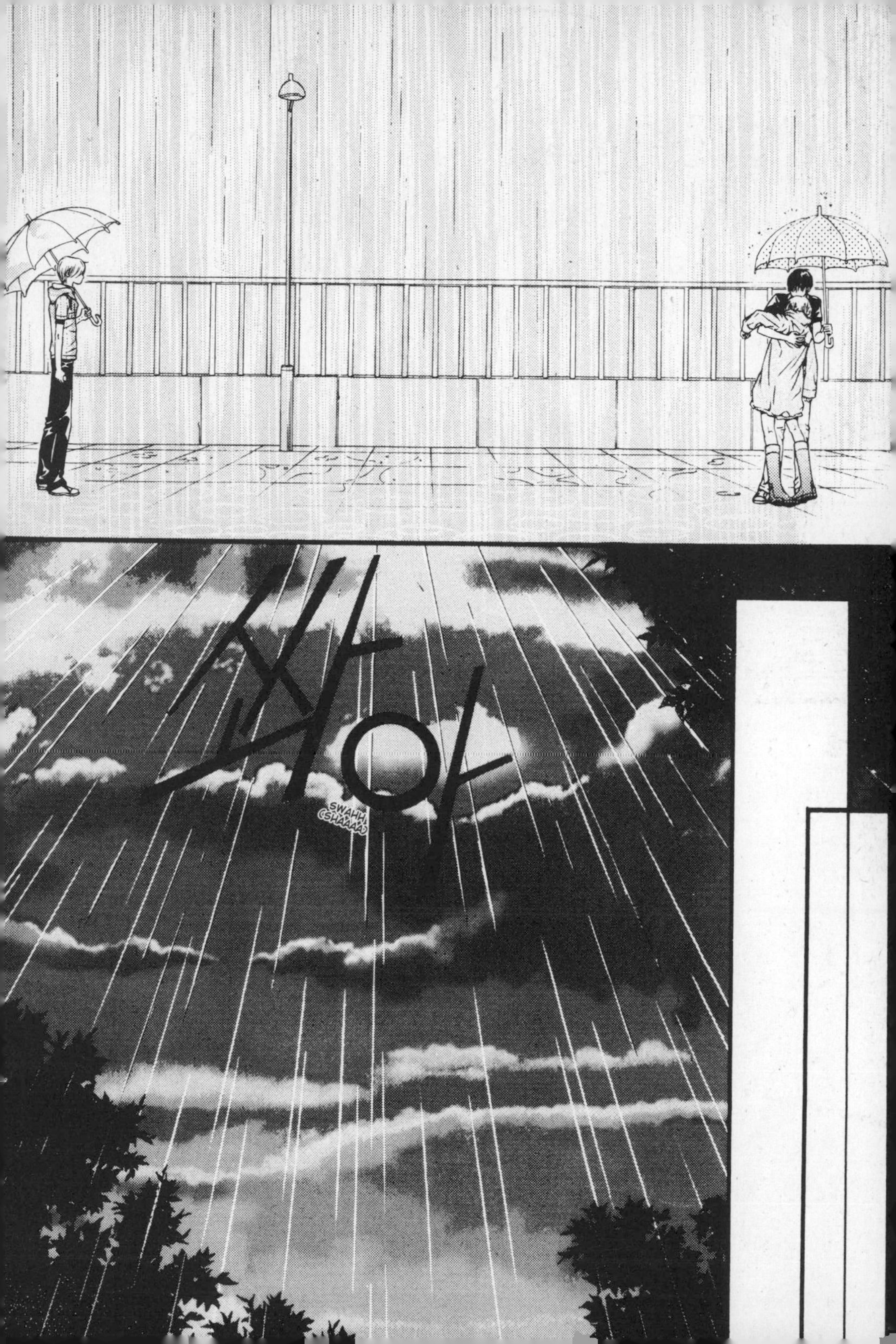
SWAHH
(SHAAAA)

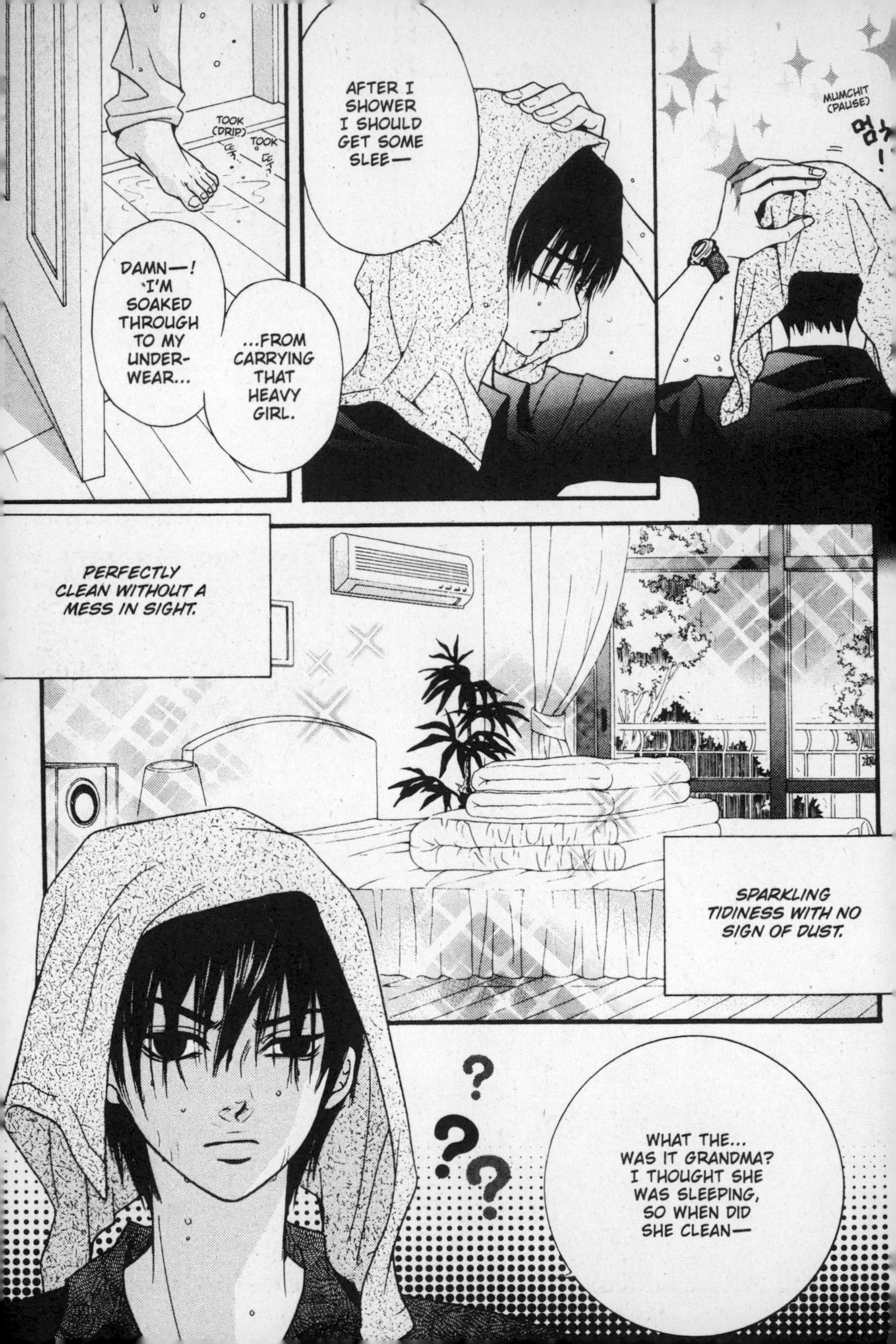

TOOK (DRIP)
TOOK
DAMN—! I'M SOAKED THROUGH TO MY UNDER-WEAR...
...FROM CARRYING THAT HEAVY GIRL.
AFTER I SHOWER I SHOULD GET SOME SLEE—
MUMCHIT (PAUSE)
멈칫!
PERFECTLY CLEAN WITHOUT A MESS IN SIGHT.
SPARKLING TIDINESS WITH NO SIGN OF DUST.
???
WHAT THE... WAS IT GRANDMA? I THOUGHT SHE WAS SLEEPING, SO WHEN DID SHE CLEAN—

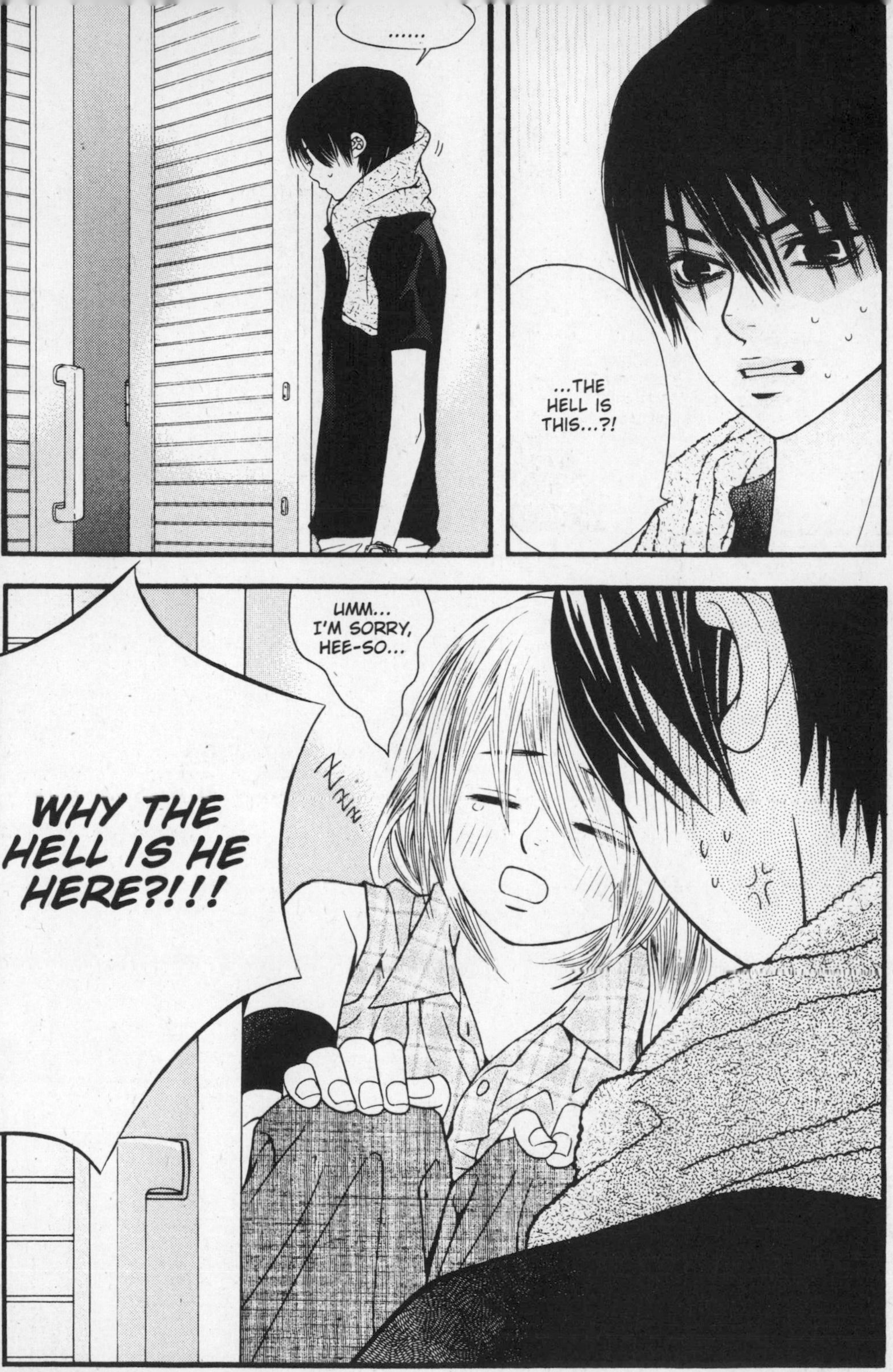
......
...THE HELL IS THIS...?!
WHY THE HELL IS HE HERE?!!!
UMM... I'M SORRY, HEE-SO...

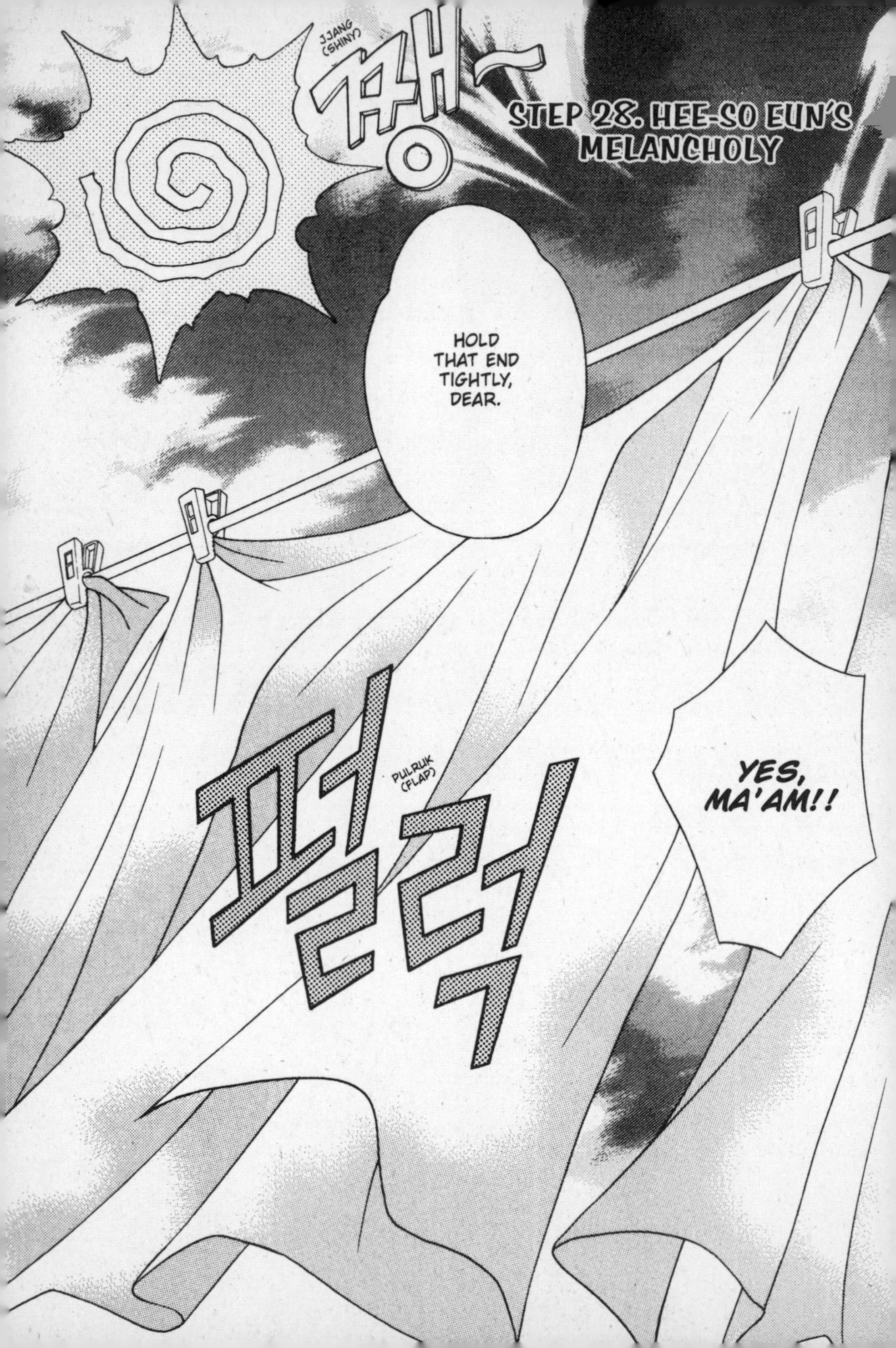
JJANG (SHINY)
짜앙
STEP 28. HEE-SO EUN'S MELANCHOLY
HOLD THAT END TIGHTLY, DEAR.
PULRUK (FLAP)
펄럭
YES, MA'AM!!

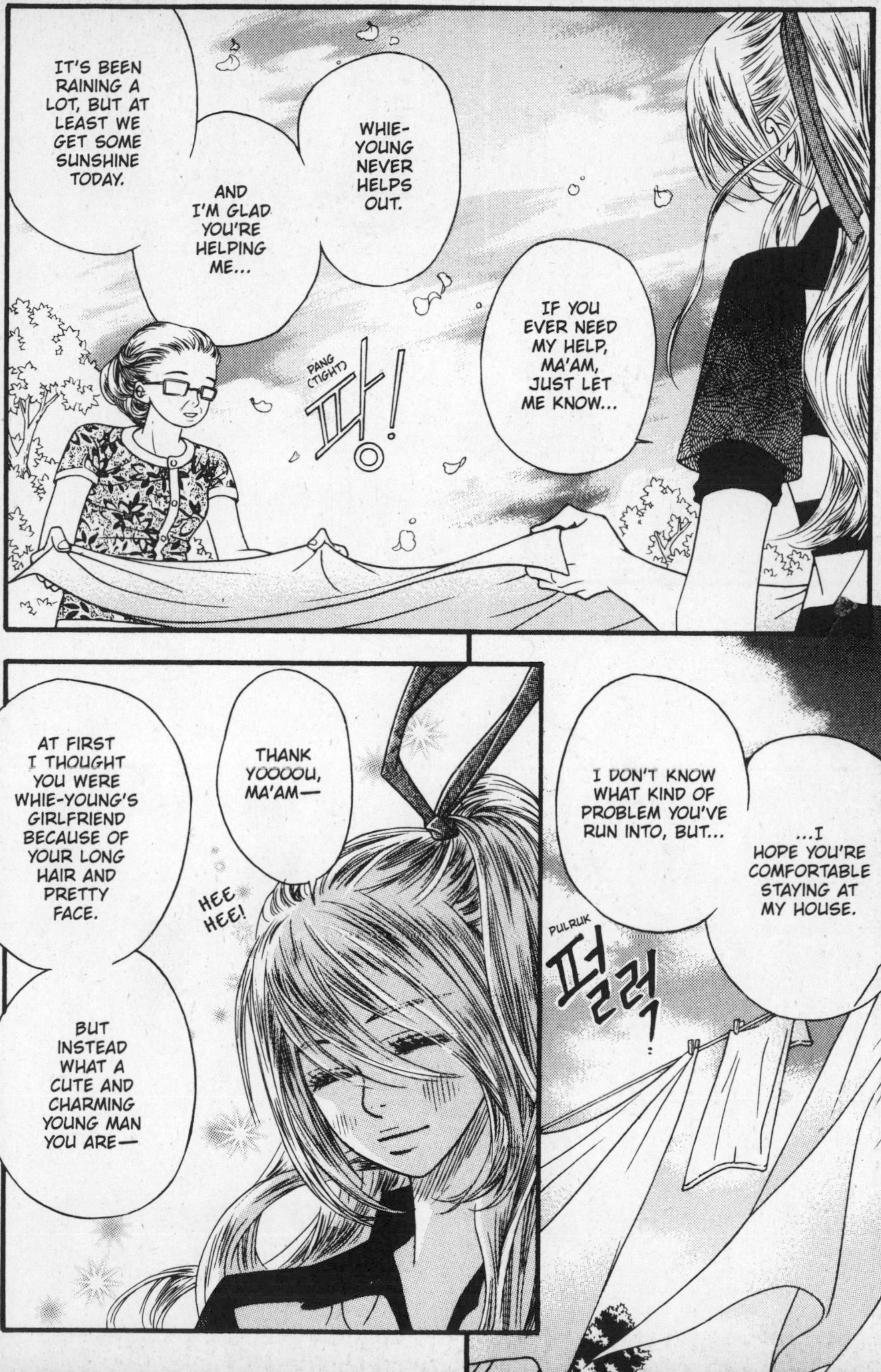
IT'S BEEN RAINING A LOT, BUT AT LEAST WE GET SOME SUNSHINE TODAY.
AND I'M GLAD YOU'RE HELPING ME...
WHIE-YOUNG NEVER HELPS OUT.
PANG (TIGHT)
팡!
IF YOU EVER NEED MY HELP, MA'AM, JUST LET ME KNOW...
AT FIRST I THOUGHT YOU WERE WHIE-YOUNG'S GIRLFRIEND BECAUSE OF YOUR LONG HAIR AND PRETTY FACE.
BUT INSTEAD WHAT A CUTE AND CHARMING YOUNG MAN YOU ARE—
THANK YOOOOU, MA'AM—
HEE HEE!
I DON'T KNOW WHAT KIND OF PROBLEM YOU'VE RUN INTO, BUT...
...I HOPE YOU'RE COMFORTABLE STAYING AT MY HOUSE.
PULRUK
펄럭!

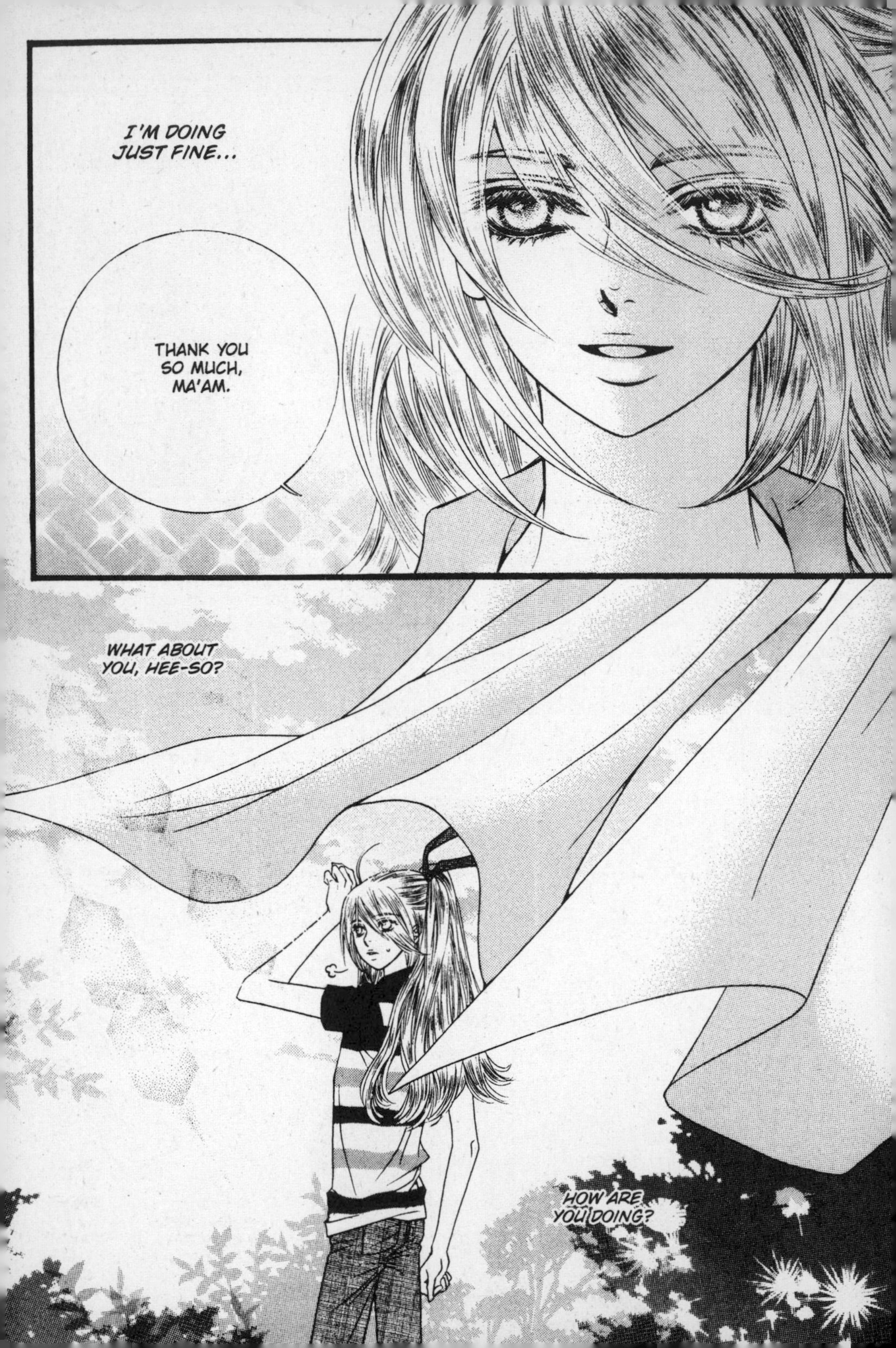
I'M DOING JUST FINE...
THANK YOU SO MUCH, MA'AM.
WHAT ABOUT YOU, HEE-SO?
HOW ARE YOU DOING?

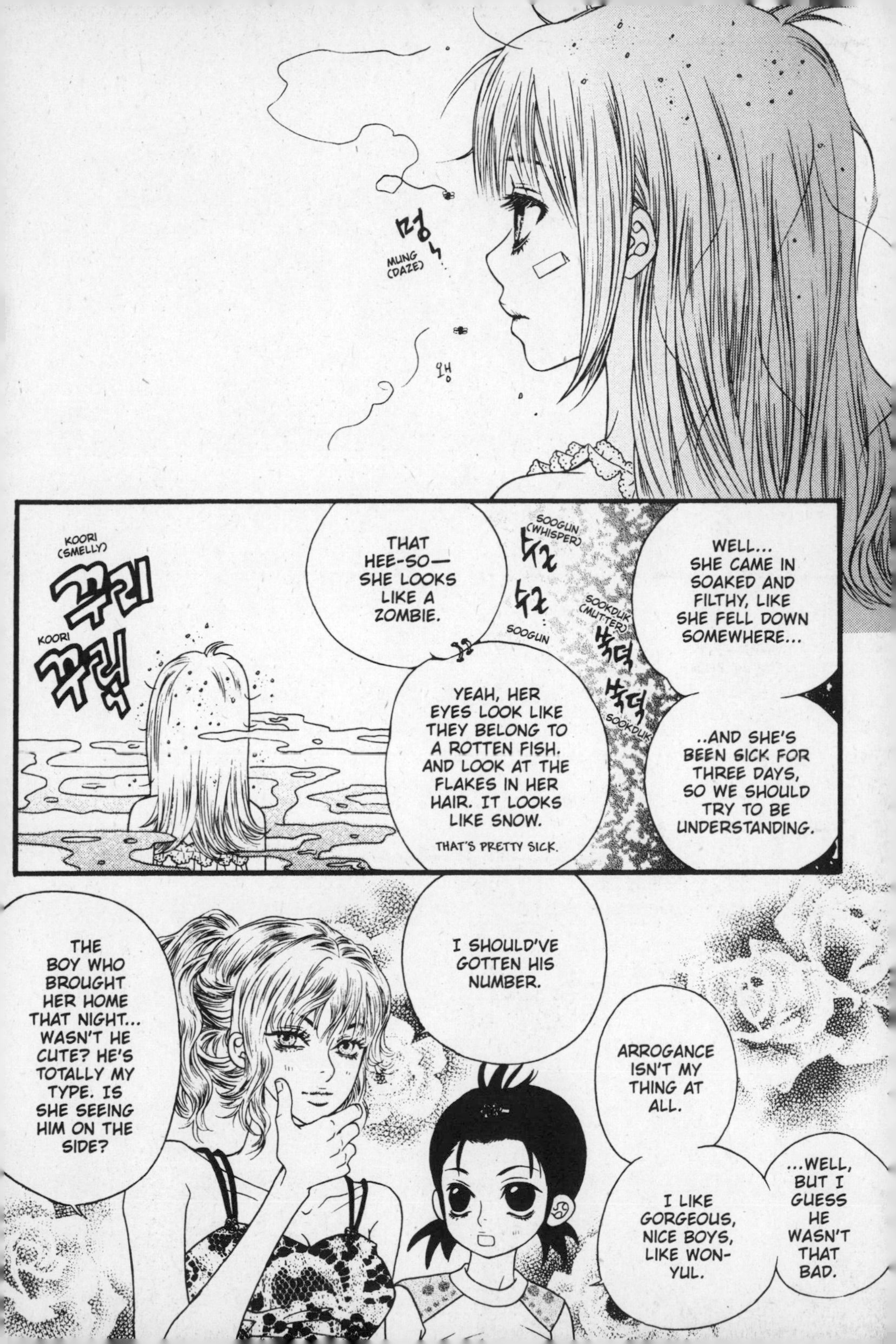

멍
MUNG (DAZE)
KOORI (SMELLY)
꾸리
KOORI
꾸릿
THAT HEE-SO— SHE LOOKS LIKE A ZOMBIE.
SOOGUN (WHISPER)
수군
수군
SOOGUN
YEAH, HER EYES LOOK LIKE THEY BELONG TO A ROTTEN FISH. AND LOOK AT THE FLAKES IN HER HAIR. IT LOOKS LIKE SNOW.
THAT'S PRETTY SICK.
SOOKDUK (MUTTER)
쑥덕
쑥덕
SOOKDUK
WELL... SHE CAME IN SOAKED AND FILTHY, LIKE SHE FELL DOWN SOMEWHERE...
..AND SHE'S BEEN SICK FOR THREE DAYS, SO WE SHOULD TRY TO BE UNDERSTANDING.
THE BOY WHO BROUGHT HER HOME THAT NIGHT... WASN'T HE CUTE? HE'S TOTALLY MY TYPE. IS SHE SEEING HIM ON THE SIDE?
I SHOULD'VE GOTTEN HIS NUMBER.
ARROGANCE ISN'T MY THING AT ALL.
I LIKE GORGEOUS, NICE BOYS, LIKE WON-YUL.
...WELL, BUT I GUESS HE WASN'T THAT BAD.

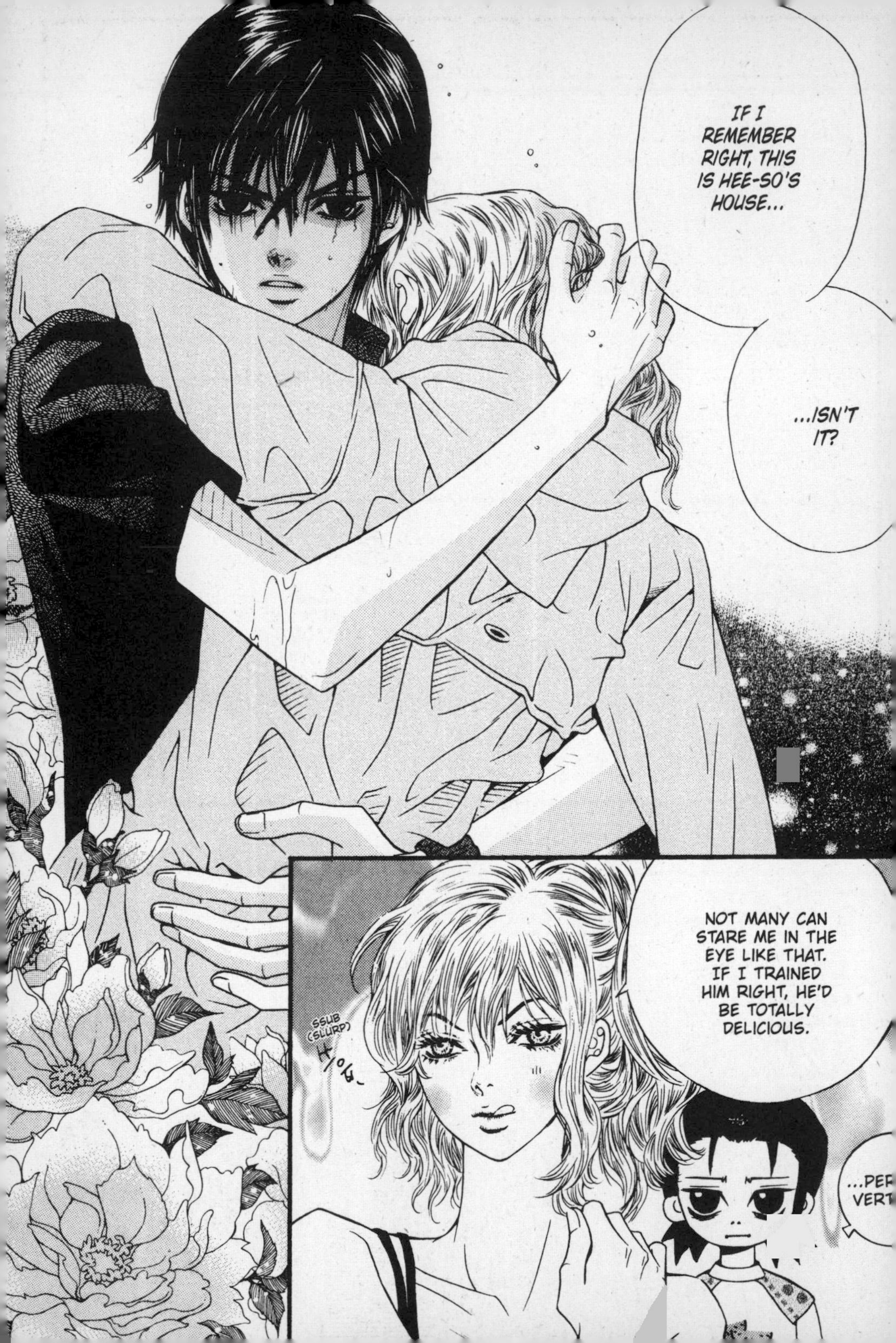
IF I REMEMBER RIGHT, THIS IS HEE-SO'S HOUSE...
...ISN'T IT?
SSUB (SLURP)
NOT MANY CAN STARE ME IN THE EYE LIKE THAT. IF I TRAINED HIM RIGHT, HE'D BE TOTALLY DELICIOUS.
...PER VERT

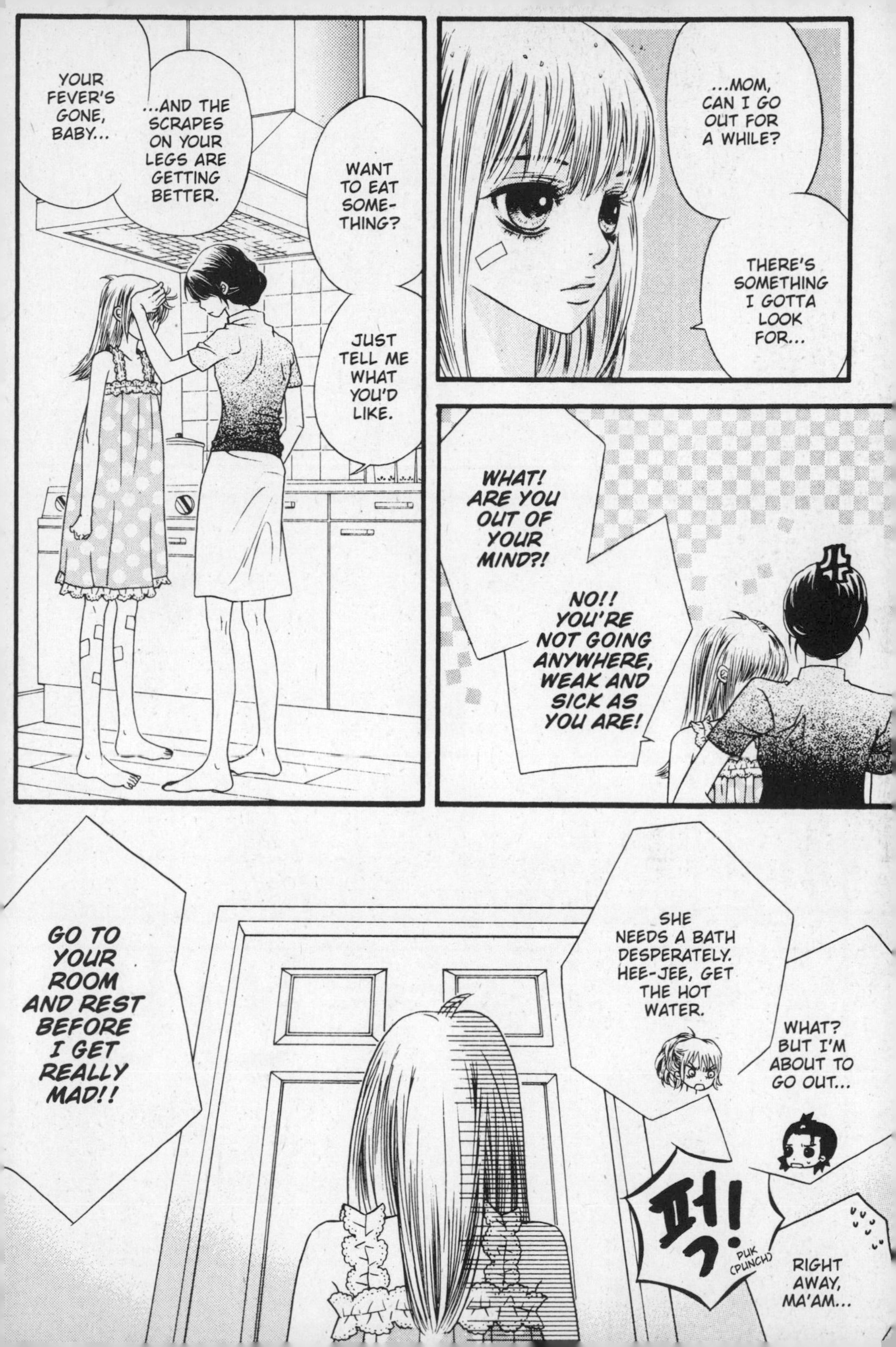
YOUR FEVER'S GONE, BABY...
...AND THE SCRAPES ON YOUR LEGS ARE GETTING BETTER.
WANT TO EAT SOME-THING?
JUST TELL ME WHAT YOU'D LIKE.
...MOM, CAN I GO OUT FOR A WHILE?
THERE'S SOMETHING I GOTTA LOOK FOR...
WHAT! ARE YOU OUT OF YOUR MIND?!
NO!! YOU'RE NOT GOING ANYWHERE, WEAK AND SICK AS YOU ARE!
GO TO YOUR ROOM AND REST BEFORE I GET REALLY MAD!!
SHE NEEDS A BATH DESPERATELY. HEE-JEE, GET THE HOT WATER.
WHAT? BUT I'M ABOUT TO GO OUT...
퍽!
PUK (PUNCH)
RIGHT AWAY, MA'AM...

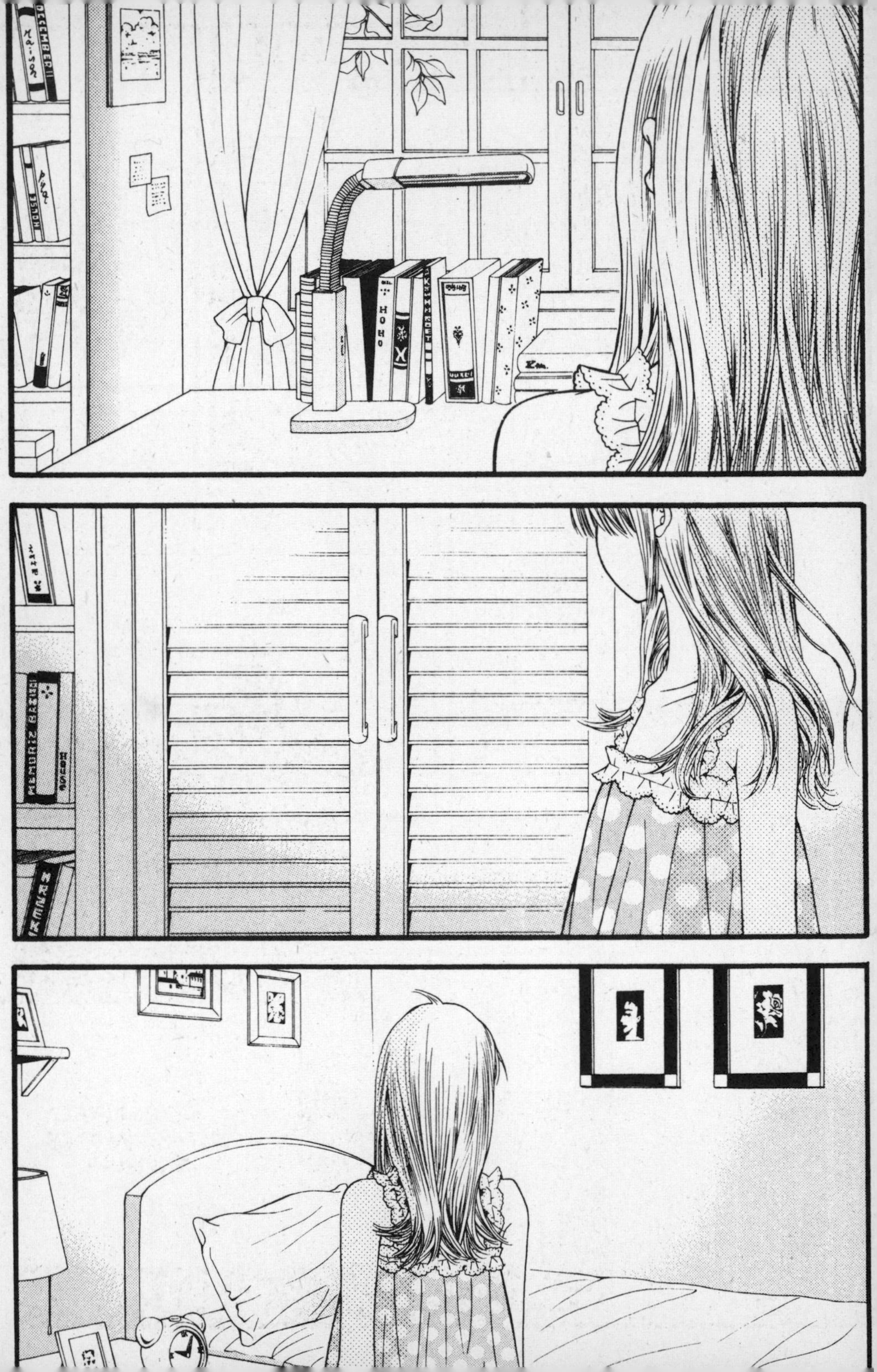

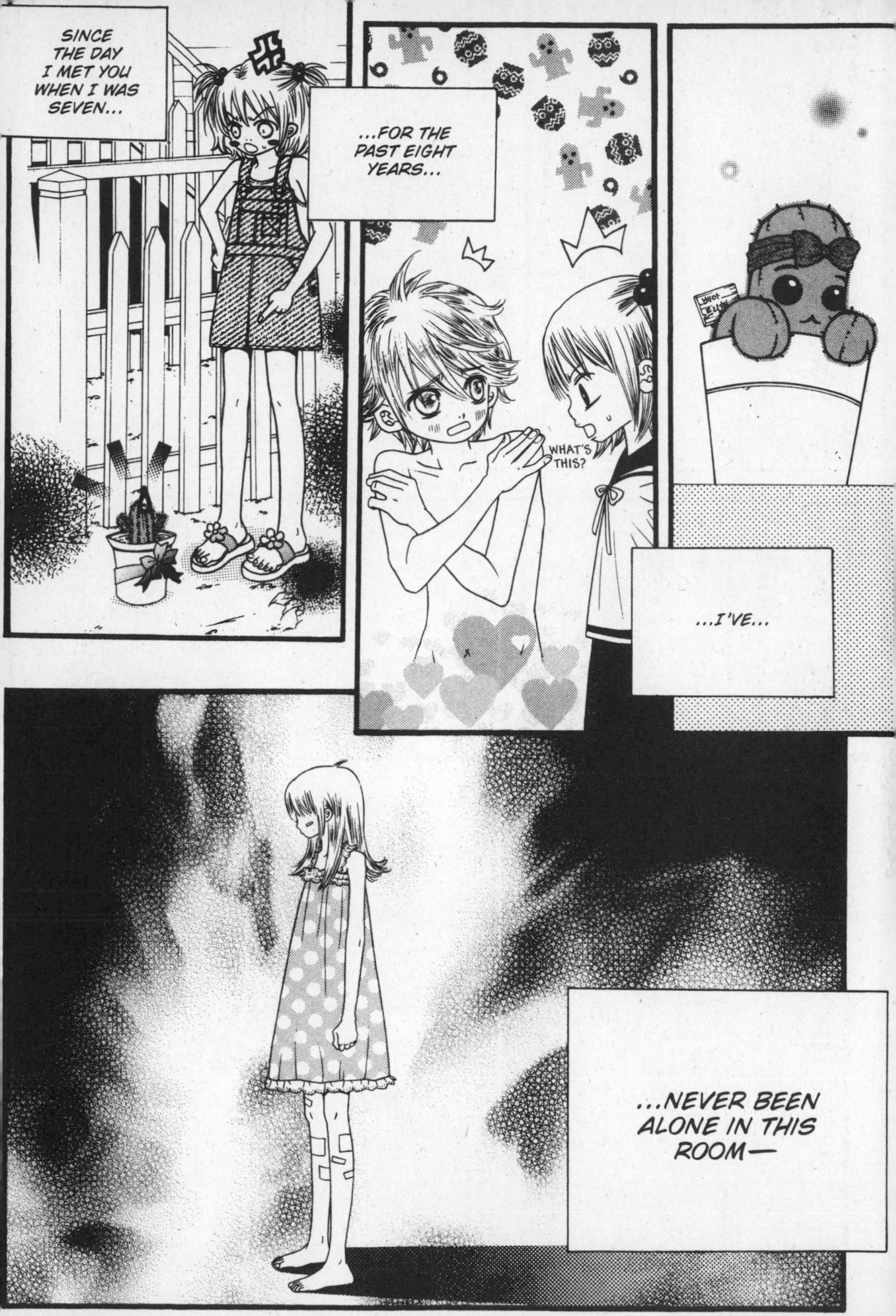
SINCE THE DAY I MET YOU WHEN I WAS SEVEN...
...FOR THE PAST EIGHT YEARS...
WHAT'S THIS?
...I'VE...
...NEVER BEEN ALONE IN THIS ROOM—

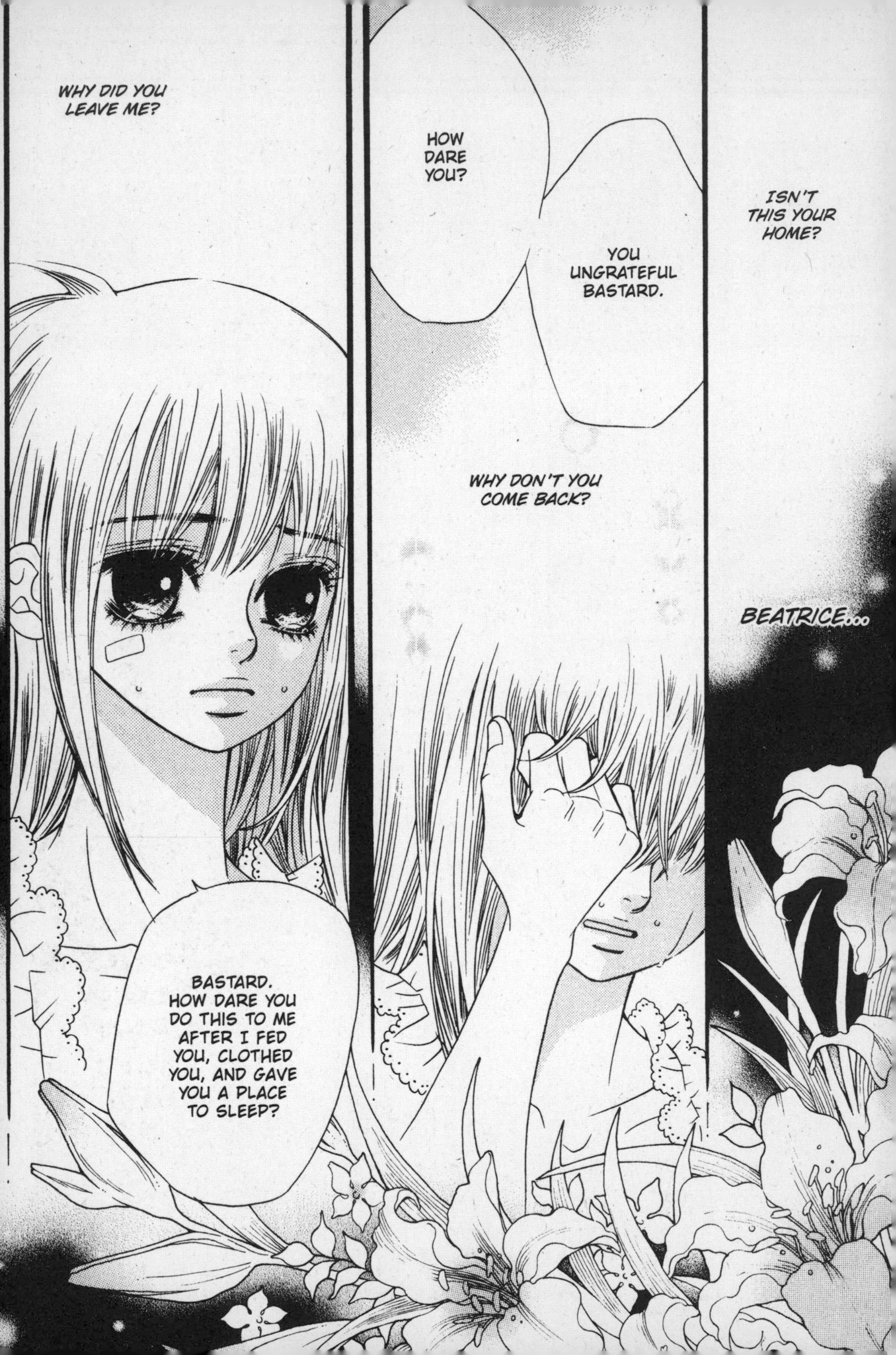
WHY DID YOU LEAVE ME?
BASTARD. HOW DARE YOU DO THIS TO ME AFTER I FED YOU, CLOTHED YOU, AND GAVE YOU A PLACE TO SLEEP?
HOW DARE YOU?
YOU UNGRATEFUL BASTARD.
WHY DON'T YOU COME BACK?
ISN'T THIS YOUR HOME?
BEATRICE...

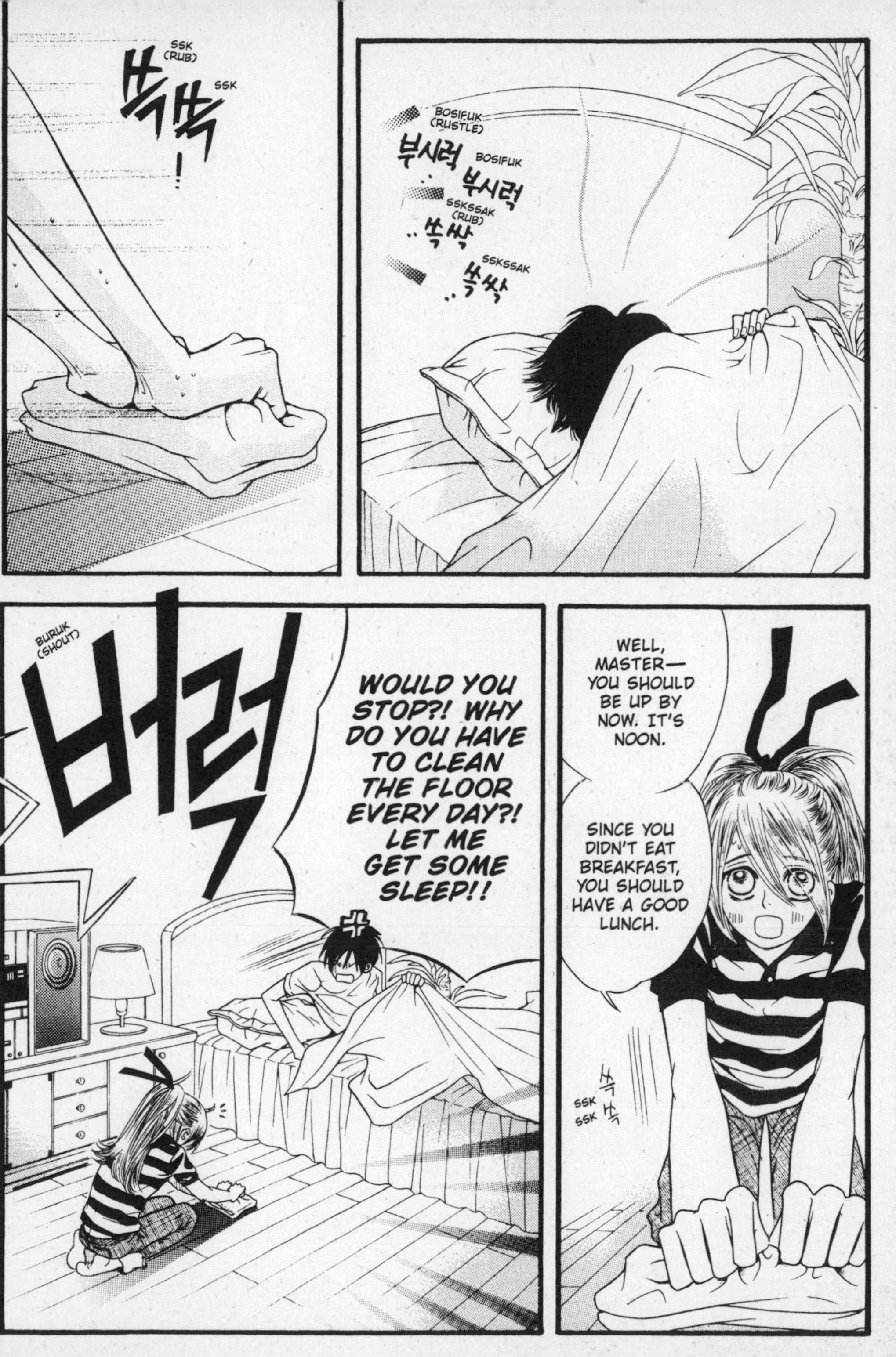
SSK (RUB)
SSK
쓱쓱!
BOSIFUK (RUSTLE)
부시럭
BOSIFUK
부시럭
SSKSSAK (RUB)
쓱싹
SSKSSAK
쓱싹
BURUK (SHOUT)
버럭
WOULD YOU STOP?! WHY DO YOU HAVE TO CLEAN THE FLOOR EVERY DAY?! LET ME GET SOME SLEEP!!
WELL, MASTER— YOU SHOULD BE UP BY NOW. IT'S NOON.
SINCE YOU DIDN'T EAT BREAKFAST, YOU SHOULD HAVE A GOOD LUNCH.
SSK 쓱
SSK 쓱

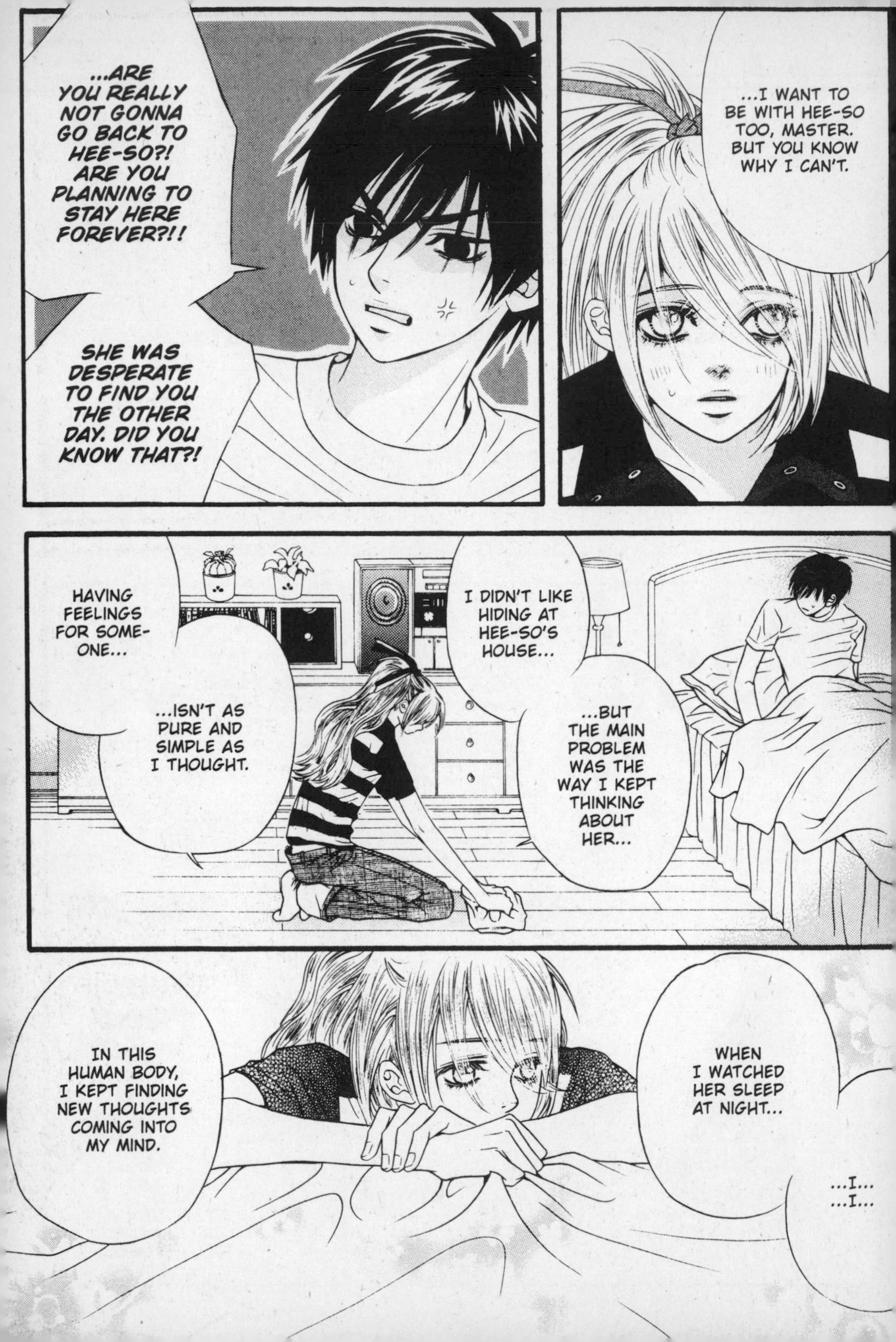
...ARE YOU REALLY NOT GONNA GO BACK TO HEE-SO?! ARE YOU PLANNING TO STAY HERE FOREVER?!!
SHE WAS DESPERATE TO FIND YOU THE OTHER DAY. DID YOU KNOW THAT?!
...I WANT TO BE WITH HEE-SO TOO, MASTER. BUT YOU KNOW WHY I CAN'T.
HAVING FEELINGS FOR SOME-ONE...
...ISN'T AS PURE AND SIMPLE AS I THOUGHT.
I DIDN'T LIKE HIDING AT HEE-SO'S HOUSE...
...BUT THE MAIN PROBLEM WAS THE WAY I KEPT THINKING ABOUT HER...
IN THIS HUMAN BODY, I KEPT FINDING NEW THOUGHTS COMING INTO MY MIND.
WHEN I WATCHED HER SLEEP AT NIGHT...
...I...
...I...

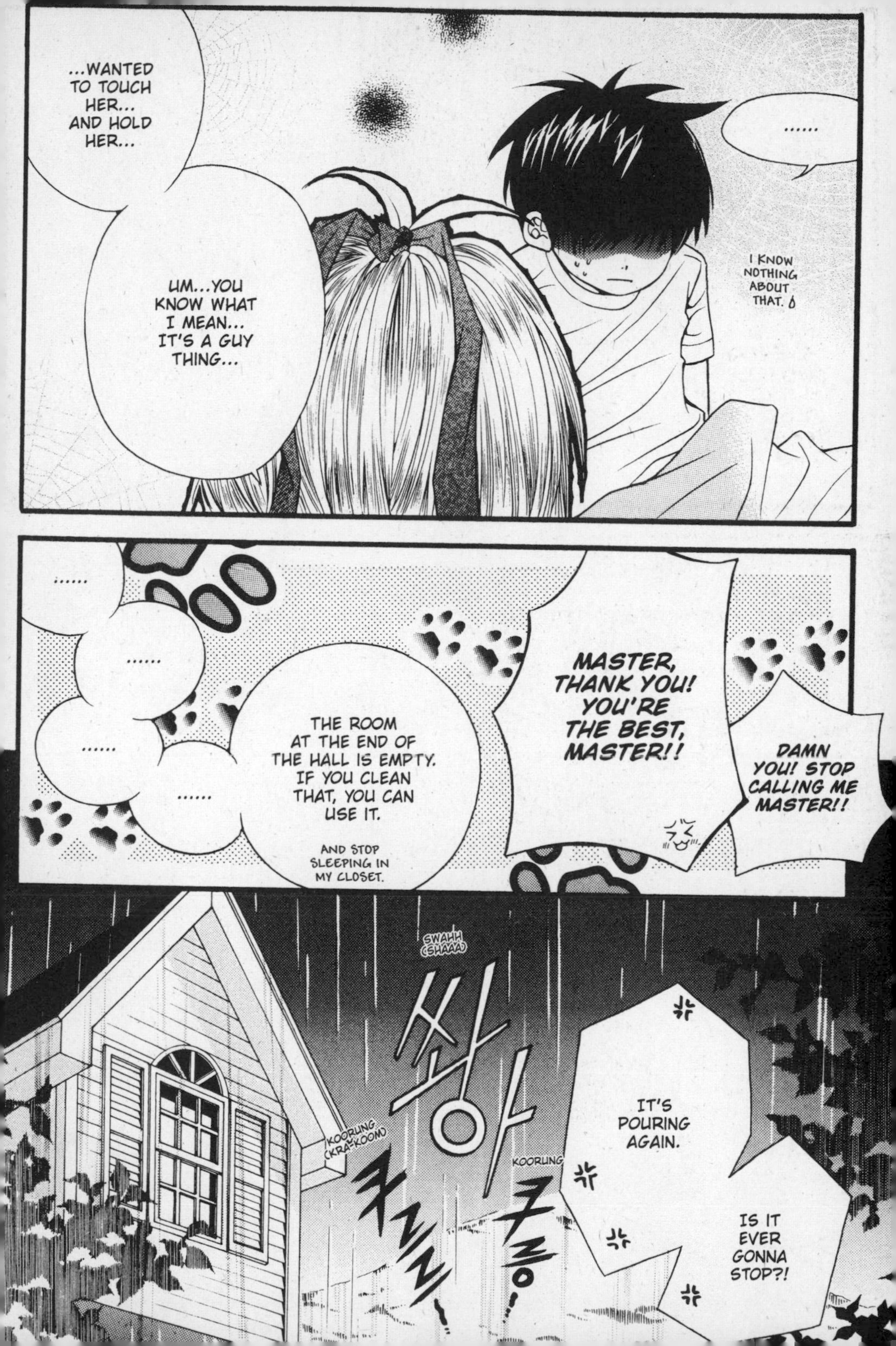
...WANTED TO TOUCH HER... AND HOLD HER...
UM...YOU KNOW WHAT I MEAN... IT'S A GUY THING...
......
I KNOW NOTHING ABOUT THAT.
......
......
......
......
THE ROOM AT THE END OF THE HALL IS EMPTY. IF YOU CLEAN THAT, YOU CAN USE IT.
AND STOP SLEEPING IN MY CLOSET.
MASTER, THANK YOU! YOU'RE THE BEST, MASTER!!
DAMN YOU! STOP CALLING ME MASTER!!
SWAHH (SHAAA)
쏴아
KOORUNG (KRA-KOOM)
KOORUNG
IT'S POURING AGAIN.
IS IT EVER GONNA STOP?!

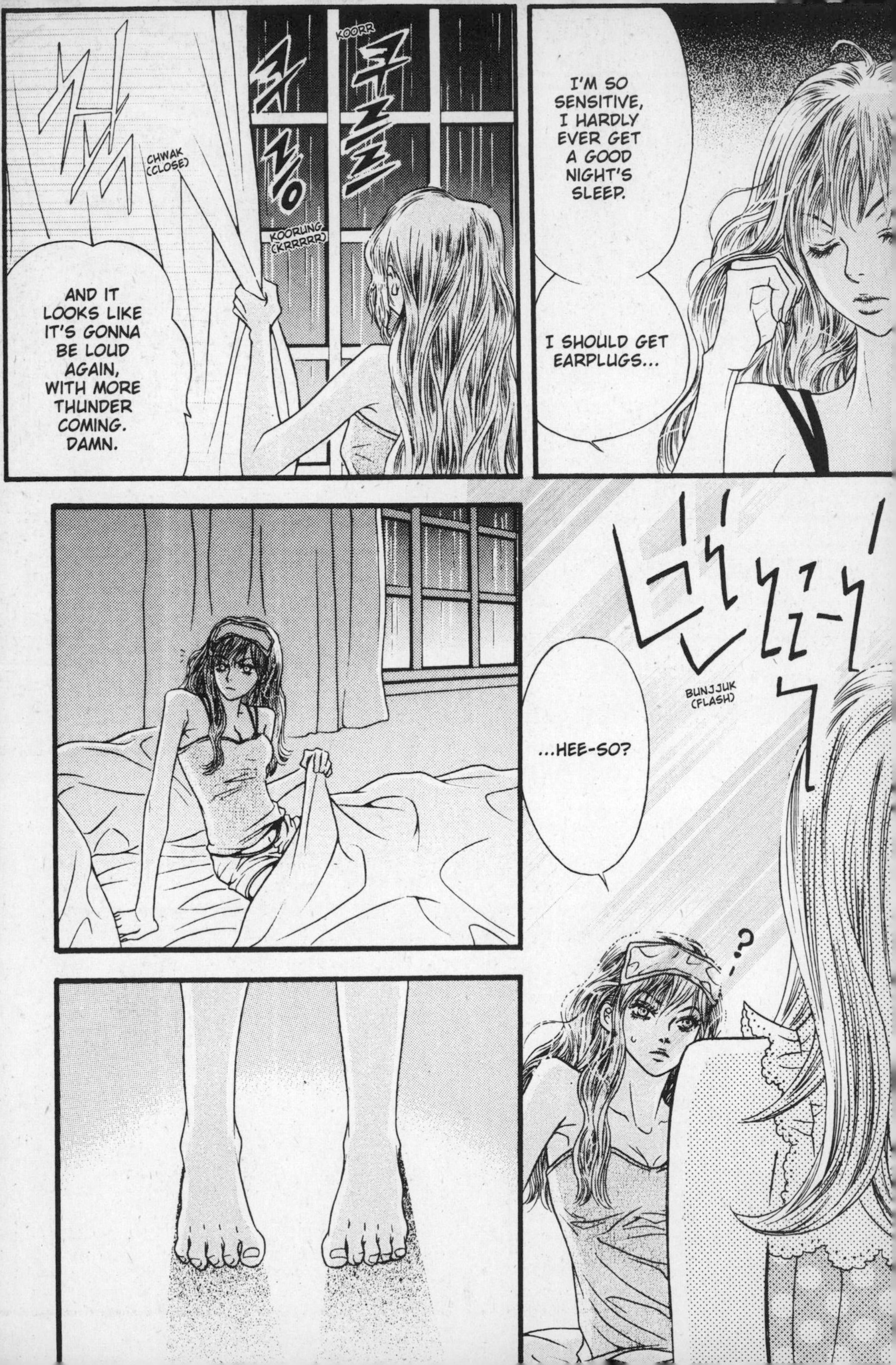
KOORR
KOORUNG (KRRRRR)
CHWAK (CLOSE)
AND IT LOOKS LIKE IT'S GONNA BE LOUD AGAIN, WITH MORE THUNDER COMING. DAMN.
I'M SO SENSITIVE, I HARDLY EVER GET A GOOD NIGHT'S SLEEP.
I SHOULD GET EARPLUGS...
BUNJJUK (FLASH)
...HEE-SO?
?

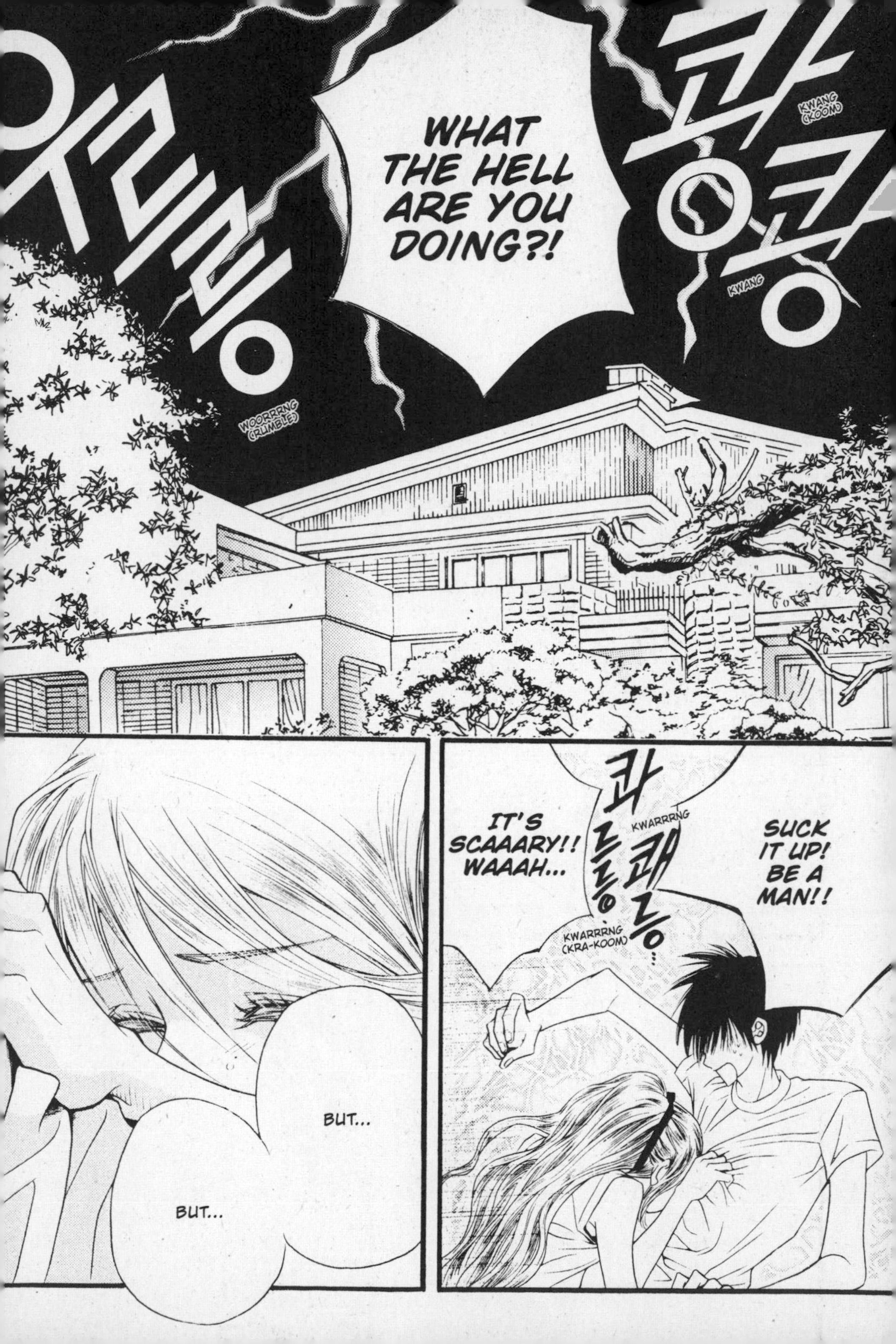
WOORRRNG (RUMBLE)
WHAT THE HELL ARE YOU DOING?!
KWANG (KOOM)
KWANG
BUT...
BUT...
IT'S SCAAARY!! WAAAH...
KWARRRNG
KWARRRNG (KRA-KOOM)
SUCK IT UP! BE A MAN!!

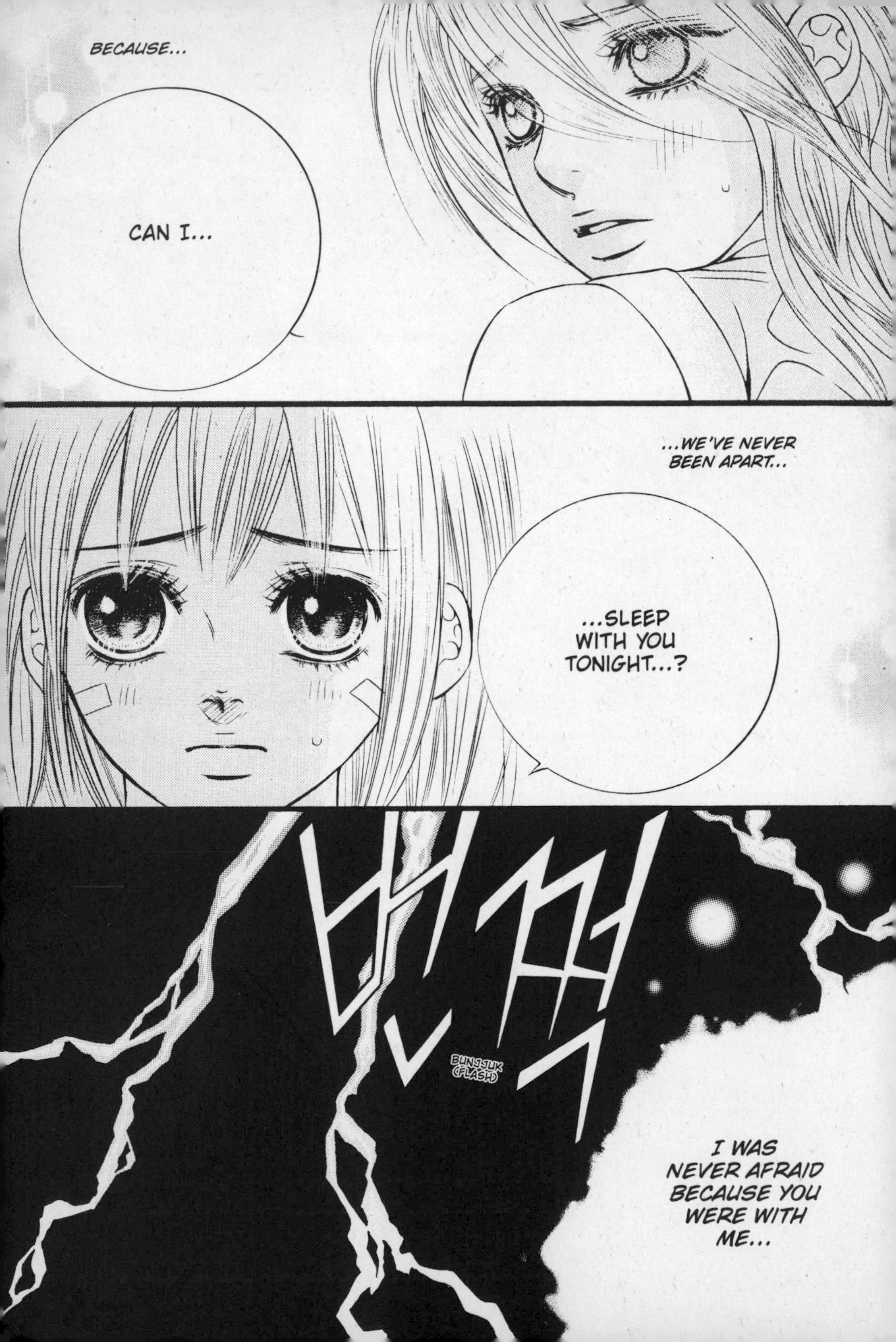
BECAUSE...
CAN I...
...WE'VE NEVER BEEN APART...
...SLEEP WITH YOU TONIGHT...?
BUNJJUK (FLASH)
I WAS NEVER AFRAID BECAUSE YOU WERE WITH ME...

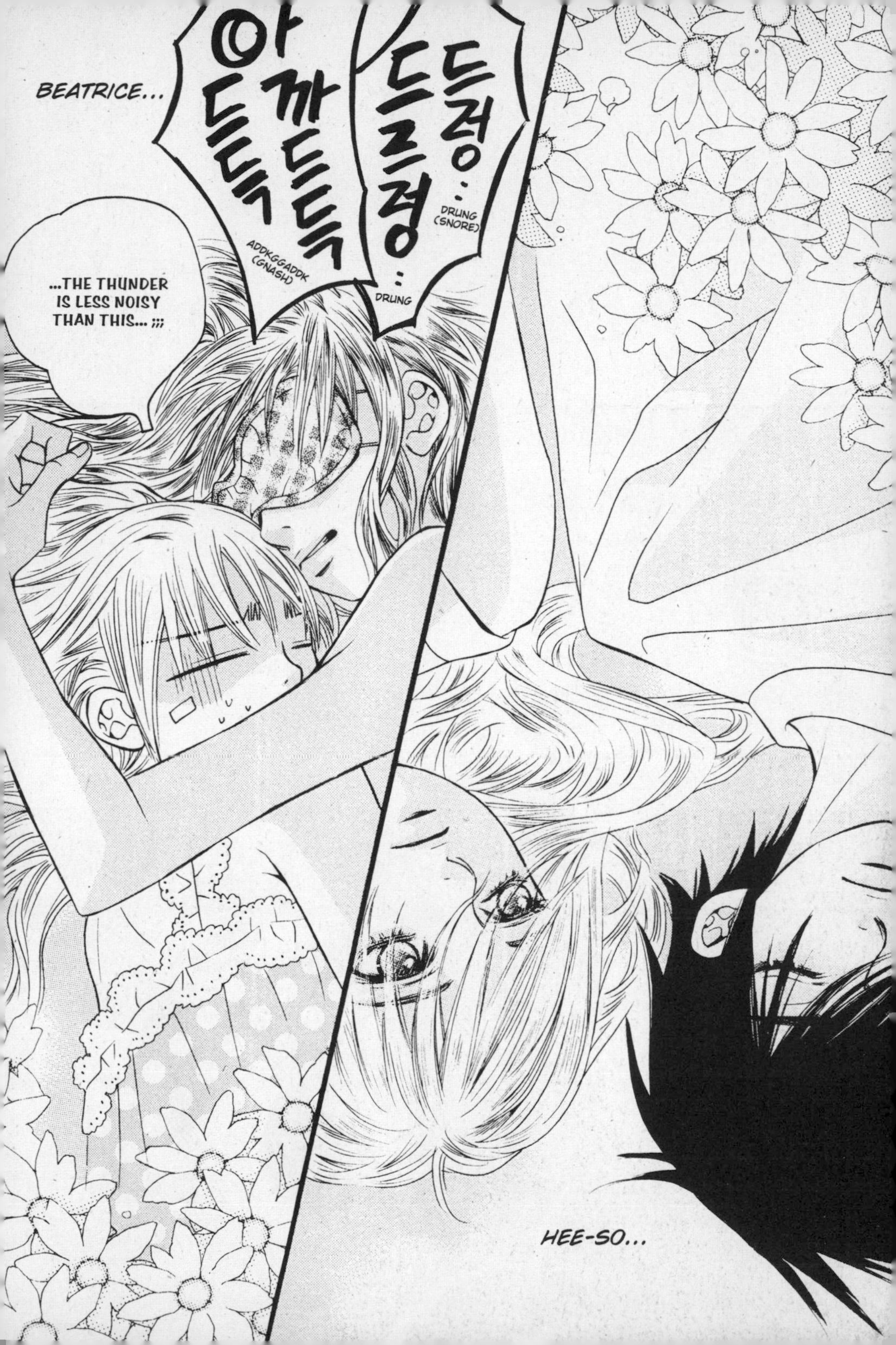
BEATRICE...
아드득 까드득
ADDKGGADDK (GNASH)
드렁: 드르렁:
DRUNG (SNORE)
DRUNG
...THE THUNDER IS LESS NOISY THAN THIS... ;;;
HEE-SO...

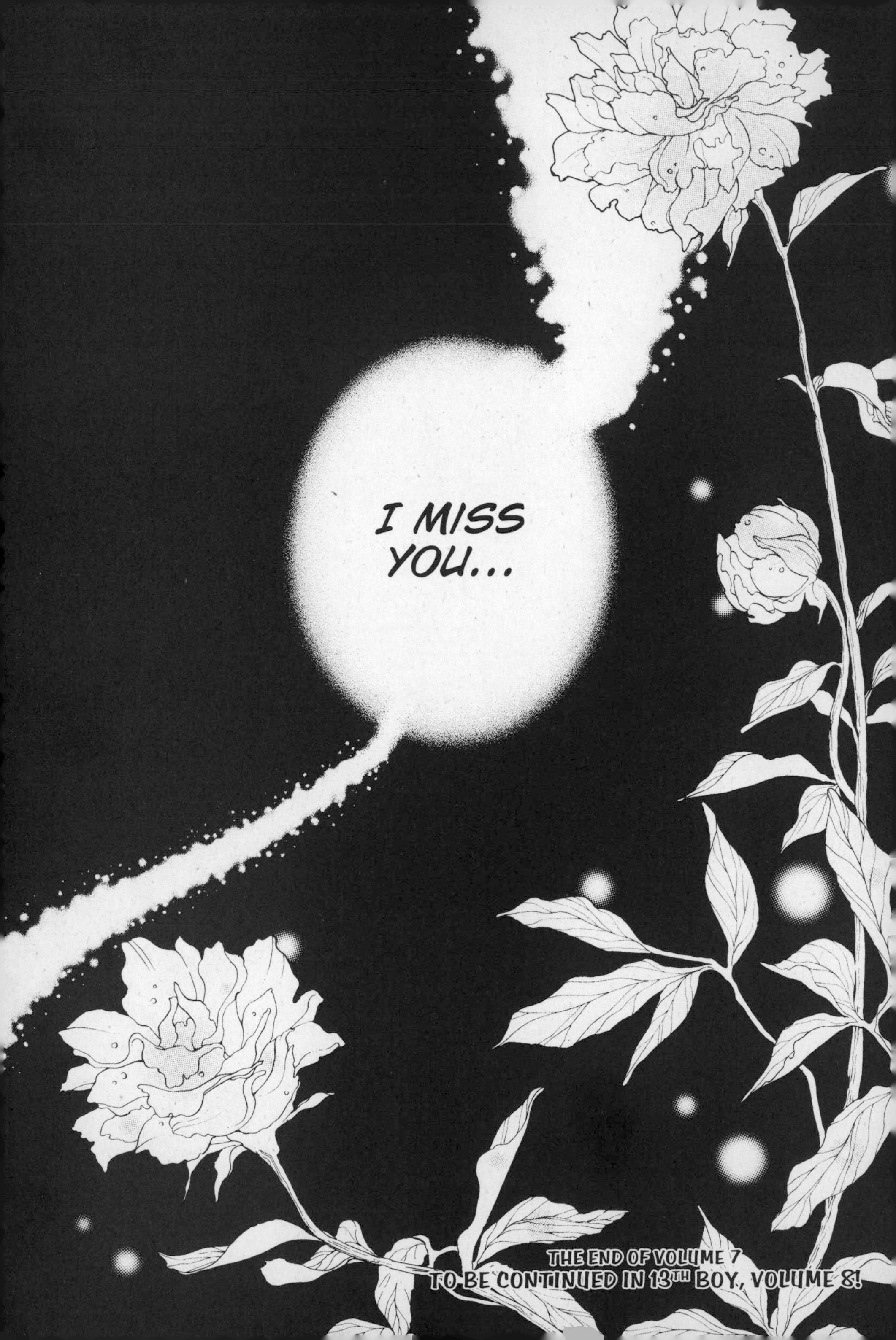
I MISS YOU...
THE END OF VOLUME 7
TO BE CONTINUED IN 13TH BOY, VOLUME 8!

13th Boy

THE POPULAR TALE OF HEE-SO'S STORMY RELATIONSHIPS!! OUR FOURTH EPISODE IS COMING UP NEXT!

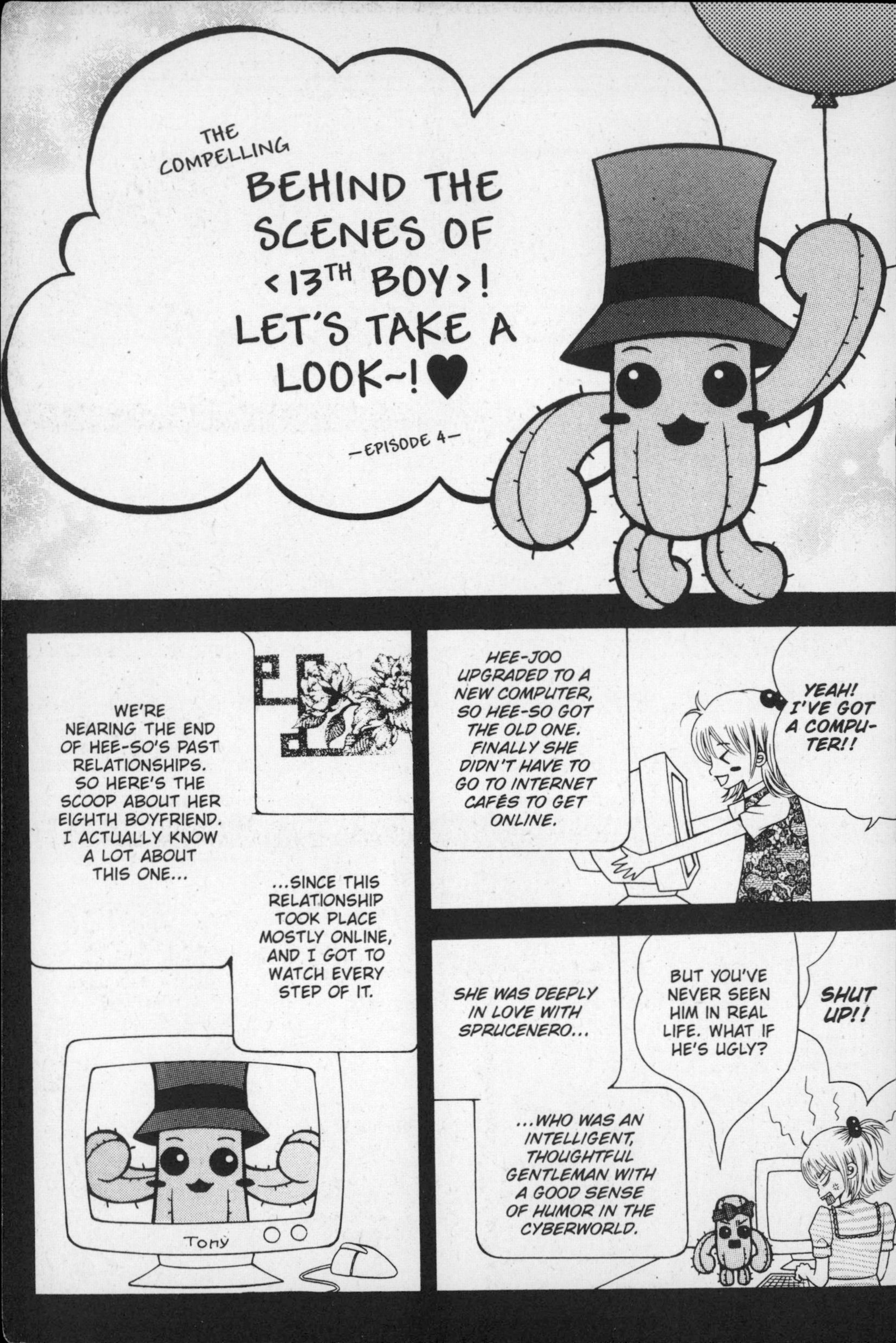
THE COMPELLING
BEHIND THE SCENES OF <13TH BOY>! LET'S TAKE A LOOK~!♥
—EPISODE 4—
WE'RE NEARING THE END OF HEE-SO'S PAST RELATIONSHIPS. SO HERE'S THE SCOOP ABOUT HER EIGHTH BOYFRIEND. I ACTUALLY KNOW A LOT ABOUT THIS ONE...
...SINCE THIS RELATIONSHIP TOOK PLACE MOSTLY ONLINE, AND I GOT TO WATCH EVERY STEP OF IT.
TONY
HEE-JOO UPGRADED TO A NEW COMPUTER, SO HEE-SO GOT THE OLD ONE. FINALLY SHE DIDN'T HAVE TO GO TO INTERNET CAFÉS TO GET ONLINE.
YEAH! I'VE GOT A COMPU-TER!!
SHE WAS DEEPLY IN LOVE WITH SPRUCENERO...
BUT YOU'VE NEVER SEEN HIM IN REAL LIFE. WHAT IF HE'S UGLY?
SHUT UP!!
...WHO WAS AN INTELLIGENT, THOUGHTFUL GENTLEMAN WITH A GOOD SENSE OF HUMOR IN THE CYBERWORLD.

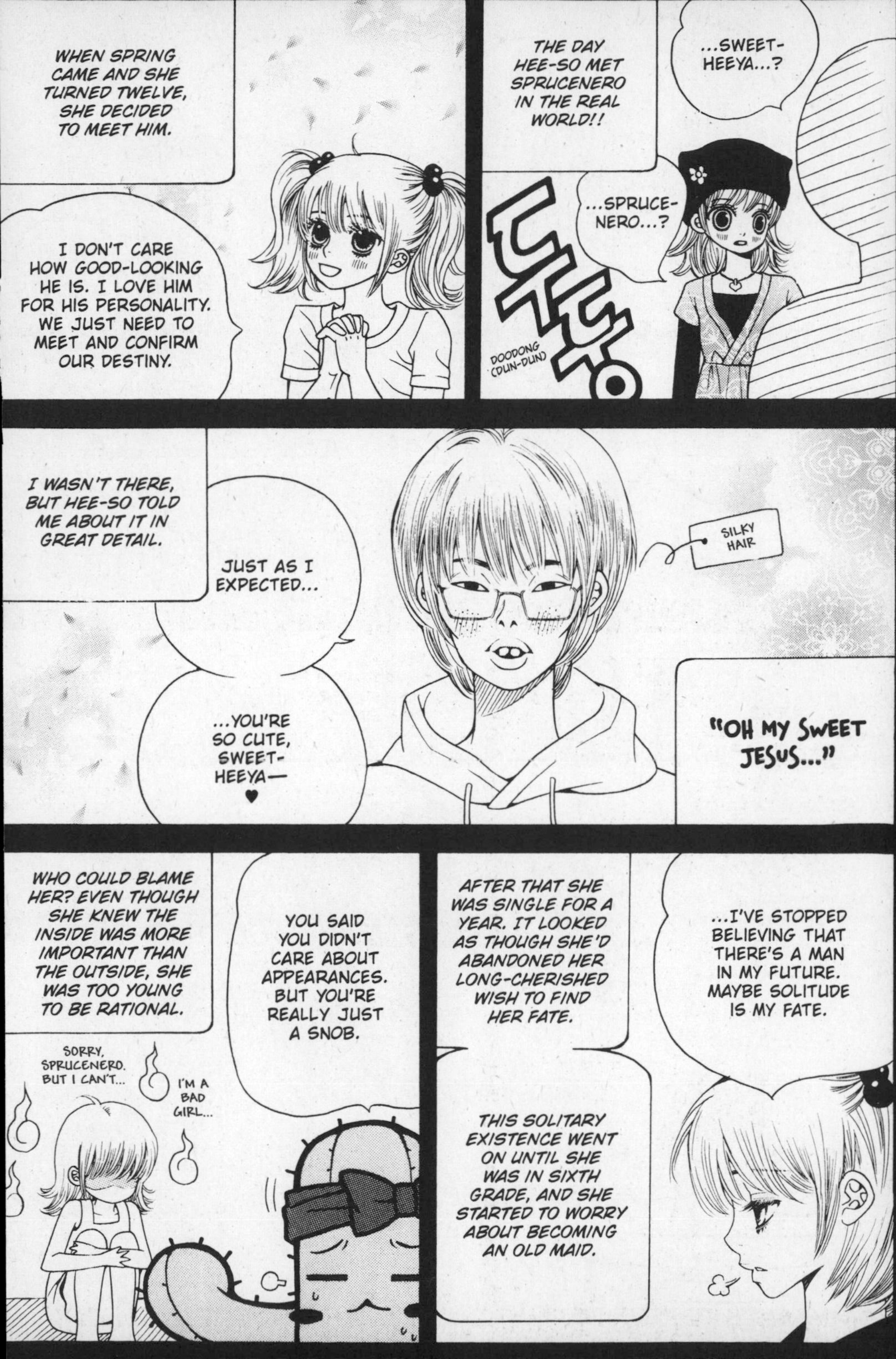
WHEN SPRING CAME AND SHE TURNED TWELVE, SHE DECIDED TO MEET HIM.
I DON'T CARE HOW GOOD-LOOKING HE IS. I LOVE HIM FOR HIS PERSONALITY. WE JUST NEED TO MEET AND CONFIRM OUR DESTINY.
THE DAY HEE-SO MET SPRUCENERO IN THE REAL WORLD!!
...SWEET-HEEYA...?
...SPRUCE-NERO...?
DOODONG (DUN-DUN)
I WASN'T THERE, BUT HEE-SO TOLD ME ABOUT IT IN GREAT DETAIL.
JUST AS I EXPECTED...
...YOU'RE SO CUTE, SWEET-HEEYA—♥
SILKY HAIR
"OH MY SWEET JESUS..."
WHO COULD BLAME HER? EVEN THOUGH SHE KNEW THE INSIDE WAS MORE IMPORTANT THAN THE OUTSIDE, SHE WAS TOO YOUNG TO BE RATIONAL.
YOU SAID YOU DIDN'T CARE ABOUT APPEARANCES. BUT YOU'RE REALLY JUST A SNOB.
SORRY, SPRUCENERO. BUT I CAN'T...
I'M A BAD GIRL...
AFTER THAT SHE WAS SINGLE FOR A YEAR. IT LOOKED AS THOUGH SHE'D ABANDONED HER LONG-CHERISHED WISH TO FIND HER FATE.
...I'VE STOPPED BELIEVING THAT THERE'S A MAN IN MY FUTURE. MAYBE SOLITUDE IS MY FATE.
THIS SOLITARY EXISTENCE WENT ON UNTIL SHE WAS IN SIXTH GRADE, AND SHE STARTED TO WORRY ABOUT BECOMING AN OLD MAID.

BUT LOVE ALWAYS COMES WITHOUT WARNING! AND IT CAME AGAIN IN THE FALL WHEN SHE WAS THIRTEEN.

SHE WAS WEARING A RED SWEATER.

OOPS!

THEIR STORY STARTED THE MOMENT HER SWEATER GOT CAUGHT ON THE BOY'S ZIPPER!

I-I'M SORRY!

ARGH! WHAT'S WRONG WITH THIS?!!

......

BUT THE TANGLE JUST GOT WORSE...

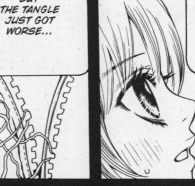

WHEN SHE LOOKED UP IN EMBARRASSMENT, SHE REALIZED HER SITUATION.

I-IS THIS...

...THE RED THREAD OF FATE...?!!

HE WAS HEE-SO'S NINTH BOYFRIEND, JAE-WOOK HAN, SEVENTH GRADE. HE WENT TO HOPEFUL JUNIOR HIGH IN THE NEXT DISTRICT OVER.

HE WAS THE SCHOOL'S TROUBLEMAKER, A WILD CHILD WHOSE FIST WAS FASTER THAN HIS WORDS. BUT DESPITE HIS LOOKS, HE HAD A GOOD HEART.

TAKE YOUR TIME. IT'S NO BIG DEAL.

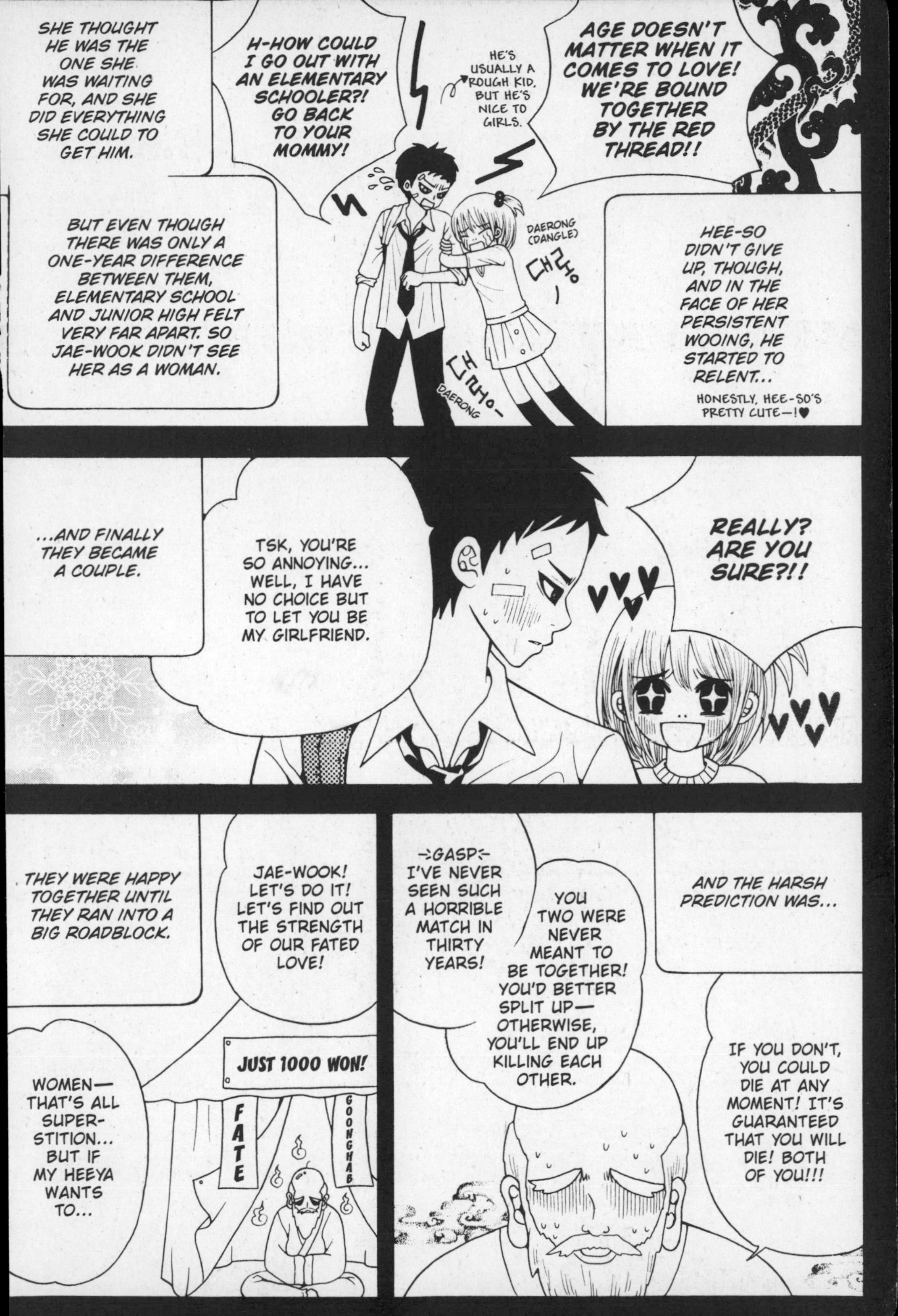
SHE THOUGHT HE WAS THE ONE SHE WAS WAITING FOR, AND SHE DID EVERYTHING SHE COULD TO GET HIM.
H-HOW COULD I GO OUT WITH AN ELEMENTARY SCHOOLER?! GO BACK TO YOUR MOMMY!
HE'S USUALLY A ROUGH KID, BUT HE'S NICE TO GIRLS.
AGE DOESN'T MATTER WHEN IT COMES TO LOVE! WE'RE BOUND TOGETHER BY THE RED THREAD!!
BUT EVEN THOUGH THERE WAS ONLY A ONE-YEAR DIFFERENCE BETWEEN THEM, ELEMENTARY SCHOOL AND JUNIOR HIGH FELT VERY FAR APART. SO JAE-WOOK DIDN'T SEE HER AS A WOMAN.
DAERONG (DANGLE)
DAERONG
HEE-SO DIDN'T GIVE UP, THOUGH, AND IN THE FACE OF HER PERSISTENT WOOING, HE STARTED TO RELENT...
HONESTLY, HEE-SO'S PRETTY CUTE—!♥
...AND FINALLY THEY BECAME A COUPLE.
TSK, YOU'RE SO ANNOYING... WELL, I HAVE NO CHOICE BUT TO LET YOU BE MY GIRLFRIEND.
REALLY? ARE YOU SURE?!!
THEY WERE HAPPY TOGETHER UNTIL THEY RAN INTO A BIG ROADBLOCK.
JAE-WOOK! LET'S DO IT! LET'S FIND OUT THE STRENGTH OF OUR FATED LOVE!
JUST 1000 WON!
FATE
GOONGHAB
WOMEN—THAT'S ALL SUPER-STITION... BUT IF MY HEEYA WANTS TO...
AND THE HARSH PREDICTION WAS...
-GASP- I'VE NEVER SEEN SUCH A HORRIBLE MATCH IN THIRTY YEARS!
YOU TWO WERE NEVER MEANT TO BE TOGETHER! YOU'D BETTER SPLIT UP—OTHERWISE, YOU'LL END UP KILLING EACH OTHER.
IF YOU DON'T, YOU COULD DIE AT ANY MOMENT! IT'S GUARANTEED THAT YOU WILL DIE! BOTH OF YOU!!!

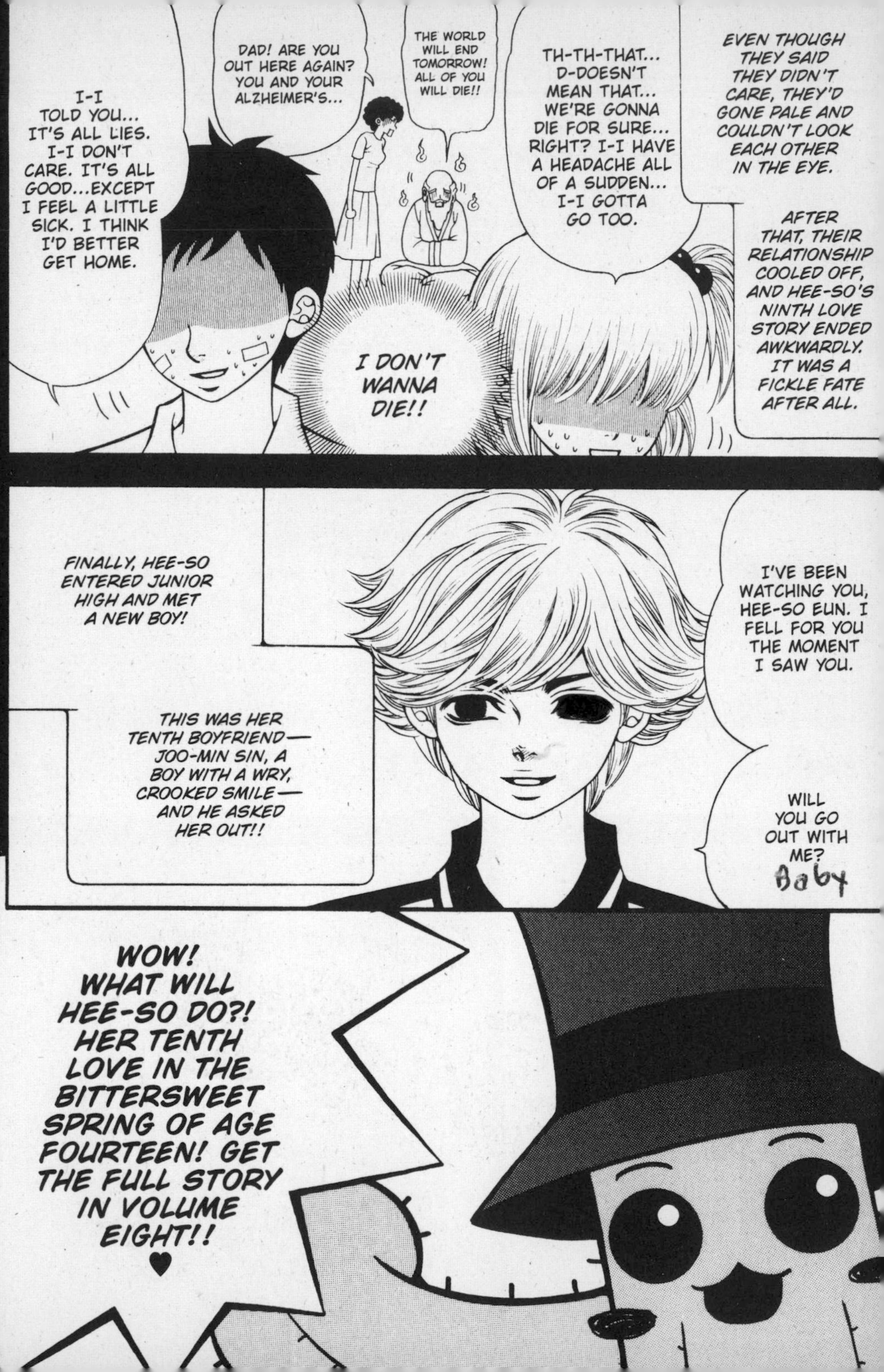
I-I TOLD YOU... IT'S ALL LIES. I-I DON'T CARE. IT'S ALL GOOD...EXCEPT I FEEL A LITTLE SICK. I THINK I'D BETTER GET HOME.
DAD! ARE YOU OUT HERE AGAIN? YOU AND YOUR ALZHEIMER'S...
THE WORLD WILL END TOMORROW! ALL OF YOU WILL DIE!!
TH-TH-THAT... D-DOESN'T MEAN THAT... WE'RE GONNA DIE FOR SURE... RIGHT? I-I HAVE A HEADACHE ALL OF A SUDDEN... I-I GOTTA GO TOO.
EVEN THOUGH THEY SAID THEY DIDN'T CARE, THEY'D GONE PALE AND COULDN'T LOOK EACH OTHER IN THE EYE.
I DON'T WANNA DIE!!
AFTER THAT, THEIR RELATIONSHIP COOLED OFF, AND HEE-SO'S NINTH LOVE STORY ENDED AWKWARDLY. IT WAS A FICKLE FATE AFTER ALL.
FINALLY, HEE-SO ENTERED JUNIOR HIGH AND MET A NEW BOY!
THIS WAS HER TENTH BOYFRIEND—JOO-MIN SIN, A BOY WITH A WRY, CROOKED SMILE—AND HE ASKED HER OUT!!
I'VE BEEN WATCHING YOU, HEE-SO EUN. I FELL FOR YOU THE MOMENT I SAW YOU.
WILL YOU GO OUT WITH ME?
Baby
WOW! WHAT WILL HEE-SO DO?! HER TENTH LOVE IN THE BITTERSWEET SPRING OF AGE FOURTEEN! GET THE FULL STORY IN VOLUME EIGHT!! ♥

Page 46
***Kimchi*:** traditional Korean dish made with cabbage and chili power.

Page 48
The story of the hatmaker and the king from the Silla dynasty: A famous story about keeping a secret. When the hatmaker finds out that the king has donkey ears, the king threatens to execute him if he ever tells anyone. But the hatmaker couldn't handle the secret, so he goes into a bamboo forest and shouts to the trees.

Page 49
KAIST: Korea Advanced Institute of Science and Technology

Page 55
***Jja-jang-myun*:** Popular Chinese noodle dish that's topped with black soy-bean paste.

Page 98
Go-Stop: Korean card game.

***Tajjang*:** The best card player.

Page 177
***Won*:** Korean monetary unit. A thousand won is worth about US$1.

***Goonghab*:** A compatibility reading that measures how well a couple are suited for each other.

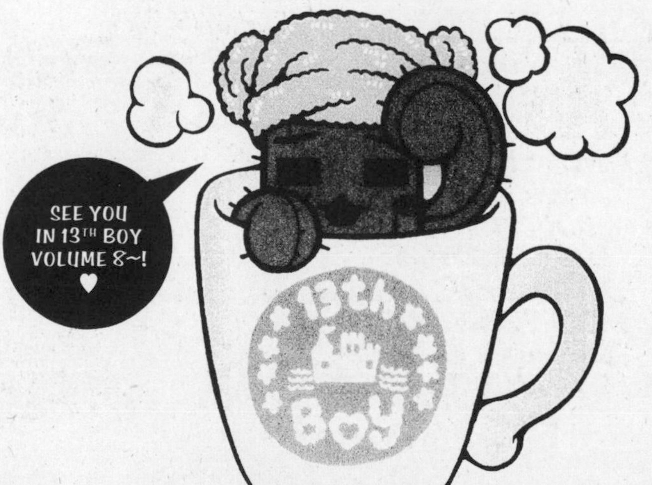
SEE YOU IN 13TH BOY VOLUME 8~! ♥
13th Boy

13th BOY ⑦

SangEun Lee

Translation: JiEun Park
English Adaptation: Natalie Baan

Lettering: Terri Delgado

13th Boy, Vol. 7 © 2007 SangEun Lee. All rights reserved. First published in Korea in 2006 by Haksan Publishing Co., Ltd. English translation rights in U.S.A., Canada, UK, and Republic of Ireland arranged with Haksan Publishing Co., Ltd.

English translation © 2011 Hachette Book Group, Inc.

Yen Press
Hachette Book Group
237 Park Avenue, New York, NY 10017

www.HachetteBookGroup.com
www.YenPress.com

Yen Press is an imprint of Hachette Book Group, Inc.
The Yen Press name and logo are trademarks of Hachette Book Group, Inc.

First Yen Press Edition: June 2011

ISBN: 978-0-7595-3000-3

10 9 8 7 6 5 4 3 2 1

BVG

Printed in the United States of America